ROYAL HISTORICAL SOCIETY

STUDIES IN HISTORY

New Series

HERESY IN MEDIEVAL FRANCE

DUALISM IN AQUITAINE AND THE AGENAIS, 1000–1249

HERESY IN MEDIEVAL FRANCE

DUALISM IN AQUITAINE AND THE AGENAIS, 1000–1249

Claire Taylor

THE ROYAL HISTORICAL SOCIETY
THE BOYDELL PRESS

First published 2005

A Royal Historical Society publication
Published by The Boydell Press
an imprint of Boydell & Brewer Ltd
PO Box 9, Woodbridge, Suffolk IP12 3DF, UK
and of Boydell & Brewer Inc.
668 Mt Hope Avenue, Rochester, NY 14620, USA
website: www.boydellandbrewer.com

ISBN 0 86193 276 5

ISSN 0269–2244

A catalogue record for this book is available
from the British Library

This book is printed on acid-free paper

Typeset by Pru Harrison, Hacheston, Suffolk
Printed in Great Britain by
Cromwell Press, Trowbridge, Wiltshire

Contents

List of Genealogies

List of Maps

TO MIKE CRAVEN

Publication of this volume was aided by a generous grant from the Scouloudi Foundation, in association with the Institute of Historical Research. It was further assisted by a grant from the History Department of the University of Nottingham.

Acknowledgements

To my supervisors Bernard Hamilton and Michael Jones go my extreme grati-
tude for expert guidance in their fields and their interest and encouragement in
my own ideas. Thanks also go to the other medievalist staff at Nottingham; Julia
Barrow, Ross Balzaretti, Gwilym Dodd, Richard Goddard and Alison McHardy.
I also wish to acknowledge how valuable the comments of the following have
been, and I am most grateful for the hours some of them have spent ploughing
through versions of what eventually resulted in publication: Malcolm Barber,
Simon Constantine, David Green, Bob Moore and especially Michael Frassetto.
I would very much also like to thank Christine Linehan of RHS. Additional
thanks are due to Michael Jones and Vic Taylor for reading the proofs. Any
errors are of course my own.

The support, enthusiasm and encouragement of family and friends were
invaluable in completing this manuscript. As such I am indebted to my husband
Mike Craven, to whom the publication is dedicated, and to to my parents Vic
and Chris Taylor and my brother and sister-in-law Joe and Andrea Taylor, and
to Jane Ellis, David Green, Simon Constantine, Konni Behr, Mike Evans, Paul
Bracken, Jeannie Alderdice, Jon Porter, Carole Mallia, Susie Curtis, Aaron
'Ananda Goshine', Didi Ananda Ragamaya and Jay Rossi.

I would have relished the opportunity of meeting Simon Walker, to thank
him in person for his invaluable suggestions concerning several important
aspects of the manuscript and for making me consider new ways of looking at the
evidence and historiography. His death has been a tragic loss for the scholars he
guided through the process of publication in this series.

Claire Taylor

Abbreviations

AD	Archives Départementales
AFP	Archivum fratrum praedicatorum, Rome
AHGi	*Archives historiques de la Gironde*
AHP	*Archives historiques du Poitou*
AM	*Annales du Midi*
AN	Archives Nationales, Paris
AS	*Acta sanctorum*, ed. J. Bolland and others, Brussels–Antwerp–Paris 1965 (repr. of 1643– original)
BN	Bibliothèque Nationale, Paris
BPH	*Bulletin philologique et historique du Comité des travaux historiques et scientifiques*
BSAHL	*Bulletin de la Société archéologique et historique du Limousin*
BSHAP	*Bulletin de la Société historique et archéologique du Périgord*
CCL	*Corpus christianorum: series Latina*, New York–London 1962
CCM	Cahiers de civilisation médievale
CF	*Cahiers de Fanjeaux*
Concilia	*Concilia*, ed. J. Mansi, Graz 1960–1 (repr. of *Sacrorum conciliorum nova et amplissima collectio*, Venice 1759–98)
EHR	*English Historical Review*
GC	*Gallia christiana in provincias ecclesiasticas distributa*, ed. D. Sainte-Marthe and others, Paris 1744–1877
HGL	*Histoire générale de Languedoc*, ed. C. de Vic and J. Vaissète, rev. A. Molinier, Toulouse 1872–1904
JMH	*Journal of Medieval History*
MA	*Le Moyen Âge*
MGH	Monumenta Germaniae historica
MGH, SS	Monumenta Germaniae historica, scriptores
MGH, Schriften	Monumenta Germaniae historica schriften
PL	*Patrologiae cursus completus, series Latina*, ed. J. P. Migne and continuators, Paris 1852–1904; 4 vols, index and 5 vols supplementum, 1958–74
RA	*Revue de l'Agenais*
RHC Occ.	*Recueil des historiens des croisades: historiens occidentaux*, Paris 1844–95
RHF	*Recueil des historiens des Gaules et de la France*, ed. M. Bouquet, rev. L. Delisle, Paris 1738–1904
RS	Rolls Series
RSASAA	*Recueil des travaux de la Société d'agriculture, sciences et arts d'Agen*
SCH	Studies in Church History
TRHS	*Transactions of the Royal Historical Society*

Note on Sources

All printed sources are cited by page or column number except where it was more useful to refer to a specific item, letter, chapter, *enquête*, verse or line, in which case the nature of the reference is indicated, along with the page number if necessary. In collections specifically of acts and charters items are cited by number, unless in *HGL*, or otherwise stated.

Introduction

My interest in this subject began whilst writing an MA dissertation on the Cathars, supervised by Bernard Hamilton. It explored Dossat's observation that the Cathar heresy, so prevalent within the French Languedoc from the second half of the twelfth century, never took root in the duchy of Aquitaine, except in the Agenais, which formed part of the duchy until 1196.[1] This was puzzling because medieval Aquitaine, and especially Gascony, was closely identified in cultural terms with the rest of Occitania. Dossat observed that the heresy did not cross the river Garonne. This could not be a simple matter of geography because the heresy had already travelled to western Europe from the Balkans. In spite of the difficulties encountered by the early bridge builders on the Garonne, which bisects the Agenais and divides the Languedoc from Aquitaine, the river was frequently crossed with ease by boats and barges.[2] There was no obvious physical impediment to the transmission of the heresy.

In addition, Aquitaine had arguably already encountered dualist heresy. Some early eleventh-century western sources warn us of a 'new heresy', others of the return of an ancient one. The emergence of such concern in Aquitaine received relatively little detailed attention in comparison with other western accounts until several 'new' sources recently came to be examined in this context. Read alongside other incidents of heresy reported throughout both eastern and western Europe in the same period, they shed a good deal of light on current perceptions of the nature of that heresy. This book examines whether the heresy in eleventh-century Aquitaine was dualist and then discusses twelfth- and thirteenth-century Catharism in an Aquitainian context. Structurally it is therefore in two parts.

Part I deals primarily with the millennial era: the society of Aquitaine (chapter 1) and evidence for heresy (chapter 2). Several accounts of heresy label and describe it as 'Manichaean'. Manichees were dualists of the classical world opposed by the Church Fathers, notably Augustine, himself a convert from the heresy. It is in part as a result of his literary legacy that Manichees were the best known dualists in the west at the end of the early Middle Ages. Dualist beliefs, most significantly Bogomilism, re-emerged and flourished also in the eleventh-century Balkans, and it is of this heresy that twelfth-century Catharism is thought to have been a variant. I have considered whether there is also a

---

[1] Y. Dossat, 'Catharisme en Gascogne', in his *Église et hérésie en France au XIIIe siècle*, London 1982, 149–68. See also his 'Catharisme et Comminges', ibid. 117–28. B. Guillemain has addressed the matter in 'Le Duché d'Aquitaine hors du Catharisme', *CF* xx (1985), 57–71.
[2] P. Delvit and others, *Garonne, de la rivière à l'homme*, Toulouse 1998, 31–2.

connection between the Bogomils and the eleventh-century dualists of Aquitaine and come to the conclusion that there almost certainly is.

When historians of religious heresy first noted features of the sources that appeared to resemble dualism it was indeed considered that the eleventh-century heretics in the west were dualist and that their heresy was a form of Bogomilism. Most recently, they have discussed the sources in a structural context, looking at social origins for dissent. They argue that not only is the previous orthodoxy wrong but that sources which claim to describe religious heresy do not identify 'heretics' at all: 'heresy' referred simply to indigenous forms of non-doctrinal dissent, the desire for a return to the simplicity of the apostolic Church being the closest that its adherents came to threatening clerical teaching, many of their complaints being related instead to localised social and economic changes that they experienced.

A comparison with related subject matter, removed by some centuries from the eleventh-century debate, might serve well to introduce this historiographical minefield. John Arnold recently noted of thirteenth-century documentation that the medieval inquisition imposed a model on the questions it put to deponents which assumed the lay witnesses to be passive receptors of externally imported beliefs. We arguably do the same when reading it. The same could be noted of the eleventh-century evidence. Yet Arnold also cites criticism of Emmanuel Le Roy Ladurie's *Montaillou*: 'The historian . . . suppresses [heresy] by giving it roots. He removes it . . . from inquisitorial condemnation by giving it the colour of earth and stone, by rendering it indiscernible from its place.'[3] The revisionists of the dualist thesis arguably do what the anthropologist is here accused of. And yet they make a very convincing case otherwise, one that incorporates some of the most important work done on the subject of medieval heresy, and I am unable and unwilling to entirely dismiss it. Instead a post-revisionism is perhaps called for, and one that, as we shall see, also has implications for the latter period with which Arnold is concerned.

Thus, if we should test the Aquitainian accounts of heresy against those from eastern Europe, we should also read them in the context of the society in which they originated. In chapter 1, therefore, I explore what the society of eleventh-century Aquitaine was like, what kinds of dissent might have arisen within it, and what kinds of dissident beliefs it might have been receptive to. Historians have established that religious dissent and heresy, not least Catharism, occurred most obviously in societies in which some people experienced insecurity and oppression and in which the orthodox Church was found wanting.[4] I therefore examine the nature and structure of lay and clerical authority in Aquitaine and its influences within a population of potential heretical recruits.

As part of this I address a modern debate about the extent to which France

---

3 J. Arnold, *Inquisition and power: Catharism and the confessing subject in the medieval Languedoc*, Philadelphia 2001, 120, 123, citing J. Rancière, *The names of history*, trans. H. Melehy, Minneapolis 1994, 73.

4 See chapter 1 below and, with reference to French Catharism specifically, chapter 3.

was undergoing what has become known as the feudal transformation, or mutation, with specific reference to the society of Aquitaine. I also attempt to establish the extent to which 'millennial anxiety' informed the actions of the laity.
Some discussion is also necessary of Gascony in the same period, as well as of
pre-Angevin Aquitaine (which incorporated Gascony from about 1060) and of
the Agenais to about 1152. Since Jane Martindale's unpublished 1965 thesis,
'The origins of the duchy of Aquitaine and the government of the counts of
Poitou, 902–1137', the political history of the region in the period covered in
part I of this book has received little attention in English. I attempt to rectify
this, albeit in less detail and in a less institutionally orientated fashion than
Martindale. Authorities on this period of Aquitainian history agree that there is
a dearth of source material, particularly for eleventh-century Aquitaine and for
Gascony well into the twelfth. This is not exclusively the case. For the political
life of Aquitaine we have charters relating to important families and an unusual
supporting document, a *conventum* recording the relationship of Hugh of
Lusignan and Duke William V. We are also well provided with monastic
cartularies for Aquitaine and thus have considerable knowledge of its economic
and religious life. However, we do lack reliable chronicle evidence. Adémar of
Chabannes is our best source for the first few decades of the eleventh century in
Aquitaine, and he refers occasionally to Gascony. Although his evidence is far
from uniformly trustworthy, as a commentator on contemporary events he is a
good deal better than the later chronicle composed in the abbey of Saint-
Maixent. But Geoffrey of Vigeois, writing in the twelfth century, can be better
informed than both of them even for events before his birth. The real poverty
comes with Gascon sources. They are lacking in economic information into the
twelfth century, and there are few political sources or sources for the religious
life before 1060. The handful of charters associated with religious foundations in
Gascony by its dukes in the late tenth and early eleventh centuries contain
almost all the information we have both about this family and the religious life
of Gascony in this period.[5]

Part II concerns the Cathar heresy in Aquitaine and the Agenais. Cathars
were dualists who believed in the existence of two principles; a good god who
created human souls and an evil god who created the physical universe and
imprisoned these souls within it, over which the good god had no influence.
They believed that these souls were imprisoned so carefully that there was little
hope of release from the world at death, because at this point the soul was rein-
carnated in another human or animal body. The only way to escape this endless
cycle was to die in a 'perfected' state. This meant that between initiation into
the heresy, through a ceremonial *consolamentum* at the hands of a *perfectus*, and
death, the adherent had to have lived a life of extreme abstinence; to have
owned nothing, renounced sexual pleasure and even family life, to have not

---

[5] For a detailed survey of the Gascon sources in the pre-Poitevin period see B. Cursente, *Des
Maisons et des hommes: la Gascogne médiévale (XIe–XVe siècle)*, Toulouse 1998, 16–17, 25–34,
111, and P. de Marca, *Histoire de Béarn*, 2nd edn, Pau 1894, 272–6.

killed any living thing and to have followed strict dietary restrictions. The Cathar *perfecti* who lived such lives spread their beliefs through preaching and through example. Male and female *perfecti* were technically equal in the movement. The *credentes*, the believers in the heresy, led more ordinary lives, except that they might flout the irrelevant rules and prescriptions of the Catholic Church and run the risk of prosecution for belief in or protection of the heresy. *Credentes* hoped to be hereticated shortly before death and so to die in the perfected state.[6]

Chapter 3 aims primarily to explain why the society of Aquitaine did not prove welcoming to the Cathars, and chapter 4 describes the impact of the Albigensian crusade, launched in 1209 against the heretics and their supporters in the Languedoc, on Aquitaine. Part II also attempts to extract information about the heretics in the Agenais from the wealth of sources relating to the heresy in southern France more generally, to find out who they were, how they came to be influenced by specific schools of Bogomil thought and how their Church operated in the thirteenth century. As a background to this I describe the Agenais as a socio-political entity, addressing in chapter 3 how and why it received the heresy initially, in chapter 4 how it reacted to the crusade, and in chapter 5 how it fared in the period of French occupation and inquisition. Chapters 4 and 5 also discuss both the Agenais and the crusade in the context of a theme introduced earlier in the book, relations between Aquitaine, by then governed by the kings of England, and Toulouse. They make reference to the influence over these events of the French crown and the papacy, both of which gained more authority in the region in this period. They also note the response of other Aquitainian parties to the crusade and attempt to explain which of them took sides in the above religious and military conflicts, and why.

When studying documentation for the inquisition I noticed that the heretics and their supporters in the Agenais appeared to be very closely involved with those in neighbouring Quercy, itself touched by Aquitainian influence as well as that of Toulouse, and also that the geographical spread of the heresy in Quercy changed significantly in the period from 1200 to 1249. I have attempted to account for this process and examine the role of the Agenais lords and heretics in it, and have outlined the status of the heresy in Quercy in the pre-crusade period as a background to this.

When examining the politics and society of Aquitaine in general, to account for the absence of heresy in this later period, I found a wealth of thematic secondary sources for the subject. With regard to the Agenais, however, even in the second half of the twelfth century, there is a comparative lack of material relating to the laity, and the structure of authority is difficult to discern.[7] I

---

6 The most recent detailed account of the Cathar church, its beliefs, hierarchy and ceremonies, is in M. Barber, *The Cathars: dualist heretics in the Languedoc in the high Middle Ages*, Harlow 2000, 71–104. For interesting discussion of the *consolamentum* see also Arnold, *Inquisition and power*, 123–30.

7 This is noted in A. Richard, *Histoire des comtes de Poitou, 779–1204*, Paris 1903, i. 270–1,

suspect that this was in part because the region was not very immediately governed by the dukes of Aquitaine, a point which will be discussed further. When looking for episcopal sources, I learned that the diocesan archives of Agen were destroyed in the Revolution.[8] The departmental archives of Lot-et-Garonne do not contain many manuscripts from our period for the Agenais in general. However, those documents which do exist, both for the diocese and the county of the Agenais, are all published and well evaluated in both local histories of the region and also in collections relating to southern France more widely, notably the *Histoire générale de Languedoc*. In addition, there are several revealing charters relating to Agen itself in the period in question contained in *Chartes d'Agen*.

The major sources for the crusade in the Agenais are three literary works, the *Chanson de la croisade albigeoise* of William of Tudela and his continuators, the *Hystoria* of Peter de-Vaux-de-Cernay and the *Chronique* of William of Puylaurens. For the heretical families of the Agenais I have used secular documents from the period of French invasion and occupation relating to the transfer of property from heretics to the northern French crusaders and their allies and, in some cases later in the thirteenth century, to Catholic relatives of the heretics. The most important single source for the heretics of the Languedoc are the inquisitorial records transcribed from October 1669 onwards from the archives of the Dominican convent at Toulouse into BN, MSS lat. fonds Doat xxi–xxvi. The Agenais does not feature centrally in these, for although the inquisitors Bernard de Caux and Jean de Saint-Pierre spent eighteen months in the Agenais and Quercy during 1243–5, not much of what survives even from the trials at Agen itself actually relates to the Agenais. What evidence we do have pertaining to Agenais heretics and their contacts in Quercy is mainly contained in Doat xxi. 185r–312v (penances given by Pierre Seilan in Quercy in 1241–2) and Doat xxii. 1r–69v (inquiry by Bernard de Caux and Jean de Saint-Pierre in the Agenais, Quercy and the northern Toulousain in 1243–5).

In discussing the development of the political and social structures in Aquitaine it became necessary to decide whether or not to use the terms 'feudal' and 'feudalism'. The criticism of the terminology by Elizabeth A. R. Brown and Susan Reynolds has proved challenging in that historians can no longer employ it as a form of shorthand, for apparently there is no accepted definition of content.[9] When investigating the families of the Agenais it was noticeable that all but a few recent accounts of the structure of authority in the region, very

---

and J. Boussard, *Le Gouvernment d'Henri II Plantagenêt*, Paris 1956, 228. For some very interesting discussion of the lack of sources for the south of France more generally and its implications for the historiography of the region see *The miracles of Our Lady of Rocamadour*, ed., trans. and intro. M. Bull, Woodbridge 1999, 20–3, 80.

8 *Inventaire sommaire des archives communales d'Agen*, ed. G. Bosvieux and G. Tholin, Paris 1884, cited in Y. Dossat, 'Les Restitutions des dîmes dans le diocèse d'Agen pendant l'épiscopat de Guillaume II, 1247–63', in his *Église et hérésie*, 549 n. 1.

9 E. A. R. Brown, 'The tyranny of a construct: feudalism and historians of medieval Europe', *American Historical Review* lxxix (1974), 1063–88, repr. in L. K. Little and B. H. Rosenwein

scholarly though they are, use terminology which can no longer be duplicated without incurring criticism.

It may be the case that the terminology needs to have its meaning clarified by further debate and the achievement of a consensus. Until this occurs we have to abandon this language, but are left with few descriptive terms by which to distinguish the Middle Ages from the ancient and modern worlds. Such terms are needed because the period contained institutions, not least in terms of landholding and its related socio-political and economic context, which were specific to it, although evolving within it and varying regionally. In addition, the debate has not as yet enabled teachers to convey an accurate picture to students where, according to Brown, they were once merely taught jargon. Indeed, a more common complaint from students encountering the Middle Ages for the very first time is surely not that they are presented with an abstraction or ideal type which informs too rigidly their understanding of the society it describes, but that they are not provided with an overview or a generalised picture of what made medieval societies different from other societies. I am therefore unconvinced that the terms 'feudal' and 'feudalism', or other such generalisations, are entirely bankrupt, although clarification of what is meant in different circumstances needs to accompany their use.

However, Aquitaine and the Agenais are certainly examples of societies in which elite social relationships cannot be easily defined by shorthand, let alone by the same shorthand applied over the 250-year period from 1000. In fact it is the rather fluid forms of social relations and their apparently uninstitutionalised nature which are most relevant in this study, and I find the use of 'feudal' terminology less than useful in this context. When used by Thomas Bisson in relation to the structure of authority in the Agenais it seems to frame the debate in artificial terms, for the lordships of the Agenais did not consider themselves feudatories.[10] Sidney Painter was sure that there must have been a hierarchy of homages at work in Poitou in the period, but failed to identify it from the available sources.[11] Because royal power was absent and other, local and aristocratic institutions evolved, the Agenais and Aquitaine had to be 'feudal' it seems. But the persistence of the allod and the reluctance of the aristocracy to enter formal relationships which threatened their free inheritance of property and titles undermines the picture of a society based around the fief. Therefore I have not used 'feudalism' or 'feudal' but attempt instead to describe what obligations and liberties were apparent and in what contexts. This seems to be the approach most comfortably taken in other recent scholarship.[12] However, I suspect that scholars able to take a more fully informed overview of medieval institutions will

(eds), *Debating the Middle Ages: issues and readings*, Oxford 1998, 148–69 (and editors' introduction at pp. 107–13); S. Reynolds, *Fiefs and vassals*, Oxford 1994.

10 Bisson's work is discussed and cited fully in chapters 3 and 5 below.

11 S. Painter, 'The lords of Lusignan in the eleventh and twelfth centuries', *Speculum* xxxii (1937), 45–7.

12 Little and Rosenwein, *Debating the Middle Ages*, editors' introduction at p. 111.

refine rather than abandon the traditional terms. In short, I approve of Benoît Cursente's attitude to the subject. He defends the use of the terminology of *la féodalité* as useful in many situations, but declares Gascony not 'feudal' but more accurately 'casal', after the specific form of land-management prevalent there.[13]

---

13 Cursente, *Des Maisons*, 48–50, 157. The text for this book was completed before I could make reference to Simon McLean's, *Kingship and policy in the late ninth century: Charles the Fat and the end of the Carolingian empire* (Cambridge 2003), which has added a great deal to debates surrounding the 'collapse' of the Carolingian empire, and the third edition of Malcolm Lambert's *Medieval heresy* (Oxford 2002), which takes discussion of early eleventh-century heresy a step further.

PART I

THE DUCHY AND DUALISM,
1000 TO THE MID-TWELFTH CENTURY

1

Aquitaine and the Agenais, 1000–1152

The counts of Poitou and Aquitainian society, to 1060

Much good work has been done on the general history of Aquitaine, notably in French, and I aim only to summarise it. However some detailed attention will be given to certain features of the early eleventh century, in which we find accounts of heresy in the sources, in order to establish what it might have been about this society that encouraged religious dissent. Important features to note are the structure of lay authority, the relationship between the laity, from its highest levels downwards, and ecclesiastical and monastic authorities, the nature of 'devolved' authority at a rural level, the impact of the year 1000 on religious and social expectations and, a phenomenon which sheds light on all of the above, the Peace of God movement.

Ducal authority over the Aquitainian nobility
As a generalisation, the second half of the tenth century saw the loss of royal power in the old Carolingian kingdom of Aquitaine no less than throughout the rest of western Francia. As this power declined, Aquitaine saw the emergence of an independent nobility. In their turn the counts of Poitou, inheritors of the authority of the old empire over what they came to style their 'duchy', sought to contain the ambitions of other noble families, themselves usually also descended from Frankish officials. Untypically for France in this period, the dukes were to have considerable success in reviving a sense of political hierarchy with regard to many leading nobles and castellans, especially within Poitou itself, in the first half of the eleventh century. The duke's presence was felt very little in the villages, towns and castles of Aquitaine, especially those beyond Poitou, but his court was attended by counts, viscounts and bishops, and much of the prestige of the royal rulers of Aquitaine was to be recovered.[1]

William III 'Tête-d'Etoupe' (d. 963) was the first count of Poitou to assume

---

[1]   The rise of the counts of Poitou in relation to the rest of the Aquitainian nobility is generally accepted by historians: G. Duby, *France in the Middle Ages, 987–1460*, trans. J. Vale, Oxford 1991, 28–9; J. Dunbabin, *France in the making, 843–1180*, Oxford 1985, 133–40, 164, 173–7; Richard, *Histoire*, i. 139–233; J.-P. Poly and E. Bournazel, *The feudal transformation, 900–1200*, trans. C. Higgitt, New York–London 1991, 9–18, 65, 69–70, 76–8 (original French 1980); J.-F. Lemarignier, *Le Gouvernement royal aux premiers temps capétien (987–1108)*, Paris 1965, 25–65 and tables. The most thorough study of this process in English is still J. Martindale's 'The origins of the duchy of Aquitaine and the government of the counts of Poitou, 902–1137', unpubl. DPhil. diss. Oxford 1965, esp. pp. iv–v, 28–61, 78, 89–98. The information in this section is drawn from these sources but in particular from the monographs

the title 'duke of Aquitaine'. His sphere of somewhat nominal authority consisted of the Carolingian counties of Limoges, Angoulême, Saintonge, Périgord, the newly created province of La Marche and Poitou itself. The duke also claimed authority over upper Berry, containing the metropolitan city of Bourges, and the Auvergne.[2] The first real advances were made by William IV 'Fier à Bras' (963–93). However it was his son William V 'the Great' (993–1030) who became one of the most successful magnates in eleventh-century France, far more so than his cousin and king, Robert I (996–1031). He made three very important marriages to improve both his position within the duchy and in relation to other European powers. They were to Almodis of Gévaudan, widow of Count Boso of La Marche-Périgord and probably a daughter of the count of Limoges, to Brisca, daughter of the duke of Gascony, in 1010, and to Agnes, daughter of the duke of Burgundy, in 1016.[3]

cited in individual footnotes concerning specific themes, regions and families. The limited influence of the crown in Aquitaine is well illustrated in a discussion of the duchy and its nobility in L. Theis, *Robert le Pieux, le roi du l'an mil*, Paris 1999, 86, 150, 160–76, 181–5. However, the picture of a rise in Poitevin power in this period does not go wholly unchallenged. From a rigidly *mutationniste* viewpoint, B. S. Bachrach sees ducal authority as weaker in 1030 than at the very end of the tenth century: 'Towards a reappraisal of William the Great, duke of Aquitaine (995–1030)', *JMH* v (1979), 11–21.

2 Over Bourges and the Auvergne the Capetian kings exercised more power than the duke of Aquitaine throughout this period, but even so its nobility was virtually autonomous. Because of this, limitations of space, and not least because the accounts of heresy which I will be discussing only originate within the counties of Aquitaine in which ducal authority was making an impact, I shall discuss the Auvergne and Berry very little. See, however, G. Devailly, *Le Berry du Xe siècle au milieu du XIIIe*, Paris–The Hague 1973, 77–84, 117–22, 239.

3 Almodis apparently poisoned Boso, and Agnes produced a daughter, also called Agnes, who married the Emperor Henry III: J. J. Escande, *Histoire de Périgord*, 2nd edn, Sarlat 1955, 63; J. Martindale, 'Succession and politics in the romance speaking world, c. 1000–1140', in M. C. E. Jones and M. Vale (eds), *England and her neighbours, 1066–1453: essays in honour of Pierre Chaplais*, London–Ronceverte 1989, 29. For the marriage to Brisca see *La Chronique de Saint-Maixent, 751–1140*, ed. and trans. J. Verdon, Paris 1979, 108–9. This is one of the few annalistic sources for the period. It ends in the year 1137, and is not always reliable: Martindale, 'Aquitaine', 114. For the duke's connections beyond Aquitaine see also D. F. Callahan, 'William the Great and the monasteries of Aquitaine', *Studia Monastica* xix (1977), 322–3. Adémar's *Chronicon* (ed. J. Chavanon, Paris 1897), is amongst the most important sources for eleventh-century Aquitaine. Born into a minor noble family of the Limousin, Adémar (989–1034) was a monk of Saint-Cybard, Angoulême, and Saint-Martial, Limoges. His chronicle is a history of Aquitaine, 814–1030, including selected events from the wider world. His third book deals with events in his lifetime and was written between 1025 and 1028. Adémar, it has been shown, is unreliable for events before his time (J. Gillingham, 'Adémar of Chabannes and the history of Aquitaine in the reign of Charles the Bald', in M. T. Gibson and J. Nelson [eds], *Charles the Bald: court and kingdom*, Aldershot 1981, esp. pp. 3–14) and also to have fabricated an apostolic *vita* of Saint-Martial and evidence supporting it (R. Landes, *Relics, Apocalypse and the deceits of history: Ademar of Chabannes, 989–1034*, Cambridge, Mass–London 1995, esp. pp. 4–9, 277). He is most useful for matters in his lifetime with which he was less personally involved and as an insight into monastic attitudes. It was not possible to include the long-awaited modern edition of his chronicle here: *Ademari Cabannensis Chronicon*, ed. P. Bourgain, R. Landes and G. Pons, Turnhout 1999.

The assertion of ducal authority was an arduous process. Great families had come to view rights to offices or property which they held of the duke as hereditary. When they submitted themselves to judicial process this did not involve his court but judgement by the peers of the two parties or, very commonly, private warfare. These factors allowed the balance of power to alter in ways which the duke could not control. Even by the time William V retired to the abbey of Maillezais in 1029 he exercised real authority only in Poitou and La Marche, less in Périgord and Limoges, and next to none within Angoulême, upper Berry and the Auvergne. He never gained control of some of the most important offices such as the Limousin viscounty of Turenne-Comborn, although by 1027 he had subdued the rebellious viscounts of Limoges themselves. But even if Adémar of Chabannes is exaggerating in saying that 'he subjected all of Aquitaine to his rule', the fairly nominal nature of the title he inherited was dramatically transformed.[4]

Within Poitou itself the castle of Lusignan dominated a forest bordering the comital demesne. From 1022 to 1028 the duke undermined the political freedom of its castellan, Hugh IV, and imposed terms which thwarted the family's hereditary claims. George Beech has argued that the *conventum* which records these events should be viewed as a form of *chanson de geste* and that this negates the specific political inferences made from it by historians. I am inclined towards Stephen White's more moderate position, that the *conventum* uses a literary device to make complaints about a very real struggle amongst the lords and castellans of Poitou.[5] That this process, if not the document itself, formed part of a deliberate policy of binding the great families to William V is indicated by his correspondence with Bishop Fulbert of Chartres, defining exactly what a lord could legally demand of his man.[6] By the time William V retired, the Poitevin lords of Thouars and Parthenay were also his vassals, and the major castles ringing Poitiers had been built by and were controlled by him.

The family which controlled La Marche-Périgord tended to ally with the counts of Anjou, the dukes' major rivals beyond Aquitaine, who were capable of exerting great influence in Saintonge and Angoulême. In part due to a rare intervention of King Robert in western France, this alliance was forcibly dissolved in 1003. As a result, William V was able to separate Périgord and La Marche into two weaker units, even though he was not able to dominate them

---

4 Adémar, *Chronicon*, 163; Geoffrey of Vigeois, *Chronica*, in *Nova bibliothecae manuscriptorum . . . collectio*, ed. P. Labbé, Paris 1657, ii. 279–342, esp. p. 281. Geoffrey wrote in the twelfth century, but recorded much concerning events, especially the viscomital wars, about which Adémar is uninformative: M. Aubrun, 'Le Prieur Geoffrey de Vigeois et sa chronique', *Revue Mabillon* lviii (1974), 313.

5 *Le Conventum (vers 1030): un précurseur aquitain des premières épopées*, ed., trans. and intro. G. T. Beech, Y. Chauvin and G. Pons, Geneva 1995, esp. pp. 21–8, 39–41, 91–111; S. White, review of *Le Conventum*, *Speculum* lxxii (1997), 430.

6 Fulbert of Chartres, *The letters and poems*, ed. F. Behrends, Oxford 1976, letter 51; 'Conventum inter Guillemum aquitanorum comes et Hugonem Chiliarchum', ed. J. Martindale, *EHR* lxxxiv (1969), 528–36; Painter, 'Lords of Lusignan', 30–2.

directly. One of the most independent-minded Aquitainians, Count William IV of Angoulême, likewise allied with the Angevins, a collaboration the duke sabotaged by binding the count to him with grants of important estates. The count was William V's voluntary *fidelis*, and he had no actual coercive powers over him, but the coming years saw Angoulême supporting ducal attempts to impose authority on other troublesome Aquitainians, not least Boso II of La Marche. A similar strategy was employed in dealing with the Angevins themselves: Count Fulk Nerra was enfeoffed with the keep at Saintes when the alliance with La Marche-Périgord was ended, and with the castle of Loudun for ending the plots with Angoulême.[7]

But this accord with Anjou was to prove hazardous after William V died. His widow Agnes married Count Geoffrey Martel of Anjou in 1032 and the couple dominated the duchy, Saintonge especially, whilst William VI 'the Fat' (1030–8) was duke, and in this context some minor lords increased their own power by supporting the Angevin intervention. Until 1044 Martel was regent for William VII 'Aigret', also known as Pierre-Guillaume and 'le Hardi', and even after Agnes and Martel divorced in the early 1050s the Angevins still sought to dominate Aigret's affairs and he was at war with them for several years. As a result there was a severe decline in ducal authority, for Aigret was unable to rule effectively outside of Poitou. It was only under Duke Guy-Geoffrey (1058–86) that a Poitevin reassertion began and the dynasty was secure. In 1061 he captured Angevin-held parts of Saintonge and the Angevin threat, with it potential plots within Aquitaine, was so effectively neutralised that his attention turned to the south, towards the acquisition of Gascony.[8]

Aquitainian religious institutions and the laity
In the process of the assimilation of Gascony into the duchy the office of archbishop of Bordeaux, technically an independent royal nominee, was in practice to be disputed between Poitevin and Gascon families. His neighbour the archbishop of Bourges, although more independent, still had to fight off Poitevin influence in the diocese of Limoges, contained within his province, in the same period as the Limousin viscounts were resisting the duke in secular affairs. In this the archbishop co-operated with the Capetian kings, the counts of the Auvergne and the viscounts themselves. Elections to the see of Limoges were not 'free', however, but contested between important local families and, along with the abbacy of Saint-Martial, were in the hands of the viscounts until civil unrest in 1019–21 allowed William V and the archbishop of Bordeaux to force reform. This had actually begun independently of the dukes: in 989 Archbishop

7 Adémar, *Chronicon*, 157, 162–5, 167, and also p. 163 n. 1; A. Debord, *La Société laïque dans les pays de la Charente: Xe–XIIe siècles*, Paris 1984, esp. pp. 104–15; B. S. Bachrach, 'A study in feudal politics: relations between Fulk Nerra and William the Great, 995–1030', *Viator* vii (1976), 111–22.
8 *Chronique Saint-Maixent*, 116–17, 130; G. T. Beech, *A rural society in medieval France: the Gâtine of Poitou in the 11th and 12th centuries*, Baltimore 1964, 45–8; Bachrach, 'Reappraisal', 16–17; Martindale, 'Succession', 29.

Gombaud of Bordeaux summoned the bishop of Limoges to the Council of Charroux, and in 990 he consecrated Limoges' new bishop, Aldouin. In 1012 another bishop was consecrated by Gombaud's Poitevin successor, Séguin, with ducal support. Duke William finally convened a council in 1021 at Saint-Junien-de-Nouaillé at which, Adémar tells us, God elected as bishop Jordan, the duke's candidate. The Bourges/Limousin faction was furious and the election was disputed, but Jordan successfully rode out the storm and held the see until 1051. In fact, wherever possible William the Great made it his business to increase his control over diocesan affairs. When he expelled the Angevins from Saintes, he quickly established his own, loyal bishop there. Other leading families also influenced the allocation of episcopal and abbatial offices, not least the families of the Angoumois who dominated its bishops and the abbacy of Saint-Cybard.[9]

At the other end of the social scale, we might speculate that the increase in influence of the wealthy laity over the Church was to the benefit of lay piety generally, for the former group took actively to church-building from the late tenth century in many areas, in and around the Gâtine of Poitou for example. Indeed, Aquitaine was not unlike Rodulfus Glaber's Burgundy: covered by a white mantle of churches. However, at least before the reforms of the mid-eleventh century there is little evidence that religious life for the majority of the population was at all improved through the activity of the aristocracy (notwithstanding the comparative lack of ecclesiatical evidence about the rural laity of the duchy generally). It was probably the church-builders themselves who benefited most from their new enthusiasm: like others in France at this time they were increasingly able to control the allocation of benefices and collect tithes into their own coffers. Nor was the Aquitainian peasantry well served by the more 'independent' churches for which the bishops were responsible. Although in parts of western France such churches and their parishes were organised and supported as part of networks of subdeaneries within a diocesan framework, there is little evidence for this in Aquitaine. In addition, the number of people comprising an Aquitainian parish was very large. The very term *parrochia*, far from implying a sense of spiritual kinship within a geographical area, merely denoted the lands associated with the *villa* on which the parish was based. It would seem that the rural laity felt very distant from spiritual leadership originating in the secular sphere. Indeed, in Aquitaine and in other parts of the Midi,

---

9 Adémar, *Chronicon*, 159, 182–3, 185. For the structure and nature of episcopal authority from archiepiscopal to parish level see J.-F. Lemarignier, J. Gaudemet and G. Mollat, 'Les Institutions ecclésiastiques en France de la fin du Xe au milieu du XIIe siècle', in F. Lot and R. Fawtier (eds), *Histoire des institutions français au moyen âge*, Paris 1957–62, iii. 7–62; Dunbabin, *France*, 98–100, 219–20, 355; Ch. Higounet, Y. Renouard and others, *Histoire de Bordeaux*, Bordeaux 1962–5, ii. 270–80; iii. 9; Martindale, 'Aquitaine', 56, 65, 122; M. Bull, *Knightly piety and the lay response to the First Crusade: the Limousin and Gascony*, c. 970–1130, Oxford 1993, 37–8; P. Imbart de la Tour, *Les Paroisses rurales du IVe au XIe siècles*, 2nd edn, Paris 1979, 108–9, 117–18, 148–53, 234–99 (esp. pp. 238, 248), 300–45; G. Lobrichon, *La Religion des laïcs en occident, XIe–XVe siècles*, Paris 1994, 49.

lay pastoral needs were more commonly met by the abbeys. The *villae* in question were typically those associated with abbeys and on which there were
monastic-run churches. The Poitevin abbey of Charroux, for example, had
dozens of such dependencies throughout the dioceses of Aquitaine and beyond.
Powerful abbeys were able to resist incursions into their parishes by the lay elite
to a greater extent than many diocesan-orientated churches. Many, and Saint-
Jean d'Angély is a good example, insisted on appointing their own priests,
perhaps in the face of opposition from important local families.[10]

There is more evidence that the peasantry and townspeople of the duchy
were increasingly drawn to the abbeys from the late tenth century. But if the
monks were able to play the greatest part in influencing the lowly laity, they
were not entirely able to escape forming relationships with the more important
on the latter's terms. Aristocratic and knightly families were hugely generous to
the abbeys, and not only those associated with their families but to those like
Sainte-Foy at Conques, beyond their obvious spheres of political or territorial
influence. This practice, which has been extensively studied, covered donations
ranging from prestigious foundations like that dedicated in 1010 by the duke to
the Apostles Peter and Paul at Maillezais, through impressive local works such as
those by the lords of Parthenay, Lusignan and La Marche, to numerous humbler
donations by knightly families. Indeed the latter, in the context of violent
disorder, perhaps gave to the religious beyond their means, and were amongst
the leading champions of saints' cults.[11] But the influence which accompanied
such generosity was not always welcome. Those who effectively owned an abbey
might distribute vicarial rights over its lands and tenants to their *fideles*.
Castellans had been responsible for the protection of monasteries in earlier
centuries when their office was an expression of public authority, but now
sources indicate that they sometimes plundered abbey lands and many monastic
immunities were effectively eroded. The Lusignans, for example, had been
installed on the lands of Saint-Maixent by the Carolingians, a very mixed
blessing for the monks because of the family's subsequent coveting of the monastery's resources.[12]

As a consequence, the support and intervention of bishops, far from being
imposed on the abbeys, was regularly sought by the monks. Bishop Grimoald of

10 Rodulfus Glaber, *The five books of the histories*, ed. and trans. J. France and N. Bulst, Oxford
1989, 126–7; *Chartes et documents pour servir à l'histoire de l'abbaye de Charroux*, ed. P. de
Monsabert, AHP xxxix (1910), p. i and no. 4; Imbart de la Tour, *Les Paroisses*, 248.
11 For illustrative examples of donations in the period see *Chronique Saint-Maixent*, 106–7,
122–3; *Cartulaire de l'abbaye royale de Notre-Dame de Saintes de l'ordre de Saint Benoît*, ed. Th.
Grasilier, Niort 1871, 1–8; *Cartulaire de l'abbaye de Cellefrouin*, ed. E. Brayer, BPH (1940–1),
no. 4 and pp. i, 91–5; 'Chartes de l'abbaye de Nouaillé de 678 à 1200', ed. P. Monsabert, AHP
xlix (1936), 173–4. For discussion of lay generosity see especially Bull, *Piety*, 115–203, 204–49,
and B. L. Venarde, *Women's monasticism and medieval society: nunneries in France and England,
890–1215*, Ithaca–London 1997, 34–40.
12 *Chartes et documents pour servir à l'histoire de l'abbaye de Saint-Maixent*, ed. A. Richard, AHP
xvi (1886), 104, 155–6; xviii (1886), 482; *Chronique Saint-Maixent*, 402; Painter, 'Lords of
Lusignan', 27–35.

Angoulême entered into conflict with viscount Guy of Limoges because of the latter's influence over the monastery of Brantôme. The matter was eventually taken to Rome, resulting in heavy sanctions against Guy. Bishop Alduin of Limoges and Count William of Angoulême built a castle in Haute-Vienne to protect the abbey of Saint-Junien from the castellan Jordan de Chabannais.[13]

The dependence of the monasteries on the support of the bishops appears to account for the very different pattern of reform in Aquitaine to that taking place in Cluniac Burgundy. Indeed, by the 1030s probably only one Aquitainian house, Saint-Sauveur at Sarlat in Périgord, was part of the Cluniac network. This seems surprising in light of the fact that it was Duke William III who, in 909, had donated the land in Burgundy on which Cluny stood. This is still not the whole picture, however, and here we must return to the growing power of the dukes in religious affairs, for it was in fact under their influence that many of the most notable reforms took place, both in the abbeys and cathedrals. William V worked between 1010 and 1020 to remove the corrupt Abbot Peter I from Charroux. He replaced him with the reformer Gombaud II, and between 1032 and 1064 a ducal charter of reform was issued for the abbey. It was also as a ducal initiative that Abbot Odilo of Cluny (994–1049), an Aquitainian himself, attempted, with limited success, to reform Saint-Jean d'Angély. It was Odilo's nominee whom the duke supported in 1012 at Limoges. By 1016 Pope Benedict VIII saw William V as a man capable, like his predecessor, of promoting and protecting the Cluniac ideal.[14]

William V's religious strategy was thus apparently as coherent as that with which he asserted political control over the elite amongst the laity. In fact, it will be argued, it was part of the same strategy: to impose peace, order and, not least, religious orthodoxy. However, ducal influence over the laity was minimal at a very local level, almost certainly less than that of the abbeys. The question of religious orthodoxy relates very closely to this absence of credible government in the countryside, and also the ultimate failure of the abbeys to impose peace themselves.

Castellans and the rural poor: *mutation ou ajustement?*

Until the 1960s the transition from the Carolingian world to that of the high Middle Ages was seen as an essentially gradual process.[15] Following Georges

---

13 Adémar, *Chronicon*, 158–60, 165–6; Callahan, 'William the Great', 328.

14 Adémar, *Chronicon*, 172, 181, 184; *Chartes Charroux*, 3; *PL* cxxxix.1601–4; J. J. Escande, *Histoire de Sarlat*, Sarlat 1903, 23–4, 30–1; Martindale, 'Aquitaine', 62–3, 164; Richard, *Histoire*, i. 196 n. 1; 220 n. 1.

15 Amongst the most influential, M. Bloch's seminal work discusses the disintegration of public authority, the transfer of power to the principalities and to castellanies and the loss of freedom by the peasantry as features of his 'first feudal age', that is to say c. 850 to c. 1050, and does not assume the need to locate them within a more specific timeframe: *Feudal society*, trans. L. A. Manyon, 2nd English edn, London–New York 1989, esp. vol. i. 255–66; ii. 359–74, 394–401.

Duby's pioneering study of the Mâconnais, first published in 1953, another model emerged which emphasised a breakdown of public authority in western Francia specifically under the last Carolingians and first Capetians, in the period 970–1030. In this context castellans began to exert independently authority originally delegated to them by higher-ranking royal officials, counts and viscounts, authority including rights to exercise justice and to fortify their property. The inability of the higher-ranking aristocracy to call these men to account meant that castellans began to make their titles hereditary and to exercise their offices for personal gain, for example in the collection of fees and fines resulting from court cases. The authority of the castellan was enforced psychologically and in real terms by the threat and use of violence, for they gathered in their castles retinues of *milites*, or knights. The social status of the knights was not originally linked to lineage, for unlike the nobility they did not claim descent from Carolingian officials, but to the right to bear arms, invested in them by their adopted lords. They rose from the very lowest ranks of the nobility and allodial land-holders, and in western France some were recruited from the peasantry. This newly assertive caste of warriors, rising in status, could not be allowed to acquire too much independent power of their own however, and so the nobility began to draw them into voluntary relationships of personal dependence, symbolised by a set of socially exclusive rituals. The emergence from the late tenth century of the private castellan and the *milites* in his castle transformed society dramatically in but a few decades.[16]

In applying this model to Aquitaine specifically, it has been demonstrated that land management practice amongst the elite, that is to say frequent subdivisions of estates through partible inheritance, coupled with probably over-

---

16 G. Duby, *La Société au xie et xiie siècle dans la region mâconnaise*, 2nd edn, Paris 1971, 150–8; *The chivalrous society*, trans. C. Postan, London 1977, 59–80, 158–70; *France in the Middle Ages*, 55–90; *The three orders: feudal society imagined*, trans. A. Goldhammer, Chicago 1982, 147–66; and *The early growth of the european economy*, trans. H. B. Clarke, Ithaca, NY 1974, 162–77. The more recent view of the social origin of the *miles* diverges from Duby's model for the Mâconnais in which the eleventh-century nobility and *milites* originated from the same families. The rest of his portrayal of change is more or less adhered to in the following regional studies: G. Bois, *La Mutation de l'an mil: Lournand, village mâconnaise de l'antiquité au féodalisme*, Paris 1989, 177–262 (English trans. Manchester 1992); P. Bonnassie, *La Catalogne au tournant de l'an mil: croissance et mutations d'une société*, Paris 1990; E. Bournazel, 'Mémoire et parenté: le problème de la continuité dans la noblesse de l'an mil', in M. Parisse and X. Barral I Altet (eds), *Le Roi de France et son royaume autour de l'an mil*, Paris 1992, 111–16; Devailly, *Le Berry*, 109–35, 161–235; J.-P. Poly, *La Provence et la société féodale (879–1166)*, Paris 1976, 112–81; M. Bourin-Derruau, *Villages et communautés villageoises en Languedoc: l'example du Biterrois (Xe–XIVe siècle)*, Paris 1987, esp. vol. i; Cursente, *Des Maisons* (on pp. 68–9 he cites charters in the cartulary of Madiran which indicate the distinction between noble castellans and *milites* in Gascony: BN, MSS lat. fonds Doat clii, fos 146–225). Duby's general principles also appear in the following thematic works: R. Boutruche, *Seigneurie et féodalité*, Paris 1959, 105–26; Poly and Bournazel, *Feudal transformation*, 9–140, esp. pp. 25–39, 98–102, 120–33; T. N. Bisson, 'The feudal revolution', *Past and Present* cxlii (1994), 6–42. J. F. Lemarignier came to very similar conclusions independently of Duby: 'La Dislocation du *pagus* et le problème des *consuetudines*', in *Mélanges Louis Halphen*, Paris 1951, 401–10; *Le Gouvernement royal*, 25–65.

generous donations to monasteries in the tenth century, reduced the economic viability of the property held by individual castellans. In truth, many probably had trouble supporting themselves peacefully off the traditional dues that their status afforded them: in Carolingian Poitou in particular they were not traditionally accorded many such rights. Castellans, even when they were still part of comital and ducal entourages, as many were, became accustomed to abusing their licence for private ends. Thus they exercised for personal gain the *bannum*, the levying of fines, called the *manament* or *mandamentum* in Aquitaine, typically held in conjunction with the right of *destreit*, to apprehend and arrest, delegated to those holding castles and, with no higher authority caring or able to stop them, extended their control over peasant communities to the extent that legal freedoms began to be eroded. The castle became the most immediately recognisable symbol of the new order. Usually wooden but none the less formidable, both theoretically public and overtly private, they increased in numbers dramatically in this period, as did private wars between those holding them and controlling the retinues within them.[17]

In the same period we find in parts of western Francia increased resentment, resistance and occasional violent uprisings by the peasantry. This was apparently as a result of the force and theft associated with the new social and economic order Although we must be careful of imposing models of resistance on groups which have left almost no trace of their own motives and objectives, they are reflected most overtly in the problematic evidence for events in Normandy in 996–7. In this revolt we hear from the earliest related source – William of Jumièges's chronicle composed around a century later – that peasants reclaimed their threatened rights to resources they perceived as communal and overthrew their servitude, forming their own assembly until the rebellion was mercilessly crushed by Count Raoul of Evreux.[18] In 1038 a popular army, mobilised by

---

[17] For illustrative examples see Adémar, *Chronicon*, 78, 136–40, 159, 185–6. Around the same time as Duby was researching the Mâconnais, S. Painter arrived independently at almost the same model for the rise of the castellans of Poitou: 'Castellans of the plain of Poitou in the eleventh and twelfth centuries', *Speculum* xxxi (1956), 246–8, 251, 253, 256–7, and 'Lords of Lusignan', 27–33. More recently see Beech, *Gâtine*, 82, 92–5; Debord, *La Société laique*, 122–62; 'The castellan revolution and the Peace of God in Aquitaine', in T. Head and R. Landes (eds), *The Peace of God: social violence and religious response in France around the year 1000*, Ithaca–London 1992, 165–83; 'Castrum et castellum chez Adémar de Chabannes', *Archéologie médiévale* ix (1979), 97–113; and *Aristocratie et pouvoir: le rôle du château dans la France médiévale*, Paris 2000, 19–88; A. R. Lewis, *The development of southern French and Catalan society, 718–1050*, Austin, Texas 1965, 312–14, 179–314; Poly and Bournazel, *Feudal transformation*, 64–5; Callahan, 'William the Great', 321–2, 327; Ch. Higounet, 'En Bordelais: *principes castella tenentes*', in P. Contamine (ed.), *La Noblesse au moyen âge, 11e–15e siècles*, Paris 1976, 97–104; R. Boutruche, *Une Société provinciale en lutte contre le regime féodale: l'alleu en Bordelais et en Bazadais du XIe au XVIIIe siècle*, Rodez 1943, 1–4, 26, 53–71; Ch. Higounet and others, *Histoire de l'Aquitaine*, Toulouse 1971, 160–4. For the condition of the peasantry in the south-west in this period see also the work of P. Bonnassie cited in n. 34 below.

[18] William of Jumièges, *Gesta normannorum ducum*, ed. A. Duchesne, Paris 1619, 823–4; Wace, *Le Roman de la rou*, cited in R. Hilton, *Bond men made free*, London 1988, 71–2; Poly and

episcopal authorities in the name of the Peace of God, took matters into its own hands and attacked castellans.[19] Few other accounts indicate this trend in Aquitaine, but it will be argued later that some alternative outlets for dissent were found.

The above model, applied to other regions of France as well, has been termed *la mutation*. The concept is employed both by those who still find the terminology of feudalism useful, and who call this process a feudal revolution, and by those who have some criticisms of it and are seeking to provide the millennial period with its own more accurate shorthand. The conclusions of the *mutationnistes* are also adopted by many who do not use the terminology itself. But the *mutationniste* school has many critics. Just as some historians have rejected 'feudalism' as an accurate or useful description of medieval society, so some also challenge *la mutation* for the homogeneity, chronologically and geographically, which it appears, to its critics, to assume. Most vehement amongst them, Dominique Barthélemy prefers a theory of *ajustements successifs* to replace *la mutation brutale*, levelling at advocates of the latter the view that 'les historiens ont trop souvent pris leurs idéaltypes pour des réalités vraies'.[20] Not least, Barthélemy disputes that there were significant numbers of free peasants who began to lose their status as a result of the rise of the castellans.[21] His own study of the Vendômois indicates that there such changes were more subtle and that the years around 1200 were more significant than those around 1000.[22]

Barthélemy is able to cite work by other historians which he feels supports his view. Janet Nelson has modified the picture of the knight as distinct from the

---

Bournazel, *Feudal transformation*, 136; R. Fossier, 'Les Mouvements populaires en occident au XIe siècle', in *Académie des Inscriptions et Belles-Lettres: comptes rendus des séances de l'année 1971*, Paris 1972, 261; Debord, *Aristocratie et pouvoir*, 56–9; C. Taylor, 'The year 1000 and "those who laboured" ', in M. Frassetto (ed.), *The year 1000: religious and social responses to the turning of the first millennium*, New York–Basingstoke 2002, 187–236.

19 *Miracles de Saint-Benoît*, ed. M. Prou and A. Vidier, Paris 1900, no. 74, pp. 196–7: see M. Aubrun, *La Paroisse en France, des origines au xve siècle*, Paris 1986, 102 and no. 24.

20 D. Barthélemy, *La Mutation de l'an mil, a-t-elle eu lieu? Servage et chevalerie dans la France des Xe et XIe siècles*, Paris 1997, esp. p. 8 (quoting H. I. Marrou, *De la Connaissance historique*, 2nd edn, Paris 1975, 157–8), 15, 28 (crediting the concept of *ajustement* to C. Duhamel-Amado, 'Les Pouvoirs et les parents autour de Béziers [980–1100]', in *Cadres de vie et société dans le Midi médiéval: homage à Charles Higounet*, AM cii [1990], 309–17), and see *L'An mil et la paix de dieu: la France chrétienne et féodale, 980–1060*, Paris 1999, 58–69. Barthélemy in fact originally coined the term *mutationniste*: *La Société dans le comté de Vendôme de l'an mil au XIVe siècle*, Paris 1993, 13, reviewed by S. White in *Speculum* lxxi (1996), 116–20 at p. 116. He does not take issue with the model proposed by Duby, but with those who 'push it to the extreme' (pp. 15–18; for the quotation see review of *La Mutation* by M. C. E. Jones, *TLS*, 6 Mar. 1998, 26). The perceived failures of *mutationniste* scholarship are also discussed in Barthélemy, *Vendôme*, 9, 11, 83, 275, and, more polemically, in A. Guerreau's review of Bois, *La Mutation*, MA xcvi (1990), 519–37. Most recently K. Thompson finds his approach appropriate when applied to the Perche: *Power and border lordship in medieval France: the Perche in the eleventh and twelfth centuries, 1000–1226*, Woodbridge 2001, for example at pp. 3, 5.

21 Barthélemy, *Mutation*, 20–3, 59–171, 175–296.

22 Ibid. and idem, *Vendôme*, 11–13, 277–8, 333–64, 441, 506, 514, 693, 709, 770.

aristocracy or as a phenomenon specific to the late tenth century onwards.[23] Whilst the accountable officials of the ninth-century Carolingian *pagi* contrast with the autonomous counts of the tenth, for most people, in terms of the experience of local justice, very little changed.[24] There is evidence that, far from being contrary to public order, private agreements complemented it and feuding, the pursuit of justice through violence, was to a great extent self-limiting in the private sphere.[25] In southern France some Carolingian terminology defining social relations did not vanish in the tenth century for it had never been widespread in the first place, whilst other terms stayed in use from the ninth century into the eleventh, implying a continuity of interpretation.[26] The very methodology by which some *mutationnistes* have reached their conclusions has been found wanting. Susan Reynolds argues that we rely too much for understanding lay social relations and the extent of violence on monastic sources, which have an interest in exaggerating the scale of the problem. She uses the *conventum* between Hugh of Lusignan and William V to modify the impression that princely power had collapsed.[27]

This debate is relevant to our subject not least because a society experiencing unprecedented levels of social injustice and the marginalisation of idealistic groups within it would, according to most models explaining the rise of heresy, be a society that could support religious as well as political dissent, perhaps depending on how well authorities responded to the concerns of the increasingly vulnerable and volatile sections of that society.[28] What kind of society, then, was millennial Aquitaine?

Many criticisms of the *mutationniste* model must be true. Common sense dictates that things did not change uniformly throughout France within the same few decades, and 'one does not safely bet against continuity in history'.[29] The unabashed assertion that in the millennial era 'an old world burst apart' in 'a time of sudden, rapid, and all-transforming change' inevitably invites qualification.[30] Another study dates the decline of 'strong comital power' in Poitou

---

23 J. Nelson, 'Ninth-century knighthood: the evidence of Nithard', in her *The Frankish world, 750–900*, London 1996, 77.

24 Idem, 'Dispute settlement in Carolingian west Francia', ibid. 68–9.

25 Barthélemy cites S. White, '*Pactum legem vincit et amor judicium*, the settlement of disputes by compromise', *American Journal of Legal History* xxii (1978), 281–308, but see also White's, 'Feuding and peace-making in the Touraine around the year 1100', *Traditio* xlii (1986), 199–200, 246–63.

26 E. Magnou-Nortier, 'Fidélité et féodalité méridionales d'après les serments de fidélité, Xe – début XIIe siècle', AM lxxx (1968), 460–70.

27 Reynolds, *Fiefs and vassals*, 124–5, 159.

28 J. Nelson, 'Society, theodicy and the origins of heresy', in D. Baker (ed.), *Schism, heresy and religious protest* (SCH ix, 1972), 65–77; T. Asad, 'Medieval heresy: an anthropological view', *Social History* xi (1986), 345–62; N. Cohn, *The pursuit of the millennium*, 3rd edn, London 1990, 53–62, 282–4; R. I. Moore, *The formation of a persecuting society*, Oxford 1987, 19–22, 102–6.

29 Bisson, 'Feudal revolution', 9.

30 R. I. Moore, 'Postcript: the Peace of God and the social revolution', in Head and Landes, *Peace of God*, 309.

specifically to the time of William V, saying that until 995 it was extensive, and asserts that this process in Aquitaine was a perfect illustration of the decline of public authority more widely.[31] Such extreme expressions of *la mutation* add weight to the view that it is a useless *idéaltype*. Simplifications and truisms should, of course, be open to modification and, if necessary, destruction. However, the studies which best support the view that significant changes marked this period provide a far more complex and qualified model than Barthélemy would have us believe.[32]

This is the case not least in relation to Aquitaine and south-western France, including Gascony. To begin with, the orthodox view itself contends that when knights eventually became dependent on noble patronage this took place in a less structured sense in Aquitaine and southern France than in the north and east.[33] Pierre Bonnassie, an apparently rigid *mutationniste*, frequently highlights regional variations in the conditions to which the peasantry were subject. He has shown his own supposed *idéaltype* to apply less to the Auvergne and Septimania, where Visigothic law was still cited and some public courts were still held. Whilst he concludes that the peasantry of France was generally 'miserable et asservie' and eventually 'vaincue', with few exceptions, around the year 1000, some were 'protégée' and others 'libre et dynamique', and whilst some were 'opprimée et soumise', some were 'rebelle'. This view of the condition of the peasantry varies regionally, and his assertion, based on the available sources, that in south-western Europe there were indeed significant numbers of free peasants who lost their status is difficult to fault. However Bonnassie himself concedes that even in Aquitaine this process does not exactly fulfil the *mutationniste* formula, for here it began in the ninth century when once-free *coloni* entered into relationships of dependency with those who could protect them from invading Normans. Bonnassie also concludes that, although there was in the south a period of freedom between that of slavery and serfdom, northern France saw a more gradual transition in which few attained freedom in between the two servitudes, and that Poitou was a society somewhere in between the two situations. André Debord notes in the Charente a *mutation* which diverges from that occurring in Duby's Mâconnais. The aims of the Peace of God were to curb knightly violence in both regions, but in Aquitaine, in contrast with Burgundy, this was in collaboration with aristocratic power. The period during which castles appear to have proliferated in Aquitaine was actually before 1000, but in the Mâconnais it was after this date. Indeed, in the Charente the duke began to increase his control over castle-building after 1000. In addition Debord qualifies uniformity in this picture by saying that there is evidence that castles were licensed by public authority relatively frequently in the northern counties of Aquitaine in comparison to the south. He thus does

---

31 Bachrach, 'Reappraisal', esp. pp. 15–16, 17.
32 S. White's review (at p. 119) of *Vendôme* also notes Barthélemy's tendency to make generalisations and overpolemicise about *mutationnisme* and its advocates.
33 See chapter 3 below.

anything but conform to the supposed orthodoxy. Beech takes the traditional view that lords in the eleventh-century Parthenay increased in actual power in relation to the duke, but stresses this less in the period 1000–30 than in 1030–8, when they were allied with enemies of William VI.[34]

For me, these historians achieve what Barthélemy accuses them of failing to do: they provide a detailed, justified and useful description of Aquitainian society in the millennial period, based on the available evidence, essentially charters and cartularies. I am happy to accept for Aquitaine the general premise that 'the years before and, above all, immediately after, 1000 appear as a turning-point in the history of rural societies in the Frankish kingdom'.[35]

In addition, some of the *ajustementist* inferences made by Barthélemy when citing 'supporting' authorities are unconvincing. White aims essentially to examine apparent contrasts between north-western France and the Languedoc from 1040 to 1250, not to show continuity or otherwise between the Carolingian and High Medieval eras. Reynolds's study of elite social relations, like Bloch's, draws material from a wide period, from 900 to 1100, and is thus certainly the sort of survey that could illustrate or disprove *la mutation*. However she does not attempt this but seeks rather to improve the terminology used in the broader time-frame, concluding only that 'the rights and obligations attached to property . . . were different in 1100 from what they had been two centuries before', not whether this changed more rapidly in a given period. Not least, she notes that the Carolingian terminology associated with the obligation of military service and attendance at public courts had in fact disappeared by the early eleventh century, and she criticises Barthélemy's own use of an *idéaltype*, 'féodalisme'. Nelson argues that there was little real contrast between the 'royal' power of the ninth century and the 'comital' power of the tenth. However the *mutationnistes* are identifying not merely an absence of royal government locally in the later tenth but also the decline of comital – and in our case ducal – authority itself, and the resultant devolution of justice to castellans. In arguing that the institution of knighthood emerged in the ninth century, she is explicitly referring only to its military and ideological facets, and nowhere implies that the delegation of judicial authority to soldiers took place in the Carolingian era. Finally, it has been noted that some of Barthélemy's own conclusions, not least his assertion that the castle was a Carolingian phenomenon, may need revising.[36]

---

[34] P. Bonnassie, *From slavery to feudalism in south-western Europe*, Cambridge 1991, 299–300; 'Les Paysans du royaume franc au temps d'Hugues Capet et Robert le Pieux (987–1031)', in Parisse and Barral I Altet, *Le Roi de France*, 118–25; and 'Survie et extinction du régime esclavagiste dans l'occident du haut moyen âge, IVe–XIe siécle', CCM xxviii (1985), 338–9 and n. 24; Debord, *La Société laique*, 116–22, 140–52, and 'Castellan revolution', 142–9; Beech, *Gâtine*, 42–8.

[35] Bonnassie, *Slavery*, 313.

[36] White, 'Pactum', 285–8, 289–98; Reynolds, *Fiefs and vassals*, 14–15, 117–19, 117 n. 4, 126–7, 157–9; Nelson, 'Dispute settlement', 68–9, and 'Knighthood'; Jones, review of *La Mutation*.

A modified *mutationniste* thesis seems appropriate to the duchy of Aquitaine and its constituent parts. To my knowledge no one has taken a region of Aquitaine to illustrate *ajustement*, and nor could they. There is simply too much evidence, including that expressed through the Peace of God movement and the fact that this began in Aquitaine, that the duchy was undergoing a rapid social transformation, that the poor felt that this was novel and unjust and that the struggling secular and religious authorities sought to bring those resistant to 'legitimate' power under their control. Certainly churchmen, and also the dukes, used such protest and the resultant movement to improve their own position, not just over the knights but also over the poor. But unless we claim that they fabricated tales of violence to achieve this – and the amount of evidence involved would mean the discovery of a most elaborate conspiracy against the poor – we must conclude that many in Aquitaine perceived that something of a *mutation* was indeed taking place.

But *la mutation* in Aquitaine does need qualifying, as it has been by its historians. Royal authority did not suddenly collapse here, for it was already comparatively weak.[37] Paradoxically, and in spite of the limitations on his power, William the Great, through what he inherited and what he achieved, was one of the most powerful rulers in this period of weak public authority.[38] Whilst, pre-empting Duby, Carl Erdmann noted that the Peace of God was necessary because princely and royal protection of monasteries had collapsed, we find, in the very same duchy in which the Peace originated, the growing devotion of lesser nobles to saints' cults.[39] If many free people were forcibly enserfed – or 'allowed' this to happen in order to protect their lives at the expense of their freedom and property, which surely amounts to the same thing – some peasant communities were successful in maintaining their liberty. Free peasants of the Gâtine, for example, apparently kept free status by supporting a lord, William de Parthenay, who did not subject them, and in 1037 they even built him a castle.[40]

On balance, however, *ajustement* does not seem to me to describe Aquitainian society very accurately. From the evidence it appears that the Aquitainian poor became increasingly frightened and insecure at the hands of the powerful and that this was largely the result of the emergence of a relatively new social group with unprecedented levels of unaccountable authority embodied in the castle, itself a relatively new phenomenon. Whether or not any of these processes had roots in the Carolingian period is not actually the central point here. What is of principal concern is the subjective interpretation of events by the peasantry, for their reaction to social conditions, not least their

---

37 Lemarignier, *Le Gouvernement royal*, 29–31, 41.

38 See, for example, his role in relation to the counts of Angoulême, as discussed in Debord, *Charente*, and to the lords of Parthenay in Beech, *Gâtine*, even though these were largely autonomous within their own territories.

39 C. Erdmann, *The origins of the idea of crusade*, trans. M. W. Baldwin and W. Goffart, Princeton 1977, esp. p. 59; Bull, *Piety*, as cited in n. 11 above.

40 Beech, *Gâtine*, 45–8, 114–16. See also chapter 3 below.

relationship with the allies whom they sought within the elite, seems to have paved the way for popular support for religious heresy.

The millennium and popular religiosity

The extent to which Aquitainian society experienced millennial 'terrors' in this period is also debated. On the one hand, what seem overtly eschatological images and apocalyptic interpretations in the sources are disputed by historians of the religious life who tend towards the view that society was only experiencing mild *ajustement*, a view encapsulated most recently in Pierre Riché's survey of Europe in the year 1000. On the other, the scale of chiliastic excitement in the millennial period and of an elite conspiracy formulated to suppress it seem to have been exaggerated by Richard Landes on the basis of very scant evidence. For example, assertions that either the pilgrims travelling to Jerusalem to mark the millennium of the Passion in 1033, or Rodulfus Glaber who tells us about them, were expecting an event of cosmological significance are not convincing: Glaber says only that 'some' people came to this conclusion 'cautiously'. Like the Roman Catholics who travelled to Rome in the year 2000, most were surely marking an anniversary. Thus, on the one hand there is convincing evidence that amongst both the pilgrims and the social commentators of the eleventh century there were indeed some who looked and even hoped for such an event and the signs prefiguring it. But on the other, if some excitable types, Adémar and Glaber amongst them, viewed events in an eschatological context, we should be aware, as Riché warns, that people had done this since the earliest Christian centuries.[41] Between the two positions there is a case for at least moderately heightened apocalyptic awareness in the period 999 to 1033, and we need to note this because 'the areas in which the age-old prophecies about the Last Days took on a new, revolutionary meaning and a new, explosive force were the areas . . . involved in a process of rapid economic and social change'.[42] Some, even amongst the clergy, looked for and found signs of The End. This dangerous activity came to the attention of conservative authorities and possibly also other extremists.

We know that some churchmen certainly saw the years 1000 and 1033 as

---

41 Glaber, *Histories*, 198–201, 204–5; P. Riché, *Les Grandeurs de l'an mil*, Paris 1999, 11–26. For evidence of apocalyptism and eschatology see relevant sections in Landes, *Relics*, and 'Giants with feet of clay' at http://www.mille.org/AHR9.html. For elite denial of the evidence see R. Landes, 'Millenarismus absconditus', and 'Sur les traces du millennium: *la via negativa*', MA xcviii (1992), 355–77; xcix (1993), 1–26. See also his 'Lest the millennium be fulfilled: apocalyptic expectation and the pattern of western chronology, 100–800', in W. Verbeke, D. Verhelst and A. Welkenhuysen (eds), *The use and abuse of eschatology in the Middle Ages*, Leuven 1988, 137–211. For discussion of views of the coming of the End as both imminent and at the same time indefinitely postponed, and as a medieval, not millennial, phenomenon see R. K. Emmerson and B. McGinn (eds), *The Apocalypse in the Middle Ages*, Ithaca–London 1992. For a good bibliography of arguments acknowledging and denying millennial 'terrors', compiled by R. Landes, see http://www.mille.org/1000-bib.htm.
42 Cohn, *Pursuit of the millennium*, 53.

significant. The problem lies in interpreting how significant and in what way. I cannot accept that Bede and his predecessors re-calculated calendars in order to postpone the dates and thereby expectation of what would accompany them.[43] The monk who wrote dates in the margins of the Angoulême Annals in 924, next to which those who followed him would note what happened in those years, stopped after writing *Mille*.[44] We could say that he merely succumbed to the attraction of round numbers, or, alternatively, that he saw no point writing 'AD1001': Christ would have returned to the world by then, marking the start of the sixth age and the end of history. Both scenarios seem equally implausible. In 999, as in 924, most clerics surely obeyed instruction from Augustine and from Christ himself and refused to speculate on what might occur and when.[45] But a minority, and there are undeniable traces of them, looked for signs if only out of human curiosity, as some people do with horoscopes: not actually expecting to find the truth, but noting with excitement occasions when 'prophecy' and 'reality' appear to coincide. A valid criticism of this view is often posited: how many lay people (i.e. the uneducated and illiterate, both rich and poor) actually knew what year it was? If the medieval laity ever knew the date it would probably be in years such as 999, 1000 and 1033, during which, whatever the apocalyptic beliefs of those clergy and monks with whom they were in communication, it might be suggested to them that, at very least, they should live in a way befitting the millennium of the Saviour's birth and suffering.

It is also certain that AntiChrist, due to appear after a thousand years, was familiar to at least a minority of the laity. It was he whom Glaber's 'cautious' people anticipated. Abbo of Fleury was appalled to hear his return predicted in a sermon in Paris in the late tenth century. In the highest secular circles around the same time Queen Gerberga of France commissioned Adso, abbot of Montier-en-Der, to write his *Libellus de Antichristo*, based on the Revelation of St John the Divine and theological commentaries. Adso wrote that AntiChrist would be born in Babylon, that is to say Cairo, in the Last Days. He would claim to be Christ but in spite of his apparent glory he could be recognised because he would declare himself greater than the Trinity. He would wreak havoc in human affairs. Non-Christians would be seduced by him easily and he would thus convert powerful rulers in the east. From there, he would send his agents, including apparently orthodox Christians, throughout the entire world. These are referred to as antichrists. The emergence of many such figures was to be a sign that the Last Days were near, and 'whatever man – layman, cleric or monk – lives contrary to justice and opposes the rule of good, he is Antichrist and the servant of Satan'. Converts would be made to their cause through false wonders

---

[43] For this view see the sources cited for Landes in n. 41 above.

[44] MS Vatican reg. lat. 1127, 1–2, cited in Gillingham, 'Adémar', 8–9, and printed in MGH, SS xvi. 485.

[45] Credit for the observation that Christ himself declared that he did not know when the End would come (Matthew xxiv.36), a fact which, curiously, is rarely noted in medieval or modern sources, goes to Bernard Hamilton.

and deception. All this, according to Revelation xx.7–9, would be met by a terrible fire from heaven.[46]

To those who were looking, contemporary events in Aquitaine seemed to confirm that the Last Days were indeed at hand. Protests against the new order of injustice and misrule abounded in this period. According to the Bonnassie model the condition of the peasantry worsened from 1000 to 1033, and Riché also proposes that the fourth decade might have seemed more momentous in secular terms than the year 1000.[47] In addition, between 990 and 1030 there were five outbreaks of ergotism. The Limousin and Gâtine were amongst the worst hit, and Adémar tells us that victims consumed by the *sacer ignis* experienced visions of heaven and hell.[48] In the years 1005–6 and 1032–3 famine throughout France reduced some to cannibalism, as reported by Glaber.[49] Good Friday fell on the feast of the Annunciation in 992, an occurrence some believed to signify the beginning of the End.[50] Adémar informs us that news from the east told of the persecution of Christians in Egypt and that, in 1010, the Holy Sepulchre had been destroyed. The result was apocalyptic visions, including one experienced by the chronicler, and attacks on Jewish communities in Aquitaine.[51] Not least, antichrists were discovered, identified by the clergy in the form of apparently orthodox religious figures recognisable because, in accordance with the predictions of 1 Timothy, they forbade marriage and commanded the refusal of certain foodstuffs put on earth by God for humankind to eat.[52] But the Last Days heralded the ultimate triumph of Christ and those aiding him, and this too appeared to be taking place. Adémar tells us of the conversion of Jews in Limoges by Bishop Alduin, the reconstruction of the Holy Sepulchre and the tribulations of Moslems in Africa including the death of the *rex Babilonius* al-Hakim, Fatimid caliph of Egypt.[53] The fight for order and orthodoxy, in east and west, was always uppermost in Adémar's mind, for if humankind was soon to be judged it would be judged, according to Revelation, by its works, and must not be found wanting.[54]

---

46 Revelation xx.1–7; 2 Peter iii.8; Psalm lxxxix (xc).4; *PL* cxxxxix.471–2; Adso of Moutier-en-Der, 'Libellus de antichristo', in *The play of AntiChrist*, ed. and trans. J. Wright, Toronto 1967, 100–10 at p. 102 (quotation), 102–7, 109–10. See also R. K. Emmerson, *AntiChrist in the Middle Ages*, Seattle 1981, 21–33, 50–62, 74–109; Theis, *Robert le Pieux*, 201; Landes, *Relics*, 16–19, 285–327, and his 'Apocalyptic dossier: 967–1033', at www.mille.org. The image of AntiChrist's reign taking the shape of rebellion against order on earth comes from medieval interpretations of 2 Thessalonians ii.3–11: Emmerson, *AntiChrist*, 38–9. The concept of 'antichrists' originates in 1 John ii.18, and was elaborated by Jerome in *De antichristo in Danielem*, CCL lxxvA. 914.
47 Bonnassie, 'Paysans du royaume franc', 118; Riché, *Les Grandeurs*, 26, 314–18.
48 Adémar, *Chronicon*, 158. Rye was the main grain crop in the Gâtine: Beech, *Gâtine*, 38.
49 Glaber, *Histories*, 81–3, 186–93.
50 R. Landes, 'Between the aristocracy and heresy: popular participation in the Limousin Peace of God, 994–1033', in Head and Landes, *Peace of God*, 188.
51 Adémar, *Chronicon*, 169.
52 1 Timothy iv.1–4. See chapter 3 below for medieval sources on identifying antichrists.
53 Adémar, *Chronicon*, 169–70.
54 Rev. xx.12–15. For Adémar's interpretation of these events and their place in medieval

The close association between the urban and rural laity and Aquitainian relic and cult sites in this period has received much attention in a millennial context: growing in proportion to social and economic uncertainty, the protests of both peasantry and monks unified in movements of pilgrimage both within and beyond the duchy. The Limousin was heavily affected. When pilgrimages to Saint-Martial were at their height, in 994–1015, its monks championed Adémar's forged apostolic *vita* for their patron. Its claims were made in the context of the discovery by the monks at Saint-Jean d'Angély of the head of John the Baptist. Miracles abounded also at Saint-Cybard, which was rewarded with a fragment of the True Cross, and at Charroux. Such events led to mass attendance at processions and ceremonies at which relics were present. Aquitainians were also attracted to the cult of Sainte-Foy at Conques, whose remains were housed in an elaborate statue-reliquary. The promotion of her cult and the emergence of that of the Limousin saint Leonard of Noblat – a figure of dubious provenance almost certainly invented in the early eleventh century and whose miracles were first recorded in the twelfth – attest to the insecurity of the times and the ingenuity of the monasteries: both saints' *vitae* feature amongst their miracles the freeing of peasants unjustly imprisoned by castellans, often held for ransom.[55] It was in this context of the renewal of popular religiosity, its championing and containment by orthodox leadership, and the quest for order and justice on earth in the millennial era, that the Peace of God movement emerged in Aquitaine.

The Peace of God: church and lay authority in alliance

The Peace of God is most usefully described in recent scholarship as an attempt by clerical authorities to re-establish public order, lost under the later Carolingians, in order to provide themselves with lay protection against encroachment on their property and liberty, and also to temper the violent excesses of private authority and place limits on *malae consuetudines*. They were aided in

apocalypticism generally see Landes, 'Aristocracy', 188–9, 216, 286–308, 322–7, and 'Giants', esp. p. 20.
55 Adémar, *Chronicon*, 162; *Chartes Charroux*, 29–41, 48–53; *Book of Saint Foy*, ed. and trans. P. Sheingorn, Philadelphia 1995, 16–17, 99–105, 128–9, 148–51, 164–5, 183, 185–7, 190–9; M. Arbellot, *Vie de Saint Léonard Solitaire en Limousin: ses miracles et son culte*, Paris 1863, 279 (manuscript tradition), 56–9, 279, 289–94, 298–301 (miracles freeing prisoners). See also Bull, *Piety*, 210–30; Landes, *Relics*, 46–9, and 'Aristocracy', 191–218; Callahan, 'William the Great', 332–6; B. Töpfer, 'The cult of relics and pilgrimage in Burgundy and Aquitaine at the time of the monastic reform', in Head and Landes, *Peace of God*, 41–57; C. W. Solt, 'The cult of saints and relics in the Romanesque art of south-western France and the impact of imported Byzantine relics and reliquaries on early gothic reliquary sculpture', unpubl. PhD diss. Catholic University of America 1977, 192–230. For an important evaluation of the sources for St Leonard and discussion of his cult see S. Sargent, 'Religious responses to social violence in eleventh-century Aquitaine', *Historical Reflections/Réflexions historiques* xii (1985), 231–2, 228–39. Adémar of Chabannes mentions the cult and implies that these miracles took place around 1010 (*Chronicon*, 181), although Sargent thinks that a date of 1028–9 is likely for their origin: 'Religious responses', 229, 232–3.

this by the highest secular powers, in whose interests it was to establish a stable social hierarchy which they could dominate. Recently the role in the peace of other groups has been highlighted: that of the rural poor, emerging communal movements and also the nobility who, on the face of it, had an interest in decentralised power. In addition, it has been shown that the peace was aimed also at clerical reform, not least against the practice of arms-bearing and the waging of war by clerics. Almost everyone, in fact, had an interest in the success of the peace, with the exception of those making their living from the violence and also of religious heretics, whom the sources claim emerged in the same period and whom the peace councils also attacked.[56]

Aquitaine was the birth place of the peace, the first such council being convened by Archbishop Gombaud of Bordeaux in 989 in the presence of the relics of St Junien. It took place at the abbey of Charroux, to which he summoned bishops Gilbert of Poitiers, Hildegar of Limoges, Frotarius of Périgueux, Abbo of Saintes and Hugh of Angoulême. Its canons, stating their intention to curb criminal activity and to promote that which was more lawful, contribute to the view of the peace now taken by historians that here 'criminal' can be defined as 'new' and 'harmful', especially to the Church. Three specific categories of violent crime are cited as being punishable, that is to say through sacramental sanctions: attacks on church property, theft of goods and cattle from *pauperes* and attacks on unarmed clergy, matters over which 'these bishops . . . clerics and monks, not to mention lay people of both sexes, have beseeched the aid of divine justice'.[57]

The council at Limoges of 994 was called in the context of an outbreak of ergotism sweeping the region. Adémar tells us that it was again convened by the men of God, on behalf of the poor, and that this time the support of the duke was sought. At it a precedent was established by which William V was to benefit greatly. As part of the council, great nobles, including the independent-minded viscount Guy of Limoges and Count William of Angoulême, took peace oaths in the presence of both the duke and of the assembled masses, on the relics of saints. But wasn't warfare the very *raison d'être* of these arms-bearers? Here, then,

---

[56] Amongst the most influential work on the Peace is Duby's *Chivalrous society*, 123–33, and *Three orders*, 13–20, 56–60, 134–9, in which it is placed in the context of social disorder c. 1000. The most important recent work is the collection of essays edited by T. Head and R. Landes, *Peace of God*. For Aquitaine see there Debord, 'The castellan revolution', 165–83; Töpfer, 'Cult of relics', 41–57; D. F. Callahan, 'The Peace of God and the cult of the saints in Aquitaine in the tenth and eleventh centuries', 80–103; Landes, 'Aristocracy', 184–218; and Moore, 'Peace of God', 308–26. For aspects of the peace aimed at clerical reform see J. Martindale, 'Peace and war in early eleventh-century Aquitaine', in C. Harper-Bill and R. Harvey (eds), *Ideals and practice of medieval knighthood*, iv, Woodbridge 1992, 147–77; A. G. Remensnyder, 'Pollution, purity and Peace: an aspect of social reform between the late tenth century and 1076', in Head and Landes, *Peace of God*, 280–307. For the historiography of the Peace see especially F. S. Paxton, 'History, historians and the Peace of God', in Head and Landes, *Peace of God*, 21–40. Problems with dating and verifying accounts of some Aquitainian councils are discussed in Martindale, 'Peace and war', 175–6.

[57] *Concilia*, xix. 89–90 (quotation at p. 89; trans. in Head and Landes, *Peace of God*, at p. 327).

we see not the banning of war but acknowledgement by the aristocracy that limitations should be placed on their conflicts, and recognition that the duke had a role in maintaining this. Here also we see the clergy conceding 'a certain rapprochement with war-like activities'. In other words, from the earliest days the peace sought not to eliminate violence but to control it and to legitimise warfare sanctioned by the duke or by the clerical authorities.[58]

Two decades later we find that William V was able to consolidate many of the ideological gains he had been making in the secular sphere. He summoned the bishops and great nobles to a council at Poitiers, in 1010 or 1014, and oaths were sworn by which magnates bound themselves to submit disputes to his court. Not only would transgressors be excommunicated but the lay lords would help the duke take measures, implicitly violent, to destroy those disregarding his authority.[59] In this we see clerical support for the imposition of ducal authority in the secular sphere: whoever opposed him, opposed the will of God as defined by Aquitainian bishops and abbots. Note also, in this context, Adémar's assumption of God's support for the duke in all his wars and His opposition to his enemies. The very location of the councils, according to Jane Martindale, expressed this duke's authority, taking place in towns which he controlled or, in the case of Charroux, where he was attempting to assert authority (it was held by the uncooperative counts of La Marche, but it was the duke who was reforming the abbey). And the new order began to extend itself through the arms-bearing elite: peace oaths between 1025 and 1040 actually included the promise that the oath-taker would not betray his lord.[60]

The subtle dynamic between the populace and the abbeys, and the cults they promoted, was an important part of the peace from the start. The laity were at Charroux in 989 and Limoges in 994 *en masse*, and in the latter Saint-Martial relieved many afflicted by the *sacer ignis*.[61] R. Landes has argued convincingly that the manipulation of the hagiography of St Martial played a part in both the recruitment of the poor to the peace and their containment within its discipline.[62] Some of the secular clergy also played an important role in mobilising the poor. Under the episcopacy of Alduin the alliance between the Church and populace of the Limousin in protesting against social violence took a symbolic yet pragmatic form: 'in response to . . . the rapine of the fighters . . . (and other

---

58 *Chartes Charroux*, 11, 15; Adémar, *Chronicon*, 158; Erdmann, *Origins*, 59 (quotation).
59 *Concilia*, xix. 265–8; Callahan, 'William the Great', 328–42. For the association between the dukes and bishops see, most recently, Barthélemy, *L'An mil et la paix de dieu*, 269–307, and Theis, *Robert le Pieux*, 203.
60 Adémar, *Chronicon*, 179–80; Lemarignier, Gaudemet and Mollat, *Institutions ecclésiastiques*, 51–2; Erdmann, *Origins*, 60–2. However, I am doubtful whether Martindale's argument about Charroux ('Peace and war', 162) holds true for the 989 council, held in William IV's time and convened by Gombaud, the new Gascon archbishop of Bordeaux and rival to Poitevin authority there (see discussion of control of Bordeaux at pp. 39–40 below).
61 *Concilia*, xix. 89; Adémar, *Chronicon*, 158.
62 Landes, 'Aristocracy', 192–3. See also H. E. J. Cowdrey, 'The Peace and Truce of God in the eleventh century', *Past and Present* xlvi (1970), 49–51.

sins) . . . churches and monasteries ceased to perform the divine cult and the holy sacrifice and the people, as pagans, ceased from divine praises, and this observance was regarded as an excommunication'.[63] It seems likely that an important role was also played by the sparsely scattered secular parish clergy of Aquitaine, that it was they who received news of the councils and rallied their flock to attend, as witnesses to and supposed beneficiaries of the legislation being enacted by the idealistic elite.[64]

But Duby and the other *mutationnistes* are convincing when they argue that the most profound impact of the peace for the poor was not emancipatory but oppressive. It both codified and justified the new order: those whose place it was to work, should work dutifully; those whose place it was to fight, should fight fairly. Whilst the councils asserted the right of those tilling the land not to be unjustly attacked by their own lord or anyone else, this served essentially to legitimise their economic exploitation: it was illegitimate to steal goods from the poor, but legitimate to take their labour and legitimate to punish those who belonged to you. There was never any question that the poor should be freed from this burden. In fact the idealistic themes contained in the 989 canons of Charroux were side-lined in later councils which concentrated on establishing ducal control. The masses were apparently not invited to the second council at Charroux in 1028. The Aquitainian clergy now apparently agreed with a criticism of the peace attributed to Bishop Gerard of Cambrai, that the poor were usurping the role of 'those who pray'.[65]

It was arguably partly out of a sense of betrayal that in 1021 the people of Limoges played reformer in the matter of the vacant abbacy of Saint-Martial. On 3 August 1029 the reinvented saint had an apostolic liturgy sung in his honour in his newly enlarged church. A Lombard, Benedict of Chiusa, publicly challenged Adémar over the legitimacy of the claims he made for the saint and convinced the populace that they had been taken in by an elaborate pretence. They abandoned the cult, destroying not only Adémar's credibility but that of the monastery, severing the ties between themselves, Saint-Martial and, by implication, the peace. The Saint-Maixent chronicler is at pains to stress the presence of 'diversorum ordinum christianorum (et) fidelibus populis' at a council at Poitou in about 1032 alongside important churchmen. However the role of the former was by now apparently largely passive.[66] Even the organisation of parish communities in Berry into peace militias in 1038, recruited by local clergy under Archbishop Aimoin of Bourges and mobilised in active defence of the peace, was intended to reinforce the institutional subjection of the *laboratores* to the *bellatores*; the peasants were armed and intended to serve an

---

63 Adémar, *Chronicon*, 161–2, trans. in Landes, 'Aristocracy', at p. 196.
64 For discussion of the roles of priests in the peace movement see Taylor, 'The year 1000'.
65 Adémar, *Chronicon*, 194; *Gesta episcoporum cameracensium*, ed. L. C. Bethmann, MGH, SS vii. 485.
66 Adémar, *Chronicon*, 174; *Chronique Saint-Maixent*, 114–15; R. I. Moore, *The first european revolution, c. 970–1215*, Oxford 2000, 105.

elite clerical agenda under the supervision of warriors. Reaction against this new order is evident also, for from Andrew of Fleury's evidence the force appears to have rejected episcopal authority and developed into a full scale anti-seigneurial revolt, a rejection not only of unfair lordship but of lordship itself according to many historians (although we should note that many non-nobles in one castle were apparently also killed). The uprising ended on 18 January when Eudes of Déols and his knights were obliged to demobilise the militia and humiliate and punish its leaders.[67] From the late tenth century the peasantry had sought protection from theft, violence and the erosion of its legal status, but by the 1030s it was experiencing instead institutionalisation of the newly oppressive rural order, a betrayal attested not least in sources for the Peace of God. A minority of the Aquitainian laity appear to have become increasingly responsive to alternatives where reform had failed, making a choice (*heresis*) which challenged the very legitimacy of secular and ecclesiastical authority.

Gascony under the Basques to 1060

There is only one account of heresy in Gascony, but the development of this medieval region is important for understanding dissent not just in the eleventh century but in the twelfth as well.

The Basque dukes and bishops of Gascony
The early history of Gascony is obscure and has been the cause of much debate and speculation because of the dearth of documentation. It seems certain that, under the Franks it was not a coherent political unit. Into the tenth century, probably as a result of land hunger in the Pyrenees, ambitious Basques extended their traditional settlements beyond Bayonne as far north as the Bordelais and as far east as the Garonne. This was probably originally with the assent of the Franks for a Basque dynasty of Carolingian officials came to dominate the region and became independent under Garsie-Sanche 'le Courbé' (886–920). His son Sanche-Garsie (c. 920–c. 960) was the creator of what Renée Mussot-Goulard calls 'Grande Gascogne', an assemblage of territories more or less corresponding to the Landes, and later including the Bazadais and the Agenais, of which he was styled 'duke'. His brothers Guillaume-Garsie and Arnaud-Garsie held Fézensac and Astarac respectively whilst other Basque families dominated the western Pyrenees. Sanche-Garsie's successor, his son Guillaume-Sanche (c. 960–97/9) was also called count of Bordeaux, but a cousin, Guillaume 'le Bon' was also likewise 'count of Bordeaux' in Guillaume-Sanche's lifetime, and thus we learn that

---

67 *Miracles de Saint-Benoît* cited at n. 19 above. See also Bonnassie, *Slavery*, 312 and n. 99; R. Fossier, *Peasant life in the medieval west*, trans J. Vale, Oxford 1988, 45, and 'Les Mouvements populaires', 263–4; Debord, *Aristocratie et pouvoir*, 59; cf. D. Barthélemy, 'La Milice de Bourges et sa défaite du 18 janvier 1038', in J. Paviot and J. Berger (eds), *Guerre, pouvoir et noblesse au moyen âge*, Paris 2000, 71–81.

the comital and ducal titles were not as synonymous as the titles 'count of Poitou' and 'duke of Aquitaine'.[68]

Guillaume-Sanche reorganised Gascon political life and asserted himself over the comital demesne from his capital at Saint-Sever. From there he established viscounts at Lomagne, Oloron, Béarn, Dax and Marsan and attempted to negotiate with Scandinavian raiders. His son Bernard-Guillaume (997/9–1009), absorbed the Bordelais into the ducal lands. He was able to extend his political horizons further northwards, for in 1004 he travelled to St Jean d'Angély on pilgrimage and there met William V of Aquitaine and King Robert.[69] It was his sister Brisca who married Duke William in 1010.[70] However, Gascony was still primarily Pyrenean in orientation; Bernard-Guillaume was the son of Guillaume-Sanche by a Navarrese princess, Urraca, and was succeeded in Gascony by his brother, Sanche-Guillaume (1010–32), already king of Navarre.[71]

Sanche-Guillaume was famous for campaigning against the Moslems in Spain, and into his Navarrese army he recruited many Gascons. Yet he could not call upon such service automatically throughout Gascony, for north of the Pyrenees the cadet lines descended from Garsie-Sanche ruled Fézensac and Astarac autonomously, as did other related lines in Béarn, Bigorre and Armagnac. The duke had some personal authority over them, stemming from familial ties rather than oaths of allegiance, but they were independent in legal terms and in the allocation of titles.[72] Yet in Bazas, Lomagne and the Agenais, as well as the Bordelais, the ducal family was seizing firmer control of secular and ecclesiastical offices.

Christianity probably came late to the Basques in general, and in the early

68 The father of Gascony history is P. de Marca. His *Histoire de Béarn*, first published at Paris in 1640, is the most thorough for the period before Gascony was politically united with Aquitaine. It is still used reverentially by Gasconists, with the occasional qualification in more recent sources. I have used, in particular, pp. 129–34, 223, 271–81, 286–93, 307–8. A political history of Gascony in this period is R. Mussot-Goulard's *Les Princes de Gascogne (768–1070)*, Lectoure–Marsolan 1982. This uses Spanish sources to fill in some of the gaps, although unfortunately says little about one of the most interesting figures in Gascon history, Bishop Gombaud. I have drawn especially from pp. 99–108, 112–29, 134–50, 178–86, 242–3. Excellent material on Gascony is included in M. Zimmerman's *Les Sociétés méridionales autour de l'an mil*, Paris 1992 (R. Mussot-Goulard, 'La Gascogne', at pp. 295–326; and Cursente, 'La Gascogne', at pp. 257–93). Cursente's *Les Castelnaux de Gascogne médiévale*, Bordeaux 1980, is excellent for aspects of social and economic history. I have also used J. J. Monluzun, *Histoire de la Gascogne depuis les temps les plus reculés jusqu'à nos jours*, Auch 1846–50, i. 390–2; R. Collins, *The Basques*, Oxford 1986, 58–66, 99–112, 170–9; J. Noulens, *Maisons historiques de Gascogne, Guienne, Béarn, Languedoc et Périgord*, Paris 1865–6, i. 28, 35–9.

69 Dunbabin, *France*, 140; Duby, *France*, 29.

70 *Chronique Saint-Maixent*, 108–9; Adémar, *Chronicon*, 161 and see p. xlvii.

71 Adémar, *Chronicon*, 194–5.

72 P. Boissonade, 'Les Premiers Croisades françaises en Espagne: Normands, Gascons, Aquitains et Bourguignons (1018–32)', *Bulletin hispanique* xxxvi (1934), 16–25; P. Ourliac, 'La Justice et la paix dans les *fors* de Béarn', in his *Les Pays de Garonne vers l'an mil*, Toulouse 1993, 195–206.

tenth century some sources still described them as pagan.[73] The early ducal family was active in Christian affairs; Aminiane (or Honorée), wife of Garsie-Sanche, rebuilt the abbey at Condom and Count Bernard of Fézensac restored Saint-Orens at Auch and founded Saint-Luper in about 980. However Gascony had relatively few religious foundations. Guillaume-Sanche founded and placed Saint-Sever-sur-l'Adour under papal authority in 988 or 989 and was to reform La Réole, but reforms were not on the scale of those taking place north of the Dordogne. Notably, we find no evidence of peace councils in Gascony.[74]

Instead it seems that the Gascon Church at the turn of the early eleventh century was primarily a resource for the ducal family, most immediately for Guillaume-Sanche and his brother Bishop Gombaud, who constructed what René Mussot-Goulard calls un principat confraternel encompassing both the secular and religious sphere in Grande Gascogne. There has been much debate about the exact structural relationship between these two aspects of Gascon life in this period, aroused in part by the family's unabashed pluralism and rendered irresolvable not only by the lack of sources but by the variable terms of self-definition which they contain. Indeed, the power held by Gombaud and his successors was apparently fluid and overlapping. It was called comital and some-times ducal when it was secular, and episcopal or monastic when it involved the manipulation of church resources. On one occasion Gombaud is styled 'episcopus et totius circumpositae regionis dux'.[75] Such labels were surely used to inform those outside the family that it held power, not to define or limit it.

Gombaud founded the majority of the monasteries established in this period and was behind the few reforms. In 977, jointly with his brother Guillaume-Sanche, dux Wasconum in this context, he refounded Charlemagne's abbey of Squirs, at La Réole, rededicated it to St Peter and gave it to Fleury. However, the family did not relinquish secular control, for the implication of the charter is that the abbey needed physical protection from violence and disorder, rein-forcing a dependency on the duke which, in the same year, allowed Guillaume-Sanche to seize the treasury of the abbey of Condom to pay ransom for Guillaume le Bon.[76] Thus we find a pattern far from unique to Gascony, the ruling family both protecting and plundering monastic property.

But Gombaud was no mere pluralist. The most interesting thing that we learn

---

73 See J. A. F. Thomson, The western Church in the Middle Ages, London 1998, 8.

74 Cartulaire de l'abbaye de Condom, in Spicilegium, ed. L. d'Achery, Paris 1723, ii. 581–3; BN, MS lat. 8878, 286 (copy of the foundation charter of Saint-Sever, repr. in J. de Jaurgain, La Vasconie, Paris 1898–1902, i. 396–8); R. Mussot-Goulard, 'Remarques sur les textes relatifs à la fondation du monastère de Saint-Orens à Auch', in C. Desplat (ed.), Terre et hommes du sud: hommage à Pierre Tucoo-Chala, Pau 1992, 81–2; A. Ducom, 'Essai sur l'histoire et l'organisation de la commune d'Agen jusqu'au traité de Brétigny, 1360', RSASAA ii/11 (1889), ii/12 (1891–3) (hereinafter cited as i and ii respectively), i. 177, 180; A. Plieux, 'Recherches sur les origines de la ville de Condom', RA i (1874), 385–95. See n. 76 below for La Réole.

75 Nova bibliothecae manuscriptorum . . . collectio, ed. P. Labbé, Paris 1657 ii. 748.

76 Ibid. ii. 743; Cartulaire Condom, 586.

from the 977 documentation is that he called himself *episcopus Wasconie*. He had created a new diocese corresponding to Grande Gascogne. This superseded the authority of the archdiocese of Auch over the diocese of Bazas in which the abbey lay, for from the same year to 980 he was also called bishop of Bazas and Aire. Indeed, from 977 to 989 he is also called bishop of Agen, a diocese pertaining to Bordeaux but clearly by this time within the Gascon sphere of influence. And by 989, under unknown circumstances, the family had also taken control of the archiepiscopal seat at Bordeaux from the Poitevins. The apparent disappearance of an independent archbishop of Auch indicates that this office too was subsumed by the new diocese. From this position, in which episcopal and secular interests were identical, the brothers exercised power and embarked on reforms which even rivalled the authority of Duke William IV.[77]

Such arrangements over this family's property and titles seem likely not least because of the nature of the power Guillaume-Sanche had inherited. In Gascony in this period we find no traces of the Roman and Visigothic law codes which provided for partible inheritance in Aquitaine and the neighbouring Toulousain.[78] However, the Gascon dukes do not appear to have adhered to traditional Basque family law, entailing strict primogeniture, the very practice that had led Basque younger sons first to colonise the Gascon plains.[79] Indeed, the Gascony of Le Courbé was divided between his heirs, although this departure has received little attention historically. Central to it was perhaps the fact that the Basques in their Pyrenean and Spanish territories did not have kings or even a recognisable aristocracy in the period in which Gascony was colonised.[80] They thus had no indigenous model by which to construct a new ruling elite. Le Courbé's family appear to have devised or copied inheritance laws, perhaps influenced by the Carolingians, to suit their circumstances; it would surely have proved impossible for one ruler to dominate or exploit efficiently the vast new territory. Indeed, in later years, when a royal family was established in Navarre, partible inheritance appears to be in evidence again, for the kingdom and the duchy were ruled by two brothers until one of them died in 1009, as we have

---

[77] The idea of a composite bishopric of Gascony was first put forward in the second half of the nineteenth century (see esp. A. Degert, 'L'Evêché de Gascogne', *Revue de Gascogne* [1900], 5–23) but was first disputed as existing in anything but name by A. Mouillé ('Le Comté d'Agenais au Xe siècle: Gombaud et son épiscopat', *RSASAA* ii/4 [1875], 136–70) and by anglophone authorities since (for example Lewis, *Southern French society*, 322; Collins, *Basques*, 176; Martindale, 'Aquitaine', 101 n. 55). Its existence has been doubted not least because the sources do not indicate a consistent geography for it. However R.-A. Sénac has, I think, convincingly demonstrated that the diocese corresponded to whichever lands the count-duke of Gascony controlled at the time: 'L'Evêché de Gascogne et ses évêques (977–1059)', in *Études sur la Gascogne au moyen âge*, Paris 1981, 131–44, and 'Essai de géographie et d'histoire de l'évêché de Gascogne (977–1059)', *BPH* (1983), 11–25.

[78] Bonnassie, *Slavery*, 401.

[79] There is evidence that primogeniture continued to be practised in lesser families: see chapter 4 below, and Collins, *Basques*, 99–100, 199–200.

[80] Collins, *Basques*, 99.

seen. Not least, in the ruling family the Basque practice whereby women succeeded in the absence of sons was apparently also abandoned, and would eventually contribute to the downfall of the dynasty.

In the late tenth century, therefore, it seems that family resources were split between Guillaume-Sanche and Gombaud in accordance with family policy, and that the latter received a lesser portion. When Gombaud took control of the see of Bordeaux, potentially exposing him to charges of pluralism which would count against him in the ecclesiastical province if not in Gascony, it was expedient for him to relinquish Agen and Bazas and an appropriate time to devolve this power to his sons Arnaud and Hugues. Eventually the family appointed a new bishop of Gascony, Arsius Racha (before 1017x1025) who, whilst probably Béarnais and not a family member, was none the less closely associated with the family seats at Saint-Sever and Condom and not at all a threat to this family firm.[81] Thus, when in 1020 Sanche-Guillaume made a donation of the villa of Tambielle to the abbey of Condom, in restitution for Guillaume-Sanche's crime against the abbey in 977, we can interpret this again as another transfer of resources within the family: Hugues, Gombaud's son, the bishop of Agen, had been Condom's abbot since 1013/14.[82] As we shall see, Gombaud and his sons also exerted comital powers in the Bazadais and Agenais.

The structure of lay authority

Under this Basque family and its cadet lines a society emerged in Gascony which was very different in many ways from that of Aquitaine. Although the dukes were, according to Abbo of Fleury, like kings in the lands they held personally, their power elsewhere in Gascony was very limited. Indeed, there were few centres of ducal authority, their fortified abbey of Saint-Sever being the most important. Auch, essentially a small fortified episcopal city, was the only significant town south of the Garonne apart from Bordeaux, and there were smaller viscomital capitals at the centres noted above. Basque law and social structure survived at local level into the eleventh century and beyond. The counts of Fézensac, Astarac, Bigorre, Armagnac and Pardiac, all related to the duke, recognised his authority and attended his court as noted above, but were masters in their own counties and castle-capitals. Formal allegiances between them took the form of agreements over property and mutual pledges not to harm each other's interest, implying little sense of hierarchy. Beyond the turn of the century these and more minor families were increasing their influence. Like Aquitaine, Gascony saw the rise and diffusion of *castella*. But centuries of governmental weakness meant that, in contrast with Aquitaine, the question of whether warriors had the right to build castles simply did not arise, and many such structures were held independently of the dukes and counts. Even in

---

81 Ducom, 'Essai', i. 185; Sénac, 'L'Evêché', 139–40. See also the unpaginated list of Agen's bishops compiled by the chief archivist of Lot-et-Garonne, J. Burias, in his *Guide des archives Lot-et-Garonne*, Agen 1972.
82 *Cartulaire Condom*, 586; Ducom, 'Essai', i. 188; Plieux, 'Condom', 394–5.

Bigorre, whose *fors* said that lords may not fortify, small, wooden constructions on mottes came to dominate the countryside. Local wars remained endemic in Gascony into the twelfth century and beyond and so, although evidence is very sparse, we can speculate that society at a local level was insecure and in many ways came to resemble that of Aquitaine.[83]

But the rise of the knightly caste in Gascony has been shown by B. Cursente to have been in many ways a different phenomenon from that which occurred north of the Dordogne. Although Gascony had little in the way of an economic infrastructure – there are no surviving records for markets and little evidence of coinage in the millennial era – the group which was to emerge as the most dynamic in this respect were the castellans. They pursued activity which resulted in the foundation of and investment in towns, those of the Garonne being particularly successful. Whilst this activity undoubtedly resulted from the increased exploitation of those on rural estates, and Gascony was not immune to revolts against the *bannum* and *pravos usos*, as 'bad' customs were known there, some groups of peasants were able to gain economically in this period. Assarting became a major feature of Gascon rural life as waste land and forests were cleared and settled, and old farms were improved by communally acquired technological knowledge. One result was that famines became rarer. In fact Gascony arguably became more populous and better fed than some regions. Most important, the system of management on Gascon rural estates, *caseux*, has its roots in earlier decades. It involved the co-opting by lords of the most successful peasant families into positions of authority as estate managers. Some of these eventually found their way into the burgeoning numbers of castellans and came to exercise the ban in their own right over their once free and now servile neighbours (Cursente follows the Bonnassie model in asserting that enserfment had occurred by 1030). Thus, whereas in Aquitaine we found a sense of grievance amongst the peasantry, in Gascony the more powerful and wealthy, those with most to lose and perhaps potentially the most vocal, benefited from the new order. In addition, in the mountain regions, whose pastoral economy was too unprofitable to attract the attentions of ambitious lordship, there remained pockets of free peasants, descendants of slaves but never subjected to the *bannum*. These, also dominated by the most powerful amongst them, adopted the legal codes of the free Basques, holding allodial land, practising primogeniture, bringing court cases and bearing arms. Indeed, in contrast with serious destruction inflicted on the Gascon economy by the Scandinavians in the ninth century, the millennial period was one of reconstruction in Gascony. This benefited, and to an extent created a sense of shared interest between, two social

---

[83] *PL* cxxxix.410. There are few Gascon sources for the ordinary laity (see M. Mousnier, 'Implantations monastiques et encadrement des populations en Gascogne toulousaine dans la première moitié du XIIe siècle', in *Crises et réformes grégorienne à la préréforme*, Paris 1991, first page of an unpaginated document) but those that exist are thoroughly exploited by Cursente, 'La Gascogne', 259–67, 295–6; *Castelnaux*, 26–32; and *Des Maisons*, 19–24, 35–40, 48–50, 71–2, 91–101, 107–16, 120–4, 157–60. *Fors*, or *fueros*, were Basque legal codes: Collins, *Basques*, 169, 200–1, 220–5.

groups almost entirely at odds with each other in Aquitaine. A form of *mutation* thus occurred in Gascony also, but again it diverges from the *idéaltype*.[84]

Religious enthusiasm in the Gascon population

Perhaps the greatest contrast of all, however, is with Aquitainian religious life. That of millennial Gascony was undynamic and apparently mainly derivative, imported from Christian Spain, especially Basque Navarre. We have observed activity in the religious sphere at the highest levels, most notably the revival of La Réole and the foundation of Condom, but this was primarily the activity of the ruling family. Interest in the monastic life only really began in Gascony in the late tenth century and by the mid-eleventh major sites were still few; most notably Blaisement and Lucq, established around the same time as Gombaud took interest in La Réole, and Sainte-Croix and Sainte-Marie at Bordeaux, and Sorde, all founded in the early eleventh century. Interest in local saints was a marginal phenomenon. Spanish centres were visited by the Gascon laity and so were Saint-Romain at Blaye, Nôtre-Dame de Rocamadour and the Pyrenean sites associated with Roland, but the relics of Saint-Seurin at Bordeaux formed the only indigenous cult of major importance, especially since the loss of the relics of Sainte-Foy from Agen in the ninth century. In fact, there was very little investment by the aristocracy and clergy in the spiritual infrastructure of the region. This was largely the result of Gascony's still small population and its economic backwardness; the coastal marshland and the wooded Landes still contained few settlements and there were very few roads, towns or markets. There was little parish structure to speak of, and although some *caseux* contained churches, local lords built far fewer chapels than their Aquitainian counterparts.[85] Although there is little else that can be said with any certainty about levels of religiosity in the millennial period, an interesting feature of its nature has been noted: by far the most popular text copied and read in churches was the Apocalypse of St John, again probably a reflection of Spanish influence.[86]

This brings us to the most famous episode in the religious life of Gascony in this period, the murder in 1004 of Abbo, abbot of Fleury, on arriving in the northern Bazadais to reform La Réole. The murder was apparently the work of townspeople, local knights and also the monks, and as such cannot be seen as purely anticlerical but as a reaction against externally imposed reform. Indeed, it has been argued by modern authorities that the act was an assertion of Gascon communal identity not just against Fleury but against France.[87] That the

---

84 Cursente, *Des Maisons*, as cited n. 83, but esp. at pp. 48–50.

85 *Book of Sainte Foy*, 36–7; Lewis, *Southern French society*, 318; Mussot-Goulard, *Les Princes*, 239–42; Cursente, 'Gascogne', 267; Bull, *Piety*, 224, 230–1; *Atlas de la France de l'an mil*, ed. M. Parisse and J. Leuridan, Paris 1994, 99.

86 Mussot-Goulard, *Les Princes*, 240. The eighth-century work of Beatus de Liébana, who wrote a commentary on the Apocalypse, became influential again in the late tenth-century: J. F. O' Callaghan, A *history of medieval Spain*, Ithaca–London 1975, 89, 137.

87 Aimoin, *Vita s. Abbonis abbatis Floriancensis*, PL cxxxix. 375–414 at 409–12; Adémar, *Chronicon*, 161; de Marca, *Béarn*, 302–3; Cursente, 'Gascogne', 260, 263–7, 278–9, 282–3.

Garonne town viewed itself as a sort of outpost of Gascon self-interest is quite possible, for the region's relative economic recovery towards the millennial period had, it has been argued, forged a sense of self-identity amongst Gascons, whose Basque tongue combined with Occitan to form a distinct regional dialect.[88] Although the complexity of motives behind this affair remain obscure, those with an interest in undermining monastic movements might have looked with interest at such subversive events in Gascony.

The duchy of Aquitaine, 1060–1152

There is little indication of dualist heresy in Aquitaine after c.1050 until the second half of the twelfth century, and so it is not necessary to establish a social context for its emergence and success. The political and social features of this period will therefore be outlined in far less detail than those of 1000–50. However, some of the religious developments in the period seem to have provided a background to attitudes towards Catharism in the duchy and are given some attention.[89]

The assimilation of Gascony into Aquitaine and the power of the dukes
It was the Gascon titles in the Bordelais, Entre-deux-Mers and the Agenais which the Poitevins were eventually to control. They were to benefit from a growing trade in wine and salt, much of which was controlled by the towns and abbeys of these regions, but their interest in Gascon politics stemmed most immediately from the struggle for control of the archiepiscopal see of Bordeaux and the influence it exerted in Aquitaine. A Poitevin family had in fact dominated the see since the ninth century, and Archbishop Gombaud's successor Séguin was one of its members. Thus the convening of the Council of Charroux in 989 by Gombaud should surely be seen in the context of Gascon ambitions north of the Dordogne: the summoning of Aquitainian bishops, including Gilbert of Poitiers, was an archiepiscopal snub to the dukes and their supporters, as was Gombaud's extensive involvement in the diocese of Limoges, whose bishop he also summoned in 989, which was likewise coveted by the Poitevins (although we may note that his successor at Bordeaux was able to continue this involvement, helping to move Limoges into the Poitevin sphere). Another Gascon, Islo (1024–7), succeeded Séguin, but was in turn succeeded by the

---

88 Cursente, 'Gascogne', 267–8; Collins, *Basques*, 104–6.

89 The political history of the second half of the century is obscure, the Saint-Maixent chronicle being almost the only annal dealing with Aquitaine, although the revival of the monastic life is well documented. Martindale's thesis is still the best political source in English: 'Aquitaine', pp. v–ix, 65–70, 97–123, 127–8, 132–9, 142–52, 154–87, 184, 210–16, 216–32. This present survey of the period, except where otherwise cited, also draws on Martindale, 'Succession', 31–7; Dunbabin, *France*, 94–100, 117, 219–20, 355; Lewis, *Southern French society*, 318–22; Higounet, Renouard and others, *Histoire de Bordeaux*, 51, 53, 91–2; Higounet and others, *Histoire de l'Aquitaine*, 169–70, 176–8; Richard, *Histoire*, i. 34, 48, 66, 95–6, 126, 278–81, 392–5; Mussot-Goulard, *Les Princes*, 187–207; Bonnassie, *Slavery*, 347–51.

Poitevin Godefred II (1027–43). An impasse between the two parties resulted in the see being vacant from 1043 to 1047, but Poitevin secular power was great enough to tip the balance in the Aquitainian direction by mid-century.[90]

The exact process by which the Poitevins attained power in Gascony is difficult to determine. The first opportunity came with the death of Sanche-Guillaume in 1032. He left only two daughters, Alausie and Garcie. One of them had married Count Aldouin of Angoulême in 1028 and their son Bérenger now claimed the Bordelais in his mother's name, in accordance with Basque rights of women to inherit in the absence of a male child. His lack of success perhaps indicates that this feature of traditional inheritance practices had also been abandoned, not least because it seems that no one within Gascony was championing the cause of this minor. In addition, there were other strong claimants. One version of events says that power shifted in the Poitevin direction under Eudes, or Odo, a son of William V and Brisca of Gascony. By 1037 he was calling himself *Vasconorum comes* and minting at Bordeaux, although he had limited influence there. His half-brother, William VII 'Aigret', expressed a less easily supported claim, but the two eventually combined forces to beat off Gascon contenders, most notably Count Bernard Tumapaler of Armagnac who was supported by Viscount Centulle-Gaston of Béarn. Other accounts attribute greater significance to the role of Guy-Geoffrey, younger brother of William VII, one saying that he secured the support of Tumapaler with 15,000 *solidi*, and another that he fought and beat his Gascon rivals near the river Adour.[91]

Whatever the truth, by 1044 it was Guy-Geoffrey, also known from this time as William VIII of Aquitaine, who had been successful. He established the Poitevin abbot of Saint-Maixent, Archibald de Parthenay, as primate at Bordeaux (1047–c. 1059), and he was succeeded by Joscelin de Parthenay (1059–c. 1080). By 1066, after his triumph over the Angevins, this duke had enough influence to lead an army of Gascons against the Moslems in Spain. He held minting and judicial rights in Bordeaux, and gained control of much new land and many churches in the Bordelais. He was also recognised by the great Gascon nobles. Indeed, some were his *fideles* by this time and an oath akin to liege homage, probably unique in the Pyrenees at this time, was taken by Centulle, viscount of Béarn and count of Bigorre, to King Alfonso of Aragon, in which he reserved his fealty to the duke and his son, the future William IX.[92]

Yet the old Aquitaine continued to be governed from Poitou and Gascony from Bordeaux, apparently quite separately. The nobility, language and culture either side of the Garonne also remained almost entirely separate, in spite of commercial exchanges. The understood status of Gascony – as a principality within a duchy or as an extension of Aquitaine proper – is consequently unclear. Guy-Geoffrey was known as its *comes* and as *princeps* and by other titles. It would seem that he viewed it as part of Aquitaine but that Aquitaine now had two

90 Adémar, *Chronicon*, 194–5.
91 Ibid. 194; de Marca, *Béarn*, 363–9.
92 Bibliothèque Municipale, Bordeaux, MS 745, 16r–v.

capitals, Bordeaux and Poitiers. In both regions he grew increasingly dominant. Indeed, although he had only partial control of the Limousin nobles and very little in Périgord by the time of his death, the other great magnates of Aquitaine and the castellans of Poitou were firmly under his influence. He did, however, make a significant enemy in his neighbour the count of Toulouse, who attacked Bordeaux in 1058 and against whom he went to war in 1060.[93]

Some of Guy-Geoffrey's achievements were lost during the minority of his son William IX, 'the Troubadour' (1086–1136). Significantly, however, the interests of the ducal house were upheld in this difficult time by the Poitevins, not least the Lusignans, and also by Centulle of Béarn. After William began to govern alone, in the early 1090s, firmer ties were forged with the other counties and great governmental advances were made in those he held directly, although this renewed tensions with the Poitevins. The ducal court was recognised, if most typically by the wronged party, even in Gascony, and many Gascons owed him some sort of military service, as did the nobles north of the Bordelais. Indeed, this duke's presence in Gascony is attested on many occasions. An alliance with Anjou was forged through marriage to Hermingarde, daughter of its count, and relations with Pyrenean and Spanish neighbours were also good.[94]

But the period saw the resumption of hostilities with Toulouse. In 1094 the duke married Philippa (or Mathilde), daughter and heiress of Count William IV of Toulouse, who had died the previous year. Her rights to the county had already been resisted by other Toulousain nobles because it would mean it being controlled by her first husband Sanche-Ramirez, king of Aragon (whom she had married after April 1085). Sometime after 1088, but probably in 1093 after her father died, the town supported the transfer of the county to her uncle, Raymond of Saint-Gilles, count of Rouergue and marquis of Provence. Philippa and Duke William pursued her claim and the dispute would affect the politics of the region well into the thirteenth century. In 1097/8 they entered the town of Toulouse with the support of its bishop, Adémar, and many of its leading families. In the following year, whilst Raymond was on crusade, they ruled unopposed, William calling himself *comes Pictavensis et Tolosae*. Reprisals were apparently not taken during William's own crusade of 1101, but in 1108 Bertrand of Saint-Gilles was able to enter the town, Bishop Adémar having

93 *Cartulaires du chapitre de l'église métropolitaine Sainte-Marie d'Auch (Cartulaires noir et blanc)*, ed. C. La Cave La Plagne-Barris, AHGi ii/3, ii/4 (hereinafter cited as i and ii respectively), i. 1; *Cartulaire de l'abbaye de Sainte-Croix de Bordeaux*, ed. P. Ducaunnès-Duval, AHGi xxvii (1892), 22; Geoffrey of Vigeois, *Chronica*, 299, 304. The cause of the conflict with Toulouse has been thought to be uncertain (Martindale, 'Aquitaine', 104–5, 124–5) but may perhaps be explained by the relationship between the houses of Toulouse and Périgord concerning the Agenais (see pp. 50–2 below).
94 Geoffrey of Vigeois, *Chronica*, 287, 289, 298; *Chronique Saint-Maixent*, 407, 420, 428; *Historia pontificum et comitum engolismensium*, ed. J. Boussard, Paris 1957, 29, 34; *Le Cartulaire de l'abbaye cardinale de la Trinité de Vendôme*, ed. Ch. Métais, Vannes 1893–1904, ii. 345; AHGi xii (1864), 319–20; GC ii, instr. 429; *Cartulaire de l'abbaye Saint-Jean de Sorde*, ed. P. Raymond, Pau 1873, 6; Painter, 'Lords of Lusignan', 35, 38; R. Favreau, 'Les Débuts de la ville de Loudun', *Bulletin de la Société des antiquaires de l'ouest* v (1988), 164–72.

changed sides. However, in 1113, when Count Bertrand was in Tripoli, William attacked the Toulousain again. His Poitevin official was in control of it until 1123, when Alphonse-Jourdain of Saint-Gilles successfully claimed it, William's divorce from Philippa in 1115 having destroyed his own claim.[95]

Eventually good relations with the French crown were cemented under William IX, essentially from a position of strength. He was an important ally of Philip I when the king was excommunicated in 1100, but when Louis VI demanded the homage of the great princes in 1108, the duke refused him. He also undermined the ultimately irresistible expansion of royal power into the Auvergne for a time, in spite of flattering the king on another occasion as 'l reis de cui ien tenc m'onor'.[96] Against this background it perhaps seems surprising that the Capetian kings were soon to hold the title 'duke of Aquitaine'. However, when it seemed inevitable that Eleanor, the eldest daughter of William X, would inherit Aquitaine, it was into Capetian protection that the duke entrusted her and thus his duchy. Eleanor and Louis VII were married in the cathedral of Saint-André at Bordeaux on either 27 July or 1 August 1137. The king had entered Aquitaine with a huge military escort, which Martindale notes must have looked more like a warning to the Poitevins than a wedding party. In practice, however, the French king had little political impact on Aquitaine, in spite of Capetian ambition. He was never *dux Aquitanorum* but governed with Eleanor's assent, perhaps realising that the way to avoid political conflict with the volatile nobility was to leave well alone.

Major religious movements in Aquitaine
We have seen that Aquitaine, and even more so Gascony, were only marginally affected by Cluniac reforms. This was to change in the second half of the eleventh century. La Réole and its associated houses grew in importance and Centulle IV of Béarn founded Sainte-Foy de Morlaas and gave it to Cluny. Between 1068 and 1167 Saint-Martial was reformed by the viscounts of Limoges and, on a more modest scale, the Duchess Agnes and Bishop Itier of Limoges reformed Saint-Leonard de Noblat in 1062. Guy-Geoffrey was especially supportive of reforming trends. He never assumed the title of abbot of Saint-Hilaire, traditional for the counts of Poitou. With his co-operation Abbot Hugh

---

95 *HGL* v. 29–31, 33, 50, 193, 849–50, 908 and *preuves* 400, 454. Geoffrey of Vigeois, *Chronica* (at p. 304) tells us about the marriage to Sanche-Ramirez, who died in June 1094. See also Robert of Torigny in *Chronicles of the reigns of Stephen, Henry II and Richard I*, ed R. Howlett (RS, 1884–9), iv. 201–2. Robert's source, Baudri of Bourgueil's *Gesta dei*, tells us that William IV sold Raymond the county in order to finance a military expedition to the Holy Land, although the date of the count's death makes a crusading expedition unlikely. See also P. Wolff, *Histoire de Toulouse*, Toulouse 1958, 77–80, 122; J. H. Mundy, *Liberty and political power in Toulouse, 1050–1250*, New York 1954, 16–17; Elizabeth Hallam, *Capetian France, 987–1328*, London 1980, 53, 60.

96 *Chronique Saint-Maixent*, 42; Suger, abbot of Saint-Denis, *Vita Ludovici Grossi*, ed. A. Molinier, Paris 1887, 127–8; A. Jeanroy (ed.), *La Poésie lyrique des troubadours*, Toulouse 1934, no. 11; Lemarignier, *Le Gouvernement royal*, 173–5.

of Cluny reformed many Aquitainian houses, including the duke's own foundation at Montierneuf. Cluniac monks Gilbert, Goderannus and Odo became
abbots of Saint-Maixent, Maillezais and Saint-Jean d'Angély respectively.
Martindale has observed that as a result of Hugh's reforming work, including
that within the chapter of Saint-Hilaire, the sons of the clergy advanced little.
Three corrupt bishops – at least one of them, Arnulf of Saintes, a simoniac –
were deposed in his time. One of the great Gregorian bishops of the period,
Archbishop Austinde of Auch (1042–68) disbanded the bishopric of Gascony
and restored the ancient diocese of Auch with the support of Guy-Geoffrey.[97]
However Guy-Geoffrey's reforms did not significantly diminish his personal
influence over the Church in Aquitaine. Initiatives inspired by the great
reformer Pope Gregory VII (1073–85) were often resisted by him and by Joscelin
de Parthenay, his archbishop of Bordeaux, especially in the matter of lay investi-
ture. Champions of clerical autonomy had cause also to complain about the
duke's insistence on hearing cases involving criminous clerics. His refusal to
support the pope in his quarrel with King Philip I of France over ecclesiastical
liberties was noted with anger in Rome.[98]

During the minority of William IX the clergy were able to break somewhat
from ducal influence. A dispute with the reformer bishop Amatus of Oloron
(1073–89) had begun under Guy-Geoffrey and the cleric had himself elected
archbishop of Bordeaux (1089–1102) against the wishes of William IX's
Poitevin advisors.[99] Relations did not improve with the majority, and the duke
was seen by many as a secular, even irreligious figure. Although still a protector
of the Church and the source of extensive grants especially to the bishopric of
Bayonne, he reduced the amount of financial and ideological support for Cluny
in the duchy. Between 1101 and 1104 he left the see of Bordeaux vacant, and
did the same with Poitiers in 1115–17 and 1123–4. Between 1114 and 1117 he
was excommunicated, although the exact cause of this is unknown, and from
1130 to 1135 flew in the face of European opinion by supporting the anti-pope
Anacletus and forcing his own schismatic candidates on episcopal sees in the

---

97 *Cartulaire du prieuré de Saint-Pierre de La Réole*, ed. C. Grellet-Balguerie, *AHGi* (1864), 99;
Martin of Montierneuf, *Fragmentum historiae monasterii novi pictavensis*, in *Thesaurus novus
anecdotorum*, ed. E. Martène and U. Durand, Paris 1717, repr. New York, 1968, iii. 1213–14;
*Recueil des actes d'Henri II, roi d'Angleterre, concernant les provinces françaises et les affaires de
France*, ed. L. Delisle and E. Berger, Paris 1916–27, ii. 431–2 (confirmation of a charter of
Guy-Geoffrey in favour of Maillezais); 'Documents pour l'histoire de l'église de Saint-Hilaire
de Poitiers (768–1300)', ed. L. Rédet, *Memoires de la Société des antiquaires de l'ouest* xv (1852),
91; *PL* cxliv.865–900; cxlvi.1320–1; J. Becquet, 'Chanoines réguliers en Limousin au XIIe
siècle: sanctuaires régularisés et dépendances étrangères', *BSAHL* ci (1974), 78–9; Ch.
Higounet, *Le Comté de Comminges de ses origines à son annexion à la couronne*, Toulouse–Paris
1949, i. 53–8, 335–41.
98 *Das Register Gregors VII*, ed. E. Caspar, Berlin 1920–3, ii. 18, cited in Erdmann, *Origins*, at p.
163. At pp. 162–6 Erdmann suggests that as a result the pope changed plans to put
Guy-Geoffrey in charge of an expedition to aid eastern Christians: *Register Gregors VII*, ii. 3.
99 Higounet and others, *Histoire de l'Aquitaine*, 169–70.

duchy.[100] His son William X was also criticised for imposing ecclesiastical and abbatial candidates.[101] In fact real reform only came under Louis VII, who renounced what was by this time an established ducal prerogative over the nomination of bishops and the right to demand oaths of loyalty from them.[102]

Ducal quarrels with reformers should be seen as a defence of princely independence rather than as anticlericalism. However, Aquitainian rulers were apparently also backward in promoting the Truce of God movement, a more pragmatic version of the Peace of God, which banned violence on feast days and was widespread throughout the rest of western Europe. The truce was observed to some extent in the duchy, however. In this context Bernard III of Bigorre protected pilgrims travelling to Santiago de Compostella, his half brother Gaston IV of Béarn was influenced by it in his dealings with his rival Bernard III of Armagnac and Périgord was among the many parts of the west in which there was an attempt to raise taxes in support of the enforcement of the truce.[103]

The Peace and Truce of God were to be over-shadowed by a movement that sought not to suppress or contain the violence of the arms-bearing caste, as they had done, but to direct it beyond Christian Europe. Aquitainians were involved in the crusading movement from its inception and in its earliest manifestations. We have seen that the proximity to Islamic Spain had produced armed responses from Christians north of the Pyrenees in previous decades, and in 1064 Guy-Geoffrey was at the head of an Aquitainian force aiding the *Reconquista*, a mission on which he was possibly entrusted with the papal banner.[104] Amongst the Aquitainians who accompanied the First Crusade of 1095 to recover the Holy Land were Gaston IV of Béarn, Amanieu IV d'Albret, Raymond-Bertrand de l'Isle-Jourdain, several Limousin vassals of William IX and a Gascon force recruited by Count Raymond of Toulouse.[105] William IX and many of his vassals took the cross at Limoges in September 1100 and undertook an expedition to the east in 1101. Amongst those destined never to return

---

100 *Chronique Saint-Maixent*, 409, 413, 425–6; GC i. instr. 201; William of Malmesbury, *De gestis pontificum*, ed. N. E. S. A. Hamilton (RS, 1870), ii. 510–11.

101 Martindale, 'Aquitaine', p. ix.

102 M. Pacaut, *Louis VII et les élections épiscopales dans le royaume de France*, Paris 1957, 54–65; I. P. Shaw, 'The ecclesiastical policy of Henry II on the continent', *Church Quarterly Review* cli (1951), 146.

103 Erdmann, *Origins*, 57–94; Bull, *Piety*, 55–6; T. N. Bisson, 'The organised peace in southern France and Catalonia, c. 1140–1233', in his *Medieval France and her Pyrenean neighbours*, London–Ronceverte 1989, 219.

104 Erdmann, *Origins*, 33–4, 63, 137–9.

105 *Gesta francorum et aliorum hierosolimitanorum*, ed. R. Hill, London 1962, 73–4, 87–9, 92, 95; Orderic Vitalis, *Ecclesiastical history*, ed. and trans. M. Chibnall, Oxford 1969–80, iii. 480–1; Raymond d'Aguilers, *Historia francorum qui ceperunt Iherusalem*, trans. J. H. Hill and L. L. Hill, Philadelphia 1968, 123; Baldric of Dol ibid. iv. 16; Fulcher of Chartres, *A history of the expedition to Jerusalem, 1095–1127*, ed. and trans. H. S. Fink and F. R. Ryan, Knoxville, Tenn. 1969, 72, 77–80; Noulens, *Maisons*, i. 425–7; J. Riley-Smith, *The First Crusaders, 1095–1131*, Cambridge 1997, 197–242; F. *l'abbé* Arbellot, *Les Chevaliers limousins à la première croisade (1096–1102)*, Paris 1881.

were Hugh VI of Lusignan, Bishop Reynaud de Thiviers of Périgueux and Viscount Herbert II of Thouars and his brother Geoffrey, who led a contingent from Bas-Poitou. Also in this Aquitainian army were William 'Fort', a ducal officer in the Saintonge and brother of the archdeacon of Poitiers, and knights and minor castellans such as Peter II of Pierre-Buffière, Guy I of Bré and Walter of Châtillon. The defeat of this crusade led to humiliation in contrast with achievements of the glorious crusade of 1098, and was blamed by churchmen on the duke's irreligious disposition.[106] Aquitainians also formed part of the army of the Second Crusade of 1146–7, led by King Louis VII, not least as part of the retinue of his wife, the Duchess Eleanor. Amongst them were Count William IV of Angoulême, Guillaume de Mauzé, the duchy's seneschal, and four members of the Limousin family of Bré.[107]

The success of Aquitainian recruitment into crusading armies resulted in no small measure from the influence on the laity of the monasteries.[108] But the professed religious life was in itself being transformed by another dynamic movement, inspired and led by eremitic preachers disillusioned with the limited impact of the Gregorian reforms, who were active especially between the Loire and Garonne. Like the crusades, it recruited from all sections of the laity. As such its adherents were initially thought suspect by church authorities. Eventually however, most of its participants were not only deemed acceptable but were able to revitalise religious orthodoxy and attract the patronage of the aristocracy of the duchy. Amongst the most influential of the new wave was Robert of Arbrissel (d. 1116). His radical foundation at Fontevrault in Poitou provided for the religious vocation of the poor and of women, groups previously neglected by the reformed abbeys. A monastery founded in about 1110 by Stephen of Muret at Grandmont, near Limoges, offered the religious life to the propertyless male faithful as well as to the nobility. Another innovator, Géraud de Sales (d. c.

---

106 *Chronique Saint-Maixent*, 172, 401, 420; Albert of Aix, *Historia hierosolymitana*, in *RHC Occ.*, iv. 581; *Cartulaires du Bas-Poitou*, ed. P. Marchegay, Les Roches-Baritaud 1877, 3–8; Geoffrey of Vigeois, *Chronica*, 296, 306; *Cartulaire de Saint-Jean-d'Angély*, ed. G. Musset, *Archives historiques de la Saintonge et de l'Aunis* xxx (1901); xxxiii (1903), 448; William of Malmesbury, *De gestis regum anglorum*, ed. W. Stubbs (RS, 1887–9), ii. 47–8, 510–11; Bardolf of Nangis in *RHF Occ.*, iii. 534; Orderic Vitalis, *Ecclesiastical history*, v. 324; *Cartulaire de l'abbaye d'Uzerche (de Xe au XIVe siècles)*, ed. J.-B. Champéval, Tulle 1901, 611; *Cartulaire de l'abbaye de Vigeois en Limousin (954–1167)*, ed. M. de Montégut, Limoges 1907, 59, 68; *Chroniques des églises d'Anjou*, ed. P. Marchegay and E. Mabille, Paris 1899, 342–3; 'Charte de Pierre, évêque de Limoges, administrateur de l'évêché de Périgueux de l'an 1101', ed. G. Babinet de Rencogne, *BSHAP* lv (1928), 156–8; J. Becquet, 'La Mort dun évêque de Périgueux à la première croisade: Reynaud de Thiviers', *BSHAP* lxxvii (1960), 66–9; Bull, *Piety*, 265 n. 78, 274–81; Riley-Smith, *First Crusaders*, 197–242. I first found most of the references in this footnote in the very thorough A. Mullinder, 'The crusading expeditions of 1101–2', unpubl. PhD diss. Swansea 1996, 9–10, 13, 32, 258–64, 264, 336–54.

107 *Ex anonimi chronici . . . ab initio mundi ad annum MCLX*, in *RHF* xii. 20, 120; Odo of Deuil, *De profectione Ludovici VII in orientem*, ed. V. G. Berry, New York 1948, esp. pp. 40–61; J. Riley-Smith, 'Family traditions and participation in the Second Crusade', in M. Gervers (ed.), *The Second Crusade and the Cistercians*, New York 1992, 101.

108 Bull, *Piety*, 155–204, 250–82; Mullinder, 'Crusading expeditions', 32, 36–7.

1120), maintained the wandering life himself, preaching in Périgord, Limoges, Poitou, Saintonge and Guyenne, as well as in the Languedoc, but advocated the establishment of autonomous eremitic communities for men and enclosed Fontevriste priories for women. Étienne d'Obazine, also initially motivated by the pastoral needs of the Aquitainian poor and of women, founded a nunnery at Coyroux in 1142. In part through his involvement in the Cistercian order, the white monks, who dominated monastic renewal in Spain, began to found and to take over monasteries for men in Gascony from the 1130s, most notably Morimond in the very south, and its daughter houses Berdoues in Astarac, Bonnefont in Comminges and Cabadour (later called l'Escale-Dieu) in Bigorre. This brought the number of abbeys for men in Gascony closer to that north of the Dordogne. In spite of the fact that in the archdiocese of Auch, where there were no foundations for women by 1000 – there were still only eight by c. 1152 – Bruce Venarde's study is able to identify the period 1080 to 1160 as a time when monastic opportunities for women living between the Loire and Dordogne increased dramatically, with twenty-three female houses founded or re-founded before 1152 in the ecclesiastical province of Bordeaux.[109]

This new movement was to be widespread and diverse in the forms it took, as well as in the responses it received from the authorities. Most relevant, an extreme wing emerged, wandering holy men who remained beyond ecclesiastical control and who wanted to revolutionise Church organisation, straying into dangerous doctrinal territory. The most famous of these, the heretics Peter of Bruys and Henry of Lausanne, attracted anticlerical followings in Gascony, Aquitaine and the Toulousain, and Robert of Arbrissel preached in the Agenais against some unidentified heresy (see chapter 2). But in the second half of the twelfth century the Agenais was to contain centres of Catharism, and so it is interesting to note that it already had a heretical history, even though it seems unlikely that these early heretics were dualist. The circumstances which eventually did give rise to dualist belief in the Agenais will receive detailed attention in

[109] *PL* clxii.1043–78; B. Barrière, 'Les Abbayes issues de l'érémitisme', *CF* xxi (1986), 71–105, and 'The Cistercian convent of Coyroux in the twelfth and thirteenth centuries', *Gesta* xxxi (1992), 76–82; J. Delarun, 'Robert of Arbrissel et les femmes', *Annales* xxxix (1984), 1142–51, and *Robert d'Arbrissel, fondateur de Fontevraud*, Paris 1986, 36–97; J. M. B. Porter, '*Compelle intrare*: monastic reform movements in twelfth-century northwestern Europe', unpubl. PhD diss. Nottingham 1997, 70–2, 82, 88–104, 133–5; C. A. Hutchinson, *The hermit monks of Grandmont*, Kalamazoo, Mich. 1989, 27–49; E. Magnou-Nortier, 'Formes féminines de vie consacrée dans les pays du Midi jusqu'au début du XIIe siècle', *CF* xxiii (1988), 193–216; J. Edouard, *Fontevrault et ses monuments*, Paris 1873–4, ii. 253–6, 276–7; Higounet and others, *Histoire de l'Aquitaine*, 156–8; O'Callaghan, *Medieval Spain*, 311; L. J. Lekai, *The Cistercians*, Kent, Ohio 1977, 41. See especially Venarde, *Women's monasticism*, pp. xi–xiii, 8–10, 32–40, 52–66, 91–102, 164, 192–205 (in opposition to the view of P. Schmitz that opportunities for women declined in this period). See also Mousnier, 'Implantations monastiques' and *La Gascogne toulousaine au XIe–XIIe siècles*, Toulouse 1997, 86–90. When Duke William IX and Philippa controlled Toulouse, they implemented reforms there too, with the aid of Robert of Arbrissel: *HGL* v. 846; M. Mousnier, 'Grandselve et la société de son temps', *CF* xxi (1986), 108–9; Mundy, *Liberty*, 17, 81.

chapter 3, but they have origins in aspects of the early history of the region which will now be outlined.

The Agenais to 1152

First what was meant by the Agenais? As a medieval county and diocese it corresponded very closely to the modern *département* of Lot-et-Garonne, except that until the creation of the diocese of Condom in 1317 it incorporated the Condomois as well. It thus extended from Périgord, to its north, to just south of the abbey of Condom, and from l'Avance, downstream from Marmande, to Auvillar and Fumel which marked its border with Quercy.[110]

The ancient and early-medieval Agenais

The features of the Agenais which help to explain its responses to heresy extend way back into the Gallo-Roman world, for then it was essentially two regions. The Garonne valley divided the southern portion from the north, and whilst Celts dominated the latter, Iberian peoples were present in great numbers to the south. From the third century the Gallo-Romans of the north were governed as part of *Aquitania Secunda*. This was the political unit upon which the archdiocese of Bordeaux was to be based, except that the ecclesiastical unit would also incorporate the Agenais south of the river. The political region between the Garonne and the Pyrenees was known by the Romans as *Novempopulana*, and from its archdiocesan metropolitan of Auch the religious affairs of what was to

---

[110] This section draws on the following histories of the Agenais and Aquitaine, except where otherwise cited: de Marca, *Béarn*, 152–7, 166–70, 251–62, 301–2; J.-F. Boudon de Saint-Amans, *Histoire ancienne et moderne du département de Lot-et-Garonne depuis l'an 56 avant Jésus-Christ, jusqu'en 1814*, i, Agen 1836, 51–2; Martindale, 'Aquitaine', 100, 104–5, 124–5, 174–9; G. Tholin, 'Causeries sur les origines de l'Agenais', *RA* xxii (1895–6), 152–62, 435–50, 516–28; Burias, *Guide*, 73 and list of bishops; Ducom, 'Essai', i. 185, 188; L. Verger and others, *Agen: hier et aujourdhui*, Agen 1979 (repr. of 1969 edn), 23, 174–6; J. l'abbé Barrère, *Histoire religieuse et monumentale du diocèse d'Agen depuis les temps les plus reculés jusqu'à nos jours*, Agen 1855–6, i. 80–6; L. F. Lagarde, *Recherches historiques sur la ville et les anciennes baronnies de Tonneins*, Agen 1833, 2–9; J. Caubet, *Histoire de Tonneins dès origines à 1870*, Tonneins n. d. [nineteenth-century], 5–7; A. Ricaud, *Marmande*, 2nd edn, Bordeaux 1975, 7; M. Esquieu and others, *Agenais occitan, 1050–1978*, Villeneuve-sur-Lot 1978, 5–7; Plieux, 'Recherches Condom', 385–95; Higounet and others, *Histoire de l'Aquitaine*, 136, 148–60, 175; Mussot-Goulard, 'La Gascogne', 322–3. However the following are by far the most important historians of the Agenais. B. Labénazie's *Annales d'Agen*, Agen–Paris 1886 edn, is regarded as the history of the Agenais in the sense that de Marca's is of Béarn (see esp. pp. 34–9), but it not nearly as reliable, and the most methodical tracing, citing and reproducing of Agenais sources was done during the nineteenth century. I have looked to more recent authorities to authenticate his claims where I have not seen his sources for myself (some of them have been lost). Ducom's detailed constitutional history extracts as much as is possible from the extant charters and customs relating to Agen (his most useful information on the pre-Poitevin period is at vol. i. 45, 164, 173–6, 185–8). M. Guignard's *Histoire de l'Agenais, dès origines au XV siècle*, Agen 1941, is perhaps the best monograph on the ancient and medieval Agenais (see esp. vol. i. 42–7, 57–80, 91–2, 98). However, J. Clémens is surely the modern authority on the early Agenais (his 'Les Oscidates campestres', *RA* cvii [1980], 91–6, is used here).

be known as Gascony would be administered. Even before the medieval period, therefore, the Agenais was a somewhat incoherent unit.[111]

Agen became Christian in the fourth century, giving rise to the stories of the martyr saints Vincent, Foy and Caprais. Its first bishop, Phoebadius (d. after 392), informed religious opinion in the Agenais against Arianism in the period immediately before the Visigothic occupation, from 412. Merovingian defeat of the Visigoths in 507 brought the Agenais and Périgord together for a time as a single political unit under Duke Desiderius. However, Gallo-Roman culture still dominated the Agenais more than that of its Germanic rulers. Shortly after 700 *Aquitania Secunda* and *Novempopulana* slipped entirely from Merovingian control, the former being governed by the mysterious Eudes and the latter being settled by invading Basques. Charlemagne had some success below the Garonne, but under the later Carolingians Gascony and Aquitaine were again two separate entities. None the less the Agenais on both sides of the Garonne remained a unit in Frankish hands into the ninth century.[112]

Internally, it was developing more complex identities. Different dialects had evolved north and south of the river. On the other hand, the process of warfare forged some sense of indigenous coherence which was still non-Frankish; local leaders faced unaided assaults on Tonneins and Marmande by a Moslem army in 726, the population both north and south of the Garonne supported Basques against the Franks, and the Agenais was decimated by raiding Norsemen in the central decades of the ninth century.[113]

Too late to save the Agenais, a champion, Vulgrinnus (or Wulfgrin), was appointed to protect the Bordeaux–Agen stretch of the river. Accounts of this warrior inform us about the opening of another very interesting and relevant chapter in Agenais history. A kinsman of Charles the Bald, he was made count of Angoulême, Périgord and the Agenais. Adémar tells us that he acquired Agen through marriage to Rogelinde, sister of Count William II of Toulouse. Although it would be unwise to take Adémar at face value for this period, counts of Toulouse-Agen – William I and then Bérengar – did indeed exist, during the wars of Pépin and Charles the Bald for control of Aquitaine. Bérengar's successor for Toulouse-Agen was Bernard II of Septimania. Bernard was neutral in the conflict but was assassinated in 844 and succeeded by his son William II.

---

111 Julius Caesar, *The gallic wars*, ed. T. E. Page, Cambridge, Mass. 1952, 388–9, 422–5, 446–9, 486–9; J. F. Drinkwater, *Roman Gaul*, London 1983, 9; R. Schmittlein, *Avec César en Gaul*, Paris 1970, 30.

112 *PL* xx.9–50; xxiii.743; *MGH* ii. 190; *Chronique dite Saintongeaise*, ed. A. de Mandach, Tübingen 1970, 269; *HGL* i. 677, 838; E. James, *The Franks*, Oxford 1988, 165–82; P. Fouracre and R. A. Gerberding, *Late Merovingian France: history and hagiography, 640–720*, Manchester 1996, 11–15; B. S. Bachrach, *The anatomy of a little war*, San Francisco–Oxford 1994, 50, 56, 94–6, 110–11, 118; I. Wood, *The Merovingian kingdoms, 450–751*, London–New York 1994, 100–1, 175–6; P. Wolff, 'L'Aquitaine et ses marges', in W. Braunfels (ed.), *Karl de Grosse: Lebenswerk und Nachleben*, i, Düsseldorf 1966, 270–1, 282–6; L. Auzias, *L'Aquitaine carolingienne, 778–982*, Paris–Toulouse 1937, 15–16, 33–5.

113 J. F. de Bladé, 'Géographie politique de sud-ouest de la Gaule franque au temps des rois d'Aquitaine', *RA* xx (1895), 47.

It was on William's death in 850 that his brother-in-law Vulgrinnus seized the Agenais in spite of William's opposition to this during his lifetime. When Vulgrinnus himself died, in 886 or 894, it passed to his son by Rogelinde, William I of Périgord, and possibly on the latter's death in 920 to William's son Bernard, although more likely to Ebles Manzer, count of Poitou (890/2–c. 935). The Poitevins then held the county until the last decades of the tenth century when it was annexed by the Basques, but we should view the Poitevins' major rivals in the county as the Toulousains rather than the Basques until this occurred.[114]

Gascon rule

It was possibly an overlap in authority between the Basques occupying the Carolingian viscounty of Lomagne and the Poitevins who held Agen that led the Gascon dukes to take control of the Agenais: the viscounts of Lomagne probably held of the counts of Agen the most important estate in the Agenais, the viscounty of Bruilhois, and also their property at Nérac, Auvillar and in the Condomois.[115] Certainly the late tenth-century counts of Poitou were not powerful enough in the Agenais to prevent the usurpation. According to the Toulousains, they had no right to it, although whether the Gascons knew or made use of the story of the illegal seizure of Agen by Vulgrinnus we cannot say (although the story was common enough currency by the 1020s for Adémar to record it).

Gombaud was Agen's count and its bishop. Sometime after his elevation to Bordeaux his son Hugues, abbot of Condom, became bishop of Agen until about 1012, when a bishop Arnaud is recorded. In addition, he held secular power south of the river in 'that part of Lomagne which pertains to the diocese of Agen' (that is to say, in Bruilhois, Nérac and the Condomois, the last of which estates he donated to his own abbey in 1014). Another of Gombaud's sons, Garsie, held comital powers north of the Garonne, perhaps even until 1043.[116] Again we see the family practising a form of partible inheritance, using a geographical demarcation by then familiar to the Agenais, with Hugues, almost certainly the eldest son, taking the most valuable share.

Setting aside the innovative intrigues at the highest levels of Agenais society, in other ways it apparently resembled the rest of south-western France quite closely in this period. Bernard Labénazie asserts that numerous independent castles were built by local lords, notably at Castillon and Puymirol, and that town residences were fortified. When the Jews of Aquitaine faced persecution, he tells us that the well-established community at Agen was likewise driven

---

114 Relevant parts of Adémar's account are cited and evaluated in Auzias, *L'Aquitaine*, 337, 352–65, 372; Wolff, 'L'Aquitaine', 290; Escande, *Périgord*, 61–3; A. Higounet-Nadal, *Histoire de Périgueux*, Toulouse 1983, 59–61; and Noulens, *Maisons*, i. 9–11. See also J. Nelson, *Charles the Bald*, London 1992, 57, 212, 233, and R. le Jan, *Famille et pouvoir dans le monde franc (VIIe–Xe siècle)*, Paris 1995, 35, 213.
115 Labénazie, *Annales d'Agen*, 34–9; Noulens, *Maisons*, i. 19–25, 63–6.
116 BN, MS lat. 5652, 10v; *Cartulaire Condom*, 581.

from its home.[117] However his portrayal of the millennial Agenais appears to have been informed more immediately by his assumption that it was naturally experiencing apocalyptic terrors than by actual evidence. Indeed, there are very few sources for the county in this period. Condom's is the only cartulary, and the few secular charters are those relating to the ducal family.

In fact a conflicting picture emerges from the documents. On the one hand, there is no evidence of peace councils in the Agenais, nor of Agen's bishops attending councils elsewhere (with the exception of Gombaud after he moved to Bordeaux). It seems safer to assume from this evidence that there was a level of spiritual demoralisation in the county, and that the ecclesiastical infrastructure of Entre-deux-Mers was not well developed, than that the Agenais was less in need of the peace. On the other hand, the political interest shown in the Agenais by the Gascon dukes and bishops might suggest that, along with the Bordelais and in contrast with most of Aquitaine and Gascony, its rulers' presence was felt relatively strongly.

This would certainly appear to have been the case by mid-century. After the death of Gombaud's son Garsie the *comitatus* reverted eventually to the dukes again, by then Poitevin, but from the episcopate of Arnaud II de Boville (1020–49) the *comitalia* had been delegated to Agen's bishop. That is to say, he held the powers that a count would exercise, but not the title itself. Henceforth the bishops of Agen held the right to mint – the coins were known as *Arnaudines* – to administer and profit from all justice in the county, and to levy taxes on the trade in weaving and milling and also on the city's Jews. Arnaud's fortune in this respect should be seen in the context of the struggle for power over Gascony taking place between the Poitevins and the count of Armagnac: Agen was important in strategic terms, dominating the Garonne as the border between Gascony and Aquitaine.[118]

Toulousain and Poitevin influences

The Agenais could also either facilitate or hinder traffic along the Garonne, i.e. into and from the Toulousain. The significance of this, and the case made that Agen belonged to Toulouse under the Carolingians, becomes clearer if we speculate that the Toulousains may have begun to revive their claim in the decades when Gascony, and with it the Agenais, was again shifting into the Poitevin sphere. It surely explains the warfare between Toulouse and Poitou in 1058–60. It has been noted that some preparatory diplomatic work appears to have been undertaken by the Toulousains with regard to Rome. Possibly also connected is the attendance of Bishop Bernard of Agen (1049–60) at a church council at Toulouse in 1056.[119]

117 Labénazie, *Annales d'Agen*, 42–3.
118 For discussion of the terminology used and what it meant see Ducom, 'Essai', i. 191–2, 300, 307, 316; *Coutume d'Agen*, ed. H. Tropamer, Bordeaux 1911, 152–3; R. L. Wolff and P. Wolff, *Évêques et comté d'Agen au XIe siècle*, Villeneuve-sur-Lot–Agen 1962, 115–20; S. Baumont, J. Burias and others, *Histoire d'Agen*, Toulouse 1991, 42–6.
119 Sources are cited in P. Bonnassie, 'L'Espace toulousain', in Zimmerman, *Les Sociétés méridionales*, 112–13, and Martindale, 'Aquitaine', 100.

This seems all the more likely given that the Toulousains were asserting a claim to the Agenais long after the Poitevins apparently had control of it. In a charter of 1079 William IV of Toulouse refers to himself as count of Agen in promising to protect those possessions of the abbey of Saint-Pons which lay in the Agenais, Périgord and Astarac. In a charter of 16 June 1080 he is 'Guillelmus Tolosanensium . . . [and] . . . Aginnensium . . . comes et dux'. Labénazie states that in 1061 'le comté d'Agenais revint aux comtes de Toulouse'. What he bases this on is unclear. However, and very curiously, after a charter of Guy-Geoffrey in 1049 granting rights at Agen to the bishop of Bazas, I find no other evidence of Poitevin influence in the Agenais until 1122, when Duke William IX made a grant at Agen itself of dues to La Chaise-Dieu. William and Philippa of Toulouse also minted *moneta decena* at Agen, on which the word *Pax* was stamped.[120]

How is this evidence to be interpreted? We have noted that William IX of Aquitaine was in control of Toulouse until 1123. It is in fact possible, therefore, that he was acting in this Toulousain capacity at Agen. If so, what had happened to the rights of the bishop-counts of Agen? Had their era of supremacy ended with Arnaud II in 1049, symbolised by Guy-Geoffrey's grant to the bishop of Bazas in that year? It seems possible that Guy-Geoffrey, in attempting to take firmer control of the important marcher land, had attempted to undermine the autonomous power invested in Arnaud II, and that Bishop Bernard had conse-quently become a Toulousain partisan. From 1097, when the duke of Aquitaine and the count of Toulouse were one and the same man, William IX, the political repercussions of this would have been negligible. Indeed, the conflict over possession of Agen had effectively been solved for a time. It is also interesting to note that around the turn of the twelfth century Agen gained new fortifications, perhaps a reflection of its importance to William IX.[121] But most interesting of all is the fact that, although historians have assumed that the *comitalia* was held by Arnaud's successors as it had been by him, there seems to be no evidence for this in the episcopates of Bernard, Guillaume (*c.* 1060–8), Elias (*c.* 1069–76) and Reynaldus (1079–83).

In fact what is usually portrayed as the confirmation of these rights by William IX to Bishop Simon II (1083–*c.* 1101) should perhaps be seen instead as their renewal. This immensely important bishop was, early in his career, a canon of Saint-Hilaire d'Agen. Then he became bishop of Saintes from where he was apparently head-hunted and brought to Agen as a Poitevin appointee to help consolidate ducal power in the Agenais. His good relationship with the duke is further illustrated by his administration of the archiepiscopal see of Bordeaux during its vacancy following the death of Archbishop Joscelin in 1086.[122] Many questions remain unanswered here and further work could be done in this area,

---

[120] HGL iii. 427–8; v. 649–50; Labénazie, *Annales d'Agen*, 46; Mundy, *Liberty*, 28.

[121] The Tour du Chapelet still stands: Verger and others, *Agen*, 82–6.

[122] GC ii. 905; *Chronique Saint-Maixent* 408; *RHF* xii. 456; *Cartulaire de l'église collégiale de Saint-Seurin de Bordeaux*, ed. A. Brutails, Bordeaux 1897, 26; *Coutume d'Agen*, 153–4; Ducom, 'Essai', i. 191, 307.

but the coins minted by William and Philippa at Agen should probably be seen strictly as a 'limited edition' and a revival of the tradition of minting in the town, for Bishop Simon and his successors were soon stamping *Arnaudines* again and the *comitalia* continued to be conferred on the bishops into the twelfth century with little erosion of their power.[123]

The religious life of the Agenais

Many bishops elected at Agen were already significant lords in their own right. Arnaud II and his successor Bernard were lords of Boville, and the family of Raymond-Bernard du Fossat (1128–49), probably an ex-monk of La Sauve-Majeure in Entre-deux-Mers, held the important seigneuries of Fossat and Medaillon. The canons of Saint-Caprais were also very influential economically, and not only in the town, for they controlled Porte-Sainte-Marie on the Garonne.[124]

Given the resources of the secular Church in Agen, it is not surprising to find its bishops among the patrons of not only important older Benedictine houses at Condom, Leyrac and Nérac, but also of the new monastic movements. Bishops Audebert (1118–28) and Raymond-Bernard assisted the foundation for nuns of Fontevriste Paravis by local lords Forto de Vic and Amalvin de Paravis on land by the river opposite Porte-Sainte-Marie, and the latter bishop founded Benedictine Renaud near Agen. But religious renewal in the Agenais had begun rather late. The first example of reform by secular lords is perhaps in 1062 when the abbey of Leyrac was given to Cluny by the viscounts of Bruilhois. There was probably a convent at Agen by the late tenth century and it was reformed on its donation to La Grande-Sauve in the Toulousain by Bishop Simon and converted into the hospital of Saint-Antoine. Sainte-Livrade and Saint-Maurin were the only other religious establishments at the start of our period, but by the 1150s there were Benedictine houses also at Penne-d'Agenais, Marmande and Gontaud (Saint-Pierre de Nogaret). There were also daughter houses of Grandmont at Garrigues (near Marmande) and le Deffès (near Agen), and Pérignac was founded by the Cistercians in 1151. Another Fontevriste house for women was founded at La Sauvetat-des-Monges (near Blanquefort).[125]

The new movement was important to the Agenais not least because the importance of Agen as a religious site had declined since the removal to Conques, in either 866 or 877–84, of the relics of Ste-Foy. Medieval accounts originating in the Agenais say that the relics were stolen by the rival abbey, although M. Guignard has suggested that, given the timing, they may have been

---

123 Ducom, 'Essai', i. 193–6, 293–7, 307–16.

124 GC ii. 902–11; Ducom, 'Essai', i. 193.

125 GC ii, instr. 316, 427; Ducom, 'Essai', i. 193; J. Clémens, 'La Maison de Béarn et les plantagenêts dans la diocèse d'Agen durant la seconde moitié du XIIe siècle', in Desplat, *Terre et hommes du sud*, 202; P. Lauzun, 'Les Hôpitaux de la ville d'Agen', *RA* xix (1892), 290–9; Barrière, 'Les Abbayes', 85; Parisse and Leuridan, *Atlas*, 99; Venarde, *Women's monasticism*, 63; J.-B. Marquette, 'Les Albret en Agenais (XIe–1366)', *RA* xcviii (1972), 302; Barrère, *Histoire*, i. 217–18, 318–25; Baumont, Burias and others, *Histoire d'Agen*, 41, 46.

removed in case of further Viking raids and never returned. Praise of once-prestigious Agen in the *Passio* of Sainte-Foy is absent from versions transcribed after this, and the eleventh-century townspeople must have followed with some jealousy the growth in popularity of the cult site at Cluniac Conques. Another calamity hit Agen in the 1090s, when the church of Saint-Etienne was destroyed by fire and the hospital of Saint-Antoine treated many sufferers of a fatal disease. The insecurity of this period, presided over by two relatively inactive bishops, Géraud I (1101–4) and Gausbert (1105–17), perhaps provides some context for adherence to the heresy against which Robert of Arbrissel came to preach in 1114. None the less, Agen and the *sauvetats* of Moirax, Sauveterre and Auvillar, all on or below the Garonne, were still visited on the route to Compostella and some economic recovery has been identified in the early years of the twelfth century, resulting in part from the clearance and cultivation of woodland by the new abbeys.[126]

Finally, a consideration of some other important points about religious life in the Agenais, most obviously, the vast majority of religious establishments that were founded either along the Garonne, concentrated around Agen itself, or south of the river in the Gascon Agenais. The same was true for parish churches. Agen had four major churches by 1100 – Saint-Etienne, Sainte-Foy, Saint-Caprais and Saint-Hilaire – and around thirty small churches were built within twenty-five kilometres of the town between the late tenth century and around 1150. Yet the Agenais as a whole had relatively few churches or religious foundations by the mid twelfth century, and the cults of the saints revered in Gascony had little impact in the region north of the Garonne. Thus the laity of the Agenais, most notably of its central and northern areas, was not as well served spiritually as that in other parts of Aquitaine.[127]

The Agenais and the Languedoc

In this respect the Agenais resembled neighbouring counties in the Languedoc, Toulouse and Quercy, which also had a somewhat sluggish religious life by the mid-twelfth century. We have noted the origins of Toulousain influence in the county but a study of the course of heresy in the Agenais should also note the related influence of Quercy. In this early period Quercy was governed by the descendants of the Carolingian counts of Rouergue, the house of Saint-Gilles. These, as we have seen, became counts of Toulouse in the early twelfth century in the face of opposition from the counts of Poitou. In other affairs too leading Quercinois families identified with the opponents of Poitou; Quercy was governed in religious matters by the bishop of Cahors, a suffragan of the arch-

---

126 *Book of Sainte Foy*, 37 n. 7; Guignard, *Histoire*, i. 80–1; Ch. Higounet, 'Les Chemins Saint-Jacques et les sauvetés de Gascogne', in his *Paysages et villages neufs de moyen-âge: recueil d'articles de Ch. Higounet*, Bordeaux 1975, 211–13.

127 Baumont, Burias and others, *Histoire d'Agen*, 37–9; Verger and others, *Agen*, 88, 94–5, 149–51; J. Clémens, 'Les Origines de la cour générale de l'Agenais', *Actes du 110e congrès national des sociétés savantes: Montpellier (section d'histoire médiévale et de philologie, iii)*, Paris 1986, 70.

bishop of Bourges, whilst its monastic life was dominated by the important abbeys to its north-east, namely Figéac, Rocamadour, Beaulieu-en-Rouergue (south-east of Caylus) and, not least, Conques, thriving economically at the expense of Agen.[128] At first glance, therefore, there would seem to be tensions between the societies of Quercy and the Agenais just as there were between Toulouse and Aquitaine. But in many ways, including at the humbler levels of society, Quercy and the Agenais were closely connected. This tendency is clearly apparent in the *Liber miraculorum Sancte Fides*, whose authors describe a socio-geographical context for the abbey's immediate influence which encompassed Quercy, Périgord and the Rouergue and also extended into the Agenais and Bazadais. In addition, families of Quercy often intermarried and allied with the noble and knightly families of Périgord, Gascony and the Agenais. Their collective estates formed minor empires crossing the boundaries of more obvious political allegiance, and their Aquitainian branches were also donors to Quercinois abbeys, as will be explored in subsequent chapters. Thus by 1152, in terms of its political history, cultural and linguistic features and its religious life, the Agenais was a region where Aquitainian, Gascon, Quercinois and Toulousain influences overlapped.[129] This was to be of vital importance in the ways in which the Agenais responded to the Cathar heresy in the second half of the century.

---

[128] See donations in AD, Lot, série F 125, esp. nos 190–2, 199–201, 216–20; F. 365.

[129] This is nowhere better illustrated than in the curious mixture of workshop styles originating in Toulouse and Saintes which are evident in building work undertaken in this period at the church of Saint-Caprais: F. T. Wands, 'The Romanesque architecture and sculpture of Saint Caprais in Agen', unpubl. PhD diss. Yale 1982, esp. pp. 242–7. See also Verger and others, *Agen*, 40–54, 94–5.

2

Heresy in Aquitaine, 1000–1150

From around the year 1000 sources for the history of Aquitaine begin to speak in alarmed tones of a 'new' heresy which had appeared in the region. Some of them refer to the heretics as 'Manichees' and say that the heresy had also taken root in other parts of the world. Until the 1950s it was as part of a wider European dualist phenomenon that historians also discussed it, taking the sources pretty much at face value and noting in them similarities with accounts of Balkan dualism.[1] In 1951 Raffaello Morghen rejected this assumption and argued instead that western heresy represented a spontaneous upsurge of lay interest in spiritual affairs which contrasted simple, moral piety with an established Church in need of reform and, consequently, on the defensive.[2] In response to this, Antoine Dondaine sought to reassert a dualist interpretation, offering a systematically comparative methodology which seemed to affirm the concept of a coherent, western phenomenon dependent on external influence.[3] The methodology Dondaine used has been the subject of criticism which has undermined the Bogomil thesis, whatever the validity of its central argument. Many of his detractors have taken Morghen's analysis further to produce alternative models for the origins of the heresy. The two most influential models are seemingly in contradiction with each other. One, which we could call the 'religious model', proposes heresy to be an extreme version of contemporary movements towards asceticism originating primarily in elite, educated circles. The other, which we could call the 'social model', also sees heresy as arising from purely localised western impulses towards clerical reform and a return to apostolic simplicity, but from a more popular milieu and incorporating appeals for the cessation of ecclesiastical encroachment into the ordinary Christian life. The former explanation was the earliest to emerge but was criticised for its failure to read the heresy within the context of social tensions and changes within the period. The most common consensus concerning the nature of heresy now stresses a culture of popular dissent. If clerics sometimes referred to it as 'Manichaean' this was not because they identified genuine dualism but because they adopted such labels in order to strengthen their polemic.

---

1 For example S. Runciman, *The medieval Manichee*, Cambridge 1947, and H. C. Lea, *A history of the inquisition of the Middle Ages* (1888), repr. New York 1955. For an overview of the early historiography see *Heresies of the high Middle Ages*, ed. W. L. Wakefield and A. P. Evans, New York 1991, 20–3.
2 R. Morghen, *Medioevo cristiano*, Bari 1951, 212–86.
3 A. Dondaine, 'L'Origine de l'hérésie médiévale: à propos d'un livre récent', *Rivista di storia della chiesa in Italia* vi (1952), 47–78.

These interpretations will be discussed as part of a critical historiography. The most thorough examination will be given to recent and current work. We should note from the outset that some of the most important has been that of Bob Moore, who provides the most convincing exposition of the connection between medieval heresy and the various movements and conflicts within and between the social, ecclesiastical and political spheres. His is a development of the social model which can account also for heresy in elite circles, and he is able to offer explanations for origins and responses to heresy which not only draw on but contribute to the most convincing models of what was occurring in the broader society of the eleventh- and twelfth-century west. As a central part of this thesis, Moore rejects entirely the concept of an alien origin for movements described in the sources as heretical. He is able to do this because the society he describes – in the process of being revolutionised by socio-economic conflicts affecting town and country, clergy and laity – was quite capable of generating such levels of dissent internally, and certainly did.[4]

I suggest that this thesis is slightly too confident in its rejection of what still appears to me, notwithstanding criticism of Dondaine's approach, to be indeed evidence of Bogomil influence. This remains the case whether or not we need such an explanation to account for the appearance of heresy in the west which, as a result of Moore's work specifically, I do not think we actually do (although I do think we need to consider Bogomil influence in order to account for some of the specific features of the sources). A discussion of Moore's work and that which it has influenced will thus feature especially centrally in this chapter. The model he initiated will be referred to as the 'conflict model'. Here 'conflict' refers not simply to a Marxist model of tensions between social classes, although this is certainly a feature of the age whether or not we employ the term 'class' to define social strata and functions, but also between other variously interested parties central to the anti-heretical discourses being expressed.

The main focus of the discussion will be on Aquitaine and as such we should also make immediate reference to two very different schools of thought emerging within the conflict model in this geographical context. Richard Landes finds in Adémar of Chabannes's accounts of heresy evidence of communities of belief which sought to prepare for 'The End' in this millennial period with the simplicity of early Christians, thus threatening the spiritual and doctrinal authority of the established Church and its conservative interpretation of historical time. Guy Lobrichon interprets an important 'new' source which claims to emanate from Périgord as a Cluniac warning against the secular

---

4 See R. I. Moore, *The birth of popular heresy*, London 1969; *The origins of european dissent*, rev. 2nd edn, Oxford 1985 (first publ. 1977, but all references are to the second edition unless otherwise stated); 'Literacy and the making of heresy, c. 1000–1150', in P. Biller and A. Hudson (eds), *Heresy and literacy, 1000–1530*, Cambridge 1994, 19–37; 'Property, marriage, and the eleventh-century revolution: a context for early medieval communism', in M. Frassetto (ed.), *Medieval purity and piety: essays on medieval clerical celibacy and religious reform*, New York–London 1998, 179–208; and *First european revolution*. These works will be cited in more detail below.

enemies of reformed monasticism, in defiance of its more obviously apparent subject matter, doctrinal heresy. Ironically, it is largely the contents of the 'new' sources which both historians have helped to highlight which have recently convinced others that a Bogomil-influenced heresy very possibly did find adherents within a society already ruptured by social and religious tension.[5] Eleventh-century Aquitaine was quite capable of giving rise to purely localised dissent that could manifest itself in religious terms. Many of the ideas and much of the behaviour exhibited by its 'heretics' were shared by later western and con-temporary eastern dualists but were by no means unique to their sects. But some resemble eastern heresy most immediately and, I shall argue, some cannot be convincingly explained outside of a dualist framework. It seems more plausible to me that the troubled duchy described in chapter 1 proved ideal ground – to borrow a tired metaphor – for various beliefs to take root in, and that amongst a potentially vast variety that could have emerged are what appear to be echoes of, and some direct borrowings from, contemporary dualism.

Things look very different when we move into the later part of the century and the early twelfth. Ascetic tendencies really begin to make themselves felt in circles which remained orthodox, arguably even as part of a response to earlier heresy. The spiritual requirements of ordinary Christians and the misgivings they shared with the reforming clergy began to be taken seriously and acted on, but in this period Bogomil influence appears entirely absent, which too can be accounted for. It will be argued that historians are wrong to extrapolate back-wards from these later ideals of reformers and ascetics, even from their appar-ently 'dualist' repugnance for the flesh, and find their strong influence in the early decades of the eleventh century. But their influence on spirituality in the eighty or so years before the earliest undisputed Bogomil influence in the west cannot be denied. Along with a surviving impulse towards further reform and, in some quarters, to the actual overthrow of clerical authority, they set the scene for the return of doctrinal dualism, arguably making its way westward again from as early as the turn of the twelfth century and certainly by the 1140s.

The number of sources for heresy in this period is not insignificant. First we will look at those that originally informed the Bogomil thesis and its revisions.

Sources which shaped interpretations of eleventh-century heresy

Six sets of sources survive for a heresy which was exposed at Orléans in 1022 but which had evidently been gaining popularity since the turn of the century. King Robert of France raised to office various of the clergy who were pious and

---

5   Landes, *Relics*, 37–9, 208–9; 'Aristocracy', 207–18; and '*Millenarismus*', 357–8; P. Bonnassie and R. Landes, 'Une Nouvelle Hérésie est née dans le monde', in Zimmerman, *Sociétés méridionales*, 435–42; G. Lobrichon, 'The chiaroscuro of heresy: early eleventh-century Aquitaine as seen from Auxerre', trans. P. Buc, in Head and Landes, *Peace of God*, 80–103, and *La Religion des laïcs en occident, XIe–XVe siècles*, Paris 1994, esp. pp. 14, 104–7, 171.

educated but not necessarily noble, and it was amongst such literate people that a new doctrine was apparently taken up and taught. It was exposed through the intervention of a Norman noble, Aréfast, and his lord Duke Richard. Initially, the heretics refused to refute directly the teachings of the Church, twisting them instead to accord with their own interpretations. When asked whether they believed that before anything was made through nature the Father created everything from nothing they replied, according to Paul of Chartres, 'You may spin stories in that way to those who have earthly wisdom and believe the fictions of carnal men, scribbled on animal skins.' They had already taught Aréfast the Docetic heresy, that Christ was not born human and thus did not suffer and die for humankind on the cross or rise from the dead. Consequently, they said, humankind could not be saved by believing this. Likewise, the veneration of saints was pointless. The sacraments were also worthless, for they did not signify the presence of the Holy Spirit or any special authority on the part of priests. The heretics instead performed their own kind of baptism by laying on hands, after which the believer apparently could not be reconverted and which he or she would never deny. Adémar of Chabannes notes that these heretics abstained from certain foods and describes them as the same sect of Manichees present in Aquitaine, from whence he claims the heresy spread.[6]

Historians' emphasis in discussing Orléans is typically on the intellectual background of the heretics. However, Rodulfus Glaber says that simple folk as well as clergy were converted, and Paul of Chartres that Herbert, a Norman monk, was taken in by them specifically because he was lacking theological knowledge, and that after his conversion he believed himself wise in such matters. We are told that recruits were educated by heretical masters who stripped away clerical learning, using the metaphor of pruning, so that a new branch could be grafted on and which would bear fruit. We may speculate that what was left after pruning was the New Testament, as special emphasis on it was an emerging trend in the period as we shall see, and that the fruit was a spiritually inspired interpretation of this, for Paul notes their insistence that they received their new knowledge from God rather than the Church.

During the trial of the heretics a canon and a nun retracted their beliefs but ten canons of Sainte-Croix, the master of the school of Saint-Pierre-le-Puellier and two lay nobles were condemned and burnt. Deodatus, former precentor of the cathedral, noted by contemporaries as devout and holy, was disinterred and burnt for being their master, and it even appears that the heretics had enjoyed the protection of Bishop Thierry of Orléans. Some people had doubts about

---

6 Paul of Chartres, *Gesta synodi aurelianensis*, in *RHF* ii. 536–9 (trans. in *Heresies of the high Middle Ages*, 76–81, quotation at p. 81); Glaber, *Histories*, 138–51; Adémar, *Chronicon*, 184–5. Fulbert of Chartres raises the possibility of heresy at Orléans as an explanation for a priest not taking communion: *Letters and poems*, letter 123. The only eye-witness accounts come from Andrew of Fleury: *Vita Gauzlini abbatis floriencis monasterii*, ed. R. H. Bautier and G. Labory, Paris 1969, 98, and John of Ripoll, whose letter on the subject is ibid. 180–3. Glaber tells of 'heresy' in evidence in c. 970 in southern Europe: *Histories*, 92–3, but this is criticism of classical knowledge and does not greatly inform understanding of popular heresy.

other clergy and laity in Orléans and throughout the archdiocese of Sens, and other royal officials were under suspicion.

Several incidents attest to heresy in north-eastern France from the turn of the century into the 1040s. In about 1000, in the village of Vertus, in the diocese of Reims, the peasant Leutard professed ideas apparently transmitted to him by a swarm of bees which entered his body through his private parts and exited through his mouth. Leutard abandoned his old way of life, repudiating his wife as he understood was commanded in the Gospel. He appeared learned and became a preacher, converting other peasants to his beliefs. We know nothing of his central doctrine, but are told that he preached against tithe and that only certain books of the Bible should be used. When the bishop of Châlons summoned him and undermined the faith of the people in him, he apparently killed himself.[7]

In 1025 some heretics at Arras were reconverted by Bishop Gerard I of Arras-Cambrai (1013–48), apparently the followers of an Italian heretic, Gundulf.[8] Gerard had heard that they venerated no church leaders living after the time of the martyrs and rejected clerical sacraments. Moore has observed of the sections of the source not apparently based immediately on answers to questions the bishop put to them, that 'the more remote the report becomes from the heretics themselves, the more elaborate and comprehensive become the doctrines which they are alleged to have held'.[9] If the recorded answers to Gerard's questions are more reliable, we learn that the heretics accepted only the authority of the New Testament and believed baptism to be inconsequential in terms of salvation, which could instead only be achieved through a set of rules governing lifestyle. These rules were

> to abandon the world, to restrain our flesh from carnal longing, to earn our bread by the labour of our hands, to wish harm to none, to show loving-kindness to all who are gripped by zeal for our way of life . . . [and] if this way of rightness be observed, there is no need of baptism; if it be transgressed, baptism does not avail for salvation.[10]

They also explicitly rejected infant baptism. If we do accept Bishop Gerard's more remote observations and inferences, they apparently also rejected baptism by water and the sacraments of the eucharist, marriage, confession and penance, the ordination of a clerical hierarchy, the existence of God in churches and worship in them, the image of Christ on the cross and the veneration of saints other than the Apostles and Martyrs. Amongst these traits attributed to them by Gerard – in so far as he has them abjure it – is also the belief that Christ was not made flesh. We gain the impression that these were simple laypeople. Whilst the

---

7 Glaber, *Histories*, 89–91. See *Heresies of the high Middle Ages*, 72–3 for the dating.
8 *Acta synodi atrebatensis in Manicheos*, PL cxlii.1269–312 (trans. in *Heresies of the high Middle Ages*, 82–5).
9 Moore, *Origins*, 11.
10 *Heresies of the high Middle Ages*, 84.

incident, like the one at Orléans, must be understood in the context of wider politics – Gerard's struggle for authority over the abbey of Saint-Vaast, perhaps – some of these curious beliefs are still not, I shall argue, satisfyingly accounted for by the religious, social or conflict models.

Further south, the diocese of Châlons-sur-Marne was a heretical centre for several decades. Those spreading the heresy to Arras had possibly come from a community there, according to Bishop Gerard.[11] As early as 1015 Bishop Roger I of Châlons (c. 1008–c. 1042) held an anti-heretical meeting and in 1043x8 his successor, also Roger, apparently wrote to Bishop Wazo of Liège asking his opinion on how to deal with 'Manichees' in the diocese, as reported by Wazo's biographer Anselm. They had first been identified as heretical simply because they were pale, the assumption being that this was the result of fanatical fasting. We also learn from Anselm that they did not kill animals or eat their meat. They rejected marriage and baptised each other by laying on hands, believing that the Holy Spirit was transmitted through this and no other ceremony. These heretics, essentially peasant converts, were burned in vast numbers.[12] There are also similarities between the Châlons heresy and an outbreak condemned at Goslar in 1051, in response to which Emperor Henry III hanged people accused by Duke Godfrey II of Upper Lorraine. Hermann of Reichenau calls them 'Manichees' and tells us that they refused to kill chickens or eat their meat even though refusal meant their own condemnation.[13]

For these incidents in northern Europe historians have long had relatively detailed accounts. Of heresy in southern Europe less was known until recently. Of the two accounts of a heresy in 1028x40 at Monforte d'Alba, in the diocese of Milan and near Turin, that of Landulf Senior gives us the most evidence, although Rodulfus Glaber is also much studied. These heretics were sheltered by the countess who lived in the castle above Monforte. At his trial, the heretic Gerard of Monforte at first declared that he believed in the Trinity but when pressed admitted that by the Son he meant the soul of man which was not really human, that the Virgin to whom He was 'born' was the Holy Scriptures, and that the Holy Spirit referred to the 'devout comprehension of the sacred Scriptures'.[14] His companions were vegetarian, fasted frequently and held their possessions in common. They did marry but remained celibate, and Gerard makes the curious statement, when it is suggested to him that humankind could not survive if everyone followed this practice, that married couples would increase without coition if celibacy became widespread. Unlike many of the other western heretics, Gerard is reported as stating explicitly that his sect used both the Old and New Testament and also other holy canons. We also hear,

11 Moore, *Origins*, 15–16 n. 15, 36.
12 *Concilia*, xix. 742 (for 1015); *Herigeri et Anselmi gesta episcoporum leodiensium*, MGH, SS viii. 226–8 (for 1043–8).
13 Herman of Reichenau in MGH, SS v. 130.
14 *Landulphi senioris mediolanensis historiae libri quatuor*, ed. L. A. Muratori, in *Rerum italicarum scriptores*, Bologna 1900, iv/2, 67–9 (trans. in *Heresies of the high Middle Ages*, 86–9, quotation at p. 88); Glaber, *Histories*, 178–9.

again apparently in contradiction of the tenets of other accounts, that the heretics put each other to death when they were perceived to have begun the process
of dying. The sect was structured hierarchically, and its leaders prayed continually all day and night in shifts. It included women. Indeed, we may have here the
only western example of a woman administering heretical rites at this time, the
countess of Monforte herself.[15]

Moving to south-western Europe, John of Ripoll, a Catalan witness to the
Orléans heresy, wrote home to his bishop, Oliba of Vich, warning him 'enquire
diligently in your bishopric and in your abbeys' for heretics who denied the role
of grace in the sacraments, never ate meat, opposed marriage and denied that
the clergy could pardon sins. He suspected these would soon cross the Pyrenees.[16] A major source for heresy in southern France is the history composed by
Adémar of Chabannes. For 1018 he tells us that 'Manichees' arose throughout
the duchy, seducing the populace, turning them from truth to error and
persuading them to deny holy baptism, the power of the cross, respect for the
saints, the Church and their Redeemer, and the eating of meat and legitimate
sexual union. Indeed they seemed to live like monks (although Adémar adds
that they were feigning chastity). They were the messengers of AntiChrist,
turning simple people from faith. For in about 1022 he tells us that the heresy at
Orléans was also 'in various parts of the west' including at Toulouse, concealing
itself carefully but still drawing many men and women to it. By 1028 the menace
was still so strong in Aquitaine that Duke William V 'called a council at
Charroux to wipe out the heresies which Manichaeans were spreading among
the common folk'.[17] Frustrating in the least for the study of heresy in Aquitaine,
no canons or further evidence for this council apparently survive.

These were the sources commonly known to historians until the identification of several more in the past few decades, and are thus the sources upon
which the various models for the origins of western-European heresy were based.
The new sources will be examined in depth later in this chapter, after an
account of what it was about the original sources that brought scholars of heresy
to their various conclusions. Before that, we should make clearer the identity of
the protagonists whom scholars such as Dondaine suggested that the composers
of the western sources faced.

The Bogomils: sources, beliefs and practices to 1050

By the late tenth century there were two dualist traditions in the Balkans,
Paulicianism and Bogomilism. The Paulicians had emerged in seventh-century
Armenia and their militarised communities were settled on the Asiatic and

---

15 Glaber, *Histories*, 177.
16 John of Ripoll, in *Vita Gauzlini*, 182.
17 Adémar, *Chronicon*, 173, 185 (first quotation), 194 (second quotation).

Thracian borders of Byzantium by its emperors.[18] By the mid-ninth century Bulgars had taken many as captives into the Balkans and by c. 872 their political autonomy had been destroyed. The heresy itself continued to thrive however, its evangelical nature being one of its major features and strengths. Paulicians were absolute dualists, teaching that there were two eternally co-existing principles, one good, the creator of the world to come, and one evil, the creator of the physical world. They rejected the Old Testament and the Epistles of St Peter, whom they considered to have abandoned Christ, but accepted the rest of the New Testament, venerating St Paul in particular. Those texts which they accepted, they took word for word to be divinely inspired, but their dualist beliefs led them to interpret them very differently from the Orthodox Church. They rejected the Incarnation, saying that Christ only appeared to be part of the physical world, and that the Virgin was not his physical mother but instead represented the heavenly Jerusalem. They likewise regarded the bread and wine of the last supper as symbolic food. When confronted with their heresy by orthodox authorities they would appear to denounce wrong belief and affirm the teachings of the Church, but it was their allegorical understanding of the holy family and the sacraments which enabled them to do this. They could, in good faith, declare their love of the body and blood of Christ, for example, for to them this meant His words.

Paulicians were still in evidence in the east during the early eleventh century at the time when dualist missions arguably appear in the west. However, it was a new heresy that appears to resemble that in Aquitaine and elsewhere most closely. It started in the reign of Tsar Peter of Bulgaria (927–69) and established itself all the more easily because the country had only recently converted to Orthodox Christianity and had more official than grass-roots adherence. A letter from Theophylact, the patriarch of Constantinople (933–56), to Tsar Peter describes the new heresy as widespread and as having a doctrine much like Paulicianism except that its adherents also rejected marriage and condemned reproduction as a sin.[19] Sometime shortly after 972 a Bulgarian priest, Cosmas, described a crisis within the disorganised semi-autonomous monasteries of Macedonia, which he identified with the rise of this heresy. Cosmas felt that many monks had entered these abbeys with worldly and not spiritual concerns. They were thus doctrinally unschooled and the chaotic abbeys unable to train them. They were therefore easy prey for heretics operating within the abbeys, and most noticeable amongst their errors was the belief that Christians living in

---

[18] The major source for the Paulicians is Peter of Sicily, Byzantine ambassador to the Paulicians at Tephrice in 869–70, where he learned of their plans to convert Bulgaria and wrote a history of the heresy in order to warn the Bulgarian Church: *Christian dualist heresies in the Byzantine world*, c. 650–1405, ed., trans. and annotation B. Hamilton and J. Hamilton, Manchester–New York 1998, 11–12, 65–92. Except where otherwise stated, the historical information on Paulicians and Bogomils and sources for them is taken from ibid. 5–43, esp. pp. 27–36; D. Obolensky, *The Bogomils*, Cambridge 1948, repr. Twickenham 1972, 29–31, 38–178; and Barber, *Cathars*, 12–21.

[19] *Christian dualist heresies*, 98–102.

the secular world could not be saved. The eremitic tradition was flourishing also, not least because many monasteries fell into disorder on the death of their founders or were disrupted by barbarian invasions, their monks left wandering and leaderless. These religious were also susceptible to heretical teaching and were responsible for preaching it in the secular world in the guise of ascetic orthodoxy.

The new heresy, which Cosmas tells us was founded by a priest called Bogomil, had rejected the essentially non-Christian absolute dualism of the Paulicians and replaced it with a more moderate concept: God had been responsible for the genesis of the evil creator of the physical universe, for he was His younger son, Christ being the elder. But like Paulicians the sect rejected the teachings of the Old Testament and treated biblical miracles as allegorical, denying that they occurred on a physical level. They refuted specifically the literal restoration of health and life to the sick and dead and asserted that the gifts of Christ's body and blood were in fact the Gospels and Acts. The miracles of the saints, on the other hand, they interpreted as works by the demiurge intended to trick humankind. Accordingly the role and power attributed to the saints by the Church was anathema to Bogomils and they rejected the veneration of their relics and icons, which they called idols, and did not observe their feast days. In addition, Bogomils did not eat meat or drink wine, fasted often, were celibate and denounced all sexual intercourse, conducted confession within their own circle as they believed instructed in James v.16 'confess your sins to one another', admitted women to the sect on an equal basis with men and prayed four times a day and four at night using only the Lord's Prayer except that 'they make His creation the creation of the devil'. Bogomils believed themselves alone to be true Christians, rejecting Orthodox writing and the authority of the clergy, the holy day of Sunday, and the validity and power of sacraments, scorning above all the eucharist which was but 'a simple food like all others'. They also found repugnant the idea that the cross should be venerated or that Christians should make its sign, symbolic of Christ's torment (even though to them His suffering was not real but apparent). This might have made them all the easier to identify except that they felt free to feign reverence of such things whilst worshipping in their own way later in secret, and even to lie under oath about their true beliefs, protesting that '[i]f our . . . works came to be known . . . then all our labour would have been wasted'.[20]

In the late tenth and early eleventh centuries great political changes took place in Bulgaria. Byzantine influence over Macedonia increased and threatened the Bogomils where they had become most successful. The provincial governor Nicholas resisted the encroachment. In 987x98 his son Samuel became tsar and fought Emperor Basil II (972–1025) until his death in 1014. Macedonia finally fell in 1018. The result of this process was that the social, political and religious institutions of Bulgaria were greatly damaged and resentment of Byzantine authority became an enduring feature of society. This, along

[20] Ibid. 114–34, quotations at pp. 130, 119, 131 respectively.

with the fact that Samuel was notoriously unconcerned with the prosecution of heresy throughout his reign, meant that Bogomilism grew stronger than ever.[21] The heretics were patronised as a symbol of resistance and discontent in Macedonia, in opposition to the now Greek-dominated aristocracy and episcopate. They had much support amongst the peasantry, enserfed as a result of the high poll and land taxes that they paid to the empire. There is little evidence that the Bogomils ever set out to become a party of political resistance, but they certainly grew in number in the atmosphere of dissent.[22] Furthermore, once Macedonia was incorporated as a province of the empire the heretics were able to spread their ideas to other regions more easily. Intermarriage between the conquered Bulgarian nobility and the most powerful Byzantine families resulted in the infiltration of Bogomilism into high society in Constantinople and other important centres.

This state of affairs is reflected in legislation passed by the Greek Church. Anathemas against Bogomils were in use in the early decades of the eleventh century, contained in versions of the *Synodikon of orthodoxy* and included in a *euchologion* produced in 1027. They attest to Bogomil rejection of the Trinity, their belief that the Holy Spirit was of a lesser nature than Father and Son, the assertion that the Son was not made flesh, and that there is consequently no salvation through this central orthodox tenet. The belief that the devil was the creator of the world is noted, as is the rejection of the eucharist as 'mere bread and ordinary drink', and also the rejection of the cross and iconic representations of the saints and the holy family. In their lifestyle, Bogomils are noted as shunning both meat and marriage but calling themselves Christians and seeming orthodox. Specifically, we learn that they espoused but reinterpreted biblical teaching, 'starting from the scriptures which we venerate; and when they have been accepted in this mask and the listeners begin to attend to them, they spew forth their poison'. On two occasions anathemas reflect concern that it was especially 'simpler' and 'rustic' people who were led astray, and that this referred to both men and women. We learn also of the exclusive use of the Lord's Prayer by Bogomils, except that they 'cannot bear to hear the ancient final sentence . . . for Thine is the kingdom, the power and the glory, Father, Son and Holy Spirit', a Trinitarian doxology used in the Orthodox Church.[23]

---

[21] Some historians assert that Samuel and his family actually supported the heresy: R. Browning, *Bulgaria and the Byzantine empire*, London 1975, 163–6. The speculation arises from the unreliable *vita* of St Vladimir: Y. Stoyanov, *The hidden tradition in Europe*, London 1994, 134–6.

[22] Cosmas the Priest claims that Bogomils taught the rejection of all secular authority and turned the ordinary Macedonian people against political and economic masters: *Christian dualist heresies*, 132. There is little other evidence to support this. Hamilton and Hamilton suggest (p. 28) that the assumption is a polemical extrapolation from Bogomil beliefs about the evils of the temporal world.

[23] Ibid. 134–9, quotations at pp. 135, 136, 137, 138. See also n. 12. The original version of the *Synodikon* was drawn up in 844 in response to the repealing of iconoclastic legislation by the iconodule regent for Emperor Michael III, Theodora, and contained anathemas against Paulicians: ibid. 21, 134.

Our final important source for the history of Bogomilism in its early period is an account composed in around 1045 by the monk Euthymius, of the Periblepton monastery in Constantinople. It describes encounters with Bogomils in various parts of the east and throughout the empire. These included some exposed in his own abbey. Indeed, as Cosmas had warned in the previous century, Bogomils were fraudulently appearing to engage in the work of the Church in both abbeys and the secular sphere. Of their beliefs he wrote that, although they called themselves Christians, 'heaven and earth and all that they contain [they say is the devil's] and say that the devil is the creator of all this, not God . . . [and] they say that there are only two things in the visible universe which belong to God's creation, the sun and the human soul' and that 'God rules all that is above and the devil rules what is on earth'. He tells us that they also believed it was possible to escape the power of the devil on dying. This was not because of faith in Christ's resurrection – they scorned also the idea that humans could be resurrected saying 'there is no resurrection from the dead' – but only through a lifestyle of extreme asceticism like that described by Cosmas and the *Synodikon of orthodoxy*; the shunning of worldly concerns and the setting aside of spouses and personal property, the refusal to kill anything living and the use of the Our Father alone, accompanied by frequent genuflection. Indeed, 'they bob their heads up and down like those who are possessed'. They would declare themselves to believe all that Christians did if challenged and would receive the sacraments of the Church if necessary for the sake of concealment. But they placed no value in any of this, rejecting the orthodox understanding of the Trinity (which he says they viewed metaphorically), the cross, all sacraments (the eucharist was again 'common bread and wine'), churches as places of worship, the special role of the priesthood, the saints and icons (which they mocked) and the Old Testament in favour of the Gospels and Epistles. They drew to them 'not just laity, but priests and monks as well' deceiving 'the ignorant and those of little faith'.[24]

Apparently unlike Cosmas's Bogomils, those encountered by Euthymius used a distinct process of initiation into the sect, involving a lengthy and rigorous period of training, lasting a year and involving fasting and prayers seven times a day and seven times a night, culminating in a ritual in which Orthodox baptism – called merely water and oil which 'neither helps not harms' – was symbolically washed off.[25]

Assuming, as seems likely, that the rite was only developed after Cosmas wrote about the Bogomils of Bulgaria, rather than solely being used by those of Constantinople and Asia Minor whom Euthymius describes, by about 1045 we have a far more sophisticated sect than the one which Cosmas encountered. The Bogomils who arguably sent missionaries to the west several decades before Euthymius wrote, lay somewhere along this path and were perhaps originating ideas and induction rituals that would vary or change. Moore has noted that

---

24 Ibid. 143–64, quotations at pp. 143, 144, 151–2, 153, 161.
25 Ibid. 149, 33.

although Cosmas is clear that Bogomils both believed that an evil force was responsible for creation and also rejected the material world and clerical sacraments, and whilst it seems logical that the one follows from the other, Cosmas himself makes no explicit link between the two.[26] Euthymius may also be read in this way (although he is more difficult to interpret, mischievously implying that the heretics actually worshiped the evil creator in acknowledging his awful power). It is therefore possible that even by 1045 Bogomils did not consistently make the link between the corruption that was creation and the rejection of its products. Bernard Hamilton is right to warn against looking for a coherent dualist system in the early eleventh-century west. By 1000 Bogomils had possibly only yet blended orthodox monastic asceticism with a moderated form of Paulician dualism, and what was to become quite a sophisticated cosmology was not yet being expressed even in the east.[27]

Evaluating theories of heretical origins

Morghen wrote before contacts between even twelfth-century Cathars and Bogomils had been accepted by most historians and was thus even less open to a global context for western heresy than are later detractors of the Bogomil thesis. But whilst rejecting eastern origins, he did note essential similarities between western accounts, indicating to him a movement rather than isolated incidents. Subsequent critics of the Bogomil thesis would continue to accept in general terms many causal factors he identified for heresy but would become divided over the extent to which such impulses constituted a movement with any coherence. Very importantly, they would also be divided over whether there was anything special about the early eleventh century. If not, heresy constituted a feature at the margins of western orthodoxy throughout the Middle Ages; if so, it was perhaps specifically the features of society in 1000, socio-political and economic as well as religious, that produced the variants and distribution of accounts we find at that time. It is far easier to discount eastern dualist influence in the former model (unless we suspect a steady trickle of Bogomilism flowing westward throughout, for which few would argue). The latter model, however, acknowledges the importance of causal factors specific to the period, but denies any possible influence by a factor which is both a feature of c. 1000 specifically and which also introduced dualism to the west in the 1100s: increased traffic in an east-west direction into regions experiencing social dissent and weak central authority.[28] This chapter argues that whilst the periodic society of the early

26 Moore, *Origins*, 153, 157–8.
27 B. Hamilton, 'Wisdom from the east: the reception by the Cathars of eastern dualist texts', in Biller and Hudson, *Heresy and literacy*, 38–60 at p. 39. In the Paulician case the lack of influence of the good god in the material world implied not that they should shun it, but merely that their actions within it were of little consequence in terms of the afterlife.
28 See chapter 3 below for discussion of twelfth-century society.

eleventh century was distinct it was far from hermetically sealed, and suggests that some scholars have too easily discounted some implications of this.

Faced with defending Bogomil origins for eleventh-century heresy with a modern methodology for perhaps the first time, Dondaine compared what he knew about eleventh-century eastern dualist doctrine and practice with the evidence in the western sources. Logically it was the account by Cosmas the Priest that formed the basis of his comparison, summarised in tabular form to accentuate the factual, or scientific, character that he clearly believed his approach to have.[29] Finding many features scattered throughout the western accounts which indeed corresponded to what was known of Bogomils, an identikit western Bogomil was revealed, based on numerous witness testimonies, each of them describing different aspects of his heresy in different locations and at different dates, each of them contributing a little more to a composite artist's impression.

Dondaine's response to Morghen was found convincing by those who already believed the western heretics to be dualists, and even to an extent by others, for example Arno Borst. However, Borst considered dualism to have been added on to and influencing an existing heresy or dissident tendency, not to form the basis of it. None the less, he found many connections between Catharism, Bogomilism and other heresies in the eleventh and twelfth centuries, the extent of which allowed him to describe a variety of phenomena as essentially the same heresy, in different guises and known by a variety of names. Thus whilst Borst noted differences between, say, the heretics of 1000 and the Bogomils of the twelfth century, he treated them as variant branches of the same tree.[30]

Not everyone was convinced. Henri-Charles Puech noted that various heretical elements revealed by the sources were being compared and contrasted rather artificially and were not only unconvincing in the sense of identifying dualism but also in implying a coherent movement. Most recently such a critique has been taken to an extreme in Mark G. Pegg's accusation that any historian who employs a comparative approach between Bogomils and western dualists, even as only one aspect of their methodology, takes an untenable position 'because this argument rests, quite weakly, on . . . simply perceiving a similarity between one set of ideas and another'. Although I feel this does not do justice to much modern scholarship, it is none the less the case that not one single incident in the west corresponds in more than a handful of ways to Cosmas's account of eastern Bogomils, and only really ever did this when Dondaine treated them together, apparently assuming that traits identified in one had lain unidentified in others. As Moore cautions, the initial assumption that these heretics were Bogomils has led historians to 'concentrate on what various groups of heretics had in common rather than to distinguish the differences between them'.[31]

[29] Dondaine, 'L'Origine', 60–1.
[30] A. Borst, *Die Katharer*, MGH, SS xii. 7, 143–222.
[31] H. C. Puech, 'Catharism médiéval et Bogomilisme', in *Oriente e occidente nel medio evo,*

Even if there were very extensive and consistent similarities between eastern and western accounts this would not in itself prove the Bogomil thesis. It would however be the case that at some point an increasing weight of evidence could be deemed to make the thesis likely. Thus Dondaine's approach is not entirely rejected by all modern historians but used as a starting point as part of better methodologies. Indeed, in Dondaine's defence we should observe that there is no earthly reason why the authors of isolated accounts of heresy should have identified all the features of the heresy which they observed. They had varying agendas – Glaber to note signs prefiguring The End, Adémar to promote a clerical and ducal alliance against disorder, as well as his own importance, Andrew of Fleury in relation to secular political factions, the episcopal staff at Arras to elevate the role of the cathedral clergy – and so they surely noted what they found useful. They had little idea of what they confronted except from what they observed or heard and if they failed to note traits by which we might identify Bogomils it does not mean that these traits were not there anymore than that they were. We should remember that the commentators on western heresy in about 1000 were not looking for Bogomils, and Dondaine was the first to do so with a modern methodology, however flawed.[32]

Something that has not always been satisfactorily addressed until more recent years is the influence of medieval writers themselves on the accounts they produced. Modern historians place more emphasis on examination of the context in which sources were composed, for knowledge of their authors and their status and circle tells us much about the events and ideas they set out to portray. Exploration of this aspect of the subject has formed the basis of much of the most recent research. It most obviously relates to the present study in terms of the use of the label 'Manichee' by some sources. Implicitly Morghen and Puech did not believe the sources on this matter, whereas Dondaine and Borst were less convinced that the label was erroneous. Central to more recent discussions is conscious examination of the basis used to evaluate a source's propensity to tell the truth or to lie, to mislead or be misled.

The question is, did those describing the heresy form prematurely the opinion that the heretics held certain beliefs that they then attributed to them? Moore argues positively yes. Bishop Gerard of Arras, for one, extrapolated from what simple Christians told him they believed and correlated it unjustly with heretical stereotypes. He may have sent his account to bishop Roger I of Châlons, and the latter's successor perhaps based his own account of 'heretics' on this, apparently adding the tidier label 'Manichee' to the heresy he reported to Wazo of

Rome 1957, 56–84, 154–61; M. G. Pegg, 'Historiographical essay: on Cathars, Albigenses, and good men of Languedoc', JMH xxvii (2001), 181–95 at p. 186; see also n. 13, and his *The corruption of angels: the Great Inquisition of 1245–1246*, Princeton 2001, 15–16; Moore, *Origins*, 19 (quotation), 42, and 'Property', 182–3.

32 See the recent discussion of Dondaine's contribution in H. Fichtenau, *Heretics and scholars in the high Middle Ages, 1000–1200*, trans. D. A. Kaiser, University Park, Penn. 1998, 110.

Liège.[33] Similarly, Adémar of Chabannes, according to Malcolm Lambert, used 'Manichee' also because it was 'one of the most infamous names in the constellation of ideas of medieval churchmen'.[34]

Discussion soon progressed to examining whether we are correct to see matters in simple terms of orthodoxy and heresy. Historians have noted that medieval movements towards lay and clerical asceticism successfully challenged and extended the boundaries of orthodoxy. Morghen's model was perhaps too simplistic therefore. Dissent that emerged in the eleventh century was as much about exploring what issues such as morality and purity meant for priests and monks as it was about dissenters exposing simoniac or married priests, for not everyone yet agreed on what constituted a corruption of the clerical life.

Herbert Grundmann asserted that the heterodox were in fact only extreme examples of a tendency to assume a very negative concept of the human condition, verging on a kind of dualism in its own repugnance of the flesh, of which a large number of exponents were to be accepted as orthodox after the dust settled in the second half of the eleventh century. Thus reformers and heretics had the same origins, in a movement born of the tension between spirit and body. It was defiance of ecclesiastical authorities, who gave or denied the clergy licence to preach, that marked 'heretics' out from the 'orthodox', but their message, essentially the same, was expressed as a current in elite and idealistic circles for some centuries. This tendency need not be heretical in a doctrinally dualist sense, even if churchmen labelled it such, nor be part of coherent networks. Some contacts with tenth- and eleventh-century Bogomilism and even ancient Manichees were in fact considered possible by Grundmann, expressed in the rejection of baptism, marriage, the eucharist and the cross, but he did not find the incidents to be organisationally linked, as having 'much in common' or being 'essentially unified' with any 'common denominator'. Where he departed entirely from Dondaine was in finding the actual impetus for dissent in an indigenous western movement which was based on religious idealism and an emphasis on the corruption of the material world, the spiritual element of Christianity and on the apostolic life as extolled in the Gospels.[35]

I would suggest some problems with his approach. First – a commonly raised criticism of Grundmann's work – he discounted any social context for the rise of the movement he identified. He assumed what Pegg has recently termed an

33 Moore, *Origins*, 9–18, 37. We should note that it is from Anselm that we hear that the heretics encountered by Roger II were Manichees, not from Roger himself, although Anselm certainly appears to report the contents of the letter to Wazo faithfully.

34 M. Lambert, *Medieval heresy: popular movements from Bogomils to Hus*, 2nd edn, Oxford 1992, 20. All references are to this edition unless otherwise stated.

35 H. Grundmann, *Religious movements in the Middle Ages*, trans. S. Rowan, Notre Dame 1995 (originally *Religiöse Bewegungen*, 2nd edn, Hildesheim 1961), 203–5, 209, 215, 219 (quotations), 222, 224, 227, 232. Bogomil links with more ancient sects were not disputed at this historiographical phase, but Grundmann goes even further in considering links between Manichees and western heretics independently of the eastern movements.

'intellectualist' approach to the question of the origins of heretical incidents, which is to find them to be 'clear philosophies . . . intellectually pure entities, able to be cleanly sifted out from other less coherent ideas and . . . never contaminated by material existence or historical specificity', thus transcending barriers of time, space and social conditions.[36] Such criticism in Grundmann's case came initially from contemporary Marxists of the Leipzig school. Although he made some concessions to their critique in his second edition, he never altered his view that those adopting and advocating the *vita apostolica* emerged most significantly from the ranks of the clergy, typically those of noble origin, and were reformers in a religious but not a social sense.[37]

This position is taken with regard to heresies from the early eleventh-century onwards, but it simply does not ring true when applied to the incidents we are examining here. Grundmann states that

> no mention of any specific social attitudes, other than general evangelical principles, ever come from [eleventh-century] heretical testimony, and even a polemic against the clergy is hardly ever to be found . . . [t]here is not yet even the idea of apostolic preaching and evangelical poverty which would dominate the heretical movement after the start of the next century.[38]

It is now widely noted that the heretical impulse amongst the peasantry and urban people is one of the period's most important features. Such popular sects regularly rejected tithe and material wealth and assumed equality between the different sexes and people of diverse social origins. This emphasis is only strengthened by the apparently communistic basis on which alms are rejected in one of the most recently studied sources. Moore emphasises their foundation in Christian ideals as much as in subjective material inequality and explains why they were felt to be important by both rich and poor converts, providing an important synthesis of the above positions. A similar view is taken by Ed Peters, who links heresy explicitly both to cultural and social changes and to the question of 'how should a Christian live in the world?'[39]

But whilst some characteristics of the eleventh-century heresies indeed appear in the manifestos of reformers, and it is thus legitimate to suggest commonality in intention and even origin between the two groups, others go far beyond this and question central Christian tenets. Most important, the belief that Christ was neither human nor born of the Virgin was not supported within reforming circles of this early period. Heretics questioned the value and substance of sacraments such as the eucharist, not merely the fitness of those performing them (the latter a heretical suggestion in itself but none the less a

---

36 Pegg, 'Historiographical essay', quotation at p. 183.
37 See R. E. Lerner's introduction to the translation of Grundmann, *Religious movements*, pp. xxiii–xxiv. The Marxist view is exemplified in E. Werner, *Häresie und Gesellschaft im 11. Jahrhundert*, Leipzig 1975.
38 Grundmann, *Religious movements*, 203–4.
39 E. Peters, *Heresy and authority in medieval Europe*, Philadelphia 1980, 57.

strand of dissent addressed by the mid-century reforms). Others opposed all sexual intercourse, even amongst the married laity, going much further than those who rejected merely the sacrament of marriage (which can be accounted for by opposition to the assertion of clerical control over what was previously a lay contract). The rejection of coition goes further even than the views of Peter Damian, to whom marriage was a quasi-legitimisation of physical corruption, his logic being that an elite of ascetics would be best fitted for heaven. No doubt to him coition for procreation was acceptable on some base level for the less deserving, whereas the logical conclusion of the heretical position was physical extinction which, if related to Bogomilism, was a perfectly reasonable prospect.

Finally, Grundmann perhaps does not extend his model into the early eleventh century as convincingly as is sometimes assumed. His thesis was developed entirely in the context of the wave of heresies beginning at the start of the twelfth century. He only applies his central thesis, that '[h]eresies are . . . only to be understood in the context of the general [i.e. indigenous] religious movement of their time', to incidents a century earlier in a frustratingly brief appendix to the 1961 second edition of his book and a short note on diversity amongst the sects as a precursor to discussion of the twelfth-century movement.[40] His comments on the earlier period are unsupported by much specific evidence. He argued that before mid-century those expressing reforming ideals were labelled heretical but were merely radical, whereas after the period of reform they could be accommodated within the extended boundaries of orthodoxy (even Peter Abelard, although he lost his battle, was no Docetist and not considered heretical by many of his contemporaries and successors). But the exponents of movements which Grundmann cites explicitly as being essentially and ultimately orthodox, if expressing a kind of dualism in their attitude to the material world, emerged exclusively *after* the eleventh-century accounts of heresy. Damian and Anselm were amongst the earliest, the likes of Robert of Arbrissel and Abelard characterising ascetic and intellectual currents in the early decades of the following century.

Grundmann gives no earlier examples of such tendencies within the elite of around 1000, but others have sought to do so. Discussions of late Carolingian neo-Platonist survival in the ideas of the tenth-century bishop Rather of Verona provide one example. Moore observes his influence on William of Volpiano, Glaber's superior at Saint-Bénigne (although he was not contemporary with accounts of heresy). William sought his inspiration 'directly from the spirit by meditation on the divine'. Moore briefly notes Abbo of Fleury and Gerbert of Aurillac (Pope Sylvester II) in this context also.[41] But this small handful does not equate with a movement even of elite let alone popular heresy. The concern of such figures not only originated in exclusive clerical circles but remained there, whereas even in Grundmann's elite interpretation idealism had none the

---

40 Grundmann, *Religious movements*, 203–5, 214, 231 (quotation).
41 Moore, *Origins*, 34, 42 (quotation). See also H. Taviani, 'Naissance d'une hérésie en Italie au xie siècle', *Annales: économies, sociétés, civilisations* xxix (1974), 1224–52.

less to spread, and downwards to an extent. These intellectuals cannot therefore be said to correspond in constituency to the heretical sphere. Neither do they do so in terms of doctrine for, most important of all, we have many accounts in which the truly heterodox concept of Docetism is present, removing them from the set of those implying merely an expansion or blurring of orthodox boundaries (if this latter point were not the case my argument would be somewhat circular, for according to Grundmann heretics were called so in c. 1000 only because their form of Christianity was not yet accepted as an orthodox current). The neo-Platonists in any case were more concerned with the role of the divine in the creation of matter,[42] not with whether Christ himself was manifested physically. The rejection of His incarnation by the heretics, and the implications of this for salvation, imply to me that something else was taking place.

None of this is to suggest that genuine issues of reform, of clerical purity and fitness for office were being raised only in heretical circles. Far from it, but I find little satisfying evidence that popular movements of laity and lowly clergy addressed them or pursued the apostolic life in response to them. Dominique Iogna-Prat and recently David C. Van Meter have demonstrated that the ideals of virginity and chastity were indeed being fiercely promoted, but in small elite circles. Exemptionist monks raised the idea that they were superior to the secular clergy in this respect. Abbo of Fleury's model of moral order noted three levels of chastity, virginity, continence and marriage, the monks represented by the first and the secular clergy by the second and less worthy classification. Charters of exemption acquired by Corbie were defended through the composition of a new *vita* of St Adelard stressing the closer proximity of the monks to the saints in terms of moral purity and asceticism. Odilo of Cluny portrayed the monks' virginity as a sacrifice to God.[43] In the opposing party, Adelbero of Laon and Gerard of Arras-Cambrai were amongst the few anti-exemptionists to fight back in the arena that the monks had defined. The secular clerics were on a sticky wicket here, but Adelbero famously chose to satirise the claims of the monks to the moral high ground. Bishop Gerard advocated celibacy for all priests in the context of his struggles against Abbot Richard of Saint-Vaast. Whilst the attention of the monastic reformers was on promoting their order as the most fit for heaven in the face of the claims of bishops to be allowed to interfere in their affairs, Gerard attempted to shift the emphasis towards seeing the clergy, both monks and priests, as being most immediately distinct from the laity, not as divided amongst themselves. He thus called for clerical chastity 'not in the hope of subverting the traditional socio-religious order but rather of

---

[42] See Fichtenau, *Heretics and scholars*, 172–96.

[43] *Liber apologeticus*, PL cxxxix.463; AS Jan. 1, at p. 111; D. Iogna-Prat, 'Continence et virginité dans la conception clunisienne de l'ordre du monde autour de l'an mil', *Académie des Inscriptions et Belles-Lettres: comptes rendus*, Paris 1985, 127–46 at pp. 132–7; D. C. Van Meter, 'Eschatological order and the moral arguments for clerical celibacy in Francia around the year 1000', in Frassetto, *Medieval purity*, esp. pp. 154–9.

preserving it against the assaults of those who would seek to erode the authority of the priesthood'.[44]

Furthermore, Grundmann's case does not really account for lay activity in heretical movements. We know they included laity – the sources are clear about this – and so his elite model of asceticism must implicitly include elite lay reformers. Yet only in the case of Duke William 'Longsword' of Normandy do we have evidence of an early eleventh-century layperson addressing the issue of whether they could get to heaven, outside of the context of indications of heretical disbelief in central Christian tenets.[45] Indeed, van Meter also makes a clear distinction between the movements in the first and second half of the century, seeing moves towards lay asceticism as widely influential only in the latter.[46] Whereas the mass movements emerging late in the century and most notably in the twelfth would involve ordinary laity as well as clergy attempting to escape from the world, the only people involved in such dialogue around 1000 appear essentially to have been in two distinct camps; the clerical elite and those they denounced as heretics. The latter are described as being part of a different movement entirely; in different accounts employing an allegorical reading of the Gospels and adult baptism without water, and as not only celibate but refusing to eat meat, to shed blood, to pray other than the *Pater Noster*, or to believe in the humanity of Christ and in the Trinity. The inner, spiritual life of the laity was not the priority of the first Gregorians or their reforming antecedents. The latter, as we have seen, were concerned with reform within the clerical sphere, with extricating the monasteries from secular claims and, through the Peace of God movement, with reducing the levels of social violence and political disorder affecting both abbeys and secular clergy. If the advocacy of lay purity were on the reformers' agenda we would surely find it expressed in the context of the Peace movement and also through relic cults, the most clear expressions of popular lay piety in the period.

Taking the religious model in a slightly different direction was Christopher Brooke, writing on the subject in the late 1960s. He declared the Dondaine and Morghen division too extreme and like Grundmann found Borst's approach more tenable, seeing the distinction between alien and native heresy as less important than either the commonality between its essential impulses or the wide variety of ways in which the new idealism was expressed. He addressed why it was that some forms of religious dissent were to survive and prove influential on a lasting basis and others not if, as Grundmann suggested, they sprang from essentially similar impulses. He concluded that the specific ideals or doctrine advocated, not only the context in which they arose, were important in deter-

---

[44] *Poéme au Roi Robert*, ed. C. Carozzi, Paris 1979, 4, 6; Van Meter, 'Eschatological order', 159–66, quotation at p. 160.

[45] In the mid-tenth century – according to Dudo of Saint-Quentin in 1015–26 – the duke had consulted Abbot Martin of Jumièges as to whether the laity would get the same reward in heaven as the clergy: Duby, *Three orders*, 83–7.

[46] Van Meter, 'Eschatological order', 160, 166.

mining the response of both authorities and society more generally. Unlike Grundmann, Brooke saw the period extending from the tenth into the eleventh century as different from the second half of the eleventh in being characterised by movements that were *either* heterodox *or* orthodox, making a carefully observed distinction between the character of what was called heretical in the earlier period and the later one, in which boundaries were certainly more blurred.[47]

But Brooke too was sceptical about emphasis on popular movements as a context for heresy, although he did suspect that it had some social as well as religious basis of appeal, suggesting that if social impulses contributing to its initial support were placated, heresy too would dwindle in favour of something less radical. This helps to explain the later elimination of Catharism but the survival of the Waldensians and growth of Mendicantism. He was talking most obviously about the thirteenth century of course, writing when it was truer that 'too little is known about popular religion in the eleventh century for precise and confident statements to be made'.[48] Recent decades have seen extensive work on the period. Although few of its scholars would now agree that 'the world of the eleventh century seems to have been a comparatively simple one',[49] we can now test models more confidently than Brooke could. We may suggest that when the Church began to reform itself mid-century the social, spiritual and, to a lesser extent, doctrinal crisis it had allowed to occur subsided, and so did the tide of heresy, a radical and reforming kind of spirituality taking its place. Again, it is only in the second half of the eleventh century that this happened. Thus, when Brooke said that '(t)he eleventh century cannot be understood unless it is seen that it found room both for a profoundly pessimistic view of the world and man's destiny',[50] this was surely to understand it by viewing it in its closing decades for, again, no evidence is offered for such a view preceding Peter Damian.

Brooke says that the century also gave rise to 'a new vision of the humanity of Jesus'. The concept is most widely addressed in the later period for, as he notes, Damian was one of the first to show an interest in reviving it. But earlier emphasis on Christ's incarnated life, for example interest in his supposed association with the 'Apostle' Martial, are indicators of earlier responses to it. Adémar and also Bishop Gerard stressed a Christ who was equally human and holy in certain sermons, the function of which was explicitly polemical and in opposition to a heresy which went further than stressing the spiritual side of Christ, denying that he had a human one at all. Arguably, the move from a transcendental to an incarnational faith was hastened, or perhaps even prompted by, responses to Docetist elements within heresy of the period. Whether or not this

---

[47] C. Brooke, 'Heresy and religious sentiment: 1000–1250', *Bulletin of the Institute of Historical Research* (1968), 115–38, repr. in his *Medieval Church and society*, London 1971, 139–61, esp. pp. 145, 148.
[48] Ibid. 157.
[49] Ibid. 158.
[50] Ibid. 155.

is the case, new interest in the human Christ again signals a clear distinction between popular religious revitalisation and the heretics as they are described; the one venerating a human Christ, the other a spiritual one. Likewise, when Brooke observed that 'the popular religious movement of the late tenth and early eleventh-centuries showed itself here and there in heresy [but] more widely and more frequently in activities which could safely be accepted under the umbrella of the Catholic Church', he makes an important distinction. Both strands were incompatible. It is very hard to see what the popular relic cults and the Peace of God mobilisations had in common with heretics who, we are told, denied the authority and power of the clerics and saints leading them.[51]

However, Brooke in no sense saw the radical tendencies of the early eleventh century as Bogomil-related, for 'before about 1140 there is very limited evidence among these heretical groups of specific dualism'.[52] In this he followed Jeffrey Burton Russell. Russell was influenced by Morghen, although he did think it possible that the Bogomil influence had been brought to Arras by the Italian heretics who had apparently converted the sect there. Unlike Brooke, however, Russell owed more to Grundmann's approach in being of the opinion that heresy was a naturally recurring phenomenon, in this case continuing from the ancient into the medieval west, not contingent on either social circumstances or new religious movements. He asserted that, although we have a great increase in extant evidence for heresy in the early eleventh century, this does not reflect changes any more profound than that the Church chose increasingly to record such incidents.[53] In response to this latter observation, a more satisfying model for the origins of medieval heresy was to be launched.

Recent scholarship reflects more awareness of material circumstances. Heresy is often represented as an impetus towards reform which has both a socio-economic and spiritual dimension. It is not usually seen as a coherent movement but a series of unconnected incidents with varying causes and explanations.[54] Some scholars have kept open the possibility of Bogomil influence, however indirect, but usually this is viewed as peripheral, incidents being seen as 'a half-way house between western dissidence and eastern dualism best described as proto-dualism',[55] social dissent in popular circles helping to explain why heresy was taken up with such apparent enthusiasm. Jean-Pierre Poly and Eric

---

[51] Ibid. (first quotation), 154, 156 (second quotation). See chapter 1 above for the cult of Martial. Bishop Gerard's sermon, part of his response to the heresy at Arras, is cited at n. 8 above. Adémar's sermons are cited and discussed at pp. 88–90 below. I would like to thank Michael Frassetto for his correspondence on this subject, which altered my own understanding of this area significantly.

[52] Brooke, 'Heresy', 143 (quotation), 146–7.

[53] J. B. Russell, *Dissent and reform in the early Middle Ages*, Berkeley–Los Angeles 1965, 21.

[54] Fossier, 'Les Mouvements populaires', 257–69; J. Musy, 'Mouvements populaires et hérésies au xie siècle en France', *Revue historique* ccliii (1975), 33–76. For a historiographical discussion of recent methodologies for the study of sources for medieval heresy see B. M. Kienzle, *Cistercians, heresy and crusade in Occitania, 1145–1229*, York 2001, 16–23.

[55] M. Lambert, *Medieval heresy*, 1st edn, London 1977, 33.

Bournazel have most obviously taken the middle path. They find material explanations for why dissident themes were taken up in the west, but that eastern dualism spoke, for different reasons, to similar concerns. As a result, they take a very open-minded approach to the sources. Although at points they assume too much continuity in the nature of heresy across the centuries after the early eleventh, they too find fault with the thesis that there was an essential continuity between heresy in the early period and popular ascetic and eremitical models. Thus the later 'eremitical movement and reforming pietism' was 'a weakening of more radical demands, a critique developing in the same area as heresy, which [by the latter half of the century] had been silenced'.[56]

Moore's account has probably proven to be the most singularly influential, and internationally so, on historians seeking an explanation of why heresy could be taken up by peasants here and nobles there, monks here and secular clergy there, and be called 'Manichee' here and 'new' there. Like others he argues that there was no clear doctrinal distinction between those idealistic reformers who were heeded in elite circles and those, the heretics, who were not. Similar arguments were used by both groups:

> The heretics were not alone in feeling a conflict between the prompting of conscience and the precepts of the church. The spiritual heroes of the day were also sustained in their struggle with evil by the inner light of the soul. An Abbo of Fleury or a Gerbert of Aurillac could appeal to his private conviction of righteousness against those who accused him of attacking the church when he argued for its reform.[57]

The heretics' enemies were those who perceived the problems inherent in the resort to private conscience and the stripping down of the faith to its bare bones, for '(t)he tension thus engendered between the urge to spiritual progress and . . . authority and discipline' undermined the path to salvation as prescribed by the clerical elite, the rituals, traditions and sacraments instituted by the Catholic Church.[58]

Moore identified two strands of heresy; intellectual and popular. The incident at Orléans, he suggests, reflects an elitist *gnosis* by-passing clerical mediation, and at Monforte he argues for a neo-Platonist survival of radical tenth-century theology. But Leutard of Vertus and those uncovered by Roger of Châlons, Gerard of Cambrai and Adémar of Chabannes were heretics who were truly popular, reflecting dissatisfaction at lower social levels with established church teachings and placing greater emphasis on the Gospels and Acts, with all the implications this had for social levelling.[59] In challenging this new-found fundamentalism, the clerical establishment portrayed the heretics as far more dangerous doctrinally than they actually were. But if many of the heretics 'were

---

56 Poly and Bournazel, *Feudal transformation*, esp. pp. 272–94, 284–94, 298, 299 (quotation).
57 Moore, *Origins*, 42–4, quotation at p. 42.
58 Ibid. 43.
59 Ibid. 25–45, esp. pp. 28–33, 40–1; see also pp. 285–9.

touched . . . by the gathering dissatisfaction with the capacity of the church to perform its spiritual duties',[60] such a state of affairs was hardly new. He asks 'whether the first popular rejection of the authority of the western church did not imply some changes in the nature of the society which the church had done so much to form'.[61] His argument relates, and has added much to, an interpretation of the eleventh century in which it would be surprising if we did not find expressions of conflict between the populace and the clergy just as we do between the peasantry and lords. Thus Moore sees heresy as merely the most radical wing of a wider spiritual pursuit, like Grundmann, but, like Morghen, as having a wider social base, one which, in explicit opposition to Russell, had recently received an impetus toward rebellion as a result of worsened material conditions.[62]

Moore rejects dualist content for early eleventh-century heresy utterly and entirely, saying recently that 'we can dismiss at once [Bogomil influence, for it] had nothing to do with anything that happened in south-western France in the early eleventh century'.[63] In explaining dualist terminology in the sources he argues that clergy encountering religious dissent 'soon remembered that such things had happened before . . . [and so] it was natural to turn to the scriptures, and to the fathers of the church'.[64] This sounds like sensible practice because several patristic authorities provide guides to different kinds of heresy; a cautious comparison between observed features and beliefs of the eleventh-century sects might have offered clues as to who they were. But this is not what Moore means, and it is his assumption as to what clergy did with the information they found with which I wish to take issue.

Moore asserts that Adémar and his colleagues did not ask the heretics or people who had encountered them what they believed but relied on what they read in biblical and patristic texts, most obviously in Paul and Augustine, to tell them. Paul warned that 'in the last times some shall depart from the faith . . . forbidding to marry, to abstain from meats, which God has created to be received with thanksgiving by the faithful', and Augustine wrote about early heretics who did likewise, called Manichees. Because of this, Moore argues, eleventh-century writers applied the term 'Manichee' to heretics who did not marry or eat meat, thus attributing to them a range of the characteristics of an ancient and extinct sect on the basis of very superficial similarities.[65] What was taking place, he argues, was a 'reaction against the impersonal and institutional framework of Carolingian religious observance and towards the search for a personal link between creature and creator'.[66] I think this is found expressed in the early eleventh century in an insignificant number of elite examples only, and not in the Peace of God or the relic cults, the biggest popular religious movements, the logic of which is in direct frustration of the personal link.

---

60 Ibid. 45.
61 Ibid. 20.
62 Ibid. p. xi.
63 Idem, 'Property', 195.

64 Idem, *Origins*, 8.
65 Ibid. 8–9.
66 Ibid. 82.

It seems possible that extrapolating backwards in such matters from the latter decades of the eleventh century to c. 1000 has become an acceptable but flawed practice, made all the more easy if the possibility of the influence of dualism is discounted before other explanations are sought. The result is a diversion from pursuing some legitimate questions resulting from similarities between accounts of western heresy and Bogomilism. Similarities alone do not prove the Bogomil thesis, as has been convincingly argued by its detractors. But similarities should make us question the assertion that several intelligent clergy, working in isolation from each other, were deceiving themselves in a similar way, with the same result, which they expressed in identical inaccurate language, thus conjuring the 'Medieval Manichee'. What of the aspects of the heresies they describe which don't make sense as part of the variety of agenda that have been attributed to the clergy who were supposedly constructing this elaborate deceit? I hope to establish that several elements only make sense within Bogomil-influenced logic. I find unsatisfying, for example, the idea that '(t)he . . . impulse to remove divinity from the language of the flesh . . . [interpreting] the Son as the soul of man',[67] is not dualist but is more likely in the period to derive from a survival of early medieval neo-Platonism, when we see that the same source, Landulf's account of the words of the heretic Gerard of Monforte, also tells us that Gerard believed that Jesus Christ was a soul born of the Holy Scriptures, the accused's interpretation of the Virgin birth. This was surely heretical even to Christian neo-Platonists, but was the kind of allegorical approach typically used by Bogomils. Likewise, Gerard's assertion of human increase without coition is highlighted as antithetical to dualism, whereas it is in fact entirely typical of Bogomil double-speak: without coition, increasing numbers would escape the physical realm.[68]

But the model I have just criticised is not the full extent of Moore's understanding of heresy. He has more recently interpreted some accounts as attacks on those actually opposed to reform. An important economic insight has been added, owing something to the work of Barbara Rosenwein on the subjectively perceived relationships between the laity and the abbeys concerning the status of donations. Heresy, Moore argues, can sometimes be understood as a form of protest on the part of the nobility who began to lose their main resource to abbeys like Cluny as the tradition and legality surrounding the nature of grants and gifts of land began to change, or rather came to be redefined by the abbeys, so that what was once understood as a benefice to which families still had access and rights became a gift outright and in perpetuity.[69] Monks viewed those protesting as enemies of the Christian ideal, as they defined it for themselves. Similarly, the secular clergy began to lose out materially as the independence of the abbeys increased and so monks and bishops portrayed each other respec-

---

67 Ibid. 34.
68 Ibid. 32–4.
69 Idem, 'Property', and *First european revolution*, esp. pp. 104–5; B. Rosenwein, *To be the neighbour of Saint Peter: the social meaning of Cluny's property*, 909–1049, Ithaca–New York 1989.

tively as enemies of reform or of traditional authority. Naturally those accusations of heresy which we are told were the expression of idealism by the *rustici* are hardly likely to fall into this category, and represent truly 'popular' heresies. But Moore has also moved away from simply stressing as an explanation for these movements for spiritual and clerical reform, involving both laity and clergy, a wave of idealism coinciding in a movement towards the *vita apostolica*. He has made a convincing case that references in the sources to common ownership of property and rejection of the marriage bond amongst heretics indicate early communistic tendencies on the part of victims and opponents of a new economic order that manifested itself in more intense exploitation of land by the elite, not least the abbeys. Betrayed, for example by the Peace of God, low status heretics were not dissimilar to the rebel peasants in Normandy noted in chapter 1. Heretics such as those warned of by Adémar, a champion of the Peace, were to Moore 'spokesmen of the less privileged who began to query whether the game of Peace was worth their candle'.[70]

This latter aspect of Moore's analysis relates clearly to the accounts of heresy in Aquitaine. But other aspects do not translate to circumstances in the duchy quite as well. This is not a criticism of his model: one of its central features is that different varieties of what was labelled heresy arose out of differing circumstances. In contrast most obviously with the incidents at Orléans, accounts in the duchy talk overwhelmingly of the support for heresy from peasants and the lowly clergy. Reformed abbeys were few in Aquitaine and, like the Peace councils, were typically the product of collaboration between abbots and reforming bishops and the highest nobility. This accord is untypical of the west in our period, and as such it makes accusations of heresy from one elite party against the other less likely in Aquitaine. In addition, we have no clear evidence for either the successful infiltration by external heresy of cathedral chapters or noble households in Aquitaine. A far simpler general model of social antagonism can thus be applied here. However, Moore has greatly influenced the responses of historians including those focusing on Aquitaine, and many now apply his model in such a way as to see heresy as reflecting tensions between rival parties as much as between social strata in the duchy. I find far more evidence for the emergence of heresy at lower social levels and that it was some of the ordinary laity and lesser clergy who formed the backbone of the heretical constituency, as much alienated from the agenda of the over-mighty lay and religious reformers as they were from the rapacious activity of the knightly caste.

If those whom the sources call heretics can be better described by these non-dualist models, then the language the clerics use to infer certain doctrines may indeed be seen as obscuring matters. It is the lifestyle and form of worship employed by the new movements which leading revisionists of the Bogomil thesis now stress, not the content of their beliefs. Moore's position has become

---

70 Moore, 'Property', and *First european revolution*, esp. pp. 102–5, quotation at p. 105. See also his *Persecuting society*, 13–19. Furthermore, Moore makes an interesting link between the wave of church building and social dissent: *First european revolution*, 106.

extreme, though no less coherent, to the extent that he no longer writes of heresy but of 'heresy'. This is a logical extension of his model, close to that of Weber in many respects, which recognises that it is assertive governing elites who decide who is within and outside society, not supposedly natural prejudices against 'otherness' on the part of the majority of the population or even the beliefs of those being demonised.[71] If 'heresy' more accurately denotes the forms of opposition to and within the eleventh-century establishment, it is consequently not an especially useful term to scholars attempting to understand what lay behind the discernible tensions of the period.

R. Bautier's approach to the Orléans sources is complementary to Moore's in this respect. Reading the trial sources with strong emphasis on Andrew of Fleury, he has stressed that the affair had very political implications, exposing factional interests within the French court and episcopacy. This important insight teaches us a good deal about the ways in which heresy might be used as a weapon both by and against the powerful explaining, for example, why matters came to a head when they did and under whose control.[72] But this surely only alters our interpretation of aspects of the accounts which are indicative of the doctrine or practice of the accused if we suspect that politics alone was at stake. The account arguably makes most sense if dissident doctrine was indeed being expressed, politics being merely the context for its unmasking.

A variety of other positions originate in the view that heretics are simply opponents in specific conflicts. One which historians appear to find least convincing is Landes's assertion that they were apostolic communities preparing for the end of historical time. This they did with the simplicity of early Christians, by pursuing the *vita apostolica*, thus threatening the spiritual authority of the medieval clergy, not to mention conservative eschatology. They opposed patristic interpretation of Scripture, not Scripture itself.[73] Landes has had to confront what he rightly identifies as an unjustifiably entrenched position that nothing of note is recorded to indicate millennial excitement in about 1000 AD. He has done so with some conviction and its influence on popular consciousness is taken seriously, if critically, as a context for the discussion of heresy in the millennial period by a few historians.[74] We have noted above the use of Paul's prediction of the behaviour that heretics would exhibit in the Last

71 This model is the central thesis of Moore's *Persecuting society*. Kienzle classes it as exemplifying the structuralist approach to the subject of heresy and its persecution: *Cistercians*, 20–1.

72 R.-H. Bautier, 'L'Hérésie d'Orléans et le mouvement intellectuel au début du xie siècle', in *Enseignement et vie intellectuelle, ixe–xvie siècles*, Paris 1975, esp. pp. 65–76.

73 See chapter 1 and specifically Landes, *Relics*, 37–9, 208–9; 'Aristocracy', 207–18; 'The dynamics of heresy and reform in Limoges: a study of popular participation in the Peace of God (994–1033)', *Historical Reflections/Réflexions historiques* xiv (1987), esp. p. 502; and '*Millenarismus*', 357–8.

74 See, for example, Bonnassie and Landes 'Une Nouvelle hérésie', 435–42; M. Frassetto, 'The writings of Adémar of Chabannes, the Peace of 994, and the "Terrors of the Year 1000" ', *JMH* xxvii (2001), 241–55 esp. p. 248; C. Taylor, 'The letter of Héribert of Périgord as a source for dualist heresy in the society of early-eleventh-century Aquitaine', *JMH* xxvi (2000), 313–49, esp. pp. 331–2, 347–9, and 'The year 1000'.

Days. Medieval authors also knew that Augustine equated heretics leaving the Church with AntiChrist. The predictions of John were also realised when 'many antichrists' appeared and behaved as expected': 'He is Antichrist, that denieth the Father and the Son', 'Antichrist (whom you heard would come) . . . even now is already in the world', and 'many deceivers are entered into the world who confess not that Jesus Christ is come in the flesh: this is the deceiver and an antichrist'.[75] Glaber's heretics accord with Revelation and are specifically 'envoys of Satan [according with] the prophecy of St. John who said that the Devil would be freed after a thousand years'.[76] In Aquitaine, Adémar called heretics antichrists and messengers of AntiChrist, and referred to Jerome's comment that AntiChrist would have many precursors. Thus patristic and biblical texts which informed medieval ideas about AntiChrist and his servants sometimes provided the language with which commentators unmasked him in the world. However, the same limitations on the actual extent of such beliefs must have applied as they did to the extent of millennial awareness in general; moreover, the heretics themselves no more referred to themselves as anticipating The End than they called themselves Manichees. Indeed Landes's case is a good deal more speculative than the Bogomil thesis. None the less, if there is evidence for some level of popular millennial anxiety, which there is, we need to take into account that this may have implications for the origin of and responses to those who were to be labelled 'heretics'.

Amongst those sometimes cited as arguing not only against Bogomil influence but also against the prevalence of doctrinal heresy in this period is Brian Stock. His model responds to the emphasis placed on literacy in a number of accounts and indicates that there was, implicitly outside formally educated circles, a congregating of those searching for an understanding of Christianity around Christian texts or, very often, around literate leaders who interpreted the texts for them. Heretical groups are thus examples of 'textual communities', groups who used literacy 'both to structure the internal behaviour of the groups' members and to provide solidarity against the outside world'.[77] Their understanding came directly from the Bible. Insular association and criticism of the established Church reinforced the particular slant which they accorded its widely known texts, the group becoming inwardly-identifying through this increasingly isolating process. Such groups need not necessarily have been avowedly heretical from the outset but may have become so through self-reinforcing discourse.

This approach has proved very valuable to scholars irrespective of their view of the origins of heresy, in terms of understanding heretical methods of organisation and forms of transmitting and developing ideas. Stock has made us think about even non-educated heretics as individual people attempting to attain and

---

[75] *De civitate dei*, CCL xl. 2, 473–4; 1 John ii.18, 22; 1 John iv.3; 2 John vii.
[76] Glaber, *Histories*, 91–3 (Revelation xx.2–3).
[77] B. Stock, *The implications of literacy: written language and models of interpretation in the eleventh and twelfth centuries*, Princeton 1983, esp. pp. 88–151, quotation at p. 90.

develop knowledge for themselves, rejecting the inaccessible and elitist communication of doctrinal ideas in forms that they did not understand. In terms of the role of parish priests, perhaps identifying with and leading their rural parishioners to a greater extent than we have sometimes assumed, Stock's model might go a long way towards explaining why several accounts of heresy refer to ordinary clerics adopting its doctrines. Perhaps they were the literate or semi-literate leaders of such groups.

But does Stock's model undermine the Bogomil thesis as much as some historians believe?[78] It indeed accounts for the rise of sects and their congregation around charismatic leaders, and groups of texts interpreted by them, in an entirely western context. It would seem to confirm Moore's view that heretics tended to see themselves as directly influenced by the Gospels and Acts without need for recourse to intermediaries. Stock does note that 'heresy . . . was reinterpreted to serve the needs of monastic and episcopal reform'.[79] But he in fact addresses the Bogomil thesis in passing only, noting Dondaine as its major but flawed exponent and assuming it by implication to have been discredited.[80] He does not in fact need to address it further: his case is that early eleventh-century heretics are examples of textual communities, not that textual communities either were or were not heretical, let alone dualist. In fact his model does not preclude a dualist context, or one that is global rather than western, and he even observes that Bogomil contacts in the period c. 1028 to 1052 cannot be ruled out.[81] There seems no reason why his chosen emphasis precludes a particular interpretation of a selected text, i.e. the New Testament, having been imported, transmitted and probably translated by central, charismatic figures originally from the east or informing the practice of proselytising western converts, for example Gundulf, the original heresiarch at Arras apparently converted in Italy. Stock's model allows for such an interpretation and could well be one of the most important for understanding both how Bogomils made and kept acolytes in the east, and how their immediate converts did likewise in the west.

Again with a strong emphasis on the text, but usually on very specific areas of conflict, a school of French scholars work from the premise that '[l'] hérésie est certes le produit d'un discours, forgé par l'institution ecclésiale'.[82] With this statement M. Lauwers begins his discussion of the changing relationship between the dead and the living in medieval society, in which context heresy is the expression of a social rupture caused by the Church's monopoly over the way Christians were buried and its claim to the ability to alter their fate after death. To him doctrinal heresy did not exist, but clerics interpreted and described as heretical for their own ends those resisting the process whereby the lay elite,

---

78 For example see Moore, *Origins*, 286–9, and Pegg, 'Historiographical essay', n. 13.

79 Stock, *Implications of literacy*, 150.

80 Ibid. 99, 102.

81 Ibid. 146.

82 M. Lauwers, '*Dicunt vivorum beneficia nihil prodesse defunctis*: Histoire d'un thème polémique', in M. Zerner (ed.), *Inventer l'hérésie? Discours polémique et pouvoirs avant l'inquisition*, Nice 1998, 157–92 at p. 157.

who previously had control of their ancestors' status and claimed their social position in reference to lineage, were manipulated into paying the clergy for burying them and praying for them. The evidence for this lies in clerical discourse against heresy from the early eleventh to the late twelfth centuries, a great deal of which refers to heretics rejecting novel sacramental institutions. Thus Lauwers reads the Arras incident, for example, with emphasis on heretical opposition to burial in consecrated ground and to paying for such services.[83] What is missing is an explanation of traits within heresies which do not fit the model, for example the rejection of the Old Testament and the apparent egalitarianism implied by the heretics' practice of earning a living by their own labours. This article also raises the question of the social origin of the Arras heretics. We are told in the source that they do not understand Latin. This could imply the type of laity – the established nobility – Lauwers suspects to be the accused. But most historians have understood the heretics to be of low status. How else may we account for their treatment at the hands of the cathedral chapter, apparently without political repercussion locally? The context for the composition of this particularly tricky source is arguably obscured even further in this model, and we are no nearer identifying who the heretics really were.

In Lauwers's study a range of texts spanning over two centuries, which claim to address a variety of doctrinal disbelief, are interpreted as a group with implications of coherency across time and space,[84] an approach criticised by other advocates of social models. More typically this French school seeks to establish contexts and explanations for circumstances under which heresy was *forgé*. Congregating around the seminar *Hérésie, stratégies d'écriture et institution ecclésiale*, their assertion is that there was more heresy in the imaginings of the clergy than in the beliefs of those they accused.[85] Lobrichon is concerned to dispense with any notion that there was doctrinal heresy in the period. He follows his earlier study of the letter of Héribert of Périgord with another discussion of the acts of the 1025 Synod of Arras, compiled for Bishop Gerard by his secretary. He deconstructs both sources so thoroughly that little trace of dissident doctrine remains, not least because the texts become almost unrecognisable to readers familiar with them. His approach is justified by the assertion that with heretical polemics 'il faut soulever le voile des apparences pour comprendre les enjeux véritables . . . la lecture littérale est le pire des mirages pour l'historien'.[86] His observations on the Héribert letter, central to modern interpretations of heresy in Aquitaine, will be examined in detail below. His case about Arras rests on his response to the discovery made by Erik van Mingroot that the synod's records were made by the same secretary who composed the portion of the *Gesta episcoporum cameracensium* covering the years 500 to 1024

---

83 Ibid. 158–9.
84 Ibid. 158–63, 166–8.
85 For other recent discussion of this school see Kienzle, *Cistercians*, 21–2 esp. n. 19.
86 G. Lobrichon, 'Arras, 1025, ou le vrai procès d'une fausse accusation', in Zerner, *Inventer*, 67–85 at p. 69.

AD. The *Gesta* is effectively a work of propaganda on behalf of its patrons, and yet it does not mention the heresy or the synod of 1025. Against van Mingroot's very plausible explanation for this – the subsequent author's work does not begin until the year 1036, and so the synod was simply missed out – Lobrichon argues that the acts do not appear in the narrative because the synod never took place, a possibility which he finds all the more likely because of the silence on the subject in other northern-French and Flemish sources.[87] He argues that the acts were constructed as part of Gerard's battle for control over exemptionist abbeys and over the new castral chapels. The heretics were implicitly the staff and patrons of such chapels who denied the Church its share of the ecclesiastical revenues derived from such control, being 'indifférents aux nécessités aux réalités matérielles de l'institution chrétienne'. In this model it makes sense, for the accused might well be portrayed as relatively unlettered. However, the context for their advocacy of clerical reform is unclear, and they appear to view all clergy since the leaders of the early Church as unworthy. This interpretation of the source also means that it is malicious indeed in implying in particular their disbelief in the incarnation. As will be asserted again below in relation to Lobrichon's treatment of Héribert, whilst we should all benefit from his advice concerning medieval documents that 'il faut . . . extirper les intentions, la fonction d'usage, et . . . les enjeux' it does not necessarily follow that these are never made explicit, or that if they are the source is trying to mislead us and we should proceed best by trying out any possible interpretation other than the one it invites. Likewise, Lobrichon is right to warn that the accumulation of 'témoinages éblouissants' to various incidents of heresy in the period tempt us to consider each as reinforcing the others' credibility. But it does not follow that by finding problems with every one of their statements, easy enough to do, the question of doctrinal heresy disappears. Nor can we suspect them simply because they emanate from monasteries with vested interests or from apologists in the service of powerful bishops.[88] There are few other places from which we would expect written sources about doctrinal matters to emanate. Not least, a problem with Lobrichon's case as it is with Lauwers's, the factionally divided western clergy seem to be pursuing a remarkably well co-ordinated strategy in constructing heretical frames with which to fit-up their adversaries.

The most recent assault on the Bogomil interpretation challenges the extent and influence of pure dualism even in the late twelfth- and thirteenth-century west, and will be given more attention in this context in chapter 3. Its central point is as applicable to the early eleventh century however. Pegg argues that historians take too remote a view of the societies they discuss in seeing heretics

---

87 *Gesta episcoporum cameracensium*, ed. L. Bethmann, MGH, SS vii. 393–510; E. van Mingroot, 'Kritisch Onderzoek om trent de datering van de *Gesta episcoporum cameracensium*', *Revue belge de philologie et d'histoire* liii (1975), 281–332, cited in Lobrichon, 'Arras, 1025', 68 n. 3 and passim, and see ibid. 75–9. For other interesting contextual commentary on the synod see Fichtenau, *Heretics and scholars*, 20–5.

88 Lobrichon, 'Arras, 1025', 80–4, 89, quotations at pp. 81, 69, 76 respectively.

where the sources say they exist. His opposition to the immutability of dualism as a historical approach has been noted. He applies a similar criticism to what I have called the social and conflict models, disputing an idea touched upon in several theses including Moore's, that dissidence arises or is identified as existing where authorities are shaping or consolidating their own power. In short, '(i)ndividuals and their societies possess no inherent tendencies, no fundamental hot-wiring, towards any particular theories, towards any particular actions'.[89] This is a challenging case with implications extending far beyond the study of heresy (although I suspect it requires expanding and rather more anthropological evidence to support it than is offered). It defies the identification of patterns and trends, which is in fact central to the historical endeavour. It seems to suggest that things were as they were in a given time and place because, quite simply, they were as they were; if something similar happened elsewhere it is pointless to compare the two or look for factors relating them. It adds to Moore's important criticism of our tendency to see patterns too readily, but it is an approach that is limited to demonstrating only what does not count as a watertight explanation for the rise of heresy or accusations of heresy in the eleventh century, whilst removing most of the tools we have at our disposal for establishing what does.

Doing the unfashionable for a moment, that is to say standing back a little from the sources, picturing their chronological and geographical distribution, surveying what they try, or rather claim, to tell us, it seems impossible to argue that there was no real perception of doctrinal heresy on the part of the clerical and lay elite. Accounts of it come from so many types of sources, many of their composers in conflict with each other, that the case that their complaints are essentially fabrications and deliberate misrepresentations seems implausibly convoluted. In moving then to viewing the sources closely, one at a time and in isolation, must we limit ourselves to reading them only as polemically distorted discourse rather than as genuine attempts at description, as though what was being said is always less important and less revealing than who said it? Some middle ground must surely be considered that obliges us to search for the origins of the accusation by attempting to examine the accused as well as the accuser. Our conclusion may be that the heresy is indeed of a purely western nature, emerging from a troubled society and only resembling dualism to some coincidental degree. But it seems impossible that the sources do not reflect a genuine fear of heresy and instead merely construct a crime with which to slander political or spiritual adversaries.

Another methodology for approaching this subject would be to do not only what Pegg rejects – identifying features of heresy which resemble each other and similarities within societies that produce heresy – and what he accepts – identifying what the sources mean within a historic specificity. In other words, we must read them in the context of the specific individuals and institutions – not just types of individuals and institutions – which gave rise to them, looking

89 Pegg, 'Historiographical essay', 188–9, 190.

'within these specific communities, (into) the worlds in which the heretics actually dwelt'.[90] This is the best that we can do, given the fact that we lack both sources composed by the heretics themselves and records indicating questioning by clerics who understood the pitfalls of deception and double-speak, such as that practised in self-preservation by contemporary Bogomils and recognised in the eastern sources.

We should also consider that we ourselves perhaps apply a sort of double standard when examining critically the terminology used in the sources. For example, Adémar says heretics gave the powdered bone or ashes of dead children to the unsuspecting in food or drink to make them instantly and irrevocably forget divine truths.[91] No one takes seriously such accusations of diabolic practices, orgies or black magic and few trouble to comment on this attempt at demonisation in any detail. This is in itself interesting: we don't believe in witches; therefore we assume Adémar is lying. Those who don't believe in eleventh-century western dualism also assume he is lying when he tells us that he knows there are Manichees in Aquitaine. Is it not more likely that there is in fact some logical basis to everything Adémar says if we read him contextually, within the framework through which he understood his world? Because the heretics opposed the Church, Adémar reasoned, they must worship Satan. But it does not follow from this that he invented everything he attributes to them. Is it not possible that in his account of the powdered bone he is unwittingly referring to a heretical ceremony that he does not understand? Paul of Chartres describes something very similar. Does Adémar's assumption of loose morals, again described by Paul, stem from the heretical untying of the marriage knot? Although we cannot rule out the possibility that Adémar's and Paul's textual accounts or the sources that informed them are related, and that they might thus share common malicious fictions, whether believed or not by the authors, nor can we be certain that the slurs they cast were not based on some easily misunderstood element of what their subjects actually did. Indeed, we know that Bogomils acknowledged the evil creator through their version of the *Pater Noster* and judging from the letter of Héribert, below, this may also have been the case in Aquitaine. Might this not be misinterpreted as 'worshipping' the Devil? It certainly was in the east, as noted in the case of Euthymius of the Periblepton. If these points are at all valid then we have every reason to ask whether Adémar's use of the term 'Manichee' also had any basis in observed or professed heretical doctrine.

Furthermore, the sources are sometimes less specific about the nature of the heretics' belief system than they are about excessive asceticism and anticlericalism. But this does not justify dismissing the existence of dualist doctrine because, as Bernard Hamilton and Dimitri Obolensky observe, the same is also true for sources which describe early Bogomilism.[92] Again, this is

---

90 Ibid. 190.
91 Adémar, *Chronicon*, 173.
92 Hamilton, 'Wisdom', 39; Obolensky, *Bogomils*, 126.

perhaps because the nature of the heresy was being concealed. Consequently it is not possible to make a systematic comparison with Bogomilism, even if we had no criticisms of Dondaine's approach, least of all with reference to the belief system of the Aquitainian heretics or their organisational structure, two areas which would be very useful in evaluating the possibility of links between these and other heretics in east and west. But we may continue to investigate the possibility of Balkan origins as new sources present themselves, as they have done since the above positions were initially taken. If we respect our sources enough to credit them with observation rather than a simple rehashing of early Christian accounts of Mani's heresy as their central methodology, as I shall argue we must, there is evidence which makes most sense if a dualist and eastern explanation is considered. It is in the recent exposure of 'new' sources for heresy in the period that we find the greatest evidence for this, and all of them shed a good deal of light on the situation in Aquitaine specifically.

'New' Aquitainian sources and their interpretation[93]

The best-known account of the activity and beliefs of the heretics in Aquitaine, and the accusation that they were 'Manichees', comes from Adémar of Chabannes and was included in various redactions of his history discussing affairs to 1028, in which year, he tells us, the duke summoned a council at the abbey of Charroux in Poitou specifically against Manichees, to which the clergy and respectable laity of the duchy were summoned. What its canons may have revealed, had any survived, is something we can only wonder at. What we do see is that unlike in those archdioceses to the north and east of Bordeaux where nobles, bishops and monks fought each other for power and autonomy in this period, the sources indicate a very different clerical agenda. The peace movement arose and prospered in Aquitaine because the governing secular and religious elites were allied in collaboration against lesser players who would usurp their power. Only with difficulty could 'heretics' be interpreted as a euphemism used by one of these parties for their enemies. The most likely candidate for the accused would thus be lawless knights. Otherwise there is little to suggest that the sources mean castellans or their retinues when they note that the simple laity were being led astray. Indeed, the armed members of society feature very little in a heretical context even in the works of Adémar and Bernard of Angers, discussed below, who otherwise frequently note the disruptive role played by this group. Who then were the dissidents? The peasantry, free and increasingly less than free, who were growing disenchanted with the Peace? But for what possible reasons are they 'Manichees' or 'Arians'? It is my contention that the variety of dissidence that probably emerged from this quarter was at points influenced by

---

[93] A useful overview of some of the 'new' sources and historians' reactions to them can be found in A. Brenon, 'Les Hérésies de l'an mil: nouvelles perspectives sur les origines du Catharisme', *Heresis* xxiv (1995), 21–36 at pp. 26–34.

external agents who gave to it the characteristics which cannot be accounted for by home-grown disillusionment and which were recognised as 'Manichaean', which is almost what they were, by those schooled enough to recognise such things. The 'new' sources for Aquitaine add weight to this case.

Some of the clearest expositions of the beliefs of the Aquitainian heretics occur in a body of sermons of Adémar of Chabannes, deposited at Saint-Martial before his departure for the Holy Land, a journey on which he died, and composed between the late 1020s and early 1030s. Without close reference to these Adémar's anti-heretical testimony can no longer be considered as understood. Recently they have received the attention of Michael Frassetto and been interpreted by him very convincingly as sources indeed indicating dualist influence in Aquitaine.[94] They describe disbelief that does much more than sound like something resembling dualism or simply have some of its characteristics.

Adémar attacks the heresy he has encountered most clearly in De eucharistia. He does not seek to undermine monks, reformed or otherwise, priests of any status or power, laymen jealously guarding their property or stealing that of others, or simple Christians seeking their own path through the New Testament. Instead he stresses two of the most important articles of Christian faith, the belief that Christ was both human and divine and that he suffered on the cross to save humankind, thereby defeating the devil. In contrast, he describes a heresy in which a Docetist Christology is present: that is to say, the heretics deny that Christ was in any sense human, and consequently deny the passion and the cross. In this they resemble dualists in the contemporary east who scorned the idea of the physical manifestation of the divine and instead asserted that His miracles should be interpreted allegorically, the resurrection being amongst these miracles of 'appearance'. Adémar goes on to discuss the role of saints, saying that the heretics deny that eternal life can be gained through their intercession, and warns Christians to look out for this. If the heretics here are secular clergy attacking monastic power through challenging saints' cults, as some revisionists might posit, his statements about their disbelief in the incarnation is indeed astonishing.

---

[94] They are in BN, MS lat. 2469, fos 1r–112v (composed at Angoulême in 1031–31) and Staatsbibliothek, Berlin, MS Lat. Phillipps 1664, fos 1r–170v (also composed at Angoulême, in 1029–33) and are transcribed in M. Frassetto, 'The sermons of Adémar of Chabannes and the origins of medieval heresy', unpubl. PhD diss. Delaware 1993, 164–229. Relevant sections are included and translated in his other works, especially in 'Reaction and reform: reception of heresy in Arras and Aquitaine in the early eleventh century', *Catholic Historical Review* lxxxiii (1997), 385–400; 'Heresy, celibacy, and reform in the sermons of Adémar of Chabannes', in Frassetto, *Medieval purity*, 131–48; and 'The sermons of Adémar of Chabannes and the letter of Héribert: new sources concerning the origins of medieval heresy', *Revue bénédictine* cix (1999), 324–40. Sections of the sermon *De eucharistia* (MS Lat. Phillipps 1664, fos 70v–78v at fos 71, 72, 75) were first published as a source for heresy in 1992: Bonnassie and Landes, 'Une Nouvelle Hérésie', 454–5. Other relevant sermons are *De chrismate sacro* (MS Lat. Phillipps 1664, fos 68r–70r), *Sermo ad sinodum de catholica fide* (fos 83v–96r), and *Sermo ad sinodo de vita clericum ex dictis Hieronimi* (fos 115r–116r).

We hear a good deal about heretical practice in *De eucharistia*. Heretics seek to fool the gullible in several ways, we are told, by feigning goodness and pretending to speak evil of no one, and refusing acclaim for leading such lives. This, Adémar says, is a sham. Likewise, they pretend to fast – wrong in itself for, as Paul noted, God created nourishment for human bodies – and renounce all worldly goods and condemn sexual intercourse, although he is sure they in fact indulge in all these things. Such accusations could be interpreted as criticism by monks of unreformed abbeys, ones co-operating with the secular sphere as Adémar's did, against the pretensions of Cluny. But Adémar was no opponent of the reformers, and would he seriously have accused Cluniac monks of disbelief in the incarnation and Trinity or the power of saints?

De eucharistia is also extremely instructive on the social basis of the heresy in Aquitaine. It appears overwhelmingly to have been taken up by the poor and uneducated, and we can certainly see the resonance of Stock's textual communities here for great emphasis was placed on the teaching of the unlettered. Once a true Christian has been won to the heretics, Adémar tells us, he or she undergoes a form of baptism involving the laying on of hands, undermining Catholic baptism. He emphasises the ability of the heretics to convince people of their message, warning priests to be on their guard in this matter and to warn their flock that heretics they may meet, no matter how eloquent, learned or saintly they appear, do not adhere to the beliefs of the Church. They are to be shunned and expelled from religious and secular society and afforded no charity. Adémar also highlights the danger of the uneducated seeking to examine the nature of God, for they might fall into heresy. It is faith and belief in the sacraments, he says, not knowledge or a pure life alone, which offer salvation. Here, perhaps, is the evidence for simple Christians pursuing the *vita apostolica*, rejecting the claims of the clergy to special powers expressed through the sacraments and the cults of saints and the claims made about their remains, as innovations and diversions from the central Christian message.

But is he indeed describing the *vita apostolica*? There are problems. A logical reaction to this from the clergy would surely have been to win support against the emerging autonomous movement and for the clerical hierarchy, monastic and/or secular, through polemic and propaganda on the part of the Peace movement, relic cults and parochial organisation (often monastic in Aquitaine). But Adémar, one of the fiercest champions of these new orthodox movements, does not advocate this, nor do we find examples of it elsewhere. This Latin sermon is not aimed at the populace. All that the clergy can try to do, implicit in the *Sermo ad sinodum de vita clericum ex dictis Hieronim* in which he addresses the question of reconversion, is lead by example, for instance with regard to celibacy. Attempts at reconversion are the concern of bishops alone, who must convince the heretics that Christ was true God and also true man (thus we may infer that the heresy was Docetic). Such activity is in any case more often than not ineffective, he notes in both sermons, for once converted the heretics cannot be won back and are irretrievably lost to the faith. Indeed, they prefer death to reconversion, such is the power of the new message and so, according to the *Sermo ad sinodum*, the heretics must be cast out like serpents and separated from good Christians whom they might contaminate.[95]

Thus we see a more sinister side to the teachings of the heretics. They cannot be countered by renewed vigour on the part of clergy, even if such clergy increased their credibility in some way. They must be treated as lost to the faith. Reform is therefore not the issue. Neither does the heresy sound like the stripping down of the faith to its bare apostolic bones, rather a far more extreme kind of conversion at the hands of skilled proselytisers untypical of those ill-trained parish clergy of the tenth and eleventh-century west, however disillusioned with their superiors they might be. Again, to labour the point perhaps, what a strange twisting of the New Testament by the leaders of such cells of simple Christians it would have been that convinced followers that Christ was not human.

Adémar's various accounts are not the only ones for the duchy, nor the earliest. We learn from the archives of Saint-Hilaire de Poitou that heretics were identified in the county at least as early as 1016, for a charter of William V refers to a heresy which was new, proliferating and 'Arian'.[96] It expresses the duke's belief that priests were flocking to them in droves, to the extent that the Church was being drained of clergy. It is specifically in order to stem this flow and to protect Saint-Hilaire that the duke says he is acting. Presumably, therefore, he and his clerical allies had good reason to fear that this house specifically was in danger of being infiltrated by such heretics. The reference to Arians is juxtaposed to William's own love of the holy and indivisible Trinity and so it seems reasonable to infer that the heretics were perceived as anti-Trinitarian, a point which will be addressed further. The duke also expresses his faith in the intercession of St Hilaire, and so it is possible that the heretics also denounced saints' cults. This important evidence of ducal involvement in monastic affairs must of course be understood within the context of the Peace of God's alliance of leading nobles, monks and bishops, again making this source difficult to interpret comfortably within the social and conflict models.

The stories recounted in the *Liber miraculorum Sancte Fides* date from the turn of the century onwards and were collected in order to promote the leading cult centre of a Gallo-Roman child martyr, Foy, whose remains had rested in the abbey of Conques since they were stolen in the ninth century from Agen, where she had lived and was killed. The stories originate in a region extending from the Bazadais to the Rouergue. The bizarre, even crude nature of some of Foy's miracles were met with embarrassment rather than joy by some of the clerical elite, and the *Liber miraculorum* was constructed not least to counter such criticism and to make the cult respectable, as skilfully explored by Amy Remensynder. The miracles in the first two books of the collection were set down between 1010 and the 1020s by Bernard of Angers, pilgrim and fanatical

---

95 MS Lat. Phillipps 1664, fos 114v, 162v (Frassetto, 'Sermons', 228, 253).
96 *Documents pour l'histoire de l'église de Saint-Hilaire de Poitiers (768–1300)*, ed. L. Rédet, *Mémoires de la Société des antiquaires de l'ouest* xiv (1847), 80–2 (published in Bonnassie and Landes, 'Une Nouvelle Hérésie', 449–50).

devotee of the saint. The third and fourth books are based on notes he made about other miracles. Those in the third were set down probably in the 1020s but certainly by 1050 by a second author, and the fourth was produced in mid-century by a variety of writers. The theme of disbelief was taken up by Bernard in stories he recounted between 1013 and 1020. He tells of two groups of people who refused to accept Foy's power and authority: lawless *milites* and religious heretics. He distinguishes clearly between the two. Whilst he is not averse to attributing supernatural causes to the misfortunes of the knights, and even refers to them as antichrists on occasion, it is the doctrinal disbelief of heretical peasants and low-ranking clergy which he sees as threatening to popular belief. The subject is addressed also by his continuators, who make the same distinction. Although the cult was not short of detractors these came from elite circles. As such they seem unlikely to have included people who would caste suspicion on the resurrection of bodies, the need for consecrating churches or for performing the sacrament of baptism, as we hear that heretics did, which is how such accounts have been interpreted elsewhere. More important, this group does not correlate with the heretics as identified by Bernard and his continuators, as lowly in origin.[97]

Pierre Bonnassie and Richard Landes brought this source to our attention in the context of discussion about heresy. They read the heretics as expressing discontent with established monasticism and disillusionment with saints' cults. Thus they include as an account of perceived heresy Bernard's tale of the terrible death of the *miles* Guy, an example of just punishment for crimes against the servants of St Foy.[98] But Bernard does not say that Guy is a heretic, merely impious. His accusations are not doctrinal, which some of those levelled at various named heretics are. I must therefore disagree with the inclusion of the story of Guy amongst incidents of heresy. If this source is discounted there is a striking consistency in what the several interpretative compilers of miracle stories in this region appear to have identified as the characteristics of popular heresy.

Several of the stories feature the ridicule of saints and their veneration. Bernard reports that heretics found absurd and actually offensive the idea that a long dead child martyr could still be active and powerful. In about 1013, we hear, some pilgrims of Bernard's acquaintance visited Le Puy en Velay and met a heretical man from the neighbourhood of Conques. When he heard that they were from Anjou he complained that Bernard had been spreading miracle stories that were lies. In particular he disputed whether it was possible for sight

---

97 The *Liber miraculorum* and other translated sources relating to the saint are published with a historical introduction to the cult in P. Sheingorn's *Book of Saint Foy*. The Latin is edited by L. Robertini, Spoleto 1994. On the nature of the miracles and Bernard's intentions see especially A. G. Remensnyder, 'Un Problème de cultures ou culture? La statue-réliquaire et les *joca* de Sainte Foy de Conques dans le *Liber miraculorum* de Bernard d'Angers', CCM xxxiii (1990), 351–79. For an extremely useful discussion of the use of miracle stories to historians more generally see Marcus Bull's introduction to *Miracles of Our Lady of Rocamadour*, at pp. 11–20.
98 Bonnassie and Landes, 'Une Nouvelle Hérésie', 445–6.

to be restored to a man whose eyes had been put out, or for mules to be raised from the dead, just some of the feats the saint had performed. Such a man, says Bernard, was surely a son of the devil and the supporter of AntiChrist, fallen into perilous error. Indeed, he is certain of the need to be vigilant against such disbelief in the Last Days.[99] Thus far, the man's heresy appears to be nothing more than opposition to saints' cults and could be accounted for on the basis that they were the novel creation of the abbeys and not derived from scriptural authority. Yet Bernard specifically refers to the belief that human corpses will not be raised from the dead for they are unworthy of entry to heaven. This attack on the doctrine of corporal resurrection really troubles Bernard and he argues at length against it, stating that by raising animals from the dead God, through the saint, is showing Christians that they too will later be raised up. In addition, he tells us that this heresy is the same as that which was reported in the time of the Holy Fathers. Like Adémar, Bernard, as well as seeing the work of heretics as having apocalyptic significance in the millennial era, appears to be responding to a dualist doctrine on the corrupt nature of physical matter and the power of God to act upon it and not merely relating a dispute about the powers of saints. He also sees it as a revival of an earlier form of disbelief, perhaps implying Manichaeism. We know that Bogomils mocked the saints and those who prayed to them, rejecting cults and ascribing miracles associated with relics to tricks played by the devil to mislead people. Their influence seems an entirely plausible explanation for this account.

In this collection we also have the only known account of eleventh-century heresy in Gascony, written down in about 1050. A monk of the Bazadais called Deusdet built a simple wooden church dedicated to St Foy in the woods near Sardan. We are told that peasants from the area never failed to incline their heads and say a prayer as they passed it. All except one heretic who was, 'profano captus errore', and mocked them for praying to a shed. Like other heretics who, we are told, had led this man into error, he denied the nature of the sacraments, failing to acknowledge that grace could change a hut into a church or water into a sanctified substance.[100] Not only are the saint and her adherents and promoters being challenged here, but established Christian belief and doctrine. Although, it is true, such transformation of physical matter does not have a New Testament basis, and it is the act of worship and ritual not the building or water concerned which is special in that context, it also seems very possible that the influence of heretics focusing closely on such matters, going much further than questioning the powers of saints and claims of the abbeys, had by now spread south of the Garonne.

The letter of Héribert of Périgord was first published in 1682 by Jean Mabillon. Scholars thought it dated from between 1145 and 1163, the dates of the earliest manuscripts in which its various versions were known, and thus to relate to twelfth-century Catharism. They had overlooked an eleventh-century

---

99 *Book of Saint Foy*, 64–5.
100 Ibid. 212–13.

version bound into a manuscript belonging to the abbey of Saint-Germain of Auxerre in c. 1050, containing documents composed from the mid-ninth century to the mid-eleventh and also Augustine's *De haeresibus*. Lobrichon suggests that this version was copied from an earlier eleventh-century original by the abbey.[101]

Nothing is known about Héribert other than what is contained in his letter and what historians can reasonably assert about him from this and from other evidence providing a context for the source. He tells us that he is a monk, 'the least of all monks'. He is traditionally taken to have written from an unnamed monastery in Périgueux because he says that the heretics have arisen 'petragorensem regionem'. But this does not seem to prove that Héribert wrote from this area, rather that he was describing heretics going into it. Indeed, he later says that time is short 'has namque ceterasque regiones occulte modo aggrediuntur'. In other words, they are not yet in his own area, but are currently entering it secretly. Thus there are still puzzles to be solved about Héribert's identity and location, but he is clearly familiar with Périgord. Given some link between the monk and Cluniac Auxerre, where the copy of his letter was made, it seems possible that he may have been a monk of Saint-Sauveur de Sarlat, Cluny's only conquest in Aquitaine by the early eleventh century.[102]

The purpose of the letter, we are told, is to inform Christendom globally of a 'new' heresy and to warn against being seduced by the heretics' appearance as ascetic holy men. Héribert opens with an appeal for the attention of all Christians, east and west, north and south, who believe in the Trinity, that is to say, in 'Peace and Mercy in God the Father, in His only Son our Lord, and in the Holy Ghost'. Lobrichon is correct that this kind of opening in a letter is 'a total oddity. Its tone . . . foreign to both contemporary and later diplomatic letter writing formulas'.[103] From the outset, Héribert is defining who is included in his address list, all Christians, and who is excluded, those who deny the Trinity. His main line of attack is to juxtapose the principle of a universal Church and belief in the Trinity with the implied doctrinal framework within which the heretics operate.

Héribert says that the heresy is perpetrated by false apostles and strikes at the very heart of what they are preaching. They do not mourn the corruption of the

---

[101] BN, MS lat. 1745. Héribert's letter is at fo. 31r, lines 1–29. The source is translated into English in Lobrichon, 'Chiaroscuro', 79–80, and its manuscript tradition given at pp. 81–102. See also G. Bounoure, 'La Lettre d'Héribert sur les hérétiques périgourdins', *BSHAP* cxx (1993), 61–72, where the 'new' letter was first described and transcribed. Interestingly, a millennial date for the letter was first suggested around the turn of the twentieth century in Escande, *Périgord*, 68, although Escande only had Mabillon's edition upon which to base this verdict: *Vetera analecta*, ed. J. Mabillon, Paris 1723, 483, although Escande cites the 1682 edn., iii. 467. See also Frassetto, 'The sermons of Adémar and the letter of Héribert'. My own views on this source and its interpretation are explored in greater depth in Taylor, 'Letter of Héribert'.

[102] See chapter 1 above.

[103] Lobrichon, 'Chiaroscuro', 88.

Church, as might those who wished to reform it, but aim 'to subvert the Christian religion at its very roots'. Not only do they loathe its elite structures and its ceremonial manifestations – mocking the mass and eschewing liturgical chant as pleasing to man rather than to God – but spurn the host, seeing the entire mass as devoid of meaning or power because the eucharist is but bread, and refuse to worship the cross or the image of Christ, calling it an idol and rebuking those who adore it. Indeed, they never go into a church except to attack it and mock it. Their belief about the sacraments, the cross and other material representations of the holy could, it is true, conceivably follow from opposition to clerical rituals and doctrines introduced since the apostolic period, although no one has yet constructed a case as to who it was that Héribert would identify in this way. On the other hand, these doctrines could also follow from the contemporary dualist belief that the divine does not interact with the physical, as did the Bogomil rejection of the cross.

Again like both the heretics described by Euthymius and Cosmas and also the simple Christians asserted by the social and conflict models, Héribert's subjects are evangelists who infiltrate orthodox circles in order to win converts. As a result, and as Adémar warns, both the simple laity and the religious in Aquitaine are being led astray. Héribert's heretics, again like Adémar's, fast to excess, as we are told of Bogomils. Fasting was not the practice only of 'heretics', of course. Ordinary Christians did it to express self-abnegation and discipline. It was part of the monastic rule by which Greek Orthodox monks lived. As a method of both worship and intercession it was common in eleventh-century France, especially amongst clerics and monks. From Adémar we learn that abstinence was employed even in the context of widespread sickness and hunger in order to solicit divine mercy at the very first peace council.[104] We might postulate that it was especially popular with those trying to follow the apostolic life. But Héribert, like the eastern sources, views his heretics as extreme in this, and we must note also that they not only fasted but never ever ate meat nor drank wine (except, says Héribert, on the third day). In this they were like Bogomils and eastern monks only, but unlike western monks and apostolic role models.

These heretics also rejected sexual intercourse, both that sanctioned by the sacrament of marriage and otherwise. Given that we are also told that they included lay adherents, we are again lost for orthodox precedents, but this tendency makes sense within a dualist framework. Héribert in fact objects that his subjects indulged themselves freely. This may be simple slander, and would be typical of polemics employed against heretics, but may also be an unwitting reference to the existence of a hierarchy of believers, initiated and non-initiated, as was the case in the Balkans by mid-century according to Euthymius. For the ordinary believers, not ready to adopt the rigorous lifestyle but entirely convinced that the authority of the Church was insupportable, what need was there for marriage? In the twelfth and thirteenth centuries Bogomils and

104 Adémar, *Chronicon*, 158; Obolensky, *Bogomils*, 127–9; Poly and Bournazel, *Feudal transformation*, 284–5.

Cathars both taught that sexual intercourse should be avoided by their uniniti-
ated supporters but that, failing this, there was little point seeking clerical sanction for it. Thus the initiated themselves were chaste, but their followers indeed
appeared wanton to the opponents of the heresy, as they perhaps did to
Héribert.

On this latter point we can only speculate, as there is no direct evidence for
such a structure in Bogomil ranks by the date attributed to this source. However,
in the case of Héribert's testimony, one form of ranking certainly existed which
very closely resembled that in Bogomil circles, whether or not there is a connection between them. Héribert is one of those sources which tell us of an intensive
programme of education undertaken by the heretical acolyte under the guidance
of teachers, a period of education during which the uneducated convert was
taught how to learn, that is to say, to read. The effect of this was striking for
Héribert states, no doubt exaggerating, that 'no one (no matter how rustic)
adheres to their sect who does not become wise in letters, writing and action
within eight days, [and] so wise that no one can overcome him in any way'.
Because we must, like Héribert, be doubtful that an illiterate adult could learn to
read well, and even implicitly learn Latin, within such a short space of time, but
unlike him do not credit supernatural goings-on as an explanation, the assertion
surely makes most sense within Stock's model. Initiates may well have been
taught to read to an extent, but what was surely most striking was their sudden
ability to cite and discuss Scripture, and to achieve this their entire being was
probably devoted to the process, which probably took place in the context of an
intensive lifestyle change. With a modern fear of religious extremism and of
'cults', we might call this process 'indoctrination'. To this we must add Moore's
observation that the simple attainment of literacy by an ordinary lay person
must have made them suspect to the elite, however they chose to use their new
skill.[105] Whilst literacy in itself would surely not have rendered them 'heretical',
it must surely have distanced them thoroughly from their peers and the sort of
lifestyle and life expectations they might otherwise have had. In this context we
can perhaps better understand the comment by Héribert amongst others that,
once corrupted, the heretic could never be reconverted to orthodoxy.
Euthymius and Cosmas tell us much about such a process in the east, and it was
evidently very effective in the conversion of people who were in any case
ill-educated in scriptural matters just as we hear from several sources was the
case in the west.[106]

Héribert's subjects resemble Bogomils even further in the egalitarian nature
of their recruitment and internal organisation. Amongst their converts are
uneducated peasants, clerks, priests, monks and nuns. Members of Bogomil
communities also included women and the ordinary male laity. They confessed
their sins to each other, subverting orthodox distinctions between laity and

---

[105] Moore, 'Literacy', 20.
[106] For which texts might have been taught, and in what languages, see Hamilton, 'Wisdom',
40–1.

clergy and between the sexes, as well as the informal but no less tangible domination of the religious life by those of socially powerful families. The whole social ethos of the Bogomils was egalitarian, with property being held and distributed in common. This is perhaps reflected also in one of Héribert's more thought-provoking assertions, that his subjects refuse to accept alms on the basis that no one should own property, from whence alms come in the first place, and instead share what resources they have communally. This latter reference has proved central to Moore's case that 'heretics' represent a communistic and challenging emulation of the apostolic life-style. What we lack, however, are contemporary accounts of such traits as Moore identifies amongst the laity outside of those which both claim to be addressing religious heresy and also carry evidence of aspects of this 'heresy' which, I think, cannot be explained in a satisfying way within a non-dualist model.

In this case, the evidence which most convincingly removes the source from a convincing non-Bogomil framework is the manner of prayer described. These heretics use exclusively the *Pater Noster*. This was also the only prayer prayed by Bogomils, but could perhaps be interpreted again as a return to the form of worship practised by the first Apostles, whom Christ told to use this prayer; no one needed a Bogomil to advocate this. However, we are told by Héribert that '[t]hey never say Glory to the Father and to the Son and to the Holy Ghost but they instead say 'For yours is the Kingdom, and you rule all creatures for ever and ever, Amen'. Thus they both adapted the prayer from the form in which it was prayed in the east by Christians – the doxology was rarely used in the west, and Héribert probably intended his audience to make a connection with the east here – and did so by distorting its Trinitarian emphasis in the way that we have heard from the *Synodikon of orthodoxy* that Bogomils did ('they cannot bear to hear the ancient final sentence . . . for Thine is the kingdom, the power and the glory, Father, Son and Holy Spirit'). The change can probably be explained by the fact that Bogomils, far from shunning all reference to the Old Testament God whom they equated with the evil demiurge, instead acknowledged him and his power over the physical world, as Cosmas tells us.[107] In addition, Euthymius tells us that as well as praying only their own form of the Lord's Prayer, Bogomils did so four times a day and four times at night, and whilst they did this they bowed or genuflected frequently but did not make the sign of the cross. The *Synodikon* notes that the cross was not signed by Bogomils. Like them, Héribert's subjects also genuflected frequently – a hundred times a day, we are told. We may safely assert from what he tells us about their attitude to the cross that they did not cross themselves either.

So far in discussing this source I have concentrated on refuting the argument that accounts merely reveal advocacy of the *vita apostolica*, in other words a life of poverty and simple devotion. However, the case for the simple Christian life is not the only way in which those opposing the Bogomil thesis have read

---

107 Moore, *Origins*, 198; Frassetto, 'The sermons of Adémar of Chabannes and the letter of Héribert', 336.

Héribert in its oldest version. Moore observes that monastic reformers were often the objects of accusations of heresy, and that 'the ideals which [reformed monks] disseminated were close to those which the heretics expressed'.[108] However, he also cautions that we in fact lack 'evidence of a direct connection between [the activity of reformed abbeys such as Cluny, Gorze and Brogne] and these earliest heresies'.[109] In spite of this *caveat*, the model has perhaps been taken too far. Lobrichon has made a daring attempt at interpreting the new source. He argues that it is not a letter, not from its apparent author 'Héribert' and its 'heresy' is a matter of Church politics at an elite level. To Lobrichon, Héribert is a code name for Cluniac interests in Aquitaine, the source a document internal to its network more likely composed in Burgundy than in western France, and its apparent content is an attack on both the secular and monastic enemies of Cluniac reform.[110] He has arrived at his conclusion through a methodology which does 'not evaluate the worth of Héribert's "letter" by testing whether it stands up to a literal reading'.[111] Instead, he urges the historian not to 'take Héribert's "letter" at its (deceptively obvious) surface meaning before he or she has exhausted other hermeneutic possibilities. It needs a careful decoding'.[112] Lobrichon's method asserts that the context in which the source was composed is what gives it meaning, not its declared content. If we accept this approach, and we would be sloppy if we entirely rejected such common-sense advice, it is surely only useful if we also have evidence external to the source as to how and where it originated. Lobrichon is asserting *both* a new content *and* a new contextual origin for the source without solid corroboratory evidence for either. Within the logic of the universe thus created, it is impossible to disprove what he says. The source is in code and the historian code-breaker may choose a range of keys – Cluniac, Bogomil, proto-communist, Apocalyptic – all of which appear, to those who have chosen them, to fit the lock perfectly. However, the fact that Lobrichon does not really address why it should be the case that 'the letter should be considered as a coded document . . . it needs a careful decoding' and why Héribert 'did not want his readers to identify these "enemies of the church" in a clear-cut manner', should in itself make us cautious about this particular interpretation.[113]

None the less, Lobrichon's interpretation has the implicit support of Monique Zerner and her colleagues and explicitly of Moore and Lambert,[114] even though, when the letter was thought to be twelfth-century, Lambert cited its doctrine as evidence for 'the origin of a portion at least of [Cathar] beliefs'.[115] Moore said it was 'suggestive of Bogomilism', the use of the eastern doxology

---

108 Moore, *Origins*, 41.
109 Ibid.
110 Lobrichon, 'Chiaroscuro', esp. pp. 80–8, 102–3.
111 Ibid. 86.
112 Ibid. 86–7.
113 Ibid. 86–7, 88.
114 Moore, 'Literacy', 20–2, and 'Property', 185; Lambert, *Medieval heresy*, 30.
115 Lambert, *Medieval heresy* (1st edn), 62–3, quotation at p. 63.

reminiscent of that which, according to Cosmas the Priest, was used by the Bogomils to appease the Lord of the (created) world, while they addressed their worship to the God of the immaterial universe', and that the 'special dislike of the cross . . . was, in the East, specifically and consistently associated with the Bogomils'.[116]

Although there are some differences between the eleventh- and twelfth-century versions of the letter, there is little variation in terms of heretical doctrine or practice to note. But now Lambert merely 'catches a whiff' of dualism from it. To Moore, Héribert now represents 'conventional avowals of the spiritual notion of apostolic poverty'. To Landes the source, along with Duke William's charter for Saint-Hilaire, describe only 'communitarian asceticism' and 'textual communities' attempting to emulate the early Apostles, 'despite the hints of some kind of eastern dualism'.[117] Of course, this is being unfair. Moore, for example, is perfectly entitled to find the twelfth-century source suggestive of Bogomilism in 1977 and still in 1985, but the eleventh-century version no longer so. He is interpreting it as he should, in the context of more recent reflection on the society in which it was written and in the context of his evolving evaluation of popular 'heresy' in that period. But one cannot help being left with the feeling that historians would have interpreted eleventh-century 'heresy' differently in earlier work had they known of BN lat. 1745.

There is another way in which we can interpret some of the contents of the letter. It is from Héribert that we get the only account of heretics in Aquitaine which declares itself to be first hand, and the penultimate passage in his letter makes reference to some strange events witnessed at that time:

[The heretics] cannot be harmed, because if they are caught, no bonds can hold them. Indeed, I, Héribert, the least of all monks and author of this letter, was there when they were loaded with chains and put in a great wine barrel. It had an open bottom, its top was shut and guards had been set over it. In the morning, they were gone, and furthermore they left no tracks until their next appearance. A vase, emptied of its wine, in which a little bit of wine was put, was found full the next morning. And they perform other marvellous deeds indeed, which I cannot relate here.

Lambert noted that this passage needed further attention.[118] Lobrichon suggests that what Héribert calls 'marvellous deeds', the *mira signa*, are incorporated at the end of the source in order to 'endow the other facts with verisimilitude' within a popular model.[119] Phillipe Buc's suggestion that the 'escape' might be a joke by Héribert, a parody of Christ's escape from the tomb, seems most plausible.[120] I suggest that Héribert is undertaking a two-pronged approach to the

---

116   Moore, *Origins* (1st edn), 198.
117   Lambert, *Medieval heresy*, 30; Moore, 'Property', 185; Landes, 'Aristocracy', 208.
118   Lambert, *Medieval heresy*, 30.
119   Lobrichon, 'Chiaroscuro', 100–1, and also p. 88.
120   Buc (as Lobrichon's English translator), ibid. 85 n. 14.

problem of heresy; having warned the elite of its duplicity and attacked its belief system, he now ridicules it. The image with which we are left is of at least two pairs of pale, emaciated and undoubtedly hairy heretical legs poking out from the bottom of an upturned barrel, its occupants blundering about whilst trying not to wake up their guards. Then, having somehow escaped without a trace, they seem to have forgotten something. They return to perform a second, equally unimpressive feat, the topping-up of a vase of wine under cover of darkness, when no one could see how they did it.

Buc suggests that the escape is a parody of the ultimate Christian miracle, but it is to a more specifically appropriate model of miracles that I think the *mira signa* make reference; to stories emerging from local saints' cults, specifically those of St Foy and St Leonard of Noblat. Indeed, Lobrichon observes echoes of their miracles in the marvellous deeds, although he cannot expand on this within the logic of his own analysis.[121] But I think that it is in the literature emanating from these cults in the first half of the eleventh century that we find both the genre, and even the specific miracles that Héribert is parodying.[122]

St Leonard of Noblat was almost certainly a fictitious character created during our period, in which his miracles were first recorded. As a result of the power to free prisoners supposedly granted to him in life, he was patron of wrongly imprisoned people after his death. Several of the stories concern the astonishing escape of such captives, held in pits or castle strongholds, typically fleeing whilst still loaded with chains.[123] Similarly, all four books of the *Liber miraculorum* of St Foy feature her freeing wrongly imprisoned victims, again typically bound and guarded in castles. In book two a good knight is chained to the inside of a barrel, and this is the closest construction to Héribert's story.[124] Reminiscent also of the wine miracle of Héribert's heretics, we have an account of an empty flask being filled through the intercession of Foy in the fourth book of her miracles.[125] A similar story is contained in the *vita* of Leonard.[126]

Both sets of miracle stories originate in the early eleventh century. Bernard of Angers tells us that the deeds of Foy were well known throughout Aquitaine and southern France, and that he himself discussed them at the court of William V at Poitiers with the daughter of Duke Richard of Normandy, who had witnessed one of the miracles.[127] To a monk looking for a model against which to measure and ridicule heretics whom he feared, a smug parody of the miracles so beloved

---

[121] Ibid. 95.

[122] Later copyists of the source apparently missed the joke, stressing instead truly impressive aspects of the *mira signa* that made them seem to Moore to have something of the 'precocious Houdini' about them: *Origins*, 198.

[123] Arbellot, *Vie de Saint Léonard*, 53, 56–7, 85–94; *The golden legend of Jacobus de Voragine*, trans. W. G. Ryan, Princeton 1993, ii. 245.

[124] *Book of Saint Foy*, 52–3, 99–101, 103–4, 104–8, 128–9, 149–51, 164–5, 185–6, 186–7, 187–9, 180–91, 191–6, 196–7, and esp. pp. 148–9.

[125] Ibid. 183.

[126] Arbellot, *Vie de Saint Léonard*, 15–16, 280.

[127] *Book of Saint Foy*, 129.

of the *rustici* of the region would have had a most satisfying resonance in the elite circles he wished to influence.

Of course, miracles of these two genres are in no way unique to saints Foy and Leonard, nor even to Aquitaine, nor to the eleventh century. The Golden Legend contains several, including those by saints on whose *vitae* Leonard's seems to have been based.[128] The late twelfth-century *miracula* attributed to the patron of Nôtre-Dame-de-Rocamadour reflect a sustained concern with wrongful imprisonment in the region, albeit less dominant in its influence than it was a century previously.[129] Furthermore, humour was in fact familiar to both ordinary and elite audiences of the genre of miracles that Héribert was parodying. As explained by Remensnyder, they bridged the gap between elite and low culture.[130] More closely related to the Héribert source in terms of genre are medieval parodies, a large Latin body of which has been highlighted by Martha Bayless. The miraculous deeds of Héribert's heretics appear to be what she terms social parody, the imitation of a form of literature in order to satirise people or their actions humorously by an inversion of the natural order to comic effect.[131] Thus, fraudulent holy-men perform pathetic miracles. Bayless also discusses several eleventh-century *centos*, which feature confused and apparently incoherent narratives as typical of the genre.[132] These read very much like the bizarre to-ings and fro-ings in Héribert's *mira signa* passage. However, in spite of the inversion of order, *centos* are in no sense subversive by implication. Indeed, they are often most conservative in intent,[133] as Héribert certainly is.

I suggest we interpret the *mira signa* passage of the letter in the following way. After exposing the heretics' intolerable beliefs and activity, Héribert provides us with parodies of locally popular miracles, themselves based on Christ's miracles, in order to hearten an elite troubled by heretical influence over the populace and disenchanted lesser clergy. If we allow for some heightened apocalyptic awareness in his audience, the letter must have struck further chords still. The coming of AntiChrist 'is according to the work of Satan in all power and in signs and in false marvels' and in the medieval interpretation Satan would empower AntiChrist and his servants to perform wonders that would test the faith of Christians.[134] In the false marvels, Héribert both mocks the heresy, by parody, yet reminds his audience, as he did at the opening of his letter, of its essentially sinister nature and the need for Christians to be vigilant. For the enemy was just as bold and capable of scorn: Héribert tells us that one of the ways heretics attacked was by parodying the mass, reporting that '(i)f one of them (in order to

---

128 *Golden legend*, i. 86; ii. 243–6.
129 *Miracles of Our Lady of Rocamadour*, 14, 38, 109, 109–10, 114, 133–4, 141–2, 153–4.
130 *Book of Saint Foy*, 136; Remensnyder, 'Un Problème', 351–79, esp. p. 355. For examples of the *joca* of the saint see especially *Book of Saint Foy*, 50, 56–7, 57–8, 104–8, 215–18.
131 M. Bayless, *Parody in the Middle Ages: the Latin tradition*, Michigan 1996, 3.
132 Ibid. 19, 32–6, 44–6, 157–67, 216, 220. See also 'Garcineida', at pp. 145–53.
133 Ibid. 175–6, 196–208.
134 2 Thessalonians ii.9. In the Middle Ages 2 Thess. ii.1–12 was interpreted as an account of AntiChrist, although 'the evil one' is not named as such by Paul: Emmerson, *AntiChrist*, 39.

corrupt) sings the mass, he does not say the canons, and turns his back, behind or on the side of the altar. As for the host, he throws it in the missal or behind the altar'. The churchmen in the east complained that Bogomils did similarly.[135]

Finally in this discussion of new sources, we should note that towards the end of the eleventh century Bishop Walran of Naumburg visited Noblat. He was told that in Leonard's day heretics who lived in the area had disputed his miracles and were responsible for the burning of his 'ancient' *vita* (which almost certainly never existed).[136] This is not evidence that dualist heretics were in Aquitaine earlier in the century. However, we should note that the monks said that the heretics in question asserted that Leonard's miracles were the work of the devil, just as Bogomils did. If Leonard was an invented figure of the millennial period, it is possible that these heretics were a product of contemporary popular consciousness also, based on figures actually encountered denouncing relic cults.

Heretics as fundamentalists or as neo-Manichees

It is correct to observe that many of the elements which Dondaine identified in western accounts could correspond to a variety of heresies which were to appear in the west other than dualism, as well as relate to issues raised by a range of medieval reformers not deemed heretical. Such elements include opposition to the extension of clerical claims and powers, especially those which were something of a novelty and an unwanted intrusion into lay life. Into this category falls Leutard's resistance to paying tithe, for example, as well as his rejection of temporal authority. Criticism of the clerical sanctioning of marriage and monopoly over baptism, burial and confession might manifest itself as general cynicism about the supernatural powers of priests which supposedly elevated them above non-ordained Christians. Opposition to infant baptism in particular was to continue to be a cause for complaint by heretics and reformers of many varieties. It is also logical to expect to find resentment of the reformed abbeys amongst the lay aristocracy, secular clergy and peasantry at whose expense monastic autonomy was being achieved. Essentially, criticism of the wealth and scepticism about the powers of the clergy may be expected as logical extensions of the sort of social dissent that many observe in the west in this period. We must accept that some aspects of what the sources tell us could have arisen spontaneously and within indigenous movements. Some are logical spiritual conclusions to social and economic features of the state of the west at the close of the tenth century, and others could have resulted from a literal reading of the

---

135 We might also note the use of sarcasm to ridicule the Bogomils by Euthymius of the Periblepton. He says that the Bogomils taught that the demiurge trapped snakes and scorpions and dogs and cats and frogs and weasels inside the first human body in order to trap its soul, and that they claimed that is why 'when a man is angry, he rages like a snake or a dog'. Euthymius adds 'I forgot to ask them . . . whether a man is angered like a weasel or a frog': *Christian dualist heresies*, 152–3.
136 AS iii. 173; Sargent, 'Religious responses', 230.

Gospels. These features alone are not convincing evidence of the presence or influence of Bogomilism.

Thus Moore says of western heretics from the early eleventh to early twelfth centuries that, '(t)aken point by point all the attitudes and opinions expressed by western heretics may be derived from the Scriptures'.[137] Many indeed may, but I question 'all'. If such a fundamentalist Christian movement was emerging, problematic observations remain. Why do we find so few references to it in the early eleventh century other than those specifically labelled heretical in the sources and typically also making allegations of dualist belief and/or of the Docetist heresy? Where are texts taking a more sympathetic or at least less polemical view before mid-century? The movement identified in accounts of 'heresy', if characterised as part of a popular movement towards clerical reform and a more direct relationship with God that also had some support even at the highest levels of the clerical elite, as demonstrated by the list of suspects most noticeably connected with the Orléans incident, apparently left little trace except in the scattered writings of what can have been only its bitterest, most alarmist and mendacious opponents. No sources survive, or none were written, defending the 'heretics' of this period as reformers who might have had a point.

There are perhaps three levels of 'heresy' revealed in the accounts. The first surely arose naturally in this society at this specific time from direct and indirect opposition to the economic claims and gains of the secular clergy and the abbeys. It includes opposition to tithe and to novel levies for clerical services, and the questioning of the value of saints and their cults to ordinary Christians. We would have to accept a large degree of credulity and passivity on the part of the medieval laity if these were not found in the late Carolingian world or early eleventh century.

Second are some slightly less moderate tenets attributed to the heretics: the rejection of the cross, of the Trinity, of the sacraments, in particular the baptism of infants, the supernatural quality of blessed bread, and the exclusive use of the Lord's Prayer and the New Testament. These arise less obviously out of circumstances in this specific period but from more general doctrinal enquiry involving a literal reading of Scripture. The Gospels make it clear, for example, that Christ's coming marked a breach with ancient tradition and authority, and so older prayers and biblical books were arguably rendered redundant by this fact. Similarly, the Gospels do not outline the doctrine of the Trinity as it came to be understood, or claim that bread broken in remembrance of the last supper had any special properties, or that the cross on which Christ died was to be revered. But their rejection was extremely challenging doctrinally, overthrowing centuries of patristic reason and clerical assumption, and was surely too radical to have emerged spontaneously out of local circumstances, especially where various elements within this category emerge in clusters as they tend to do. They need not arise out of a dualist logic, admittedly, but neither is there enough here to convince me of a spontaneous popular ascetic or reforming movement either.

---

[137] Moore, *Origins*, 165.

One might argue at least as convincingly that a movement rejecting the Law and the Prophets was an expression of early antisemitism. In addition, the identification of a movement claiming to adhere to the New Testament primarily does not in any sense weaken the Bogomil thesis on its own. Such an approach to the apostolic life advocated in the Gospels was also at the heart of Bogomil teaching, given that they interpreted aspects of the Gospels and Acts in an idiosyncratic way.

The final category of heretical tenets is doctrines which are not merely either radical or fundamentalist but heterodox. They were as heretical after the Gregorian reforms as they were in around 1000. They include, most importantly, that Christ was not born human, or of a human, and did not therefore die to save humankind, which cannot be saved by belief that He did. The second is that baptism should be performed by the laying on of hands and not by water, in conflict with New Testament precedent. Third is the form of the Lord's Prayer used by Héribert's subjects, a form which is at the same time eastern, deletes reference to the Trinity and, perhaps most under-examined of all, seems to acknowledge the fearful power of the demiurge in the detested physical universe. This evidence is something we would not expect to find in a movement which, we are led to believe, tended towards the ascetic and spiritual in a quasi-dualist sense, anticipating Peter Damian amongst others but in no way acknowledging a dualist cosmology. Fourth, we have the evidence that, far from reverting to a simple form of worship and rejecting innovative rituals, some heretics performed frequent recitations of their prayer accompanied by frantic genuflection. Finally, we are told that heretical groups rejected not merely the clerical sanctioning of lay unions by marriages, but of any sexual intercourse for anyone. Some idealistic and reforming elements may have wanted to move lay practice closer to monastic regulation or an imitation of the Apostles. This is the case that Landes argues in the context of apocalyptic communities. In this sense it holds water: the purity of humanity was what mattered in preparation for judgement, but its procreation was an irrelevancy. More likely, or perhaps existing side by side, could be the dualist case that the death of the body was of greatest concern and the increase of even the Christian community undesirable.

On the issue of what heretics believed would happen on the death of the body we run into problems of course, as we are unclear exactly what Bogomils understood to occur at death by c. 1000. Did they believe that the soul would escape? Or only after a good death, as dualists later came to believe? Thus we cannot say for sure whether Héribert's 'they have been swallowed up [by heresy] to the extent that they seek to find men who might torture and deliver them to death', or the accusation levelled at the Orléans heretics by Paul of Chartres, or assertions that the Monforte group actually killed each other, derived from belief that they would escape the physical world by dying in a perfected state. It may merely reflect a recurring slander against heretics that we find into the thirteenth century. On the other hand, it is very difficult satisfactorily to explain such accusations outside of a dualist framework. I do not think historians have ever accounted for their inclusion as opposed, for example, to the more obvious fiction of the murder of innocent orthodox Christians, such as was to be later levelled at Jews. The transmigration of souls into other bodies upon a non-perfected death and eventually into a non-physical universe is actually a logical conclusion of dualist cosmology and arrived at much earlier by Mani. The fact that it was almost certainly not transmitted down the centuries to dualists, who apparently eventually arrived at this and other of his conclusions independently, surely supports its inevitability. Indeed, if dualists believed that 'death' meant literal death, there would have been little incentive for initiation into the heresy and the rigorous, persecuted lifestyle assumed thereafter. The only alternative is to assume a certain nihilism towards the physical realm as Paulicians did. Thus, when Euthymius of the Periblepton says in mid-century that Bogomils did not believe in the resurrection of the dead, he surely means in the orthodox sense of a resurrection of the body, as we also find in Bernard of Angers's account. We should also note that although accusations of intra-sect murders amongst dualists are almost certainly greatly exaggerated in later centuries, in which we have more evidence of what was really taking place, they are not without some foundation, for some Cathars indeed practised *endura* – fasting to death and refusing medical aid – in extreme circumstances. Neither was the allegation levelled at any non-dualist groups to my knowledge.

We at last address directly the most commonly raised query about the credibility of the sources: why do they accuse heretics of being Manichaean? This label is used outside Aquitaine by Anselm of Liège as attributed to his bishop's correspondent Roger of Châlons and by Hermann of Reichenau in relation to the Goslar incident. In Aquitaine it is used by Adémar on several occasions, and Bernard of Angers perhaps had it in mind. We should also note that scorn is levelled at Manichees in the sermon *De nativitate beatae Mariae virginis* of Abbot Odilo of Cluny (994–1048/9), in which the heresy is discussed in the present tense as though Odilo was addressing a contemporary enemy. He proclaims that 'God, the creator of man and of the Son of Man says "This women whom you despise, Manichee, is my mother, but she was made by my hand . . . What are you doing, Manichee? You oppress the mother of Christ, and you do not defend Christ" '.[138] Did Odilo also believe there were contemporary Manichees? Cluny was a hub of information about Christian affairs but establishing exactly why its abbot came to be alarmed by Manichees to the extent that he thought it necessary to preach to his monks against them may be difficult. Two possibilities seem most likely. Cluny perhaps came across Aquitainian heretics in the context of its efforts in support of the reformer Duke William, to whom Odilo sent abbots for Saint-Jean-d'Angély (in 1018) and Charroux (in 1020).[139] The former date coincides with Adémar's assertion that Manichees were in Aquitaine, and Charroux was the site of the council summoned to combat heresy in 1028. Alternatively, Poly and Bournazel have suggested that Odilo was invoking devotion to the cult of the Virgin in support of the efforts of Fulbert of Chartres

---

138 *PL* cxlii.1028–9 at 1029.
139 See Landes, *Relics*, 122.

in relation to the heresy at Orléans.[140] In either case Odilo possibly both knew of the belief that heretical groups were present in the west and agreed with Adémar about their nature.

However, the possibility that those describing heresy formulated their interpretations of its nature on the basis of what they expected to encounter, as opposed to actual examination of doctrines being expressed, or out of a desire to slander those whose opposition they feared, is justifiably troubling to opponents of the Bogomil thesis and we must address it methodically. We are told that '(w)hen [the clergy] did not get the answers which they expected they were less inclined to attribute it to their having been misled by their own preconceptions than to the mendacity, or lack of frankness, of their witnesses'.[141] In particular, it is argued that the term Manichee was chosen simply because it was 'one of the most infamous names in the constellation of ideas of medieval churchmen'.[142] Moore is more specific, arguing that '(f)or a thousand years after his death Christian commentators everywhere greeted as 'Manichaeism' every manifestation of irregularity which had any point of similarity with what they knew of his teaching, and some which had none'.[143] Thus, because the conclusions of a range of clergy dealing with several incidents of heresy in the Châlons area were similar when it came to the nature of that heresy, 'the preconceptions of the bishops led them to assume rather than to establish that each of these threats to the faith proceeded from the same source'.[144] On the other hand, we could at least leave open the possibility that some eleventh-century clergy sought, albeit it in a less systematic way than their inquisitorial heirs were to do, to isolate what it was about dissidents that made them 'heretical', and that in doing so some of them used patristic and early medieval writings on Christian heresies to see if there was a category to which they corresponded. Not all of them chose this methodology, not the commentators on the Orléans and Monforte incidents, and we must note that the excitable Glaber avoided this avenue of accusation entirely. Héribert for one amongst the newly identified sources not only chooses not to use 'Manichee' but identifies the heresy as 'new'. But, some authors did assert a revival of the ancient horror and we must address why.

In doing so we might make comparisons with the way they use other apparently erroneous terms. 'Arian' is one that we find in Aquitaine, used in the charter for Saint-Hilaire and in Adémar's sermon *De nativitate Beatae Mariae Virginis*. Heretics are also referred to as Arian by Anselm of Liège. The term has been called 'a common designation for all heretics and specifically those Christians who denied the full divinity of Jesus Christ'.[145] This is not what various of

---

[140] Poly and Bournazel, *Feudal transformation*, 276 and n. 10.
[141] Moore, *Origins*, 18.
[142] Lambert, *Medieval heresy*, 20.
[143] Moore, *Origins*, 146.
[144] Ibid. 37.
[145] Y. Congar, ' "*Arriana haeresis*" comme désignation du néo-manichéisme au xiie siècle', *Revue des sciences philosophiques et théologique* xliii (1959), 449–61 at p. 454.

the heretics we hear about asserted. They believed Christ only to be divine and not flesh. But might it also have been applied to heretics who disputed the orthodox account of the Trinity? As we shall see, Bogomils already thought the Holy Spirit to be lesser than the Father and Son, and were coming to understand the Son as lesser than the Father, as a temporary and apparent manifestation of the godhead, eventually reincorporated by it.[146] Might the term even indicate an allegorical reading of the Trinity such as we also find in Héribert's account and that of Landulf Senior, who both choose not to employ the Arian label? In using a terminology which approximated to what they witnessed, the sources are as likely to be trying to help us, the reader of their record, understand what they encountered, as to be trying to mislead us. Although the composer of the Saint-Hilaire charter, for example, was using a strictly inappropriate term, for there were no true Arians left in the west by this date, why not consider that he was trying to find some useful shorthand to describe a heresy which indeed denied the Trinity, if on a different basis from Ari?[147]

Another comparison may be made with the use of eschatological terminology in reference to heretics. There was enough correlation between the behaviour of the heretics and biblical and patristic predictions about the ministers of AntiChrist to justify the perceptions of Adémar, Glaber and Bernard of Angers, for example, that they witnessed one of the signs of the End, because they were of that predisposition anyway. But none of these writers felt themselves to be bound by their adoption of this terminology. Far from constructing their 'heretics' so that their features fitted those of antichrists, the easiest path, they describe characteristics that deviate from their apocalyptic starting point. Adémar says that messengers of AntiChrist will deny the intervention of saints.[148] He thus introduces a contemporary concern into his warning. As the process of identifying and labelling Bogomilism was taking place in the east, the same apocalyptic language was being used by eastern commentators on heresy. Anathemas in the *Synodikon of orthodoxy* in circulation in the area of Athens, and both Cosmas the Priest in Bulgaria and Euthymius of the Periblepton in Constantinople, saw the appearance of Bogomils as precursors of the End, referring to the predictions of Paul that deceivers will arise then, forbidding marriage and commanding the refusal of certain foodstuffs put on earth by God for the faithful to eat.[149] The theme is especially central to Euthymius' interpretation of what the heresy signifies. He begins his letter by making reference to the Last Days, to the fact that 'false Christs and false prophets . . . shall arise . . . The apostles of AntiChrist'.[150] Yet we know for certain that these supposed allies of AntiChrist, whilst they acted just as Paul had predicted, were in fact real

---

146 See p. 133 below.

147 See also Frassetto, 'Sermons', 251–3, 304, 315.

148 Adémar, *Chronicon*, 173; MS Lat. Phillips 1664, fos 40r–57r, 75r, 90v, 96v, 114v (cited in Frassetto, 'Sermons', 199).

149 1 Tim. iv.1–4; *Christian dualist heresies*, 28–9, 116, 128, 132, 136, 158–9; Moore, *Origins*, 8.

150 *Christian dualist heresies*, 143.

dualists, and apocalyptic language, though we know it to be wide of the mark, does not mislead us for one minute as to the content of the heresy for we have corroboratory evidence for the nature of what is being described.

The Arian label and apocalyptic images used in the west were thus not necessarily meant to have been understood restrictively or in literal terms but as starting points for descriptions by those who encountered heretics but were at a loss as to how to categorise what they found more accurately, not even having a name for it such as was emerging in the east. Both designations give us an insight into why and how eleventh-century clergy used older sources to help them interpret and convey what they saw. It was surely sometimes the case that they used 'Manichee' because what they saw was a bit like Manichaeism. This lazy use of the term does not exclude the possibility that their subjects were very like Manichees indeed. If it was not used with some degree of accuracy and with some logic, this either means that a variety of commentators independently yet simultaneously decided to defame their subjects by employing an erroneous terminology, or they conspired with each other to do so. Both of these possibilities seem unlikely.

Of course even if the clergy using the term were indeed applying it to dualists whom they recognised as such, 'Manichee' is an inaccurate label. Not only can no plausible link between the ancient heresy and the incidents in our period be established, but, as Janet and Bernard Hamilton have noted of the heresy founded by the Persian Mani (216–77), neither was Christianity its starting point nor dualism its point of departure from it, as was the case with Christian dualists of the Middle Ages. Christ did not occupy a central place within the path to salvation as understood within this doctrine, and so Manicheaism should not really be classified as a Christian heresy.[151] It was, however, a heresy to which many brought up in the early Christian world were adherents, including most famously St Augustine, and it was as a heretical sect within the sphere of those calling themselves Christian that early medieval and eleventh-century authors also regarded it.

Mani and his followers were absolute dualists, believing the material world to be evil in substance and nature and to have been created by a demiurge of darkness, independent from but co-eternal with his antithesis, a benevolent god of the world of light. Goodness was trapped in the physical world as light particles mingled with dark matter, but could be released from reincarnation in physical form if freed by Manichees. Until this happened, darkness and evil was inherent in the human condition, perpetuated by sexual reproduction, speaking evil and blaspheming, consuming wine and meat or otherwise harming living creatures,

---

[151] Ibid. 1–3, 10. Other information on Manichees in this section is taken from G. Widengren, *Mani and Manichaeism*, trans. C. Kessler, London 1965; H.-C. Puech, *Le Manichéisme: son fondateur – sa doctrine*, Paris 1949, esp. pp. 69–72; S. N. C. Lieu, *Manichaeism in the later Roman empire and medieval China: a historical survey*, Manchester 1985, 5–24, 37–54; G. Bonner, *St Augustine of Hippo: life and controversies*, 2nd edn, Norwich 1986, 157–92; N. J. Torchia, *Creatio ex nihilo and the theology of St Augustine: the anti-Manichean polemic and beyond*, New York 1999, 65–96.

and also if plants, fire or water were harmed. Thus the Manichee elect did not prepare their own food but were supported by followers bound by a less austere regime. They believed Mani to have been a prophet and identified him, as he identified himself, with the Paraclete. Christ, they believed, had only appeared to be real, as did his miracles. They none the less called themselves Christian, although they accepted the authority of only selected books in the New Testament in addition to works composed by Mani himself.

In examining the basis on which the clergy of the eleventh-century west used the term 'Manichee', another useful comparison may be made with the way it was employed in relation to genuine dualism in the contemporary east, where it was applied to Bogomils on occasion and regularly to Paulicians. Peter of Sicily and his abridger Peter the Higoumenos claim that Paulicians were, in spite of their denials, actually disciples of Mani. Theophylact Lecapenus and the tenth-century abjuration formulae for Paulician converts also imply that they revered him. Euthymius of the Periblepton tells us, equally fancifully, that Bogomils did likewise. But eastern clergy did not necessarily believe the heresy to have been derived directly from Mani or his followers (although Peter of Sicily thought a link existed but that they were ignorant of it).[152] We know that what they mean in using the term is that the new heresy was *like* that of Mani, and they say so justifiably. We do not dismiss their accounts or suspect that they encountered merely simple, pious Christians who threatened their authority any more than we do when they employ apocalyptic terminology. When we consider what Mani taught about the origination of the material world, its implications for the doctrine of incarnation, and the austere lifestyle adopted by his sect, it is not difficult to understand how the similarities between his heresy and Christian dualism struck the clergy in the east and why they assumed a connection. Far from it popping into their heads as the most frightening of a variety of outlawed beliefs, they appear to have done what modern scholars might do: they made observations, then went to their books to see whether what they saw correlated with an established pattern, and how closely. Euthymius tells us that he consulted definitions of heresies in *On the Christian faith*, by St John of Damascus (c. 675 and c. 749), the standard text on ancient heresies in the east, and that, in his own words, he 'went through the whole . . . book to try to discover what sort of evil heresy and blasphemy this was, and what it was called'.[153] He tells us that he could not in fact find the heresy in this work and could only determine, from his observation, that it was new but related to Paulicianism.[154] We may suspect that Héribert did something similar, telling us of a 'new' heresy. Cosmas the Priest, giving us the earliest account of observed Bogomil belief and practice, evidently used a similar methodology. He begins his own treatise on Bogomilism by rehearsing a list of the earlier anathematised heresiarchs very like those lists

---

[152] *Christian dualist heresies*, 1–4, 7–8, 12, 29–30, 66 and n. 2, 74–7, 93, 95, 101, 107, 154. Peter of Sicily goes as far as to state (p. 74) that Paulicians had Manichaean books.
[153] Ibid. 157.
[154] Ibid. 158.

produced by the early Christian authors, which he had presumably consulted.[155]
And when easterners did identify the heresy with the teachings of Mani, far
from finding something of a correlation and thence attributing its other features
to contemporary incidents, they give us a very original account of what they
observed. Like the later patriarch Cosmas of Jerusalem (1075–81), who wrote
'[t]he darkness of Manichaeanism [was] brought to nothing by the holy fathers,
but now . . . has secretly entered . . . the country of the Bulgars',[156] they felt it was
simultaneously and paradoxically both a thing eliminated and a doctrine
returned. Such reasoning is clearly evident in Peter of Sicily, who asserts both
that the Christian emperors 'have killed the Manichaeans . . . wherever and
whenever they were found', and yet believed the tradition to live on.[157]

We may usefully compare eleventh-century accounts of 'Manichees' with
both those of churchmen who were the heretics' contemporaries and encountered a living doctrine, and also those of early medieval authors, a handful of
whom, although the heresy was dead, drew on patristic writings and early legislation in composing new and compiling older sources. We may then see whether
traits they identified form the basis of an *idéaltype* reproduced in eleventh-
century accounts as the revisionists suspect.

Augustine himself spent nine years of his early life as a Manichee convert. He
tells us that to him at that time the heresy contained the answer to the origins of
evil as part of what seemed a logical and coherent cosmological system, allowing
him to free himself from the guilt of sin: sin had been imposed upon humanity by
evil, over which it had no control. In this Manichees shared something in
common with the neo-Platonist view that evil was somehow an independent
and inevitable counterpart to goodness within creation. Eventually, however,
Augustine failed to find answers to subtler questions within the sect, even from
one of its leading heresiarchs, Faustus of Milevis. On reconversion to orthodox
Christianity he attacked the heresy in polemics composed from 388 to 401
AD.[158] To him it now seemed that God had created everything from nothing at
the start of history, a central tenet of monotheism and as described in Genesis.
Everything created was thus naturally good, a concept entirely at odds with the

---

[155] Ibid. 115 and n. 1.
[156] Ibid. 165–6.
[157] Ibid. 75.
[158] References are to volumes of *PL*. See especially *Confessionum* bk 3, xxxii.683–92, and relevant sections of bk 5 at 705–17; *De libero arbitrio*, xxxii.1221–310 and *Contra Faustum
manichaeum*, xlii.207–518. For other discussion of the heresy see also *De moribus ecclesiae
catholicae et de moribus manichaeorum*, xxxii.1310–76; *De Genesi contra manichaeos*,
xxxiii.171–219; *De vera religione*, xxxiv.122–69; *De Genesi ad litteram imperfectus liber*,
xxxiv.219–484; *De utilitate credendi*, xlii.63–92; *De duabus animabus contra manichaeos: acta
contra Fortunatum manichaeum*, xlii.93–112; *Contra Fortunatum manichaeum*, xlii.111–30;
Contra Adimantum Manichaei disciplum, xlii.129–72; *Contra epistolam Manichaei*, xlii.173–206;
De actis cum Felice manichaeo, xlii.519–52; *De natura boni contra manichaeos*, xlii.551–72; and
Contra secundinum manichaeum, xlii.577–638. For discussion of his work on creation see espe-
cially Torchia, *Creatio ex nihilo*, passim; Bonner, *St Augustine*, 193–236, esp. pp. 204–10; Lieu,
Manichaeism, 117–54, esp. pp. 119–20.

Manichaean view. Evil, on the other hand, was the result of the corruption of creation by sin, for which mankind was responsible through the misuse of free will. Such a view is at the heart of the Christianity of even Rather of Verona and of those morose theologians of the later eleventh century onwards who found God primarily in the non-physical world, stressing the introduction of corruption and impurity into what He had created. To them, like Augustine, creation was in its origin and original nature pure, and as a result the manifestation of Christ in human form was also tenable. Being manifested as both created and pure He was at once potentially corruptible but able to redeem humanity by overcoming its frailties and dying for it.

The logic of this was central to those who followed Augustine. To Eusebius Hieronymus it was the insistence of the Manichees on their counter-logic that condemned them: the material world was corrupt and so a good Christ could consequently only appear to be human.[159] Pope Anastasius I (399–402) and Pope Leo I 'The Great' (440–61) anathematised and otherwise persecuted Manichees primarily for their central beliefs about the origin and nature of creation and of the Son and His relation to the Father (although they were not exempt from throwing in accusations of orgiastic behaviour as did eleventh-century clergy).[160] The incorrect doctrines of two principles, creation by the demiurge, the non-human nature of Christ and the rejection of Mosiac law are central to the affirmation of faith by Prosper (390–c. 460). But here we are also informed about some of the more bizarre aspects of the heresy, such as the belief that light particles trapped in fruits like cucumbers and melons could be released when the plant was eaten by the Manichee elect. The affirmation is also untypical of sources for the period in informing us of some of the theological and practical consequences arising from central Manichaean beliefs about the physical world, for example their disbelief in the resurrection of the body and their rejection of sexual intercourse.[161]

We may start to doubt Lambert's assertion that Manichees were one of 'the most infamous names in the constellation of ideas of medieval churchmen' when we come to the early Middle Ages. After the period in which Manichaeism was eliminated in the west, clerics are in fact scarcely concerned with Manichees at all. Only a handful recorded the nature of their beliefs and the ways they had been dealt with. Sometimes this was done in the context of compiling encyclopaedic accounts of human affairs. In book viii of the *Etymologia*, Isidore of Seville (c. 560–636) notes Mani's teaching that there were two principles, good and evil, and that human souls came from the good.[162] St Paul, patriarch of Aquila (804–23), discusses a variety of heresies and bases his

---

159 *PL* xxiii.213, 360, 371; xxvi.54, 48, 59, 84–5, 94, 98, 100, 102, 105, 107, 211; xxii.494, 742, 747, 925, 1085, 1150, 1157; xxv.1297.
160 *PL* xx.75 (Anastasius); liv.163, 178–9, 198, 206, 278–9; lxv.23; *Concilia*, vi. 431–4 (Leo). See also J. Stevenson (ed.), *Creeds, councils and controversies: documents illustrative of the early Church, AD 337–461*, London 1966, 95, 263–4, 307–8.
161 *PL* lxv.23–30, esp. pp. 24–6.
162 *PL* lxxxii.300.

account of Manichees on Augustine and Leo, telling us that Manichees believed the devil to have created and to rule all perversity.[163] Isidore and Paul are discussing Manichees as parts of broader categories and as such we do not get the impression that the heresy was especially important to them. They are joined by Pope Gregory the Great (595–604) in regarding the heresy in a historical context. He includes condemnations of the belief in the two principles in his *Moralium*, books ix and xxxii.[164] Paschasius Radbertus, abbot of Corbie (843–c. 850), addressed the Manichaean rejection of the Old Testament, essentially the Law and the Prophets, and acceptance only of the New, as part of illustrating his own interpretation of Matthew, and in this context he disputes the Manichaean concept of equality between all living creatures through the possession of an eternal transmigrating soul.[165]

Gregory, Paschasius, Paul and also Hrabanus Maurus – abbot of Fulda (823–42) and archbishop of Mainz (847–56) – and also Alcuin of York (c. 730–804), all note the Manichaean denial of the humanity of Christ and belief that his earthly incarnation was illusory. Manichees taught, says Alcuin, that the disciples first suspected that He was an 'apparition' when they saw Him walk on water, and that He was 'only God and not man', not brought about by birth to the Virgin nor killed in the mortal sense by crucifixion.[166] To all of them, the Docetist aspect of the heresy is by far the most important reason for discussing it at all, and in doing so they draw on Augustine. Only briefly, in contrast, does Pope Gregory observe, in describing a varieties of heresies, that Manichees applauded virginity and condemned marriage, whilst the other issue concerning Paschasius was that, like Ari, Mani did not believe the Son to be equal to the Father.[167]

Amongst other ninth-century sources on which eleventh-century clergy might have drawn is the *History of the Roman pontiffs* by Anastasius Biblio-thecarius. Like Isidore and Paul of Aquila, Anastasius' account is part of a set, describing the activities of early popes. Those whom he notes as acting against the heresy, apart from Anastasius and Leo, were Siricius (384–98), Gelasius I (492–6), Symmachus (498–514) and Hormisda (514–23). His accounts draw only indirectly, if at all, on Augustine's discussions of Manichaean teachings and are primarily concerned with the sanctions placed upon them. However, in discussing Pope Gelasius he does draw on Leo's sermon for Quadrigisima to inform us that Manichees considered wine to be the poisonous creation of the demiurge.[168] The ninth-century decretal collector Isidore Mercatoris was naturally also primarily concerned with the legislative aspects of the subject. From

---

163 *PL* xcix.476–7.
164 *PL* lxxv.899; lxxvi.60, 646.
165 *PL* cxx.38, 364, 770.
166 *PL* lxxviii.290 (Gregory); cxx.37–8, 388 (Paschasius); xcix.476–7 (Paul); ci.1330 (Alcuin, quotations); cx.365 (Hrabanus).
167 *PL* lxxvi.115 (Gregory); cxx.364, 761 (Paschasius).
168 *PL* cxxviii.109–11, 113, 116, 123, 125–6 (on Sirichius), 129–30 (on Anastasius), 413–14, 430–1 (on Gelasius), 451, 472 (on Symmchus), 475 (on Hormisda).

the sources he compiled we get an idea of what clergy of his period knew about the beliefs of the heretics. For example his decretals of Pope Anastasius tells us that Manichees found in Rome in the fourth century believed Christ not to have been born in human form and that an apparition, not a man, was crucified.[169]

Very noticeably, in early medieval sources we only rarely find discussion illustrative of some of the logical consequences of the central tenets of the heresy as they manifested themselves in daily practice, such as we do in Augustine's personal writings or the affirmation of faith by Prosper. Exceptions to this are Pope Gregory's observation that Manichees denounced sexual intercourse and Anastasius Bibliothecarius' inclusion of Pope Leo's observation about wine. In general such secondary matters, resulting out of more serious disbelief, appear to have been of little interest to early medieval scholars. They focus instead on the action taken against the sect and especially on the central doctrines of the Manichees on the nature and origins of the physical world and Incarnation. Like the earliest papal legislators, and also like Gratian in the twelfth century, early medieval writers were overwhelmingly interested in the most central tenets of a long-dead heresy.[170]

So to what extent do the 'Manichees' described in the high Middle Ages correlate with earlier writings on the sect? Whilst it is probably true that Adémar and his colleagues who used the term Manichee relied to some extent on ancient Christian writings, they did so rather differently from the way they were used by early medieval scholars. In the early eleventh century, where the sources are concerned with what they apparently considered to be a living heresy, they in fact employ very little of what was written about Manichees from patristic and early medieval authors. Specifically, aside from the implication contained by the use of the term Manichee itself, they not once assert the heretical belief in two gods. This is in spite of the fact that many of them read Augustine and Bishop Gerard of Arras-Cambrai at least also used Gregory the Great and Isidore of Seville.[171] Of the central Manichaean beliefs, only the non-human nature of Christ and rejection of the Old Testament are overtly attributed to eleventh-century heretics. If some of the most central aspects of patristic and early medieval accounts of the fearful heresy are neglected, why

---

169 PL cxxxix.691–2 (on Anastasius, whose decretal is also at xx.75), 820 (on Leo).

170 Gratian uses Augustine as the basis for approximately one third of the *Decretals* (see *The treatise on laws: [Decretum DD. 1–20]*, trans. A. Thompson and J. Gordley, Washington, DC 1993, at p. xiii). Thus he is naturally his major source for the Manichaean heresy: PL cdlxx.60, 201, 858, 1163, 1196, 1307, 1314, 1315; *Treatise on laws*, 40, 58. Gratian does, however, also refer to early papal writings and councils for its treatment and for definitions of correct belief on the nature of Christ and the Trinity, and in listing the apocrypha used by heretics (see esp. PL cdlxx.78, 163, 168, 172) he uses a letter of Pope Leo (*Concilia*, vi. 431–6; *Treatise on laws*, 56), and probably read Isidore of Seville on Manichaeism as he cites him in many other decretals: *Treatise on laws*, pp. xiii–xxiv, 56, 57–8.

171 Bishop Gerard's use of these authorities is noted in Lobrichon, 'Arras, 1025', 81–3. Poly and Bournazel think Isidore, not Augustine, the likeliest source for the use of 'Manichee': *Feudal transformation*, 293. See below for discussion of Adémar's sources in this context.

should we accept that eleventh-century clergy effectively based their accounts on them?

The elements of 'Manichaean' belief on which eleventh-century clerics mainly concentrate are details with which their immediate predecessors were concerned very little: the rejection of sex, the refusal to drink wine, eat meat or otherwise harm living creatures, a predilection for fasting and the refusal to speak evil. It seems unlikely that they chose to pluck such minor traits from an external source whilst ignoring its central points. It seems more likely that they were observed. On the other hand, traits such as the Manichaean belief about the nature of goodness – as light particles which had to be freed – and the refusal of the elect to harm plants, fire or water are not attributed to the eleventh-century heretics. If Augustine's Manichees and not the heretics observed are the basis for these accounts, it seems strange that, unlike early medieval writers, their authors derived little from patristic texts by way of fundamental Manichaean characteristics and central doctrine.

It is very important that we should also note features of the millennial heresies which do not at all conform to the model produced in the early Christian centuries and reiterated in the early Middle Ages. These include an emphasis on literacy and other forms of social equality within the sect, specific opposition to the cross as an object of veneration, the rejection of all prayers but the Lord's Prayer in its eastern form accompanied by elaborate ritual as noted by Héribert. These are amongst the traits that some groups of western heretics in our period shared only with dualists in the Balkans.

Arguably eleventh-century accounts, far from being based upon textual sources and early idéaltypes, were the result most immediately of observation of what the subjects of the accounts did and said. For some, such as Héribert, that is where their attempts to identify the heresy stopped, and we can congratulate them on their methodology. Others felt the need to find an established yardstick by which to measure the heresy. But it does not follow automatically that they drew much other than the label from other sources. Thus Adémar chose 'Manichee' because it 'seemed to describe kinds of beliefs similar to those he had heard about in Aquitaine'.[172] I find little convincing evidence that he took much else from Augustine's account or from Isidore's list of heresies, of which he in fact made a copy,[173] and attributed their content to those he observed or of whom he had heard. Had he been attempting instead to impose an ancient or early medieval Manichaean model on his subjects, he would surely have given us lurid details about their polytheism and disputation of the Augustinian account of the origin of evil.

Through his studies we can see that Adémar gained some knowledge of a vast array of dissident ancient beliefs. But far from it being the case that Manichee

---

[172] See Peters, Heresy, 61, although Peters thinks (p. 62) that the question of actual dualism is open to question.

[173] Michael Frassetto is working on Adémar's copy of Isidore's list of heresies (BN, MS lat. 2400, fo. 130v). I thank him for his correspondence in this context.

was a term which, if not selected randomly from a list of heresies with which to frighten clerics and laymen, was chosen because, historians have decided, it was the worst, it seems possible that he and other clergy knew enough about dualist teaching to recognise it when they encountered it and label it as such, albeit with an anachronistic title. Whilst it is surely the case that of those encountering heretics in the west 'not a few supposed that these outbreaks of heresy were linked to a revival and spread of Manichaeism',[174] it does not follow automatically that clergy such as those whom Moore calls 'skilful and important writers', merely 'sedulously accumulated a set of commonplaces deriving from Augustine's *De haeresibus*, polished and refined at length by tradition'.[175] In his concentration on heretical practice as opposed to cosmology, Adémar, like others of the period, diverges significantly from the supposed patristic *idéaltype*. In fact, given his knowledge of the east and his contacts with its clergy, discussed further below, during the period when he wrote his original accounts of heresy, it even seems possible that there is a textual or oral relationship between his use of the very term 'Manichee' itself and that by easterners: even the label need not have come directly from patristic sources.

However, if the sources are using earlier authors in the manner I suggest, why do they not refer explicitly to the doctrine of two principles if this was indeed being expressed by the heretics they encountered? It is implied by 'Manichee', but why is the worst crime of all not discussed further? We return to the case that western heresy could have been Bogomil-derived without the dualist doctrine being clearly articulated or understood. Moore has noted that the rejection of the physical world perhaps existed independently of Bogomil cosmology in the east, and Hamilton observes that such concepts had not yet converged as clearly as they would. It seems plausible that the five teachings and tenets which, I have argued above, can derive only from eastern dualism in this period, could have been articulated in the west without the two principles. Schooled in the ancient heresies as they were, clergy may even have understood the implications of what are arguably fragments of dualism better than their earliest western exponents did. It seems certain that some clergy indeed thought they were encountering revived Manicheaism. The argument that they were over-confident, inaccurate or even mendacious in asserting the label does not disprove the possibility that what they encountered none the less derived from dualism.

A number of other historians have responded to the accusations of Manichaeism more sympathetically than exponents of the social and conflict models. Frassetto elucidates open-mindedly such accusations made in various parts of France and argues that we should take the assertions of the sources more seriously because he finds much evidence to support the possible importation of Bogomil influence. Although Anne Brenon does not think that these heretics, whom she does consider dualist, were connected to Bogomils, she notes that the

---

174 Van Meter, 'Eschatological order', 161.
175 Moore refers to Glaber, Adémar, Anselm of Liège and Landulf Senior: *Origins*, 40 (first quotation); Lobrichon, 'Chiaroscuro', 100 (second quotation).

lack of coherent dualism in the eleventh-century sources is far from unique to this ambiguous era. As Hamilton observes of the contemporary east, many accounts of dualists even by the thirteenth century are very unspecific about the cosmological understanding that was, by the later date, undeniably in place.[176]

Peters accounts for the use of 'Manichee' by suggesting that medieval churchmen were less concerned with the extant status or otherwise of the ancient heresy than with its content. Thus in 1143 or 1144 St Bernard compared early Cathars identified at Cologne with Manichees by saying that they were like them in their rejection of the material world but different because they had no leaders. Bernard's conclusion was that the heresy could easily be refuted because it contained nothing 'new or strange . . . but that which is worn by use . . . and which has been well thrashed and winnowed by our theologians'.[177] Like some clergy in the eleventh century, to Bernard Mani's teachings were at once both dead and living. If he was wrong to imply a continuation of dualist belief, we do not doubt that he was attempting to define the new heresy usefully and accurately.

As Malcolm Barber puts it of the period before about 1045, when the Bogomil label began to be used in the east, 'it is difficult to see how [sources] could have described what they believed to be dualist heresy other than as Manichaean'. He finds it difficult to believe that Italians at least would not have come into contact with Bogomils or their influence by such a date.[178] Heinrich Fichtenau also suggests specific cases where Bogomil contacts might have happened, the likeliest to him being those of Leutard of Vertus and of Châlons and Orléans.[179] Bernard Hamilton finds it most plausible that there might be some connection between these 'new Manichees', and 'the Bogomilism which was evolving in the Balkans'.[180] We should now turn to evidence of why it in fact seems far more likely that dualist ideas or even missionaries did reach the west than did not, whatever their actual influence was to be.

---

[176] See Brenon, 'Les Hérésies de l'an mil', 28–31, 35, and Le Vrai Visage du catharisme, Portet-sur-Garonne 1988, 45–8, 98–9. She surely goes too far in seeing a continuation of dualist belief from the ancient period however. For a historiographical account of historians who trace the roots of medieval dualism into the ancient period, most famously S. Runciman in Medieval Manichee, see Barber, Cathars, 11–12.

[177] See Peters, Heresy, 63, where quotation from On the Song of Songs is translated, and Kienzle, Cistercians, 85–90, esp. pp. 88–9 for discussion of sermons 65 and 66 and their dating.

[178] Barber, Cathars, 29 (quotation), 32.

[179] Fichtenau, Heretics and scholars, 17–18, 26, 37.

[180] Hamilton, 'Wisdom', 39. D. Callahan suspects Bogomil influence in Aquitaine, not least since the discovery of an eleventh-century Héribert, and is currently also writing on the subject.

Bogomil inroads to the west

Dualist beliefs had been encountered in southern Italy well before our period. Byzantine influence there was strong and shortly before 872 Paulician mercenaries, defeated survivors of some of the Armenian communities, were settled there. They were deployed in the region by Greek armies in 1038–41. Armenian Paulicians were probably also using the trade routes and mercantile communities between Constantinople and central and northern Europe to spread their heresy into Bulgaria. Many Balkan dualists were associated specifically with the cloth industry and its merchants were amongst those who travelled to the west, perhaps sometimes bringing an unorthodox religious outlook with their Byzantine fabrics.[181]

Contacts between Byzantium and the west were strengthened in the late Carolingian and Ottonian period. Cultural and artistic influences came westwards, and eastern saints were venerated by westerners and their relics brought home. Greeks were present at the secular and ecclesiastical courts of Europe in both a cultural and diplomatic capacity, and many westerners journeyed into Byzantium for the same purposes. In Italy, Greek monks were frequently used in diplomacy between their Latin patrons and Byzantine superiors. Abbots and bishops from all over Europe travelled to Constantinople on papal and imperial business, such as the marriage arranged between Emperor Otto II and the Byzantine princess Theophano in 972. After her husband's death in 983, Theophano was co-regent for their son Otto until her death in 991. Byzantine influence was thus at the heart of western Imperial court life.[182]

Greek intellectuals were engaged in debates at lay and also ecclesiastical courts, some of them having been taught Latin in Byzantium. Greek patristic works were in circulation in the west in the early eleventh century and the Greek language was read and spoken not only by monks but even by some nobles. Greek cultural and linguistic influence was in evidence even in early eleventh-century Aquitaine: in subscription clauses in charters of the abbey of Bourgueil, founded by Emma of Poitou, mother of Duke William III; in the nickname *Chiliarch*, leader of a thousand, attributed to Hugh of Lusignan in the *Conventum*; and in the inclusion of the Greek alphabet in what is very probably an autograph manuscript of Adémar of Chabannes. Greek art remained influential in spite of the mid-century schism.[183]

---

[181] The major sources establishing the extent of east–west contact in this period, which is not an especially contentious issue in debates around the origins of heresy, are J. Ebersolt, *Orient et occident: recherches sur les influences byzantines et orientales en France avant et pendant les croisades*, 2nd edn, Paris 1954, and also B. Hamilton and P. A. McNulty, 'Orientale lumen et magistra latinitis: Greek influences of western monasticism (900–1100)', in B. Hamilton, *Monastic reform, Catharism and crusades (900–1300)*, London 1979, passim. See also *Christian dualist heresies*, 23, 139–40, 167; Obolensky, *Bogomils*, 82–3, 287, 289; Browning, *Byzantium*, 151; Runciman, *Medieval Manichee*, 169; Fichtenau, *Heretics and scholars*, 18.

[182] A. Davids (ed.), *The Empress Theophano: Byzantium and the west at the turn of the first millennium*, Cambridge 1995; Riché, *Les Grandeurs*, 94–8.

[183] Examples of the use of Greek are detailed in Martindale's 'Conventum', 528 n. 3.

In addition to those pilgrims travelling from various parts of western Europe into, across and throughout Aquitaine, were many travelling from eastern Europe and Asia Minor to the west, and vice versa. These were aided by the fact that Crete and Cyprus were captured by the Greeks in the second half of the tenth century, and traffic increased in the millennial era in part because the conquest of Bulgaria by Byzantium led to the opening up of a new land route to the Holy Land. Duke Richard of Normandy used it and in 1026 contingents from Verdun, Trier, Limoges and Angoulême were led along it by Abbot Richard of Saint-Vanne, returning the following year. In 1034 Bishop Lietbert of Arras-Cambrai and others used this route as far as Laodicea, but the Fatimids then closed the frontier to Christian traffic. Thus we see that pilgrims from several of the regions which experienced heresy in our period journeyed through Bulgaria, the Byzantine empire and parts of Asia Minor. Pilgrims to Jerusalem, many Aquitainians amongst them, met Greeks and orientals on their travels, and easterners were welcomed into French communities in return. Amongst those Aquitainians who attempted the journey to the Holy Land in the millennial period were Duke William V, Bishop Isembert of Poitou and Bishop Jordan of Limoges, Mainard, abbot of Saint-Cybard in Angoulême, and Adémar himself, who never returned. Gascons making the journey include a knight, Raimond Paba, who travelled to Jerusalem as penance for a murder of a noble of his region. One of the easterners who came west was the Armenian saint Symeon the Hermit. He arrived in Italy in 983 and stayed in the west until at least the 1020s, spending time in Gascony and also Aquitaine amongst other places, then settling for a time at Padolirone near Mantua. Indeed, wandering preachers from southern Italy were amongst the earliest initiators of the eremitic movement in Europe, and an Armenian hermit is known to have lived at Orléans in the early eleventh century.[184]

The 1026–7 pilgrimage led by Count William Taillefer of Angoulême gives us a good example of the ways in which some easterners came into contact with Aquitainians. Saint Symeon of Trier, a Greek Calabrian raised in Constantinople, eventually went to live at Saint-Vanne, Verdun, after meeting Abbot Richard in Antioch in 1027. The Greeks in this party went with Richard as far as Belgrade but then took a route via Rome and then France. They spent time in Aquitaine as guests of William V at Poitiers, where they became acquainted with the clergy of Angoulême, residing for a time at Adémar's abbey, Saint-Cybard, and accompanying him on one of his few extra-mural journeys, to Limoges. The Angoumois was greatly impressed by the intellect and devotion of

---

Adémar's alphabet, which she cites (BN, MS lat. 2400, fo. 182r), was not known to R. L. Wolff when he stated that Adémar knew no Greek in 'How the news was brought from Byzantium to Angoulême; or, the pursuit of a hare in an ox cart', *Byzantine and Modern Greek Studies* iv (1978), 139–89 at p. 149.

184 Adémar, *Chronicon*, 194; *Cartulaires Sainte-Marie d'Auch*, ii. 134; *Book of Saint Foy*, 4–13; Mussot-Goulard, *Les Princes*, 242; Landes, *Relics*, 39, 309–27; Hamilton, 'Wisdom', 39–40; Poly and Bournazel, *Feudal transformation*, 288.

Symeon and his companion Cosmas, and by Symeon's fondness for fasting. Adémar was to be affected in another way by this pilgrimage. One of the pilgrims was his abbot, also called Richard, who died in Byzantium, upon which William Taillefer nominated a fellow pilgrim, Amalfred, as his successor.[185]

Through either his connection with the Greeks Cosmas and Symeon, or with his new abbot or with other pilgrims returning from the east in the same year, Adémar attained some limited knowledge of eastern affairs and provides some possibly revealing observations. He accounts for the fourteen-year struggle of the Byzantine emperor Basil against the Bulgarians (1000–14) thus:

> At this time the rebelling Bulgarians were greatly annoying the Greeks and the Emperor Basil in particular. He promised God that if he could subject them he would become a monk. He struggled with that enemy for fifteen years and triumphed in two great battles. At last, he got all the land of the great kings of the Bulgars, Samuel and Aaron, not by public battle but when they had been killed by Greek cunning, and the strongest cities and castles were destroyed and most of the Bulgar population was held in the Greek camps everywhere established against them. As he had vowed, he put on the habit of a Greek monk for the rest of his life, abstaining from sensual pleasure and meat.[186]

It is an intriguing account. Adémar is factually incorrect.[187] Yet his mistakes may be revealing in themselves. Are we reading here a confused account of the struggle between orthodoxy and heresy? Adémar refers neither to the Bulgarians nor their tsar as heretics, yet the moral triumph and sacrifice of the Christian Basil is contrasted with the rebellious and dissident nature of the Bulgars and their leaders, and we must not forget the scurrilous claims made elsewhere about Samuel's support of Bogomils. Most interestingly, it was after Adémar came into contact with the two Greek pilgrims that he wrote his sermons and account of Aquitainian heretics for the year 1022, who he says were in various parts of the world.[188] At the end of the 1020s, was Adémar beginning to understand the significance of certain contacts between Aquitaine and the Balkans?

The Normans were the cause of many contacts between Byzantium, Italy and France. In the early decades of the eleventh century Norman adventurers, in alliance with autonomous elements in Byzantine Italy, gained control of much

---

185 Adémar, *Chronicon*, 189; Wolff, 'News from Byzantium', passim; Landes, *Relics*, 154–70. It was on this visit to Limoges with the Greek monks that Adémar composed the first version of the account of the Bulgarian war, as *marginalia* in his abbey's copy of the *Chronicon aquitanicum*: Landes, *Relics*, 163–5; Wolff, 'News from Byzantium', 139–89.
186 Adémar, *Chronicon*, 155.
187 He is confusing several events. The reference to monasticism is probably a confusion with the 'monastic reign' of Tsar Peter of Bulgaria during which orthodox religious life in Bulgaria was revitalised and which ended when Peter himself became a monk after a Russian invasion. Tsar Samuel fought the Greeks till the end. He collapsed and died in 1014 at the sight of thousands of prisoners of war whom Basil had had blinded.
188 The account does not appear in the first version of his history, written 1025–7, but was added to it later in notes and included in the later two versions, although the Orléans and Toulousain heretics appear in the earlier account: Landes, *Relics*, 175–7.

of Apulia and Campania and from there encroached on Moslem Sicily. Then, supported by the papacy, which hoped to disrupt Byzantine influence over southern Italian monasteries and bishops, they threatened Byzantium and the Balkans. It is not impossible that Balkan missionaries, refugees from the turbulence afflicting their own countries, could have travelled back to Sicily and thence through France along established Norman lines of communication. Indeed, the close collaboration between Norman colonists in different parts of the world was a causal feature of their success at this time. We should not overlook the possible role of the Paulician communities which had remained in Sicily under Moslem rule and which now perhaps also had access to the most westerly parts of Europe.[189] Indeed, Norman communications with southwesterly regions of France existed from the time of the Norse raids and establishment of their duchy in France. As we have seen, negotiations between Normandy and Gascony in the 970s resulted in the release of prisoners captured along the Garonne. Adémar was especially familiar with Norman affairs and the extensive political contacts between Norman and Aquitainian rulers.[190] In the context of the Orléans heresy, Duke Richard of Normandy seems to have been well enough acquainted with heresy to recognise a serious problem when he saw one. His knowledge might well have come from a combination of contacts with Aquitainian and Greek clergy: St Symeon of Trier had actually been *en route* to Normandy to the court of Duke Richard, on the business of the monks of Mount Sinai, when he met Richard of Saint-Vanne. Bernard of Angers attests that the subject of heresy was even discussed with Normans at the ducal court at Poitiers.

Links between Byzantine and Roman monastic institutions by the late tenth century resulted in extensive activity by easterners in the west; in their own Orthodox communities in southern Italy, the Papal States, Lombardy, Lorraine and the west of France; in Latin houses such as Gorze and most notably Saint-Bonifatius in Rome and Monte Cassino in Benevento; and as widely tolerated and patronised hermits. If, like Euthymius' heretics at the Periblepton, Bogomils attempted to use Orthodox monasticism as a cover for their missions, they would not have been short of opportunities to enter western houses. Indeed, the eastern habit continued to suit them well, for Orthodox monks were noted for their preoccupation with the simple life. St Nilus and his monks lived frugally on the abbey estates of Monte Cassino, engaging in debate about the rites of the Greek and Latin churches until the abbacy of Manso (from 984) when they left, offended by the lax practices which had crept in and influencing others at the abbey to do likewise. Austerity was also noted amongst those Greeks at Mount Gargano in Benevento and those visiting Saint-Michael the Archangel in Apulia.

In all this evidence we have not one single account of an obviously Bogomil mission. However, if such activity took place it must have been as deliberately covert in the west as it was in the east. It was certainly far from difficult for here-

---

[189] Adémar, *Chronicon*, 178; G. Tabacco, *The struggle for power in medieval Italy*, trans. R. B. Jensen, Cambridge 1989, 179–81.
[190] Adémar, *Chronicon*, 146–50, 178, 188–9.

tics to conceal themselves within the foreign traffic, toward which there was clearly familiarity and tolerance. This was not uniformly the case of course. Pope Benedict VIII (1012–24) had to rescue Symeon the Hermit from the hands of an angry mob who suspected that he was a heretic.[191] It was widely believed in the west that all Armenians were heretics because their rite had been labelled as suspect by the Greek Church.[192] But even this evidence suggests that at some level in popular consciousness there was a connection between the east and religious heresy, perhaps because heterodox ideas were indeed being expressed in the west by apparently orthodox easterners.[193] We have pertinent evidence that a pilgrim's guise could render a stranger inconspicuous in this period. The *Translatio* of St Foy, composed between 1020 and 1060, tells us that the monk Arinisdus, planning to steal the saint's relics from their resting place in Agen in 866, needed to discard his own Benedictine garb and dress himself instead as a pilgrim in order to win the trust of the Agenais people. Heretical 'pilgrims' might deceive all the better if, like Bogomils, they had the appearance of saintliness: Arinisdus was all the more successful in his deception because of his virtuous and humble demeanour and his chastity.[194]

We should add to this the contemporary experience of Bogomilism in the east for, as we have seen, it entered a period of simultaneous persecution by Byzantine rule and the ability to extend its horizons when in 1018 Macedonia was absorbed by the empire and Bulgaria became part of the wider Christian world. It seems plausible, because of the inherently evangelical nature of the heresy, that the early eleventh century was a time to 'go west', and that Bogomil missionaries concealed themselves in the columns of travellers already doing so. Such journeys as orthodox pilgrims undertook were often encounters with the unknown, and on long journeys there is nothing as good as contemplating the meaning of life to while away the time. Euthymius of the Periblepton tells us that he encountered the heretics in this way. Without over-stressing the point, we should note that he was writing of the year 1018 when Adémar first raised the alarm about Manichees in Aquitaine.

Turning more specifically to evidence that the west was experiencing more than localised disturbances, there is a strong case to be made for the identification by Aquitainian contemporaries of an organised dualist network with eastern origins which goes beyond the simple identification of its adherents as 'Manichees'. In his *Sermo ad sinodum de catholica fide* Adémar states that the reason that heretics had not found their mission easy in Gaul was because St Martial protected it, and he explicitly contrasts this with their success in the east.[195] In his chronicle the account of heretics in Aquitaine appears with his

---

191 AS vi. 324. For the dating of this event see Hamilton, 'Wisdom', 40 n. 10.
192 For the schism between the Byzantine Church and the Monophysite Armenians see J. Strayer (ed.), *Dictionary of the Middle Ages*, New York 1982–9, i. 498–500.
193 This is noted in Hamilton, 'Wisdom', 40.
194 *Book of Saint Foy*, 26, 267. Cathars also disguised themselves as Catholic pilgrims: Doat xxii, fo. 20r.
195 MS Lat. Phillipps 1664, fo. 85r (Frassetto, 'Sermons', 213, 336, 338).

account of the heresy at Orléans, whence he says the heresy was taken by a peasant from Périgord. Here we should surely consider a link with Héribert's account of heretics infiltrating the very same county. Even Lobrichon admits that 'one must allow the possibility that Héribert's pamphlet and Adémar's historical work are either textually linked or, more likely, independently describe the same phenomenon in the Périgord',[196] a statement which rather undermines his view that the heretics were a coded metaphor for the enemies of Cluny, for this is most certainly not the way in which Adémar was writing, either about them or in code. Héribert's warning that 'a new heresy is born into this world . . . [and] right now [heretics] are secretly invading these parts and others' implies that it originally came from elsewhere and would spread further, as we know contemporaries believed it to have done within Aquitaine by 1028. Adémar also tells us that there were Manichees at Toulouse who had been involved in spreading their teachings 'in various parts of the west'.[197] Bernard of Anger's continuators found heresy as far south as Millau, and the heretic encountered by Deusdet of Gascony was identified as being part of a wider sect.

Sources refer to several routes of contact for heresy. We have seen that John of Ripoll warned his Catalan bishop that it might cross the Pyrenees. The heretics who originally brought the new doctrine to Arras, we are told, came thence from Italy and said that they were disciples of the heresiarch Gundulf, although we are not told whether they were themselves Italian. Glaber tells us that Italians were also behind the case at Orléans, and this time the bearer of the heresy was a woman who quietly moved on 'elsewhere' after she had made her converts.[198] Transmission of eastern heretical ideas via Italy in fact makes much sense, as Barber notes. However, the case is somewhat compromised by the fact that we have accounts of only one possibly dualist incident there. It is in itself revealing however. Landulf Senior tells us of the Monforte incident that the heretics had come from 'some unknown part of the world . . . [and appeared to be] like good priests'. Gerard of Monforte declared that his sect was spread throughout the world and had a leader whom he likened to the pope but who he said had not received holy orders.[199] Glaber perhaps even links these heretics to the Graeco/Bulgarian conflict for he says that the 'demon' whom they worshipped had been making mischief in Byzantium, murdering an emperor, before he came to Italy.[200] Other sources imply transmission not limited to the west. Several scholars have noted that the heretic Stephen was referred to retrospectively, in 1063, as *bulgarellus*.[201] Both Héribert's heretics and his form of address are universal and seem to be describing a form of prayer that was recog-

---

[196] Lobrichon, 'Chiaroscuro', 100 n. 46.

[197] Adémar, *Chronicon*, 185.

[198] Glaber, *Histories*, 138–9.

[199] *Heresies of the high Middle Ages*, 88.

[200] Glaber, *Histories*, 178–9. Glaber is, however, confused (n. 2) about which murder he is referring to.

[201] GC viii. 494; Poly and Bournazel, *Feudal transformation*, 287. From Paul of Chartres we learn that Stephen was once confessor to the queen, Constance of Aquitaine. This is cited as

nisably eastern. Whatever we may conclude about whether incidents of heresy in the west in this period were related to each other and to the east, those writing about them at the time seem far from confused about the matter.

The early eleventh-century evidence

There are problems with the traditional 'Bogomil' interpretation and a variety of plausible candidates for 'heretics' within the non-dualist models. There are many aspects of the accounts of popular heresy which resemble later reforming and ascetic tendencies and anticlerical currents extending towards the Reformation. But, aside from those accounts of indications in early eleventh-century tendencies and beliefs which, I consider, are not very convincingly explained outside of a dualist model, I find little evidence of expressions of the *vita apostolica*, in the range of social circles in which it needs to have been expressed, to make a revision of the Bogomil thesis really convincing. Simple piety that overtly challenged the clerical monopoly is often expressed in 1000 alongside ideas that also challenge essential and non-negotiable doctrine. That is to say, ideas that not only threatened the pre-Gregorian, pre-Fontevriste, pre-mendicant, or pre-vernacular Church but central beliefs, most importantly the incarnation and its implications for salvation. Also we have to account logically for traits such as novel rituals, baptism without water, the rejection of any and all sexual contact and implicitly of procreation, the spurning of wine, and a Bogomil form of prayer. We also find striking similarities in the ways in which heretical ideas were transmitted in the west, in particular from Héribert, and accounts of Bogomils. The westerners' heretical ideas, on first hearing, appeared orthodox as well as devout, but then heterodox concepts, presumably the allegorical nature of Scripture, were introduced. Those whom the heretics managed to mislead in this way were then drawn into intensive training in which it appears that, far from them being encouraged to seek a personal relationship with God, they were schooled in what to believe by practised teachers and certain forms of interpretation and practice imparted to them. Furthermore, far from choosing a heretical label arbitrarily and then attributing its facets to their enemies, commentators on heresy often seem to have done the reverse, calling heretics by a dualist label because, when their assertions and practices were examined, they more closely resembled Manichees than anything else. Yet they stop short of extrapolating Manichaean cosmology from this, and possibly a coherent dualism was in any case not yet being expressed. I thus suggest that it is the reliance on a purely comparative methodology such as Dondaine's that undermines the Bogomil case, not problems inherent in the evidential discourse. We must consider the possibility that warnings about Manichees should be taken as possible indicators of Bogomil influence, provided by clergy

---

proof of a link with Aquitaine: Runciman, *Medieval Manichee*, 117. However, there is no evidence that Stephen himself came from Aquitaine.

who knew neither the term Bogomil nor the content of the eastern sources but only the name of some ancient dualists.

If the Bogomil thesis can be shown to hold water, then what appears to have been happening in Aquitaine in the first few decades of the eleventh century is that Bogomils were spreading their ideas into the region via communication routes that were busier than ever. They were probably doing this either by disguising themselves as priests, hermits, pilgrims and monks, or Bogomil converts made in Italy were doing it for them. Euthymius tells us that Bogomils drew lots to decide who would travel where to proselytise, and perhaps does not exaggerate too wildly in stating that they covered the whole world. This perhaps accounts for the several similarities between accounts of heresy from western regions. The model I support does not deny the many differences, however. I suggest these arose out of factors such as differing local circumstances and long-standing influences, the result of the varying cultural and social backgrounds from which the heretics appear to have recruited in different places; the clerics raised from humble ranks in Orléans perhaps already influenced to some degree by elite post-Carolingian neo-Platonism; the unlettered peasants of north-eastern France and the Low Countries; and powerful lay circles at Monforte in which a socially dominant woman retained her status and performed heretical rites. In Aquitaine, the secular and lay elite were less at odds with each other than elsewhere, the militarily and politically powerful dukes having formed a 'peace club' with favoured clergy which various high and middle-ranking nobles scrambled to join. Excluded were the peasants, both the unfree and, perhaps more influentially, those whose freedom was threatened in this period, and the castellans and knights whom both the populace and the 'in-group' blamed for social disorder.

It is members of the former group who seem to have been most attracted to heresy. Their reasons are not difficult to discern. Subjected to violence from one elite party, and to the encoding of oppression and the interests of authorities within the solution to the rapine from the other, a disillusioned minority appear to have become increasingly responsive to a range of alternatives. In this we may speculate that they were led most immediately by low-ranking clergy, also *pauperes* in the language of the Peace. Landes and Moore agree that when Adémar warns us of heresy arisen in Aquitaine he links its genesis to the disillusionment of the masses with the elite monastic solution to their troubles, a mentality symbolised tragically by the death of many pilgrims in the basilica of Saint-Martial in c. 1018.[202] Others sought apocalyptic explanations for human suffering. The extent to which this was the case at the humbler levels of society remains impossible to ascertain, but Bogomils may have over-estimated the extent of millennial anxiety in the west just as Glaber probably did. Apocalypticism in itself emphasises that the power of evil is in evidence in the cosmos as well as the power of good, for history becomes an account of the interaction of these forces – of God and Satan, of Christ and AntiChrist, of saints and

---

[202] Adémar, *Chronicon*, 173; Landes, 'Dynamics', 499–503; *Relics*, 165–6, 176; and 'Aristocracy and heresy', 209 n. 117; Moore, 'Property', 194–6.

demons – for influence over creation. Of course this is not dualism in the sense understood by the Bogomils. To orthodox Christians AntiChrist was not eternal but was eventually to be destroyed. But to dualists encountering or travelling as part of increasing east-west traffic in this period, 'The End' was to be a momentous non-event giving rise, as Landes has suggested, to debate, expectation and ultimately disappointment and disillusionment. Western Christians might then seek new answers. At the same time a few in the intellectual elite were debating the relative importance of chastity, in terms of salvation, to different social groups: the lay elite, secular clergy, monks, and labouring Christians. Bogomils, fully capable of infiltrating the circles in which these debates took place as well as lower social levels to which they might filter down, had coherent suggestions of their own to make on the subject, as they had evidently done successfully in the Byzantine empire. Thus we do not only hear of a rejection of the elite life of contemplation or of hostility towards its monks, as might be implied by the reference made at the Council of Charroux to the heresy 'being spread amongst the common folk'. We also hear of the infiltration of abbeys and the recruitment of monks and nuns, threatening the communities of Saint-Hilaire, Conques, an abbey – probably Sarlat – in Périgord, more doubtfully Saint-Léonard, but perhaps even Saint-Cybard and Saint-Martial, given the detailed knowledge Adémar claimed of heresy. They give us examples of belief and practice which, although also ascetic, egalitarian and sometimes anti-clerical, are more typically found in dualist circles in global terms in the period.

Amongst the variety of forms of dissent which faced them a few appear to have made a choice, *heresis*, which not only challenged the very legitimacy of secular and ecclesiastical authority but accounted for the paradoxical behaviour of a loving God who let his creatures suffer so. Such a message might gain purchase in miserable millennial Aquitaine if transmitted deliberately by opportunists. The case for His impotence within creation has its own internal logic and it is not inconceivable that it could be arrived at spontaneously. But the *bona fide* medieval dualists of whom we know tended to arrive at their belief systems through contacts with other groups, and that such a belief in this instance arose as a result of Bogomil contacts is surely possible given the correlation between the sectarians, only beginning with those similarities identified by Dondaine, and culminating most convincingly in the form of prayer noted by Héribert. What was almost certainly a primitive and not always coherent form of dualism from the Balkans must have become even more diluted in the west when the beliefs, experience and social priorities of the recruited initiates are taken into account. We should not look for pure expressions of Balkan dualism, for we certainly shall not find them. But as Brenon has noted of western dualism in general, the origins of the belief and its core doctrine were arguably not as important on a day-to-day basis as the social function which it fulfilled, and dualist theology was thus perhaps 'réel mais non fondamental' to many of its adherents.[203]

---

[203] Brenon, 'Les Hérésies de l'an mil', 22–3, quotation at p. 23.

Advocates of the Bogomil case are thus not envisaging shabby Greeks openly setting up stall beneath abbey walls in the west and declaring the existence of two co-eternal gods . . . and in the local vernacular. The heretics they identify no more did this than they did in the east. None the less, elements of such beliefs were discernible to orthodox clerics after frequent or sustained exposure to the heresy. Some of those thus exposed in the east found it convincing and converted; others reported it to the authorities. I suggest a similar situation in Aquitaine, but with fewer Bogomils, fewer elite converts to protect them, some element of language barrier and, above all, a cautious approach which entailed revealing the whole picture about the heresy only to schooled initiates, as Héribert implies, and its concealment from inquisitive outsiders such as Bernard of Angers, Adémar and Héribert himself. But the evangelising aspect of the heresy seems to have brought it to the attention of authorities equipped and informed enough to identify it as like Manichaeism and to employ an arsenal of weapons, from imprisonment and execution to parody, with which to fight back.

Scholarship in the area of eleventh-century heresy can only be said to have been strengthened by work done to find its origins within the society in which it expressed itself. We are left with a picture of the west in turmoil and hungry for explanations for human misery and appropriate responses to it, a situation in which a variety of 'heretical' ideas could arise. But to me this does not fully explain all the elements contained within the sources and it excludes any influence by Bogomil missions. An agnostic position if not a thorough post-revisionism seems most tenable, even if one concedes only that 'the question [of the influence of Bogomilism on western heretical movements in the eleventh century] seems to me to be by no means closed'.[204]

The question of orthodoxy, 1050–1150

The period in which the west saw the rise of great intellectual currents, the beginnings of the universities and of the scholastic tradition, also gave rise to important clerical reform and moves towards devotional simplicity and spiritual asceticism. Thus, we see Peter Damian, truly radical in his perception of divine distance from the physical world, exploring the personal austerity which came to be adopted also by the Cistercians. But not a few of the period's innovators were branded suspect by theological conservatives. Robert of Arbrissel and his ilk were initially frowned upon as they distanced themselves from accepted monastic models. Those who were rehabilitated and ultimately accepted were allowed this room for manoeuvre more because they did not fall foul of those whose understanding was needed for new ideas to gain currency than because their ideas were inherently less subversive than those who were to be destroyed as heretics. Amongst the acceptable group were some whose understanding of the very indistinct difference between reforming orthodoxy and heresy was what

204 Hamilton, 'Wisdom', 39.

equipped them to fight those who went too far – the rehabilitated Robert of Arbrissel, as we shall see, was employed in the fight against 'real' heresy – whilst Christopher Brooke points out that Peter of Bruys was in the company of radicals as orthodox as Bernard of Clairvaux in attacking the adorned abbeys of Cluny as distractions from worship.[205] It was other features which led Peter to be branded as a heretic and executed, and which have even led scholars to wonder if he was influenced by Bogomils. But most heretics who were to be persecuted for their apparent threat to orthodoxy had much in common with that reforming current which was to dominate successful religious innovation in the period 1050 to 1150.

It has been said that the Gregorian reforms were fuelled in large part by the move towards a more apostolic Church by the heretics.[206] If we deny dualist content in the heresies, this in itself probably explains to a great degree why popular heresy all but disappears from the central decades onwards. Whether or not the eleventh-century heretics were dualists, their converts were surely won in part through various perceived failures of the clergy and addressing this crisis played a large part in eradicating heretical adherence. Questions pertaining to the character and conduct of the ministers of Christ were considered and partly resolved by about 1100 within the parameters of orthodoxy. Lay power over the clergy and over clerical possessions was lessened, and the secular clergy was moved further from worldly concerns. In the monastic sphere, the Cistercians rejected the cosy, collective wealth of the Cluniac order and embraced simplicity, even discomfort, installing themselves in stark abbeys that dominated the wilderness. Some took things even further in terms of the austerity of the communities they established. The hermit monks, even those such as Stephen of Muret, Bernard of Tiron and Robert of Arbrissel who later embraced a coenobitic structure, drew on the experience of the earliest Christian ascetics in renouncing even the cloister to begin with. Several included women and people from humble backgrounds within their spiritual milieu in an attempt to be closer still to the *vita apostolica*, heeding the guidance of the New Testament above that of authors of established monastic rules.

It is in this twelfth-century context that the Grundmann thesis comes into its own, stressing the common heritage and shared idealism of those who were to be seen as reformers, i.e. as orthodox and progressive, and those who would be deemed heretical. Brooke stresses that this movement was characterised by a doctrinal emphasis on the rejection of the physical, not only by a simple life-style, and it is in this rejection that the orthodox and heretical, even the dualist, seem so close. But amongst the most extreme, Peter Damian, whose opinion of the flesh almost appears to deny its creation by the same benevolent force that created human souls, did not consider creation evil, only its, admittedly extensive, corruption. He thus conforms to the model by which Augustine had countered both Manichees and neo-Platonists. He did not deny Christ's

---

205 Brooke, 'Heresy', 148–9.
206 See, for example, Moore, *Origins*, 46, 51.

accommodation of the human condition by coming to earth as a man, the central tenet of Christianity, one which, Brooke notes, he not only accepted but enthusiastically rejoiced in (if he rejoiced in anything).[207]

But there were many deemed beyond the pale on examination by twelfth-century authorities. They represent a wave of heretical outbreaks throughout western Europe, but most concentrated in the north-east of France, the Low Countries and Italy. Many of them, Tanchelm of Utrecht, for example, had once been priests themselves, frustrated at the shortfall in reforming zeal by their bishops. One of the issues over which they frequently fell foul of clerical power was that in addressing the suitability of priests to perform sacraments they strayed too far towards Donatism, denying the effectiveness of a sacrament performed by an unworthy cleric. Others like Eon of the Star, uneducated laymen, responded to the emphasis on New Testament values by identifying with ideas they erroneously believed to lie therein, interpreting the Gospels in some very curious ways. Yet others were more clearly social as well as religious dissenters, challenging, in Italian towns in particular, forms of authority as well as forms of worship. Arnold of Brescia may be seen in this way.[208]

That these incidents occurred partly in response to the perceived shortcomings of the reformers' agenda seems certain. Where expectations were not realised, dissent might follow. However, the interpretation of sources informing us about these heretics has been varied. At one extreme, Grundmann shied away from the idea that their causes were other than religious and their social make-up essentially privileged and clerical, for 'they did not speak in the first instance to the urban population and not primarily to the lower level'. The reason for the acceptance of some and persecution of others depended on the way and circumstances in which they interpreted the *vita apostolica* and how this was viewed from above, for 'there were no heretics in this period . . . who did not assert that they were "true Christians" '. Those who were accepted as such limited themselves to insisting that only ordained priests could serve, whereas 'heretics' insisted that they should also be worthy of their office, thus pushing the reforms further. Other historians responded to Grundmann that heresy was not so much the language of religious idealism as of social and economic conflict, a more secular arena nowhere existing as yet. Grundmann found this approach entirely anachronistic, the result of 'social prejudices' amongst his contemporaries.[209]

Most now interpret sources as indicating that heresies were largely initiated by disillusioned clerics who founded their central tenets but who spoke to and recruited from 'the workless and rootless poor [ultimately in towns], who joined with vigour the attack upon those whom they saw as the sources of their misfor-

---

[207] Brooke, 'Heresy', 153–4.

[208] The best overview of the variety of heresies in this period is still that in Moore, *Origins*.

[209] Grundmann reviewed and responded to the literature on the twelfth century and offers his explanations for what occurred in *Religious movements*, 213–16, 219–21, 227, 231–5, quotations at pp. 219, 227, 232. See also Lerner's introduction to that volume at pp. xxiii–xxiv.

tune'.[210] Thus heresy was not typically the voice of those opposing the clerical caste, but opposing the abuse of the claims it made spiritually and economically (i.e. to the material resources of ordinary Christians, to which the reforms now gave it a moral right). In Moore's eyes the early twelfth-century heresies were indeed born of economic and social change, closely related to the growth of urban life and to the situation of ordinary Christians whose security within the emerging order was uncertain. In many instances the heresiarchs were social and political reformers rather than anti-clericalists *per se* or people who denied central Christian doctrines, something observed even by some contemporaries.[211] But Moore also argues that there were a few genuine heretics in the period who did not want the clergy reformed but deposed. Two in particular proposed coherent alternative doctrines. The influence of Peter of Bruys and Henry of Lausanne, on both popular consciousness and on the clergy who encountered and combated their ideas, was profound and also far from marginal to the history of dualism in the south-west of France.[212]

Peter of Bruys, originally from the Dauphiné where he began preaching in 1112 or 1113, was by 1115x18 operating near Soissons in the district containing the manor of Bucy-le-Long. He was thus a contemporary of other heretics of that area whom historians have suspected were dualist. He had a huge impact in southern France, perhaps helping to sow the seeds of dissent from which Catharism benefited some decades later, and his followers were to be found as far west as the Gascon Pyrenees. Peter was a theological opponent of Catholicism, and Moore notes the relative sophistication and coherence of his teachings, which we know about in some detail as a result of probably the most important single source for heresy before the thirteenth century, Peter the Venerable's *Tractatus contra Petrobrusianos*. A similarity between some of these teachings and those of eastern dualists has been noticed. Peter preached against services for the dead and in general against the mass and the priesthood, and also against the veneration of both the cross and the body of Christ. Indeed, he thought churches and crosses should be destroyed. He also denounced infant baptism and possibly rebaptised adults without water, and rejected the Old Testament. His death, soon after 1131, followed his construction of a huge pile of wooden crosses to be burnt at Saint-Gilles. Local orthodox zealots threw him onto the burning pyre.[213]

[210] Moore, *Origins*, 77.
[211] For discussion of heretics in such terms see especially ibid. 63–81, 115–36. See also Peters, *Heresy*, 62.
[212] Moore, *Origins*, 82–114. We should note also that in October 1079 the heretic Berengar of Tours had made his submission to the Council of Bordeaux: *Chronique Saint-Maixent*, 407. One of the earliest of the scholastics, he denied the doctrine of transubstantiation and accused Pope Leo IX of corruption, but he cannot be said to have affected the laity of Aquitaine significantly, and he was certainly not a dualist.
[213] The *Tractatus contra petrobrusianos* was composed by the abbot of Cluny sometime after his opponent's death, in 1138x41. The best edition is that of J. V. Fearns, *Corpus Christianorum, Continuatio Mediaevalis*, x, Turnhout 1968. See also Fearns's own summary of the heretic's life and teachings and discussion of the source in his 'Peter von Bruis und die

The similarity between Peter's teachings and those of contemporary Bogomils led Brooke to observe that 'it would be unduly sceptical to deny a link' between them.[214] James V. Fearns in particular argued that the style and content of Peter's polemic, his hatred for the cross and possibly his attitude to the Old Testament plausibly had eastern origins.[215] We could also note that, like Bogomils and like Héribert's heretics, Peter was critical of the notion of charity. Possibly this and some other ideas were indeed influenced by Bogomils. However, Fearns does not see Peter as a Bogomil convert *per se* but believes that the time and circumstances were right for some radicals to echo distantly their beliefs, or even to have arrived at these positions independently and coincidentally.[216] Fearns's position is thus not unlike a very agnostic approach to the early eleventh century. But he holds, even if such contacts could be proven for Peter, that '(t)he acceptance of a Bogomil influence does not diminish the significance of the ruling religious climate in the west for the development of heresy'.[217]

In Peter's case this seems sensible, for other features of the heresy argue against it being at all influenced by Bogomils. His denial of the mass was on different grounds to that of Bogomils (he believed that the last supper was not intended to be replicated by Christians but was undertaken by Christ and the Apostles for themselves alone). Unlike both dualist and non-dualist heretics of the period, he places little emphasis on the 'symbolic relationship between [Christ's] life and [that of] his future followers'. Significantly, he does not seem to have believed that His physical manifestation should be understood allegorically. Fearns also notes that it is by no means certain that Peter baptised his followers without water. These followers seem yet a further step removed from contemporary eastern dualism. Peter the Venerable alludes to violence committed on their part and, more conclusively, they outraged Catholics by cooking and eating meat on Good Friday. Fichtenau observes that Peter the Venerable does not refer to dualism on their part even though he was well acquainted with the teachings of historical Manichees. Poly and Bournazel urge us to consider the abbot's observation, addressed to the heretics, that '(y)ou have banished the Latins from the throne and from heaven, but perhaps you spare the Greeks'.[218] But overall the evidence does not incline scholars of heresy

---

religiöse Bewegung des 12 Jahrhunderts', *Archiv für Kulturgeschichte* xlviii (1966), 311–35, esp. pp. 317–26. For an important discussion of the source as part of Peter the Venerable's 'triptique polémique' against the enemies of Christianity on behalf of Cluny, along with his *Adversus judeos* and *Contra sectam sarracenorum*, see D. Iogna-Prat, 'L'Argumentation défensive: de la polémique grégorienne au *Contre petrobrusianos* de Pierre le Vénérable (1140)', in Zerner, *Inventer*, 87–118, quotation at p. 87. See also Moore, *Origins*, 102–7.

[214] Brooke, 'Heresy', 146.

[215] Fearns, 'Peter von Bruis', 327–32.

[216] Ibid. 327, 331.

[217] Ibid. 333.

[218] Ibid. 321–2 (quotation), 329–30; Peter the Venerable, *Tractatus*, 10; Moore, *Origins*, 102–14, esp. pp. 102–7; Poly and Bournazel, *Feudal transformation*, 278–9, 290–2; Fichtenau, *Heretics and scholars*, 58.

to cite Peter as evidence of Bogomilism in the west by the second decade of the twelfth century, whether or not they concede the possibility a hundred years previously.[219]

A heretic rather more rooted in the temporal world, Henry of Lausanne was most successful at Le Mans, where he had begun his heretical career in about 1115, and at Toulouse. Both towns were gaining autonomy in the early 1100s. The latter was arguably prone to dualist heresy in the early eleventh century, and perhaps in this period too. In 1135 Henry recanted his heresy but was preaching again at Toulouse in 1145 when his followers, many of them skilled workers, many of them very important citizens, were confronted by Bernard of Clairvaux. Henry had apparently fled at news of Bernard's approach, and here he disappears from the record. Like many heretics, including dualists, he exploited discontent with the standards set by the authorities and, noted Bernard, the absence of both parochial organisation and regular practice of the sacraments that already characterised the south.[220]

Unlike some who fell foul of the Church for continually pushing the envelope of reform and refusing to accept the limits of what the eleventh-century had achieved, Henry challenged some of the central tenets of reform itself in rejecting the need for a priesthood and the central, mediating and socially dominant role assigned to it by the reforms.[221] In this he resembles dualist attitudes to the orthodox Churches. Like Bogomils, for example, he opposed the confinement of worship to church buildings and denied the utility of monastic prayers for the dead. But Henry was no dualist. He stressed direct communication between the believer and God, a relationship not possible within the universe Bogomils depicted. While Henry denied the right of the Church to sanction marriage, he did not deny the need for the marriage contract but advocated it as something performed amongst ordinary Christians for themselves. The same goes for his view of the other sacraments: he did not reject them, only the monopoly of the priests over them. Also, unlike Bogomils he was deliberately socially subversive in the towns in which he operated, taking control at Le Mans for a time.

Both of these heresiarchs had some degree of success in Aquitaine. It lay *en route* from Maine to the Languedoc and we know that Henry preached in Poitou and at Bordeaux. In July 1154 St Bernard preached against his ideas at Bordeaux itself and also in Périgord and the Cahorsain before doing so in Toulouse. Peter the Venerable tells us that the teachings of both Henry and Peter of Bruys were

---

219 He is not treated in this way by, for example, either Barber (*Cathars*, 31) or Lambert (*The Cathars*, Oxford 1998, 14–16, 41).

220 *Actus pontificum cenomannis in urbie degentium*, ed. G. Busson and A. Ledru, Le Mans 1901, 407–15, 437–8; *RHF* xii. 547–51; *Sancti Bernardi . . . epistolae*, letter 241, in *PL* clxxxv.312–13, and *Sancti Bernardi . . . vita et . . . Gaufridi monacho*, *PL* clxxxii.434–6. For accounts and appraisals of Henry's career see Russell, *Dissent*, 72, 77–8; Moore, *Origins*, 83–106, 108–13. See also M. Zerner, 'Au Temps de l'appel aux armes contre les hérétiques: du *Contra Henricum* du moine Gullaume aux *Contra hereticos*', in Zerner, *Inventer*, 119–56.

221 Moore, *Origins*, 96.

influential in *Novempopulana*, that is to say in Gascony. Clerical concern about the heretics' successes in the archdiocese of Bordeaux was probably what led a papal legate to bring together St Bernard, the bishop of Chartres and Bishop Raymond-Bernard of Agen at a meeting in the city in the spring of 1145, for it was here that Bernard's preaching mission to Toulouse was arranged.[222] The wave of dissent is presumably also the context for the copying in about 1145 of Héribert's letter of *c*. 1000 concerning heresy in the duchy.[223]

Is it also possible that Henry and/or the Petrobrusians might have been influential in the Agenais, part of the archdiocese in question but also part of classical *Novempopulana*? There is some evidence for this in Henry's case. If we assume that St Bernard followed Henry's itinerary exactly the answer is perhaps no, for he did not use the Garonne, the major communications artery in the region. However, we have no actual record of Henry himself in the Cahorsain or Périgord and so it seems most likely that he travelled up the Garonne from Bordeaux to Toulouse. This would have taken him to Agen and, whilst there is no direct evidence of his activity there, there seems a strong possibility, and the presence of bishop Raymond-Bernard at Bordeaux perhaps indicates that he was to undertake preaching against heresy in his diocese to complement the work of Bernard of Clairvaux elsewhere.

The Agenais may in fact have attracted Henry because it had already been home to some unidentified heresy. All we know about this is that Robert of Arbrissel came south to preach against it in 1114.[224] In chapter 1 we saw that this was an uncertain time in the Agenais generally, making it a society in which dissident ideas might implant themselves all the more easily. But in terms of date, this is almost certainly too early to be associated with Peter of Bruys, and his reported influence in *Novempopulana* was also later. It is, however, contemporary with the start of his career and with other heresy at Bucy thought by some to bear dualist traits, and is also a decade and a half after the first possible arrival of Bogomil-derived heresy in the west.[225] However, we know nothing of its content and it is too early and too isolated from the earliest good evidence for dualism in the Agenais in the second half of the twelfth century to be at all convincing on Bogomil activity.

Some attempt at interpreting it, however, may be made. Given the evidence that in the early years of the twelfth century there was indeed a fairly indistinct boundary between reformers and those 'heretics' who were reformers gone too far, we could perhaps attempt to read this frustratingly brief reference in that

---

[222] *PL* clxxxxv.410–11; clxxxxix.721. St Bernard's route appears in map form in Moore, *Origins*, p. xii, and is discussed in Kienzle, *Cistercians*, 91. See also P. Wolff, *Voix et images de Toulouse*, Toulouse 1962, 54; Russell, *Dissent*, 77–8.

[223] We should note also that J. B. Russell observed how dubious was the connection between the heresy of Henry and the letter of Héribert even before the eleventh-century version of the latter was discovered because of how dissimilar the two heresies sound: *Dissent*, 77–8.

[224] *Monumenta conventus tolosani ordinis fratrum praedicatorum*, ed. J. J. Percin, Toulouse 1693, ii. 3.

[225] See pp. 134–5 below.

context. Robert of Arbrissel represented the ultimately acceptable wing of ascetic reform and spiritual renewal that characterised a much wider movement. One sense in which he proved himself an ally of the reforming Church and not, like Henry and Peter, an opponent of it, was in his adoption of the enclosed monastic life for his followers, after some time alone in the forest of Craon and at the head of autonomous eremitic communities with not untarnished reputations. Recruits from all walks of life were welcomed into Fontevriste houses, but the sexes were now safely separated and the communities established along more conservative lines.[226] What, therefore, might have been the nature of those whom Arbrissel, once under suspicion himself, deemed heretical at Agen? Were they, like he had been, fundamentalist adherents of the *vita apostolica* whom conservatives considered a threat? Perhaps the incident reflects his attempts to bring an unacceptable wing of the movement from which he himself sprang into the fold, maybe by challenging the style rather than the content of their heresy. In other words, perhaps he was trying to persuade them to leave behind the itinerant life and take up coenobitic discipline, a central distinction between who was deemed 'heretical' and 'orthodox' in this period according to Brooke.[227] If this was the case, we might speculate that Henry of Lausanne heard of such early radicalism in the Agenais and it seems plausible that his influence indeed extended into the county as local historians there have over-confidently asserted.[228] Whatever the case, as Moore notes and as will be explored in chapters 3–5, the region north-east of the Gascon Garonne, between the Bordelais and Cahorsain, was to be the second strongest arena of Catharism in France.[229]

Bogomilism in the east after 1050

The growth of Catharism in this geographical area was not to occur for some decades, but as a background to it we should give a brief account of the position that the dualists had reached in the east.[230] The removal of political boundaries between Macedonia and Byzantium allowed Bogomils to infiltrate urban and rural monasteries. Euthymius of the Periblepton attests to this occurring in Constantinople and in western Asia Minor. He asserts that by 1050 the heretics had divided the world up between them into zones for conversion. They were more sophisticated doctrinally than those identified by Cosmas the Priest, more articulate in denying divine influence over earthly matter and possessing a more developed form of prayer. From the 1080s the Byzantine government was forced

---

226 See chapter 1 above.
227 Brooke, 'Heresy', 148.
228 See, in particular, Guignard, *Agenais*, 107–8.
229 Moore, *Origins*, 114.
230 For the history of the heresy in this period in general see Obolensky, *Bogomils*, 168–219, and *Christian dualist heresies*, 35–40.

to confront dualism. Most immediately the reaction was against the Paulicians. At Philippopolis they proved a great menace to Christians, according to Anna Comnena, daughter of the Emperor Alexius I Comnenus, and when challenged in disputations they proved as skilled in knowledge of Scripture and in debate as the Bogomils, although they were more ready to convert. Bogomils, on the other hand, lived more covert lives and were harder to detect. Their persecution came later, after they were well established in the Byzantine capital, disguising them-selves in monkish garb and gaining the support of some very high ranking families. Between 1097 and 1104 Alexius imprisoned those who recanted and burned their leader Basil, after which their presence at Constantinople appears to have declined.[231]

To help in his fight against heresy Alexius commissioned the *Panoplia dogmatica* of Euthymius Zigabenus, the most systematic first-hand source for the history of the Bogomils. From this it emerges that the sect at Constantinople believed that Satanael, elder son of God, had created the world and that he imitated his father's heavenly power in the physical realm. He created demons who inhabit water, human bodies and also the relics of saints. The Docetist element of the heresy was strengthened by the understanding that Christ came into the physical world through the Virgin's right ear as the Word. He returned to heaven after taking away Satanael's divine nature and became one with the Father. Thus the Bogomils now more coherently denied the Trinity and redemption through Christ's suffering. Zigabenus attests that converted men and women underwent rigorous instruction and then a double baptism in which the Gospel of John was laid upon the head, once as believers and then once as fully-fledged members of the elect. They then undertook the rigorous life-style described for earlier Bogomil adherents with its chastity, frequent genuflection and prayer, fasting and dietary restrictions, which now explicitly also excluded dairy products and eggs. By this time we know for certain that they believed that when they died they escaped the physical world and went to live with angels.[232]

It has been suggested above that the western reform movement beginning in the mid-eleventh century did away with the need for a message as radical as dualism, for the social fractures into which it had embedded itself began to be healed. In addition, the insecure lot of the unfree, though not significantly ameliorated, was no longer a novel phenomenon, and whatever millennial anxiety existed had passed. This seems to have been a period of expectation and optimism in ordinary circles, even if the majority of the sources which we have for popular demands and desires emanate from the elite. But other explanations also offer themselves for a decline of dualist influence in the context of its emanation from the east. Most obviously, friendly discourse and traffic between

[231] Anna Comnena, *Alexiad*, trans. E. R. A. Sewter, Harmondsworth 1969, 14–15, 141, 463, 496–504; M. Angold, *Church and society in Byzantium under the Comneni, 1081–1261*, London 1995, 496; Stoyanov, *Hidden tradition*, 135–6.
[232] *Patrologiae cursus completus, series Graeco-Latina*, ed. J.-P. Migne, Paris 1857–66, cxxx.1289–332 (extracts in *Christian dualist heresies* at pp. 180–207).

the Churches of east and west was interrupted by the mid-century schism. There were fewer opportunities for Bogomils to conceal themselves in western monasteries, for hostility between the Greek and Latin Churches increased and fewer eastern monks entered the west. It is certainly not the case that diplomatic contact ceased entirely in 1054, and western pilgrims continued to travel eastward. However the route through Serbia and Bulgaria fell into relative disuse from 1064, the journey becoming too dangerous after the Seljuk invasion of Anatolia. It was some decades before the way was again clear for such varied traffic as these routes had and would yet carry.[233]

The first dualists in the twelfth-century west

Dualist churches were established on a large scale in the west in the second half of the twelfth century, but the extent to which they were active before this is open to some dispute. The earliest manifestation of Catharism in the west which is generally undisputed is an incident at Cologne in 1143, to which Everwin, prior of Premonstratensian Steinfeld, alerted St Bernard, noting its eastern origins. This is the earliest incident which Moore will accept as dualist, and he cites increased persecution of the heretics in the east in the early 1140s as the likely cause of their movement. This heresy was of the moderate dualist variety, apparently reflecting the still predominant Bogomil belief that the good God had given rise to evil, although a clearer relationship to Bogomilism may be found in the heretics described by Eckbert of Schönau in 1163.[234]

However, this wave of infiltration may have begun much earlier. In the 1080s, a seventeenth-century source informs us, foreign Arians were in the valleys of Aran and Andorra in the diocese of Urgel in northern Spain, including in a castle called Monléo.[235] We have seen that, like the term Manichee, Arian is not an entirely inappropriate term to apply to Bogomils if it was being used to alert Christians to their teachings against the Trinity, which were becoming more pronounced and coherent in this period. It would appear to have been the term preferred by William of Puylaurens, referring to the Cathar *perfectus* Bernard Raimundi in 1178, and this writer was most certainly familiar

233 Hamilton and McNulty, 'Orientale lumen', 190–3, 206; S. Runciman, The crusades, 5th edn, London 1991, i. 117.
234 PL clxxxii.676–80 (letter of Everwin); cxcv.13–18 (the first of Eckbert's Sermones contra catharos); Annales brunwilarenses, MGH, SS xvi. 727. For Moore see Origins, 168–71, 174, 212–13; Birth of popular heresy, 28; and 'Saint Bernard's mission to the Languedoc in 1145', Bulletin of the Institute of Historical Research xlvii (1974), 1–10, esp. pp. 1–4, 10. Barber gives a good overview of the evidence and historiography of early Catharism in Cathars, 21–33, and important issues in a European context are raised in Lambert, Cathars, 32–44.
235 D. D. Monfar y Sors, Historia de los condes de Urgel, i, reproduced in Collección de documentos inéditos del archivo general de la corona de Aragón, ix, ed. D. Próspero de Bofarull y Mascaró, Barcelona 1853, 354. This reference was discovered by Philip Banks and kindly passed on to me by Bernard Hamilton. Unfortunately Monfar y Sors does not give his source.

with Cathar theology, as was Bernard Gui who used it of Cathars in the early fourteenth century.[236] However the 1080s would be very early for the origins of western Catharism. Between the executions at Goslar and c. 1100 we really have only the examples of the 'heretical' Paterines and the martyred Ramhirdus of Cambrai, who were clearly reformers and certainly not dualists. There is little else at Monléo in content and nothing in its context to allow a serious case to be made that it indicates dualism.

A much stronger case has been made that a wave of Bogomil influence had begun by as early as 1101. The date is deduced by Bernard Hamilton from the words of Hildegard of Bingen, who gives either 1083 or 1101 for the first arrival of Cathars in the west, and the account of the inquisitor Anselm of Alessandria, who possibly indicates a connection with the 1101 crusade of William IX of Aquitaine. Anselm, writing in about 1270, says that Franks who 'went to Constantinople to conquer the land' met there Greek merchant converts of the Bulgarian Bogomils, established a flourishing Latin branch of the dualist faith in the city with its own heretical bishop and then returned home where they established the Bogomil diocese of 'France'. There is no corroborating evidence for this from French sources, and we should note that Anselm is not entirely reliable, believing as he did that the heresy had remained hidden in the east since Mani first preached it there. Lambert in particular disputes that Anselm was referring to the 1101 crusade, and Moore has more general reservations about crusades as a medium for the transmission of the heresy. None the less we still have to account for the observations made by Hildegard and Anselm, and Hamilton's theory ties them together on a sound methodological basis. It must at least be considered plausible, as indeed it is by Barber, that the first Cathar church in the west was founded by crusaders returning from Constantinople in 1101.[237]

Other crusaders may also have come into contact with heretical ideas on the First Crusade or in 1101. On the journey to Constantinople in 1095 the contingents of Peter the Hermit and Godfrey de Bouillon took a route via Bogomil-infested Bulgaria and visited Philippopolis, where Bogomils, and especially Paulicians, were still influential.[238] Normans from southern Italy, Toulousains and Gascons in other contingents also passed through Constantinople.[239] The Lombard, Rhineland and Bavarian-Aquitainian contingents on the 1100–1

---

[236] William of Puylaurens, *Chronique*, 2nd edn, ed. J. Duvernoy, Toulouse 1997, 34–5; Bernard Gui, *Practica inquisitionis heretice pravitatis*, ed. C. Douais, Paris 1886, 235–355 passim; E. Griffe, *Les Débuts de l'aventure Cathare en Languedoc*, Paris 1969, 21–52. See also chapter 3 below.

[237] Anselm of Alessandria, 'Tractatus de hereticis', in Dondaine, *La Hiérarchie cathare en Italie*, AFP xx (1950), 308; Hamilton, 'Wisdom', 43–5, 59–60; Lambert, *Cathars*, 19, 36–7; Moore, *Origins*, 172–3; Barber, *Cathars*, 27–8, esp. n. 62.

[238] Albert of Aix, *Historia hierosolymitana*, in *RHC Occ.* iv. 274–8, 303–9; Anna Comnena, *Alexiad*, 463; *Christian dualist heresies*, 259–60; Obolensky, *Bogomils*, 195.

[239] Raymond d'Aguilers, *Historia francorum qui ceperunt Iherusalem*, trans. J. H. Hill and L. L. Hill, Philadelphia 1968, 16–24; Fulcher of Chartres, *A history*, 72, 77–80.

expedition almost certainly travelled a similar route, the Bavarians and Aquitainians journeying also through Serbia, and Lombards spending the winter of 1100–1 camped outside the walls of Philippopolis. All of them spent time in Constantinople and Asia Minor.[240] We thus see a correlation between the home regions of some crusaders who travelled in lands where the Bogomils were influential and regions which were to receive the Cathar heresy in later years. Bogomils remained active in the city of Constantinople. The Greek Bogomil Church suffered a major blow under Alexius I, but the Cathar-turned-inquisitor Rainier Sacconi informs us of its survival in the city into the thirteenth century.[241] Heretical contacts could also have been made in 1148 for, amongst others, the contingent of Alphonse Jordan, count of Toulouse, and Queen Eleanor's Aquitainian courtiers passed through the capital as part of the Second Crusade, having already visited Philippopolis.[242] The German contingent travelled via Philadelphia, where Sacconi tells us a Bogomil bishopric also operated.[243] But again there is no actual evidence of the transmission of heterodox ideas back to the west in this context.

However, the crusades are not the only means by which eastern heretical ideas might have influenced westerners. Normans encountered Paulicians in 1081 when the heretics fought under the leadership of Xantas and Kauleon in the army of Alexius I. In 1087 the hermit Nilus was discovered by the Byzantine authorities to hold the Bogomil belief that God had two sons. He was dealt with as a dualist, being forced to renounce his beliefs using the same formula as had been previously demanded of Paulicians. Nilus, we should note, had spent some time in Italy. In this same imperial army were Anglo-Saxon refugees from England who had fled after the Conquest.[244] Thus western Christians could still come into contact with eastern dualism through a wide range of circumstances.

The argument for the inadvertent role of the crusading movement in transmitting dualist heresy westwards would be weakened by the fact that there are no universally accepted accounts of the activities of Cathars in the west until the 1140s, implying that the Frankish-speaking mission from Constantinople had been a failure, were it not for four incidents in the intervening years which can perhaps be viewed as hinting at dualism, adding weight to the argument that an open mind should be kept. The first, an outbreak of heresy at Bucy-le-Long near Soissons in c. 1114, and thus conceivably related to the heresy of Peter of Bruys, bears some traits shared with contemporary Bogomilism: the rejection of child baptism and marriage, the mass, the virgin birth, eating of meat and burial

---

[240] S. Runciman, 'The crusade of 1101', *Jahrbuch der Österreichischen Byzantinischen Gesellschaft* i (1951), 3–12; Mullinder, 'Crusading expeditions', 86–131, 286.

[241] Rainerius Sacconi, 'Summa de catharis et pauperibus de Lugduno', in 'Un Traité néo-manichéen du XIIIe siècle: *Le liber du duobus principiis*, suivi d'un fragment de rituel cathare', ed. A. Dondaine, Rome 1939, 64–78.

[242] Odo of Deuil, *De profectione*, 40–61; Runciman, *Crusades*, ii. 260–1.

[243] J. Riley-Smith (ed.), *Atlas of the crusades*, London 1991, 51.

[244] Anna Comnena, *Alexiad*, 141, 160; Poly and Bournazel, *Feudal transformation*, 288; Obolensky, *Bogomils*, 191.

in church grounds. Guibert of Nogent says these heretics were like Manichees, a terminology I hope to have demonstrated does not necessarily discredit the source. The second is a pronouncement of anathema in the third canon of the 1119 Council of Toulouse against heretics who rejected the sacraments and denied the supernatural power of priests. The third is an outbreak of heresy at Ivoy near Trier, not a great distance east from Soissons again, in about 1120. The heresy resembles dualism in that the sect denied the efficacy of child baptism and refused to accept transubstantiation. The source refutes them in what its author believes, incorrectly, to be Augustinian language, and affirms that Christ was born in flesh as though the heretics denied this also. A fourth incident occurred at Liège in 1135 and sounds very similar to what occurred there a century previously, the heretics appearing to lead a holy life, refusing sacraments and prayers for the dead.[245]

Moore is quite right to point out that such concerns had been at the heart of reform and the *vita apostolica* for many decades before they emerge here and so may well reflect this rather than external dualist influence.[246] None the less, there are traits at Bucy in particular which do not quite fit this explanation: rejection of the virgin birth, of the eating of meat and the use of 'Manichee'. Indeed, although again far from certain, this account may even imply a survival of dualism in the region for the 'dregs' of this heresy were once held in ancient times by the educated, says Guibert, and 'sank down to the countryfolk, who, boasting that they hold to the way of life of the Apostles, choose only to read their Acts'.[247] Here then, implicitly, we also have a case of peasants who could apparently read Latin or, in Stock's model, were familiar with and able to utilise Scripture, perhaps in translation, under the guidance of an elect.

Whatever the nature of these early incidents, dualists appear to have recruited adherents in large numbers only from the 1140s. From that decade they spread into Italy and southern France. It seems likely that they proclaimed the truths of the moderate dualist Bogomil Churches at first but, perhaps in about 1167 although more likely 1174–7, were apparently converted to the absolute *ordo* of Drugunthia. The evidence for this is still controversial and will be addressed further in chapter 3. It does however indicate that they were well

---

[245] Guibert of Nogent, *Histoire de sa vie (1053–1124)*, ed. G. Bourgin, Paris 1907, 212–15; *Concilia*, xxi. 226–7; *Gesta treverorum: additamentum et continuatio prima* xx, in MGH, SS viii, 193; *Annales rodenses*, MGH, SS xvi. 711. See also C. Thouzellier, 'Hérésie et croisade au xiie siècle', *Revue d'histoire ecclésiastique* xlix (1954), 855–72, and Hamilton, 'Wisdom', 45. B. M. Kienzle thinks that the 'Arians' discovered by St Bernard at Toulouse in 1145, whilst he was preaching against Henry of Lausanne, may have been Cathars: *Cistercians*, 92, 96. She suggests this because of the possibility that the term 'Arian', used by Bernard's secretary Geoffrey of Auxerre, could imply dualism. Bernard's knowledge of early Catharism, gained over the previous two years, probably makes it unlikely that he would neglect to observe a correlation between the ideas of heretics encountered at Toulouse and those described by Everwin of Steinfeld at Cologne. For debate as to whether Bernard even identified two distinct sets of heretics at Toulouse see Kienzle, *Cistercians*, n. 54.

[246] Moore, *Origins*, 69.

[247] *Heresies of the high Middle Ages*, 103.

enough established at Agen by the latter date to warrant the foundation of a Cathar bishopric in Aquitaine.

Reported incidents of heresy between c. 1000 and the 1140s appear to fall into two groups in several senses. Obviously they are separated chronologically by the decades immediately after the Gregorian reforms, in which we hear very rarely the word 'heretic'. The beginnings of the reform process sounded the death knell for what may well have been early western dualism. It had stressed the rejection of the material world and of the clerical structures which legitimised it, and also added to medieval heresy the rejection of several central orthodox tenets. In this it resembled eastern heretical practice but, like Bogomilism, it was not fully mature in the sense of being able to communicate explicit or coherent reference to the existence of two opposed principles.

By the end of the century, however, the rejection of the world by religious radicals was more typically couched in different terms. The emphasis was on eliminating corruption as far as possible from the lives of both the ordained clergy and of the laity. For a time, indeed, clerical and lay agendas and even those of rich and poor seemed to coincide and be reconcilable in the recovery and defence of the Holy Places. That this triumph, and the creeping disillusionment that followed the erosion of Christian gains in the east, was temporary, and that many of the concrete problems which had shown themselves in the eleventh century remained, may be witnessed by the success of social and clerical reformers; some, like Robert of Arbrissel, whose more egalitarian vision for the organisation of Christian communities found favour and patronage, and others, like Henry of Lausanne, who challenged not only the established structure of such communities but also the claim to authority of those with the power to sanction reform. Above all, a new strand of Christian spirituality emerged as if in response to the deeper message of dualism: the eternal conflict between body and soul. That orthodox Christians were in fact duty bound to address this message seems possible. The crisis it implied had arguably already allowed in the west for the rejection of the physical world as evil in its very incarnation and for the belief in God's impotence within it, as it continued to do in the east.

PART II

CATHARISM, AQUITAINE AND THE AGENAIS, TO 1249

3

Aquitaine and its Cathars, 1152–1207

Bogomils, or at least their teachings, arguably returned to the west as early as 1101. Although there is no universally agreed version of the processes which established the first Cathar churches, by 1143 the heresy was in the Rhineland and consisted of people indigenous to the region, second generation converts, if not third. Their teachings were so similar as to be indisputably derived from the moderate dualism of the Bogomils. By the 1160s Cathars had established themselves also in northern France, Lombardy and the Languedoc.[1]

The Cathar church was not a branch of the Bogomil church however, but a fully independent movement. Lambert notes that in many ways it was more mature and coherent, both in terms of doctrine and organisation. Relations with the east were perhaps maintained to some degree, but were renewed in the 1170s when the Bogomil Nicetas came to the west. His mission had important structural implications for the Cathar church, including the founding of a Cathar diocese of Agen, and most historians regard him also as recruiting western dualists to the absolute dualist doctrine which had been adopted by the Bogomils of Constantinople since the last contact, resulting in schism in eastern Europe and subsequently also in Italy. This evidence and the various ways in

---

[1] The entry of Cathars into the south by this date is supported even by R. I. Moore. His judgement was based upon two pieces of evidence: the 'letter of Héribert' copied into the *Annales de Margam* for the year 1163, and the canons of the Council of Tours of the same year: *Annales de Margam*, in *Annales monastici*, ed. H. R. Luard ((RS, 1864–9), i. 15; *Concilia*, xxi. 1177). He found the contents of the former to be 'suggestive of Bogomilism' in various respects, and the declaration of the Tours canons that a 'new' heresy was spreading from the Toulousain to other parts of the south to add weight to the argument that Catharism first appeared in the region in this decade: *Origins*, 197–9 at p. 198. On the evidence available this judgement was sensible, but so was his desire (p. 199) for better evidence in this context. Conclusions drawn through the body of sources have surely been affected by the discovery in the 1990s of an early eleventh-century version of the Héribert source. The evidence which Moore had found convincing as explicit proof of dualism in the 1160s came from this, not from the canons of Tours, which are far less specific about the nature of what the heretics believed, as are the records of a similar assembly at Lombers in 1165, which in no way attribute clearly dualist belief to the *boni homines* they describe: *Concilia*, xxii. 157–68; Moore, *Origins*, 203. It may therefore be the case that Moore will now reject the 1160s as the earliest evidence for Bogomilism in the south of France and accept only what he considers to be the next clear account, the Saint-Félix source, on which he accepts B. Hamilton's interpretation and dating to the mid-1170s (see n. 83 below). On the other hand, the latter evidence relates explicitly to an already well-established heresy. If Cathars were active by the 1140s in Germany, even by Moore's exacting standards the 1160s still seems a conservative date for the earliest Bogomil successes in the Languedoc. As he in any case notes (p. 198), the Margam annalist would have copied the Héribert source into his narrative of 1163 'where he thought it belonged'.

which it has been interpreted will be addressed in some detail. What seems certain is that with Nicetas's help the Cathars were able greatly to increase their numbers and influence in Occitania.[2]

Catharism and Aquitaine

When Pope Innocent III was elected in 1198 one of his first actions was to write to the metropolitans of Auch and Narbonne instructing them, amongst other things, to challenge the strength of the heresy in their archdioceses, not least in parts of Gascony. This task was in turn entrusted to the bishops of Bazas, Comminges, Lodève and Agen.[3] It was a response to an assertion by many churchmen that the Cathar heresy had been flourishing in Gascony in preceding decades. Several councils reported the fact: Reims in 1148, Tours in 1163 and the Third Lateran of 1179. Chroniclers of the kings of England believed that there were Cathars in Aquitaine, and in 1181 Robert of Auxerre stated that they were 'in Gascogna'.[4]

However, there is no evidence that the bishops of 1198 found tolerance of heresy in Aquitaine, and pontifical directives soon ceased to claim that there were heretics there. Bishop Navarre of Couserans, papal legate from 1207–9, never once mentioned heresy in his diocese. Although there was to be Gascon opposition to the Albigensian Crusade – launched in 1209 against the heretics and their protectors – from Béarn, Comminges, Bigorre and central Gascony, like the attacks which prompted it, it was to have a secular and territorial basis and not one of support for the heresy. We can be reasonably sure that William of Newburgh 'conjured' a heresiarch in Gascony 'out of the air', and Geoffrey of Vigeois's lurid account of the heretical depravity indicates that there was little first hand knowledge of Catharism in the Limousin.[5]

---

2   For the western situation as a whole see Lambert, *Cathars,* esp. pp. 29–44, which is, moreover, excellent in historiographical terms.
3   *PL* ccxiv.71–2; M. Roquebert, *L'Épopée cathare,* Toulouse 1970–89, i. 147–54. Roquebert is a journalist not a historian by training and so his work is unpopular with some historians of the heresy: C. M. Dutton criticises his unscholarly Occitan partisanship ('Aspects of the institutional history of the Albigensian Crusade, 1198–1229', unpubl. PhD diss. London 1993, introduction), whilst others simply do not cite him. I find his investigative technique and methodical cross-referencing of sources illuminating. Perhaps he sometimes extrapolates too much from documents, but his citations are generally sound and so his conclusions can be tested. In addition Roquebert, *L'Épopée* is one of the most thorough accounts of the heresy in southern France.
4   *Concilia,* xxi. 718 (for 1148), 1177 (for 1163); xxii. 232 (for 1179); William of Newburgh in *Chronicles of Stephen, Henry and Richard,* i. 329–30; Walter Map, *De nugis curialium,* ed. T. Wright, London 1850, 62; Gervais of Canterbury, *Opera historica,* ed. W. Stubbs (RS, 1879–80), i. 285.
5   Geoffrey of Vigeois, *Chronica,* ii. 326–7; P. Biller, 'William of Newburgh and the Cathar mission to England', in D. Wood (ed.), *Life and thought in the northern Church, c. 1100–c. 1700* (SCH, subsidia xxii, 1999), 11–30 at p. 20; Dossat, 'Comminges', esp. p. 120. The central

But although churchmen assessed the geographical spread of the heresy incorrectly, they were not entirely wrong to attribute heretical belief to Gascons before 1198 or, more accurately, 1196, for before it passed to the house of Toulouse, the Agenais, infested with the heresy at least since the time of Nicetas's visit, pertained to the duchy. Thus, of the above sources, the 1163 Council of Tours was probably the most accurate in warning that heresy was spreading from the Toulousain into Gascony. In fact the Cathars of Agen were so infamous that they made the duchy of Aquitaine appear doctrinally suspect into the next century; Matthew Paris, discussing events for 1209–13, repeats the suspicion that heretics were in Gascony, and William of Tudela, first author of the *chanson* recording the Albigensian Crusade, says that their influence extended to Bordeaux.[6]

Yet apart from in the Agenais Cathars in fact appear to have had little if any presence in Aquitaine at any point. There still are a handful of possible late exceptions to this pattern. The cleric Yves of Narbonne, who worked for the archbishop of Bordeaux, fled to Italy in *c*. 1214 after denying accusations of heresy, and we have a reference to a 'diachonum haereticorum' of Saintonge who was in the Languedoc in *c*. 1237.[7] Some of the heretics and heretical sympathisers interviewed by the inquisition in the 1230s and 1240s had names implying that their families were of Aquitainian descent, although this does not provide a record of heresy in the duchy.[8] As late as the early fourteenth century, it has been suggested, heretics could conceal themselves in Gascony.[9]

Thus the Bogomil heresy, by now containing many eastern branches although rent by schism by the early 1170s, had travelled as far as the western Languedoc, and the diocese founded at Agen constituted the most westerly outpost of organised dualism. This requires explanation, for in many ways the societies of the Languedoc and Aquitaine were very similar. Linda Paterson has

---

thesis of a work claiming that there were Cathars in Périgord is very unsatisfactory: R. Bordes, *En Périgord: l'hérésie cathare*, Eglise Neuve d'Issac–Castelnaud-la-Chapelle 1996, esp. pp. 77–93, 135–53. Bordes knows that Héribert's letter has been discounted as a twelfth-century source, but cites the following as Cathars in Périgord: those of the Languedoc with Périgordian names, which is not proof of heresy in Périgord, those of Gourdon which is actually in Quercy, 'heretics' at Cistercian Gondon and Cadouin, accusations related to a struggle for control of the abbeys within the order and not to do with doctrine (see Barrière, 'Les abbayes', 94–102), and heretics in the castles of the *faidit* Bernard de Cazenac, for which I find no evidence (see chapter 4 below). He cites failure to act against heresy as the reason for the deposition of bishop Raymond of Périgord in 1210 by the pope, although again no evidence for this is offered.

6 Matthew Paris, *Chronica majora*, ed. H. R. Luard (RS, 1872–83), ii. 554; William of Tudela and continuator, *La Chanson de la croisade albigeoise*, ed. and French trans. E. Martin-Chabot, Paris 1960–72, i. 8–9, 18–19.

7 Matthew Paris, *Chronica majora*, iv. 270–2; Doat xxiii, fo. 135v.

8 Such names include 'Poitevin', 'Gasc', 'Engolesme' and 'de Limoges'. See depositions contained in Doat xxi, fos 168r–169r, 191–3v, 206v, 211v–213v, 227r–v, 286v, 302r; xxii. 17r–v, 23r–v, 29v–31r; xxiii. 108–9; xxiv. 135r–136v, 141r; xxv. 248r–271r.

9 J. Duvernoy, *Le Catharisme*, II: *L'Histoire des Cathares*, Toulouse 1979, 331.

asked 'why should the Cathar heresy have taken such a strong hold in Occitania, or more particularly in the Languedoc?' Moore has pointed out how wisely Henry of Lausanne chose the region between Toulouse, Carcassonne and Albi for his work earlier in the twelfth century, for it turned out to be especially susceptible both to his heresy and to dualism.[10] But Henry had also worked in Aquitaine, with much less success.

A little work has been done previously to establish why Aquitaine was largely immune to the heresy. Dossat noted that the river Garonne separated the lands which accepted the heresy from those that were resistant to it, even though the societies of eastern and western Occitania were essentially the same and offered the same opportunities for heretics, Gascon Comminges being especially Languedocian in orientation. He points to a linguistic difference between Gascony and the Languedoc: outside of Gascony, Gascon was only spoken in Couserans. He concludes that whilst we might therefore expect to find the heresy in the Couserans-Comminges region, its linguistic distinction from the Languedoc means that this was not the case.[11] However, far greater barriers were overcome in spreading the heresy from the Balkans to southern France. Gascon, by this period, was a variant of the Occitan tongue of the Languedoc, and there is no indication that speakers either side of the river had trouble understanding each other.[12] The Garonne was, as we have seen, a major artery for communications of all kinds in the Midi, and was to be used frequently by the heretics who could easily have crossed into Gascony to undertake missionary work had they so wished.

How can we therefore account for the lack of heresy in Aquitaine in the period during which it manifested itself so forcefully in the Languedoc? In spite of a prevailing view that 'il semble assez vain de chercher une explication dans l'inexistence des raisons qui peuvent être invoquées en Languedoc pour justifier la crise',[13] it seems that this is exactly what we should do. Indeed, a study of the relevant features of Aquitainian society with reference to elements that compare or contrast with the circumstances in which Catharism flourished in the Languedoc does perhaps provide a few clues.

The duchy of Aquitaine

Our starting point is the political structure of Aquitaine in the relevant period, which also provides a background to the response of the duchy to the coming crusade. In 1152 Henry, count of Anjou, Maine and Touraine and duke of

---

[10] L. Paterson, *The world of the troubadours*, Cambridge 1993, 336; Moore, *Origins*, 114.

[11] Dossat, 'Comminges', 117–18, and 'Gascogne', 162–8. See also P. Bec, *Les Interférences linguistiques entre Gascon et Languedocion dans les parlers du Comminges et Couserans*, Paris 1968, 24.

[12] B. Guillemain is also unhappy with this explanation: 'Le Duché', 66.

[13] Ibid. 67. See also Higounet and others, *Histoire de l'Aquitaine*, 182.

Normandy, married Eleanor, divorced queen of Louis VII of France and duchess of Aquitaine. In 1154 he became king of England and began to increase his influence over Brittany. Thus, all western France was ruled by the king of England, his territory dwarfing that of the king of France, his lord for some of it. The threat that this posed to Capetian power produced war or truce, as opposed to actual peace, between the rulers of the two lands for the rest of our period.

Internally Aquitaine, like the other Angevin dominions, was rent by the wars waged amongst Henry and Eleanor's sons the young Henry, Richard, Geoffrey and John. Richard did homage to Philip II 'Augustus' of France for the duchy and in 1189 succeeded his father as king of England. In 1190 he went on crusade and on returning in 1192 became the prisoner of Duke Leopold of Austria. John began to plot with Philip Augustus to undermine him. The brothers were reconciled on Richard's release in 1194, but this did not stop Capetian attempts to dislodge him in France. Philip attacked Angevin territories at their weak points, making most progress after Richard's death in 1199 by supporting the claims of Arthur, posthumous son of Geoffrey, against his uncle John in accordance with Angevin law. Crucially, Eleanor supported John. She secured allies amongst the Poitevin lords then did homage herself to the French king for Poitou. She subsequently ceded Poitou to John who formally gave her the whole duchy, including the allod of Gascony, to rule on his behalf as *domina*. The pair thus attached the principality of Aquitaine to the English crown without Philip's approval.[14] But at its highest social level Aquitaine was still far from stable or securely part of any Angevin 'empire' and John was still not free of his complex status as king of England and a prince of France. In 1200 he and Arthur made their peace but the treaty involved John's submission to Philip for his lands in France, an acknowledgement of authority which he was soon to regret. In 1202 the Poitevin Hugh IX 'le Brun' of Lusignan brought to the French *curia regis* a case against John, his lord. John refused to acknowledge Philip's authority in the affair and so the latter declared the Angevin territories forfeit and began the process of conquest. In 1204–5 Normandy, Anjou, Maine and the Touraine were seized, Brittany also passed into Capetian hands, and many Poitevins did homage to Philip. With Angevin authority weakened, Gascon nobles looked temporarily to Castile for leadership. John was able to recover his position in Aquitaine, largely due to the efforts of his Poitevin seneschal Savary de Mauléon and Elie de Malemort, archbishop of Bordeaux (1188–1207). However, his continental possessions were now geographically isolated from England, and the French still

---

14 Robert of Torigny in *Chronicles of Stephen, Henry and Richard*, iv. 240; Gervais of Canterbury, *Opera historica*, i. 513–4, 529; Geoffrey of Vigeois, *Chronica*, 282, 284, 290, 302; J. C. Holt, 'Aliénor d'Aquitaine, Jean sans Terre et la succéssion de 1199', CCM xxix (1986), 95–100; P. Chaplais, 'Le Traité de Paris de 1259 et l'inféodation de la Gascogne allodiale', MA lxi (1955), 121–37. The rulers of Gascony were probably not considered to owe homage to the crown, which was reviving its control over other French princes in this period, because the Basque rulers of Gascony had been invaders and not royal officials who had usurped power from their Carolingian masters: see chapter 1 above, and Higounet and others, *Histoire de l'Aquitaine*, 174–5.

threatened Poitou. From 1204–14 John's priority was the recovery of his lost lands, and even in those parts of the duchy which he still ruled, now from Bordeaux, his authority was weakened.

John's position was partly the result of the traditionally looser structure of authority in Aquitaine compared with the bonds forged in England, Anjou and Normandy. Due to the strength of provincial customs much of the Aquitainian aristocracy was in many ways autonomous. But if it was true in general that in the time of duke Henry 'les grands fiefs . . . étaient trop anarchiques pour être dangereux',[15] John managed to provoke them to serious rebellion. Neither was local loyalty encouraged by John's innovative practice of appointing foreigners to the position of seneschal, and the English knights Robert of Turnham, Hubert de Burgh and Geoffrey de Neville, and Martin Algaïs, a Spanish mercenary, were not well received. Savary de Mauléon was in fact John's only Poitevin appointment.

Thus, although north of the Dordogne most of the major lords were vassals of the duke, they were to assert themselves against ducal power on many occasions, and in Périgord that authority remained minimal. The castellans controlling the frontiers with France, most notably the Lusignans, were prepared to exploit to the full the advantage of their geographical position. This was a tendency John seriously exacerbated when in 1200 he forced the count of Angoulême to give him his daughter and heir Isabella in marriage, although she had already been promised to Hugh le Brun of Lusignan by Richard.[16] Hugh, also count of La Marche, and other Lusignans had been vital to John in securing control of Angevin territories in 1199. Now they were robbed of the prize of Angoulême, and not only did John not compensate them but he confiscated La Marche. This was why Hugh had appealed to Philip Augustus, precipitating the process whereby John lost control of many of his continental possessions. This was not the first or last occasion on which the Lusignans were to play a key role in Anglo-French relations.

Gascony was the region perhaps most likely to be the focus of a Cathar mission, for it was most like the Languedoc.[17] By 1152 it consisted of thirteen virtually independent counties and viscounties and much allodial land, real ducal authority still being limited to the demesne around Bordeaux. Its nobility was still beyond ducal control. Those of the plains, even ducal tenants-in-chief,

---

15 Boussard, *Gouvernement*, 548.

16 Roger of Wendover, *Flores historiarum*, ed. R. G. Hewlett (RS, 1886–9), i. 295.

17 There are few secondary works for the political structure of Gascony in this period. Unless otherwise cited see J. F. Samazeuilh, *Histoire de l'Agenais, du Condomois et du Bazadais*, Auch 1846–7, i. 147–8; M. Bordes and others, *Histoire de la Gascogne, dès origines à nos jours*, Roanne 1982, 61–70; Boussard, *Gouvernement*, 122–55, 226–9; J. Ellis, 'Gaston de Béarn: a study in anglo-gascon relations (1229–1290)', unpubl. DPhil. diss. Oxford 1952, esp. pp. i–v, 24b, 204, 379–84 and appendices; E. Lodge, *Gascony under English rule*, London 1926, esp. pp. 25–6; Cursente, 'Castelnaux', 40, 48–50, and *Des Hommes*, 80–4, 128; and R. Studd, 'The marriage of Henry of Almain and Constance of Béarn', in S. D. Lloyd and P. R. Cross (eds), *Thirteenth century England*, iii, Woodbridge 1991, esp. p. 162.

recognised no legal superiority in the court at Bordeaux. The most powerful amongst them were by now the counts of Armagnac and Fézensac, but fluid social bonds allowed also for the emergence of a dynamic group of barons between the aristocracy and the castellans. Relatively minor families such as the Biran and Marestaing associated themselves with major houses of Astarac, Comminges and L'Isle-Jourdain; others, such as the Montesquiou, began as minor cadet lines and grew in importance, in this case as part of the house of Fézensac. Most successful amongst the newcomers was the house of Albret. Of their exact origins little is known, but Amanieu I (in 1050), Amanieu II (in 1096), Amanieu III (in 1130) and Bernard (in 1140) held the majority of their lands at Labrit in the diocese of Aire. Meagre evidence for their early period reveals that they patronised La Sauve-Majeure in the 1130s. By the mid-twelfth century, however, they too were tenants-in-chief of the dukes and had come to hold estates in the Bazadais and Agenais.[18]

The Pyrenean powers clearly had divided allegiances, being part of the Spanish world as much as that of Aquitaine. The viscounts of Béarn did homage to the duke for Bruilhois, Marsan and Gabardan but to the kings of Aragon for Béarn itself since 1170, and for the Aragonese valleys of Roncal and la Tena. In spite of the fact that in 1187 Gaston VI's homage to Aragon expressly reserved his obligations to Duke Richard, Béarn was in fact allied with the expanding Aragonese sphere in the Pyrenees, and in the viscounty they had all the prestige of independent rulers, such that they could practise rights of justice and coinage like those more usually held by counts. As such the twelfth-century arrangements of loyalty owed much to those discussed in chapter 1 for the eleventh. By the end of our period the viscounts had reformed the administrative and legal processes of the viscounty in their own favour and renewed its *fors* to undermine ducal powers. The counts of Bigorre controlled many castles and *caseux* from their capital at Lourdes. In the early 1190s after the death of Count Centulle III, also a vassal of Aragon, Petronilla, heiress to Bigorre, was given in marriage to Gaston VI of Béarn, increasing the relative power of the viscounts in Gascony. The counts of Comminges spanned the Spanish, Gascon and Toulousain worlds, being vassals of their relatives the counts of Toulouse for the strategically important towns of Samatan and Muret, whilst choosing when and how to ally with the kings of Aragon to improve their position. By the early thirteenth century the count of Toulouse also had influence in Armagnac-Fézensac and Astarac, and the marcher viscounts of Lomagne performed homage to him. Thus we should see the Gascon plains and mountain lordships as very much part of the Occitan world which welcomed the heresy, even though they themselves did not, and note that their place within that world would perhaps inform their response to the northern invasion which the heresy would provoke.

This pan-Occitan sphere was not an alien one to the dukes themselves, for

---

18 J.-B. Marquette, 'Les Albret en Agenais (XIe siècle–1366)', *RA* xcviii (1972), 301–2; *Dictionniare de la noblesse*, ed. A. de la Chenaye-Desbois and others, 3rd edn, Paris 1969 (repr. of 1868–76 edn), i. 276–7.

they were at various times the enemies and allies of the major Languedocian and Pyrenean houses. As we have seen, William IX asserted with some success Philippa's claim to Toulouse, occupied since about 1093 by the house of Saint-Gilles. Louis VII of France did likewise on behalf of her descendant the duchess Eleanor, notably in 1141. However after Eleanor's marriage to Henry of Anjou, Louis supported his brother-in-law Raymond V of Toulouse, husband of his sister Constance of France. Henry consequently entered the Languedoc in 1159 and held Cahors briefly, but was ultimately unwilling to wage war against his suzerain and a truce was agreed in 1162 and renewed the following year. By 1167 Raymond had repudiated Constance and so Henry pressurised the county again until, in 1173, Raymond was forced to perform homage for his county to the Angevins at Limoges. The king of England, as duke of Aquitaine, thus became overlord of Toulouse, this time recognised as such by its counts.[19]

During 1183 the new accord was disturbed. Henry and the young Henry were at war. The king, John and Richard formed an alliance with Alfonso II of Aragon and Ermengarde, countess of Narbonne, whilst Raymond of Toulouse threw in his lot with the young Henry and his Aquitainian allies. In 1188 Richard occupied parts of Quercy held by the house of Saint-Gilles, to which the count retaliated in 1191–2. Raymond V died in 1194 and Richard initiated a peace with Raymond VI, giving his sister Jeanne in marriage to the new count in 1196 with the Agenais as her dowry. It was to be held by Raymond, and his heirs by Jeanne, of Richard and his heirs in return for liege homage by the count. As part of the same settlement Richard abandoned the claim to Toulouse and restored, unconditionally, parts of Quercy and the Rouergue which he had invaded. Thus ended ninety-nine years of intermittent warfare between the dukes of Aquitaine and the house of Saint-Gilles, now their in-laws and vassals for the Agenais. Jeanne died in 1199, but homage was performed again in 1200 by Raymond VI to John.[20]

In the years leading up to the Albigensian Crusade, therefore, we see a strong Anglo-Toulousain alliance which was by implication anti-Capetian. In 1207/8 Philip Augustus apparently told the pope that he was more than happy for a crusade to enter the heretical Toulousain, for the house of Saint-Gilles had

---

[19] Robert of Torigny in *Chronicles of Stephen, Henry and Richard*, iv. 201–2, 225; Gervais of Canterbury, *Opera*, i. 167; Roger of Wendover, *Flores*, ii. 75; Geoffrey of Vigeois, *Chronica*, 318; *HGL* iii. 718–20; v. 29–30, 33, 50; vi. 24–5, 34–5, 38, 41, 51–6 (pp. 53–4 note that Ralph Diceto says that this homage for Toulouse was saving Raymond's homage to the king of France, but speculates that it may in fact have been liege homage); Wolff, *Histoire de Toulouse*, 77–80, 122.

[20] Gervais of Canterbury, *Opera historica*, ii. 432; Roger of Hoveden, *Chronica*, ed. W. Stubbs (RS, 1868–71), ii. 339–40; *HGL* vi. 102–5, 144–5, 173–5, 179–80, 189–91; vii. 22–4; Mundy, *Liberty*, 59–60. No copy of the marriage contract survives but see William of Puylaurens, *Chronique*, 44–7; Peter des Vaux-de-Cernay, *Histoire albigeoise*, ed. and French trans. P. Guebin and H. Maisonneuve, Paris 1951, 17–18, 126. The anonymous second author of the *Chanson de la croisade albigeiose* refers to it in his account (see vol. ii. 73–7) of the Fourth Lateran Council of 1215 where he claims, although there is no supporting evidence, that the agreement was approved by Rome.

greatly offended him: Philip and his father had given it aid against Henry and Richard in the wars before 1196, but Raymond had taken Richard's part against France in 1198 and in 1204 had sent troops to help John at the siege of Falaise. As recently as 1208 the French king had quarrelled with Raymond again because of a visit made by the latter to Otto of Brunswick, enemy of Philip and ally of John.[21] A crusade against Raymond would have predictable repercussions within the broader conflict between John and Philip: a defeat for Raymond would bring French influence into the south, whereas a victory with John's assistance might bring Angevin influence to bear more directly in the Languedoc.

More typically, however, it was not the dukes of Aquitaine or counts of Toulouse but the house of Aragon that was the arbiter of Occitan events. Its influence in 1173 was decisive, for it was a southern alliance formed against Toulouse in 1172, involving both Aquitaine and Aragon, which was largely responsible for the submission of Raymond V at Limoges. In 1183 it tipped the balance of power against Toulouse and the young Henry. Elsewhere in the Languedoc the kings of Aragon were overlords of the Trencavel viscounts of Béziers, leading rivals of the counts of Toulouse. Through a voluntary association with the kings of Aragon, Count Bernard IV of Comminges (1176–1225) was able to realise his ambitions in the Languedoc. In 1181 he and Alfonso II went to war against his uncle and lord Raymond V, and in 1201 he became the vassal of King Peter for Comminges in return for a new fief, the Val d'Aran, which Comminges had been disputing with Bigorre since c. 1143. Through this alliance Bernard also gained the viscounties of Marsan and Astarac and temporarily the county of Bigorre itself. Peter II was a capable politician and eventually sought peace with Toulouse, so that between 1204 and the start of the crusade in 1209 an alliance was achieved by marriages between the two families (although in the case of Raymond VI, this was understood as secondary to his liege homage to the duke of Aquitaine for the Agenais).[22]

The king-dukes had also been seeking allies across the Pyrenees. In 1170 Henry gave his daughter Eleanor to Alfonso VIII of Castile. Her dowry was the whole of Gascony, to be handed over on the death of the duchess Eleanor. In 1204 that time came but John was unwilling to comply, providing an opportunity for rebellion in Gascony. Until 1206 the viscounts of Tartas and Orthez, the lord of Trencaléon and even the bishops of Bayonne, Dax and Bazas supported some nearly successful campaigns by Castile, and it was perhaps only the kingdom's commitment to the Reconquista that saved John from further attempts on the duchy.[23] Thus the influence of other powers within Aquitaine was viable because of a shared Occitan political identity, and Gascony and the

---

[21] PL ccxvi.127; William of Tudela, Chanson, i. 98–9; HGL vi. 185–6, 271; A. Luchaire, Innocent III, Paris 1905–8, ii. 125.

[22] HGL v. 52–3; Higounet, Comminges, i. 34–48, 73–89; Roquebert, L'Épopée, i. 166–7, 171–4; Mundy, Liberty, 52.

[23] Robert of Torigny, in Chronicles of Stephen, Henry and Richard, iv. 247; R. V. Turner, King John, London 1994, 124, 130.

Languedoc, including their Pyrenean regions, had very similar societies. Similar, that is, but not identical, and it is perhaps in the differences between these neighbours that the clues to their different approaches to religious diversity lie.

Aquitainian society *hors du Catharisme*

In essence, and to generalise, two related features distinguished the Languedoc from northern France and made it susceptible to heresy: its decentralised political structure and its looser forms of social cohesion. A complex and fluid network of allegiances existed in place of the more clearly recognised hierarchies and obligations of the northern and royal lands. The greatest powers formed 'an aristocracy without vassals', for they did not command military support from those lesser lordships with whom they allied, the latter forming a patchwork of competing castellanies between whom counts and viscounts could not always arbitrate. This situation resulted in part from Occitan family law, which favoured partible inheritance, and the resultant features of noble poverty and the economic unviability of systems of dependence based on the landed fief. Indeed competition for land, or more specifically its revenues, made for frequent local warfare and the predominance of paid military service as opposed to that resulting from the performance of homage for an estate, a system which could define and contain private wars in the north. A frequent cause of conflict was control of the administration of tithes, and so the Church itself and those dependent on it were often the target of military activity in the campaigning season and of the brutality of the discharged *routiers* pillaging the countryside in the winter. The poor, if they looked to the Church for reassurance, found it largely worldly and indifferent to their spiritual and physical well-being. It was also almost exclusively aristocratic and male in its recruitment. As a consequence, anticlericalism was widespread amongst the powerful and powerless laity in a society typified by material insecurity and social disquiet: a perfect breeding ground for religious dissent. Into this came a heresy from the Balkans which was quite indifferent to the theft of property from the Catholic Church. Indeed, it shared many of the criticisms of those in opposition to and neglected by it. Unlike the monasteries, it gave expression to the vocation of women and men irrespective of social status, it welcomed the patronage of aristocratic heiresses and, I suspect, offered the poor a better explanation for their misery and clearer path out of it than that offered by ill-educated parish priests. At the same time the autonomy of *castra*, small fortified communities, allowed new and dissident ideas to flourish if the lesser nobility who protected and influenced them were themselves tolerant or sympathetic. We shall see that the minor nobles of such communities were, from the outset, the most important protectors of heresy in the northern Languedoc.[24]

24 Of the many modern accounts of the medieval Languedoc as a context for the rise of heresy, the works on which this chapter most depends are Moore, *Origins*, 232–7; Roquebert, *L'Épopée*, i. 95–126; J. Sumption, *The Albigensian Crusade*, London 1978, 15–31; Paterson, *World of the troubadors*, 66–89; Magnou-Nortier, 'Fidélité et féodalité', quotation at p. 476;

Many of the features of Languedocian society which encouraged support for the heresy were also present in Aquitaine. Most obviously, the western and eastern counties of southern France shared a language, Occitan, unique to them, to whose speakers the northern French *Langue d'oïl* was alien, and which predominated over Latin in legal and other profane literature. South of the Garonne a Gascon-Béarnaise form was spoken, whilst between the Garonne and Blaye, Ruffec and Périgord, and in the Limousin and the Auvergne, a mixture of Occitan and northern dialects had evolved. Aquitainian court life was cultured, intellectual, cosmopolitan and liberal by comparison with many parts of France. The noble code of *paratge* dominated court life as far north as Poitou. Northern, clerical and ethical concepts of knighthood were largely absent in that most noble of pastimes, warfare. The soldier's income was still frequently supplemented by mercenary activity, the castellan's by raids on

Mundy, *Liberty*, esp. pp. 60, 203; P. Wolff, 'La Noblesse toulousain: essai sur son histoire médiévale', in P. Contamine (ed.), *La Noblesse au moyen âge, xie–xve siècles*, Paris 1976, 154–74, and *Histoire*, esp. pp. 36, 58, 118, 201, 206–7; J. Given, *Inquisition and medieval society: power, discipline and resitance in Languedoc*, Ithaca–London 1997, 5–9; M. Humbert-Vicaire, 'L'Action de Saint Dominique sur la vie régulière des femmes en Languedoc', CF xxiii, 219–40; Mousnier, 'Grandselve'. See also Barber, *Cathars*, 55–70. Barber challenges (pp. 60–3) the view that the clergy did little to oppose heresy or to promote popular orthodoxy, although there is little evidence of them intervening in the northern Languedoc until it was too late. Likewise he challenges (pp. 63–8) both the traditional view of the towns of the region as attaining communal status especially early in a European context, and that the nature of large-scale urbanisation in any case played a major part in allowing the growth of heresy. Although B. M. Kienzle's study of the region adheres to a more traditional view of the rise of its urban centres, she too is sceptical about the relationship of cities and the rise of the heresy: *Cistercians*, 38–9, 47–8. T. Bisson has sought to moderate the picture of weak social institutions and bonds by emphasising the survival and institutionalised growth of the eleventh-century peace movement: 'The organised peace', 215–36. However, the legislative initiatives on which he draws as evidence of a move towards a Catholic and peaceful hegemony rather strengthen the impression of continuing disorder and abuse of secular power, against which they were reacting, as argued by R. Bonnaud-Delamere whose views he disputes ('Légende des associations de la Paix', BPH [1936–7], 47–65). The *routier* problem was so bad by the turn of the century that it ranked as highly as heresy in papal complaints about the Languedoc and, according to William of Tudela, was the cause of the excommunication of Count Raymond VI of Toulouse in 1209: PL ccxv.1166; William of Tudela, *Chanson*, i. 14–15; H. Tillman, *Pope Innocent III*, trans. W. Sax, Amsterdam–New York–Oxford 1980, 240. An Italian source, overlooked in English until recently, highlights that the picture of a lawless Languedoc lived on in the memories of unfortunate Italian merchants forced to travel through it: A. Vauchez, 'Les Origines de l'hérésie cathare en Languedoc, d'après un sermon de l'archevêque de Pise Federico Visconti (1277)', in *Società, istituzioni, spiritualità: studi in onore di Cinzio Violante ii*, Spoleto 1994, 1023–36, cited in Lambert, *Cathars*, 41. The extent of the appeal of Catharism to women is still a moot point: see most recently Lambert, *Cathars*, 152, where it is argued that women did not independently adhere to the heresy but followed their families and husbands. Whilst it is undoubtedly true that families were important in the recruitment of believers of both sexes, the fact remains that women in the twelfth-century Languedoc wanting a life of religious observance could, with few exceptions, only enter the heretical life: CF xxiii. 217–37, 299–309. Examples of such women show them influencing as well as being influenced by male relatives.

neighbouring estates. This tendency was, if anything, increasing, and as far north as the Loire the *chevauchée* was favoured over 'chivalrous' warfare.[25]

Income from noble estates was low in areas where partible inheritance was still the predominant means of transmitting family property. This practice, influenced by that of the Aquitainian ruling families as well as those of Toulouse, was widespread even in Gascony in this period. It is enshrined in the laws of Soule in an act of 1170. The castle and lands of Durfort supported the families of its three co-heirs by 1215, and the Montesquiou family and others in Fézensac and Astarac, previously generous to the Church, seized back donations in the twelfth century to provide for heirs and fortified requisitioned churches in order to prepare for warfare against their neighbours. Although essentially still castle-based, Gascon nobles sometimes lived in towns or married into commercial families. Indeed, most noble revenues in Gascony were derived, directly or indirectly, from the trading community. This activity strengthened the links between Gascony and the Toulousain with which much trade was transacted. The nobility of Gascony thus played a supportive role in the growing urban assertiveness of the Languedoc, appearing frequently in urban charters, and also profited by levying *péage* on goods transported through their lands.[26]

Urban life, though it came late to Aquitaine, became relatively vibrant from the late eleventh century, and towns in the duchy began to aspire to political independence. Geoffrey of Vigeois attests to the growth in confidence of the urban elites in the Limousin, and the *bourg* of Saint-Martial in Limoges itself was administered by *consuls* from early in the twelfth century. Poitiers briefly proclaimed a commune in 1138, and Bayonne, Dax and Saint-Gaudens achieved partial economic and political autonomy. In the far north of the duchy too there was a shift from a castle-orientated society to one which was becoming more urbanised.[27]

---

25 The secondary works that in general reveal most about Aquitaine in this context are Higounet, *Comminges*, i. 40–8, 51–66, 85–9, 339–41; *Aquitaine*, at pp. 160–73; and 'Nouvelle Approche sur les bastides du sud-ouest aquitain', in his *Paysages et villages neufs de moyen-âge*, Bordeaux 1975; Paterson, *World of the troubadors*, esp. pp. 63–115, 141–5, 175–85, 241–55, 324–7; Bull, *Knightly piety*, 1–20; Barthélemy, *Vendôme*, esp. pp. 724–35, 749–70; Cursente, *Des Hommes*, esp. pp. 157–62, and *Castelnaux*, 29–49; Beech, *Gâtine*, esp. pp. 42–70, 125–7; Debord, *La Société laique*, 323–6; Ch. Petit-Dutaillis, *Les Communes françaises: caractères et évolution des origines au XVIIIe siècle*, Paris 1947, 155–7; Bonnasie, *Slavery*, 1–59, 104–31, 355–7, 382–92; Lodge, *Gascony*, esp. pp. 152–5, 189–223; Shaw, 'Ecclesiastical policy'; Samazeuilh, *Histoire*, i. 219–20; Higounet, Renouard and others, *Histoire de Bordeaux*, iii. 22–35; R.-H. Bautier, *The economic development of medieval Europe*, trans. H. Karolyi, London 1971, 79–86; Boussard, *Le Gouvernement*, 178–92, 247–51; R. Crozet, *Villes d'entre Loire et Gironde*, Paris 1949, 39–78; L. Papy, *La Côte atlantique, de Loire à la Gironde*, Bordeaux 1941, ii. 15–16; Petit-Dutaillis, *Les Communes*, esp. pp. 117–21; Favreau, 'Loudun', at pp. 163–4; Collins, *Basques*, 238–41; Mousnier, *Gascogne toulousaine*, 94–8, 102, and 'Grandselve'; Boutruche, *Seigneurie*, 146, and *Une Société provinciale*, 53–71, 113–16.
26 *Cartulaire de Sorde*, 179; *Cartulaire de l'abbaye de Berdoues*, ed. *l'abbé* Cazauran, The Hague 1905, 91, 104, 110, 116–17, 120–2, 192, 448; *Cartulaire de l'abbaye de Gimont*, ed. *l'abbé* Clergeac, Paris–Auch 1905, 16, 18, 35, 82, 135, 137–8.
27 Geoffrey of Vigeois, *Chronica*, 284, 308, 313–14, 317–18.

Secular authority in Aquitaine, as we have seen, was decentralised and patchy even under the Angevins. Justice was still often dominated by local custom rather than by the ducal court, so that disputes were settled by the peer group of the interested parties. This sometimes involved violent feuding, considered perfectly legal and proper process. Legal bonds between individuals were weak and temporary and ill-defined alliances were the commonest form of social relation. Because of land-hunger, not least that resulting from the inheritance of unviably small plots of family land, the period did see a partial shift from allodial land-holding to that involving some service or responsibility. Yet there was no established framework for the duration or nature of services rendered and the term *fevum*, fairly common terminology by this period in texts from the Languedoc, was rarely employed in Gascony (*casal* perhaps carried some of the same connotations, but neither of these terms had an implicitly understood type of tenure or service, and property held in this way appears in many cases to have been regarded as simple payment and to remain allodial). Thus, 'until the thirteenth century the whole of south-west Aquitaine was virtually foreign to ties of obligation or dependence'. Not least, it seems that land actually became increasingly allodial in Gascony and also in Saintonge, Périgord, Angoulême and the Limousin, for the concept of the fief is decreasingly employed in charters of alienation after 1050.[28]

As in the Languedoc the real victim of warfare was the peasantry, for armies mobilised by either public or private authority supported and amused themselves largely by plunder. And who was to stop them? The Church had ultimately failed to moderate the behaviour of the Aquitainian soldiery in spite of the earlier success of the Peace movement. The Church in Gascony was relatively insignificant, the province of Auch comprising even in the later twelfth century a collection of ten unimportant sees. Until the 1170s the archbishopric of Auch was the family property of the counts of Armagnac. When the election of Géraud de Labarthe (c. 1172–92) brought independence, lands pertaining to the see were decimated by the aggrieved Count Bernard IV. Archbishop Bernard III de Montaut (1200–14), whose election never had the approval of Rome, was so negligent of the pastoral needs of his flock in this period when heresy was flourishing in the neighbouring Languedoc that the pope was to demand his resignation. At parish level, in spite of reform in the last century, the clergy was frequently the beneficiaries of nepotism. Often they appear to have had little knowledge of the Church's teachings and to have been ill-suited to ministering either to the spiritual or pastoral needs of the poor. Cistercian monasteries were responsible for the displacement of peasants on established holdings and the transformation of those not entering the order as *conversi* into day-labourers. Other monasteries exacted as harshly from their tenants as any lay lords, and bishops were the resented recipients of tithes much of the peas-

---

[28] Paterson, *World of the troubadors*, 19 (quotation).

antry could ill-afford to contribute. As a result, anti-clericalism was common amongst the poor.[29]

The poor were also still largely excluded from religious life in spite of the ideals of some early twelfth-century reformers. Indeed, the new abbeys were amongst those most closely associated with aristocratic piety at its highest level and foundations such as that at La Rochelle by Eleanor of Aquitaine in 1180 epitomised this relationship; Fontevrault became the family abbey of the Angevins and by the 1170s Grandmont was supported by endowments from both the dukes of Aquitaine and the French kings. In both the role played by the humble laity became less significant. After the death of their founder Gérard de Sales, simple autonomous Geraldine hermitages either became larger, and wealthier, Benedictine abbeys – for example Fontdouce in Saintonge – or formed family groups under the authority of a house such as Cistercian Cadouin in southern Périgord (Cadouin was itself Geraldine when founded in 1115, but became Cistercian in 1119). Etienne d'Obazine found his ultimate inspiration in La Grande Chartreuse and formed a larger coenobitic community on a Cistercian-inspired model. Significantly, there were still few religious outlets for women south of the Loire. At the point when Catharism was gaining strength, the new monasticism had already reached its peak in Aquitaine, with the foundation of probably only two houses accepting women in the archdiocese of Bordeaux between 1150 and 1215 and one in that of Auch. The Cistercians only formally associated female houses with their order after 1213.[30]

Thus we find in Aquitaine many of the same characteristics of the society in which Catharism was successful; weak central government, a culturally adventurous nobility thriving on warfare, towns which were socially fluid and cosmopolitan, anti-clericalism amongst a vulnerable peasantry, and frustration of the religious aspirations of the ordinary laity including women. But when we look beyond this superficial and generalised picture we find that many important features necessary for confessional diversity were missing.

Perhaps the most striking contrast between Aquitaine and the Languedoc is that its highest authorities were actively orthodox and largely co-operative with ecclesiastical authorities. Duke Henry had little formal influence over archiepis-

---

29 *Cartulaires Sainte-Marie d'Auch*, i. 113; GC i. instr. 163–4. Constance Berman argues that the traditional concept of early Cistercian landlords having opened up wilderness for settlement and cultivation is incorrect, and that established farmland was taken over by them and its tenants displaced: *Medieval agriculture in the southern French countryside and the early Cistercians*, Philadephia 1986, 11–60.

30 *Chartes de Fontevrauld concernanat l'Aunis et La Rochelle*, ed. P. Marchegay, Paris 1858, esp. pp. 130–6; Venarde, *Women's monasticism*, 10–11, 142, 192–205; Barrière, 'Les Abbayes', 74–85; Porter, *Compelle intrare*, esp. pp. 71–99; J. Verdon, 'Les Moniales dans la France de l'ouest au xie et xiie siècles', CCM xix (1976), 247–64, and 'Recherches sur les monastères féminines dans la France du sud au ixe–xie siècles', AM lxxxviii (1976), 117–22, 127–8; S. Thompson, 'The problem of Cistercian nuns in the twelfth and early thirteenth centuries', in D. Baker (ed.), *Medieval women* (SCH subsidia i, 1978), 227–52; C. Douais, *Les Frères prêcheurs en Gascogne au xiiie et xiv siècles*, Paris–Auch 1885, 17–19, 282–93; Hutchinson, *Hermit monks*, 51–90.

copal elections to Bordeaux, but when he exercised it informally the result was often good partnerships with prelates. Although he tried unsuccessfully to influence an election in 1158, he was decisive in that of Hardouin, dean of Le Mans, to Bordeaux in 1162, and this new ally campaigned against Toulouse on his behalf in 1164. William de Temple, abbot of Reading, another ducal nominee and ally, was elected to Bordeaux in 1173 and supported Henry against his sons. There is less evidence of ducal influence at Auch, a much less important office. None the less, its bishops were willing ducal officials and allies; Gérard de Labarthe was justiciar and chief chaplain on Richard's crusade, Bertrand de Montaut of Lectoure (1162–74) worked closely with Henry and was an opponent of Thomas Becket. Indeed, the king's quarrel with the archbishop of Canterbury did not jeopardise his relationship with the Aquitainian bishops in the slightest.[31]

When heresy was infiltrating the Languedoc, the Aquitainian bishops can have been sure that Henry would support them if Cathars entered the duchy for in 1166 when a group of about thirty continental dualist *Populicani*, a heresy thought by many to have been related to Catharism, were discovered in England, it was the king who took the initiative, commissioning an episcopal synod to try them. When the synod handed them over to the crown for punishment, they were beaten, branded and cast out into the snow. Royal legislation followed in the same year: article 21 of the Assizes of Clarendon forbids Christians from giving succour to condemned heretics. This constituted the first secular legislation against the heresy anywhere in Europe and influenced the form of the imperial and papal decree *ad abolendam* of 1184.[32]

In 1178 Henry also acted against heretics and their defenders in the Languedoc at the request of his vassal Raymond V of Toulouse. He sent bishops Jean de Bellesmains of Poitiers and Reginald of Bath to Toulouse with the papal legate Peter of Saint-Chrysogonus (also known as Peter of Pavia) in a mission sanctioned by Pope Alexander III. To protect them Henry sent a vassal of both Aquitaine and Toulouse, Raymond II of Turenne. The delegation confronted Bernard Raimundi, the Cathar bishop of Toulouse, and the *credens* Peter Maurand. The bishop of Bath then excommunicated Roger II Trencavel,

---

[31] Benedict of Peterborough, *Gesta regis Henrici Secundi*, ed. W. Stubbs (RS, 1867), ii. 110. Geoffrey of Vigeois even tells us that the martyr intervened to aid the king's army against the Scots: *Chronica*, 319.

[32] William of Newburgh in *Chronicles of Stephen, Henry and Richard*, i. 131–4; *Councils and synods, I: AD 871–1204*, ed. D. Whitelock, M. Brett and C. N. L. Brooke, Oxford 1981, ii. 923–6; *Select charters from the beginning to 1307*, ed. W. Stubbs, Oxford 1913, 145–6, 173; Moore, *Formation*, 111, and *Origins*, 182–3. Moore, however, notes differences between the Oxford heretics and Cathars: *Origins*, 183–5; *First european revolution*, 160–4. M. Lambert's observation that Paul instructed that heretics, twice warned, should be shunned (Titus iii.10) may shed some light on the shape the legislation took. In 1210/11 at least one Cathar was reported in London, and burnt: *De antiquis legibus liber . . . cronica maiorum et vicecomitum Londoniarum, 1188–1274*, ed. T. Stapleton, London 1846, 3; Ralph of Coggeshall, *Chronicon anglicanum*, MGH, SS xxvii (1885), 357 (RS, 1875, 121–5); Borst, *Die Katharer*, 103. Biller, 'William of Newburgh' adds important discussion of English knowledge about heresy.

viscount of Béziers (who had imprisoned the Catholic bishop of Albi and was more accommodating to the Cathars than the count of Toulouse). In fact he was openly challenged in the names of the kings of France and England, two monarchs who had no political authority over him. Thus this mission, with the threat of physical force, should be seen as a precursor to the Albigensian Crusade.[33]

A second exception to the generalisation that Aquitaine and the Languedoc were very similar is that the nobility north of the Dordogne began slowly to reform its inheritance practices in favour of male primogeniture in our period. In the Gâtine of Poitou, for example, a practice emerged whereby the estate remained essentially intact and was passed to the eldest brother of the deceased. Women in Poitou consequently inherited less property. This was exacerbated by the shift from an 'aristocratic' to 'ecclesiastical' model of marriage, resulting in a loss of control of dowry lands by women. The case should not be overstated. Even by the 1250s the titles and lands of the house of Turenne were claimed by rival daughters of previous viscounts Raymond IV and Boso III, until a royal judgement divided the lands between them. Thus neither female succession nor partible inheritance was dead north of the Dordogne, but both were being successfully challenged. Women may have been losing their inheritance rights in parts of Gascony too. In the period before 1050 some important castellanies were inherited and held by women; Marie de Esconboeuf brought the castles of Marmont and Tourecoupe into her family through marriage to Hugh de Panassac and Guillaume-Raymond du Brouilh, and the castle of Estang was held by Alemane d'Estang in the second half of the eleventh century. But male primogeniture was adopted by families in Comminges during the twelfth century. By 1256 *caseux* were typically inherited by elder sons who had most rights when it came to disposing of family property, as reflected in an entry in the cartulary of Sorde. Bernard, Pierre and Pons de Condom donated property at Vieilaigue (modern Grenade-sur-Garonne) to Grandselve. Their sister Guillemette approved this alienation but does not seem to have been a co-owner herself.[34] Thus some of the economic causes of instability on which the heresy throve in the Languedoc had been ameliorated in Aquitaine to some

---

33 Benedict of Peterborough, *Gesta*, i. 198–202; Roger of Hoveden, *Chronica*, ii. 155–66; *HGL* vi. 78; Duvernoy, *Catharisme*, ii. 219–29. This was the start of an extensive military involvement against the heresy by the house of Turenne, whose viscounty spanned the Dordogne from Brive to Souillac and Saint-Céré: 'Documents relatifs à l'histoire de la maison de Turenne', ed. A. Vaissière, *Bulletin de la Société historique et archéologique de la Corrèze* vii (1885), 312, 330–2; *Dictionnaire de la noblesse*, 256–7; Roquebert, *L'Épopée*, i. 239–40; ii. 110–13. For recent discussion of their relationship with the Angevins see also *Miracles of our lady of Rocamadour*, 77–9, 81. See also chapter 4 below.

34 *Cartulaire de Sorde*, 60; *HGL* viii. 1799; Beech, *Gâtine*, 42–70, 98–9; J. A. McNamara, 'Victims of progress: women and the twelfth century', in K. Glente and L. Winther–Jensen (eds), *Female power in the Middle Ages*, Copenhagen 1989, esp. pp. 28–33; G. Duby, *Medieval marriage*, trans. E. Forster, Baltimore 1978; B. B. Rezak, 'Women, seals and power in medieval France', in M. Erler and M. Kowaleski (eds), *Women and power in the Middle Ages*, Athens, Georgia–London 1988, esp. pp. 65–6; 'Documents de la maison de Turenne', 313–15, 347–9.

extent, not least in Comminges, and by the same process we find women unable to patronise independently the orthodox religious, let alone the heretical.

Thirdly, in spite of the undoubted growth of urban life, a result of demographic growth and land hunger which was a feature of Aquitaine as much as of other parts of France at this time, it cannot be justly compared with that of the Languedoc. The duchy was far less urbanised and at a later date, none of its centres attaining consulates as early as Béziers (1131) or Narbonne (1132). In addition, although the economy of the duchy was almost entirely centred on towns – La Rochelle and Oloron in the north and Bordeaux and Bayonne in the south dominated the lucrative river and sea transport of wine and salt to England, Brittany and Flanders, and the import of wool – their prosperity was dependent on the dukes and not achieved at their expense. The best trade in wine, for example, occurred at times when the Angevins were at war and had troops to support. Urban elites thus had an economic interest in the political ambition of the Angevins. In 1173–4 La Rochelle aided Henry against Richard, for it was Henry who offered access to markets throughout the Angevin territories. And it was specifically in this context of support for Angevin authority that towns won political autonomy; Bordeaux's first customs were conceded by Eleanor and confirmed by John in 1199 because its support was needed against Arthur, further liberties were granted when it closed its gates to Alfonso of Castile in 1205–6 and a commune was recognised 1224 when it refused to submit to Hugh of Lusignan. Bayonne, Dax, Oloron, Niort, Poitiers and Saintes were also granted communal status under the Angevins for their loyalty. In the Languedoc, in contrast, urban independence was exacted at the expense of the seigneurial prerogative. Toulouse offered its economic resources in 1141, 1159 and 1188–9 in exchange for concessions from its counts extending as far as self-government by a consulate. Urban prosperity in Aquitaine thus lay in identification with conservative priorities, perhaps explaining why town life was less liberal and tolerant than in the Languedoc at a comparable date; Jewish moneylenders, persecuted in southern France as elsewhere in Europe, were more oppressed in Aquitaine than in the Languedoc, and the customs of Bordeaux eventually decreed that anyone found guilty of heresy would immediately lose their burgess-ship.[35] Catharism thrived in many urban centres in the Languedoc and its advocates often experienced great freedom of speech in them. It is difficult to imagine a Cathar being able to preach in the conservative centres of Aquitaine, let alone make converts there. In any case, it is the support of lesser nobles in urban centres that is emerging as most significant in the rise of Catharism, not the existence of large and autonomous mercantile centres in themselves.

Fourthly, many communities in the Aquitainian countryside managed to resist the erosion of free status and even to improve their condition. The

---

[35] Robert of Torigny, in *Chronicles of Stephen, Henry and Richard*, iv. 282; *Rotuli litterarum patentium*, i, ed. T. D. Hardy, London 1835, i. 36; *Livre des coutumes de Bordeaux*, ed. K. Barckhausen, Bordeaux 1890, 445, 518.

francaus of Entre-deux-Mers held allods over which the only higher authority was the duke himself, and he provided protection in exchange for a payment, rendered communally, which was considered neither as rent nor payment in lieu of military service. Legal freedom and freely held land could also be attained by immigration into *castelnaux* and *salvetats*, the predecessors of the *bastide*. Established by the Church since the second half of the eleventh century, the duchy had far more of these than the Languedoc. They were built in regions subject to attack by soldiery, such as the Bordelais, ravaged in 1179 by Basque, Navarrese and Flemish mercenaries, Périgord, where peasant holdings were attacked by discharged *routiers* during periods of fighting between Toulouse and Aquitaine in 1183–5, and the Limousin, where Brabançon mercenaries provoked an organised defence by the population in 1192. These communities were granted a degree of communal self-government. Again, therefore, we find communities who very much identified with the interests and values of the orthodox authorities in Aquitaine.

In contrast, some communities defined themselves by their distance from higher authority. In the valleys of the Gascon Pyrenees survived villages never subjected to the *ban* and influenced instead by the Basque-Navarese law codes of the free. The *fors* of Soule stated that its inhabitants were 'free and of free status without any stain of servitude'. Those of Bigorre indicate that its inhabitants were answerable only to the count and could bear arms in self defence even against knights. In such self-governing communities authority rested with *baziaus*, village assemblies. These were dominated by those who held the most land. Usually this meant the eldest male heir, for Basque family law, and primogeniture with it, survived here. It also allowed for a daughter to inherit if there were no sons. However, if a man married an heiress he took on her family name, for most important of all was the transmission of land intact within one family. Thus the strict observance of family law was the very basis of authority in the Gascon Pyrenees: these laws invested property and the legitimacy of marriage with great economic and psychological significance, values antithetical to Catharism. In addition we should note again the inherent conservatism of the heads of some *casal* communities in Gascony, themselves free but acting as agents of the *ban* over their servile neighbours, and their identification with the values, noted above as Catholic, of the social elite they aspired to enter.[36] Thus we find that in many subtle ways the society of Aquitaine was developing along different lines from that of the Languedoc in the twelfth century, which may well have had an important impact on the extent to which the Cathar heresy would be received if heretics had attempted to carry it there.

In addition to these differences, and perhaps more important than all of them, is the fact that since the eleventh century the Church in Aquitaine had been able to confront and eliminate heretical tendencies, most recently that of Henry of Lausanne, and eventually to distinguish them from orthodox radicals

---

[36] The *fors* of Soule are cited in Lodge, *Gascony*, 189, and those of Bigorre in Cursente, *Des Hommes*, 91, 159, where discussion can be found at pp. 157–62.

like Robert of Arbrissel. In challenging attitudes to the vocation of women and the poor, the new movements fulfilled some of the important social and spiritual roles later played by the Cathars in the Languedoc. There was indeed a decline in interest by the new monasteries in simple lay piety and so it would be going too far to say that the new monasticism revolutionised the relationship of the Church to the vocation of the laity. None the less, a model channel for the expression of simple piety had been firmly established, and that path was orthodox.

The Gascon nobility often proved notable benefactors of abbeys within and beyond the counties south and west of the Garonne, although it was still only in Comminges and Couserans that the religious life was relatively healthy. In these counties, Fontevriste daughter houses of Lespinasse were established and Bernard IV of Comminges was a generous patron. J. Duvernoy has noted that the Fontevriste presence goes some way towards explaining the lack of heresy in these very regions in which historians once expected to find it. We should also note that Comminges had seen by far the biggest increase in Gascony of abbeys belonging to older orders. The Benedictine dependants of Lézat were well patronised after its reform in 1073, Cistercian monasteries abounded there by the mid-twelfth century and a prestigious new abbey, La Bénisson-Dieu, daughter house of Bonnefont, was founded at Nisors between 1180 and 1184. The knightly orders had a strong presence in Comminges too from about 1114 and in Couserans from 1176. It is hard to imagine Cathars infiltrating such houses or having success in the communities they dominated. When, in an astonishing show of defiance against its abbey in 1208, the town of Saint-Sever in Aire underwent what has been termed a revolution and renounced political and economic domination by the monks – refusing to pay fees and dues to the abbey, blockading it against those who tried, declaring municipal authority, symbolically raising a rival bell-tower and even levying taxes on the abbey – there is no evidence of heretical attempts to take advantage of the rebellion and not one accusation of incorrect doctrine levelled against the rebels, who in any case accepted the unfavourable ruling of the papal legate, Bishop Navarre of Couserans on the matter.[37]

North of the Dordogne the new monasticism had had a huge and well documented impact. By 1149 Fontevriste houses had 4–5,000 nuns. Venarde has shown that although the demand for female monasticism increased in proportion to the numbers of propertyless unmarried women, such women chose the religious life for themselves and were not typically coerced by their families. In contrast with religious apathy of the leaders in the Languedoc, the support of bishops and of noble families had been vital in this trend.[38]

[37] Duvernoy, *Catharisme*, ii. 196; Dossat, 'Comminges', 122; Barrière, 'Les Abbayes', 84–5; Mousnier, 'Grandselves', 109–10; B. Cursente, 'Une Affaire de non-hérésie en Gascogne, en l'année 1208', in Zerner, *Inventer*, 257–62.
[38] See, for example, charters and donations to the new abbeys in *Recueil des actes d'Henri II*, esp. vol. i/1, nos xxiii–xxx; i/2, nos xxv, cxxv, cxxxii, cxliii, ccxliv, cclxxviii. See also M. Faye,

It thus seems possible that from an early date the Fontevriste movement in Aquitaine had been catering for the vocation of a social group from which the Cathars made some of their most prestigious conversions in the Languedoc, aristocratic women. These, as other evidence has indicated, had fewer resources at their disposal with which to patronise any variety of religious life. The only house in the Languedoc which came close to offering noble women and the poor of both sexes a similar orthodox outlet, Prouillé, founded near Fanjeaux by Dominic Guzman, was not established until 1206. This was far too late to prevent heresy taking root, but Dominic does appear to have looked to accommodate the religious vocation of social categories that the Fontevriste houses served in other regions. The women at Prouillé lived an enclosed existence and did not preach, in contrast with both male Dominicans and Cathars of both sexes, and the foundation was never patronised as extensively by the native nobility as by the northern crusaders. None the less, Prouillé was approved of by the southerners, and when lands seized by the Albigensian Crusade and handed over to the Church began to be retaken by the southern party in the 1220s those pertaining to this abbey were left untouched. The Franciscans may have consciously noted that female houses undermined heresy, for of the twenty-five houses they founded for women in western Europe before 1260 most of them were in regions containing Cathars. The Cistercians also first accepted women in this period when the order was in close contact with Catharism and its supporters.[39]

The reformers had thus removed some of the causes of grievance which had enabled Catharism to thrive in the Languedoc and, as their foundations did not challenge Catholic doctrine or ecclesiastical power, they were acceptable to the secular authorities whose worldliness they had sought only to escape, not to destroy, and whose patronage they had come to accept. Because of this, and because some of the economic causes of warfare had lessened, the Aquitainian Church shaped aristocratic understanding of religious issues. We should not imagine that the Aquitainian nobles never attacked church property. The abbey of Grandselve's complaints of thefts from monastic lands included those by the ill-disciplined retinues of some of the same Aquitainian nobles who at other times patronised it, even those of the viscounts of Turenne, themselves great allies of the Church. But the nobility of Aquitaine now rarely waged war on the clergy, and one of the most impressive mobilisations of Gascon soldiery was for a religious cause, Richard's crusade of 1190, on which at least sixteen lords, including Bernard of Armagnac, Bernard of Bezaume, Gaston of Béarn, Pierre of

'Notice sur le monastère de Montazai, de l'ordre de Fontevrauld', *Memoires de la Société des antiquaires de l'ouest* xx (1853), 120–8; P.-R. Gaussin, 'Y a-t-il eu une politique monastique de Plantagenêt', CCM xxix (1986), 83–94; and, especially, Venarde, *Women's monasticism*, 84, 91–132, 152–5.

39 Humbert-Vicaire, 'St Dominique', esp. pp. 221–5, 133–6; Roquebert, *L'Épopée*, i. 189–92, 491–4; Lambert, *Cathars*, 132–3; Venarde, *Women's monasticism*, 171–5; Thompson, 'Cistercian nuns', 227–52.

Castillon, Guillaume of Mont-de-Marsan, and Amanieu d'Albret, led contingents in the company of leading clergy and abbots of Aquitaine.

Because both the religious and secular establishment had already made a distinction between acceptable innovation and dangerous heresy, Cathar missionaries to Aquitaine would perhaps have been judged by all sections of society in the context of these two models. The exception to this is the Agenais, part of Aquitaine until 1196 but home to Cathars from the 1170s at the latest.

The Agenais and its Cathars

In 1152, when Henry of Anjou became duke of Aquitaine, he assumed the title count of Agen. Although little is known of the region's early administration under the Plantagenets, it seems very likely that they installed seneschals to govern it.[40] Economic concessions were soon made to Agen itself, an indicator of the importance of the Garonne towns to the security of the frontier between Aquitaine and Toulouse, not least because the house of Toulouse disputed the Aquitainian claim to the Agenais. To resolve this conflict Duke Richard gave his sister Jeanne in marriage to Raymond VI in 1196, and so although the counts of Toulouse became vassals of the kings of England the Agenais itself moved further into the world of the Languedoc. By 1207 it was divided into twelve *bailliages* under the immediate authority of its first Toulousain seneschal, Hugues d'Alfaro, a Navarrese mercenary captain to whom Raymond gave his natural daughter Guillemette in marriage. The seat of the seneschalsy was Richard's castle Penne d'Agenais on the Lot.[41]

Perhaps one reason for the dearth of documentary evidence on the ducal administration of the Agenais is the fact that the bishops of Agen continued to have the most immediate influence. Their possession of the *comitalia* meant that, like his predecessors, Bishop Elie II de Castillon (1149–82) was count of Agen in all but name when Henry assumed the actual title in 1152. Elie was probably from Castillon-en-Couserans and was appointed from the chapter of Saint-André de Bordeaux. We shall see that he took steps against what he considered some kind of heresy in the 1150s. In 1158 he was called back to Bordeaux to arbitrate in the dispute over the election of the new archbishop. His judgement in this matter undermined the attempted interference of the duke. Perhaps as a result, in around 1174 he found Henry uncooperative when he petitioned him to transfer the benefices of Saint-Caprais to Saint-Etienne at Agen. None the less, when Duke Richard conferred the *comitalia* on Bishop Bertrand de Béceyras (*c.* 1183–1209) in 1190–1 it still entailed the exclusive right to

---

[40] Ducom assumes this to have been the case: 'Essai', i. 283. This is logical because when the Agenais and Aquitainian-held Quercy were again governed by Toulouse seneschals were appointed to them. The office was essentially alien to the Languedoc and so it seems likely that it was inherited from the ducal administration, which employed seneschals widely elsewhere.
[41] Boussard, *Gouvernement*, 148–51; Burias, *Guide*, 35; Ducom, 'Essai', i. 273, 282–8.

mint *Arnaudines*, to administer justice and receive the revenues thereof in the diocese, and to raise various other moneys in a secular context.[42]

Not all the clergy originating in the Agenais were as dynamic as Bishop Elie. Given the major political and religious events in the Agenais, the episcopate of Bertrand de Béceyras was unremarkable. His most notable activity in defence of orthodoxy took place outside the Agenais, for he apparently went on the Third Crusade with Duke Richard. A famous clerical scandal took place during his episcopate. Bernard de Rabestans, archdeacon of Agen, became bishop of Toulouse through fraud and was deposed in 1205.[43] Thus in the period around the turn of the century, after heretics had already established themselves in the county, its ecclesiastical and secular authorities were only as capable, or incapable, of challenging the subversion as those of the rest of the Languedoc. But this does not enable us to explain how the heresy had originally become established in the Aquitainian county.

Thomas Bisson observes that 'even in the twelfth century the men of the Agenais were understood to form a kind of regional community, with common rights and responsibilities'. The clearest expression of this, he says, was the *cour d'Agenais*, a secular body which consisted of representatives of Agenais villages and approximately twenty significant towns and one hundred and fifty nobles. It would convene at Agen when convoked by the count or his seneschal. This, says Bisson, was the institutionalisation of local customary practice that recognised responsibility to, but also some autonomy from, the region's higher authorities. He asserts that it began in Duke Richard's day, initially to support him militarily but also to offer advice and to arbitrate amongst its members. Bisson's argument for a twelfth-century *cour* is based on the implication of regional responsibility in certain articles of the general customs of the Agenais, not least common liability for military service and regional regulation of relationships relating to land-holding and inheritance. The earliest reference to such articles is in the customs of Marmande, the earliest extant copy of which claims that they date to 1182. Such was the emphasis on this regionally constituted body that oaths of homage from individual nobles and towns to the counts of the Agenais are unknown until the imposition of northern practices by the crusaders in the next century.[44]

However, Bisson may have inferred too much from the contents of early documentation in asserting that the origins of the *cour* lay in regional tradition and in the twelfth century. The origins of the customs of Marmande in 1182, and thus the early date for the articles relating to the Agenais, have been called into question by Jacques Clémens who argues convincingly that the mention of

---

42 Ducom, 'Essai', esp. i. 294–318; Labénazie, *Annales d'Agen*, 47, 50–3.

43 William of Puylaurens, *Chronique*, 48–9; *PL* ccxv.682–83; Samazeuilh, *Histoire*, i. 219–20; Roquebert, *L'Épopée*, i. 150–1, 180.

44 T. N. Bisson, 'The general court of Agenais in the thirteenth century', in his *Medieval France*, 4–11, 29, quotation at p. 4; P. Ourliac, 'Note sur les coutumes successorales de l'Agenais', *Annales de la faculté de droit d'Aix* xliii (1950), 253–8. See n. 55 below for the customs of Marmande.

a *cour* is a mid thirteenth-century interpolation.[45] It does seem likely that, as in the thirteenth century, early seneschals of Agen had the power to convoke gatherings of its lords and to summon an army.[46] However, even if the articles cited by Bisson imply the existence of a general court, which Clémens is surely correct to dispute, such a body probably did not exist by 1182, not least because the *cour* is nowhere mentioned until 1212.[47]

Bisson's hypothesis of political self-identity relies heavily on the assumption of a homogenous culture throughout the Agenais. This might in turn lead us to expect to find a unified response to heresy within the region. Neither of these appears to have been the case, and frequently the opposite is true. Indeed, in seeking to understand the religious preferences of the people of the Agenais, we should note that Gascon, Toulousain and Poitevin-Aquitainian influences met and overlapped in this region and produced a very diverse society.

The southern third of the Agenais was distinct in many ways from its northern portion. By the mid-twelfth century the region spanning the Garonne's broad fertile plain and extending into Bas-Quercy formed a region of assarted agricultural land and commercial towns which the foreign crusaders were later to find a more pleasant environment than the area to the north, consisting of wooded hills and river gorges like those of the Lède and the Canaule, and dotted with castles and tiny settlements dominated by those of the river Lot. These contrasts in environment and settlement meant that the Agenais of the Garonne had a great deal more in common with Bas-Quercy. Indeed, it has been observed that the pre-Revolutionary demarcation of the 'Agenais' and 'Bas-Quercy' is in many ways arbitrary and that the region stretching from Marmande into the Aveyron, Tarn and Garonne basin were self-defining *pays de la moyenne-Garonne*. This association is reflected in the treaties of mutual support struck between the towns of the two regions after they began to gain self-government, notably the ports of Agen, Mas-d'Agenais, Marmande, Porte-Sainte-Marie, Montauban, Moissac and Castelsarrasin. Thus the Agenais was neither homogenous nor clearly defined in geographical or economic terms, and parts of it associated most immediately with places beyond its political boundary: Bas-Quercy in the case of the towns of the Garonne, and in the case of the Lot parts of Haut-Quercy brought into the Aquitainian sphere (the Cahorsain by Henry in 1159 and by Richard from 1188 to 1191, and even Cahors itself until the settlement of 1196). Indeed, on several occasions after 1196 Quercy and the Agenais were administered by a single seneschal.[48]

---

45 Clémens, 'Cour', 69–80.

46 Ducom, 'Essai', i. 283.

47 Clémens, 'Cour', 72; Samazeuilh, *Histoire*, i. 187.

48 *Archives municipales d'Agen: chartes première série (1189–1328)*, ed. A. Magen and G. Tholin, Villeneuve-sur-Lot 1876, nos xiv–xix; AD, Lot, F 97, 104; *HGL* iii. 810–11; vi. 174; vii. 22–4; Robert of Torigny, in *Chronicles of Stephen, Henry and Richard*, iv. 201–2; P. Deffontaines, *Les Hommes et leur travaux dans les pays de la moyenne Garonne (Agenais et Bas Quercy)*, Lille 1932, esp. pp. 1–8, 247–56; *Inventaire des archives municipales de Cahors*, ed. E. Albe, i/1, Cahors 1998, 36; Clémens, 'Cour', 69–70.

Cultural distinctions, in contrast, are most notable either side of the Garonne. A linguistic mapping of the region reveals the presence of a distinct subdialect within Occitan extending from just south of the abbey of Blasimon in Entre-deux-Mers into the Lot region and down towards Agen. It was a dialect closer to that of Quercy and the Languedoc, but even containing elements of medieval French. South of the river, however, the dialect was more obviously Gascon.[49]

In contrast to Bisson, I find that the people within the Agenais do not in fact appear to have assumed a distinct regional identity. The towns of the Garonne and the seigneuries of the Lot were very different from each other in their orientation. The bishops and the orthodox nobility north of the Garonne presented only the veneer of an institutionally Catholic hegemony. The powerful Gascon lords south of the river were both actively Catholic and had little to do with Agenais political life. These differences are very important when we examine the way in which the region reacted to heresy.[50]

None of the towns of the Agenais were thriving commercial centres by the standards of Bordeaux or Toulouse, but some of the ports on the right bank of the Garonne were amongst the largest and most important of the *pays de la moyenne Garonne*. Land-owners adjoining the river were becoming increasingly aware of its economic potential. Thus in 1210 Honor de la Tour and her husband Gaubert de Pis were attempting to undermine the right of Grandselve to import salt along their stretch of the river without paying duties for it, a right granted to the abbey, argued Bishop Arnaud de Rovinha (1209–28), by Richard I.[51]

Agen and Marmande both contained busy mercantile communities, collecting *péage* and developing their own consular authorities, and resisting most other secular interests except for those permitted to the clergy by the

[49] H. Guiter, 'Limites linguistiques dans la région bordelaise', in *Actes du 104e congrès des Sociétés Savantes*, Paris 1981, 65–7; Esquieu and others, *Agenais occitan*, 11–12, 23–7; Verger and others, *Agen*, 433; J. Séguy, *Atlas linguistique et ethnographique de la Gascogne*, Toulouse 1954–6, for example vol. i, maps 4, 11, 25, 33; ii, maps 275, 296; iii, maps 704, 741, 761, 778, 786.

[50] Information about the major towns and lordships of the Agenais comes from the following books and articles, except where otherwise cited: *Coutumes d'Agenais*, ed. P. Ourliac, AM lxxiv (1962), 241–53; Labénazie, *Annales d'Agen*, 5–53; Clémens, 'Cour'; 'L'Espace coutumier d'Agen au moyen âge', RA cix (1982), 3–19; 'La Coutume d'Agen au xive siècle', RA cxiii (1986); and 'La Maison de Béarn', 303–11; Bisson, 'General court'; Ducom, 'Essai', i. 194–200, 288–94, 319–20; ii. 133–234, 319–20; Guignard, *Agenais*, 100–6; Baumont, Burias and others, *Histoire d'Agen*, 38–50; Higounet, *Paysages et villages neufs*, 325–34, and *Le Développement urbain et le rôle de Marmande au moyen-âge*, Agen 1952, 1–5, 14; Ricaud, *Marmande*, 7, 35, 41–3; A. Lagarde, *Notes historiques sur la ville de Tonneins*, Agen 1882, 6–9, 12, 38–9; Samazeuilh, *Histoire*, i. 147–58, 186, 219–20; J. B. Delrieu, 'Les Puits de Richard-Coeur-de-Lion à Penne', RA i (1874), 181–9; Marquette, 'Les Albret'; J. Lacoste, 'Le Château de Nérac', RA iv (1877), 193–8.

[51] HGL viii. 1853–4 (see also pp. 1828, 1834, 1848, 1855). For discussion of such rights pertaining to Grandselve and other Cistercian abbeys in the region see Berman, *Medieval agriculture*, 82–3.

counts and those of the counts themselves. The articles of the customs of the town of Agen itself were conceded in 1196–7; significant economic rights were granted by the duke, the limited authority of its consuls was recognised and the town's seal was issued.[52] These privileges were not all new, for the charter confirms some exceptions to comital power already in existence, and in 1189 the town had been granted the right to finance and build a bridge.[53] The charters of 1189 and 1196–7 thus provide us with a picture of a town that was economically and communally assertive. The greatest economic wealth, however, was that of the chapter of Saint-Caprais, and there is evidence by 1216 that its dominance was resented by the townspeople, expressed over the charges made for performing religious ceremonies and the size of wine measures sold by the canons.[54] The bishop too, in spite of his own extensive economic and judicial powers, was somewhat alienated politically from the town, having no say at all in the running of the commune in spite of the homage performed to him by the consuls.

The next most important town on this stretch of the Garonne was Marmande, with strategic importance for the control of the river. It was established by the dukes of Aquitaine although its exact origins are a matter of some debate. This is not made easier by the uncertainty of the original wording and date of its customs. The earliest extant version of these, claiming to have been based on an older version conceded by Duke Richard in around 1182, dates from 1340.[55] What is certain is that by the late twelfth century this was a relatively thriving town for the Agenais, home to numerous mercantile and noble families and a monastic priory, protected by walls and a castle. By the outbreak of the Albigensian Crusade it dominated the very border between the lands of Toulouse and Aquitaine.

The towns of the more hilly region through which the river Lot ran were *castra*, fortified settlements, often with a small castle, dominated by local seigneurial families (who, we might speculate, did not trouble much with a literate administration, for secular records pertaining to them are few and far between and originate almost exclusively in the chanceries of higher authorities). One of the most important was the de Rovinha family. Their origins are uncertain. During the thirteenth century they acquired numerous titles, but in the late twelfth century they seem simply to have been lords of Casseneuil, which nestles low in the gorge where the Lède meets the Lot, and also of Tonneins-Dessus, just above the meandering confluence of the Lot and Garonne.

The first reference we have to a de Rovinha is to Racinto-Bernard de *Roviniano* who, at Agen in *c.* 1185, witnessed a charter of Duke Richard in

---

52 *Chartes Agen*, no. ii.

53 Ibid. no. i. This bridge was not completed until the late thirteenth century.

54 Ibid. nos iv, v.

55 *Coutûmes de l'Agenais*, I: *Les Coutumes du groupe Marmande: Marmande, Caumont, Gontaud, Tonneins-Dessous, La Sauvetat-du-Dropt*, ed. P. Ourliac and M. Gilles, Montpellier 1976, 5.

favour of the abbey of Candeil (Tarn).[56] The next is to Raymond-Bernard de Rovinha and his son Centulle, who co-operated in 1197 with an abbot Guillaume, exempting his monks from *péage*. This charter most likely refers to the abbey of Grandselve, and is perhaps the oldest record of a branch of the family at Tonneins-Dessus.[57] The most famous members of the family are Agen's bishop Arnaud de Rovinha and his brother Hugues, lord of Casseneuil, the family's most important seigneury in the period and one that was possibly held of Raymond VI of Toulouse.[58] There was apparently little love lost between this fascinating pair and in 1209 the former was literally to declare war on the latter. Perhaps their animosity had some origin in family politics; we can only speculate. What is certain is that Arnaud was determined to rid the Agenais of the Cathar pestilence and that the crowded *castrum* of Casseneuil had, under Hugues's protection, become a major, if not the major foyer of heresy in the Agenais.[59]

In spite of the dearth of documentation relating to the towns of the Lot valley, we also know a little of another family connected with Casseneuil. Séguin de Balenx was to be in charge its defence in 1209 and 1214.[60] *Balencs* itself was situated somewhere in the *bailliage* of Monflanquin, north-east of Casseneuil on the Lède, a region which was arguably the earliest in the Agenais to be infected by the heresy. A woman, Hartemanda de Balenx was to feature in the records of the inquisition. The close association of the family both with a lord who was sympathetic to the heresy and their activity in its defence – very typical for the Languedoc in this and later periods, but for which the sparse evidence provides few clear examples for the Agenais – makes this an early example of one means by which heretical lords protected themselves from the enemies of the heretics in James Given's schema.[61] By drawing servants, retainers and clients into relationships with the heresy, they built networks of support also for themselves. Given discusses this most obviously for the inquisitorial period, but because of the difficulty faced by authorities of the region in raising military support, a result of the fluid and indistinct bonds that bound fighting men to each other, mutual implication in the heresy can only have helped strengthen such ties in this earlier time of crisis also.

Neighbouring Tonneins-Dessus was Tonneins-Dessous. This was controlled by another family, the Ferréols, present in the town since ancient times (Tonneins supposedly takes its name from the fifth-century Frankish official Tonnantius Ferréolus). They would appear to have been owed some sort of homage for Tonneins-Dessus from the de Rovinhas, rendered at least in

---

56 *HGL* viii. 388.

57 Ibid. 1849. In 1289 Ranfred de Montpezat followed the earlier example of a Raymond-Bernard de Rovinha of Tonneins and Auterive (alive in 1261) who had exempted Grandselve from *péage*: ibid. viii. 1878.

58 A. Cassany-Mazet, *Annales de Villeneuve-sur-Lot et de son arrondissement*, Agen 1846, 49.

59 Peter des Vaux-de-Cernay, *Histoire*, 198–9.

60 William of Tudela, *Chanson*, iii. 341.

61 A central theme in his *Inquisition*.

symbolic form by the presentation of thirteen bread rolls on a silver dish. The family had some influence at Gontaud also in the early thirteenth century, and elsewhere in the Languedoc, and was to be involved in the coming wars.[62]

Sainte-Livrade was apparently less heretical than some towns on the Agenais Lot. The lord of Madaillan, a leading vassal of the bishop, was also a lord of Sainte-Livrade, and it was one of the few towns of the area containing a monastic foundation. The town was never attacked in the Albigensian wars. Instead, the abbey hosted the crusader army for some time and there an important document was drawn up by the northern party in 1214. Apparently the only notorious heretical sympathiser was Guillaume Amanieu. His goods were confiscated because of his belief before 1214 and on 13 April of that year were given to a relative, Pons Amanieu, who did homage at Penne d'Agenais to Simon de Montfort, the crusade's commander. Guillaume was not a *perfectus* however, at least not in 1217 when he helped to liberate Toulouse.[63]

Penne d'Agenais was the most significant political centre on the Agenais Lot. When Henry II pacified Richard in 1173 with a portion of the Aquitainian revenues, the latter immediately used them to set about building this fortified town and castle high above the river, later known locally as *castrum regum*. It was granted after 1196 to Hugues d'Alfaro by Raymond VI as the administrative base of the seneschalsy, and the lord of Fumel, a vassal of Agen's bishop for other lands, also controlled property in its town.

In general terms, as elsewhere in the Languedoc, nobility in the Agenais was defined far more clearly by land-holding than by birth, and property ownership within towns as well as in the countryside conferred great status.[64] Yet this would only seem to be true as a generalisation north of the Garonne. The estates of the left bank were dominated down the years by minor local and major Aquitainian dynasties holding towns and estates there because they pertained to their titles and they could exploit them, not acquiring *noblesse* through urban activity. The lords on this side of the river were also most actively Catholic. Those of Caumont had a very close relationship with the abbots of Grandselve, donating property to the abbey in the late twelfth and early thirteenth century and allowing its monks to transport goods unhindered along this rural stretch of the river. The viscounts of Lomagne also had influence south of the Garonne and as lords of Auvillars on the right bank.[65]

The viscounty of Bruilhois remained the largest and most important estate in the Agenais. Its somewhat confusing history – it was held at different times by the viscounts of Béarn and the Aquitainian de Faye family – has been clarified by Clémens. An act of King John of 1199 recognises Raoul de Faye as its viscount, and so we see that it did not pass to Toulouse with the rest of the

---

62 *HGL* viii. 308, 363–4, 411–12, 789, 846–7; G. Tholin, 'Notes sur la féodalité en Agenais au milieu du XIIIe siècle', *RA* xxvi (1899), 77.
63 *Catalogue des actes de Simon et Amaury de Montfort*, ed. A. Molinier, Paris 1874, 78.
64 See Mundy, *Liberty*, 9–13.
65 *HGL* viii. 1795, 1816, 1849, 1854, 1857; William of Tudela, *Chanson*, iii. 139 n. 5.

Agenais. In c. 1170 the viscounty had been granted to Raoul's father of the same name, uncle of Duchess Eleanor and seneschal of Saintonge in 1163. Yet by 1193/5 Bruilhois had evidently been transferred to Gaston de Béarn, who founded there the abbey of Laplume. This transfer, Clémens demonstrates, probably occurred in 1183. In the 1190s however, Gaston fell out of favour with the Plantagenets, as did the powerful Boville family of the Agenais with whom he was associated. It was in an attempt to limit rival power with the Agenais, therefore, that one of John's first acts as ruler of Aquitaine was to re-allocate Bruilhois to the de Faye family. As part of this process in which the Bovilles were undermined, their castle of Castilou, near Agen, was also destroyed.[66]

Other Gascons, Bernard (c. 1140) and Amanieu IV (1174–1209) d'Albret, had influence in three major towns in the Agenais. It is unclear how the family acquired rights at Casteljaloux, but by the time Amanieu IV made his will, in the year he died, they had overcome the claims of the bishop of Bazas, although by the late twelfth century Bishop Galhard de Lamothe (1186–1214) still shared some power with them there. At Meilhan they were at least co-lords by the end of the century, and in 1200 Amanieu IV granted an exemption from *péage* there to the monks of Grandselve. It also seems likely that another lord of the town, Fort Guillaume de Meilhan, was an Albret. The town of Nérac was theoretically the possession of the monks of Condom, having been granted to the abbey by the sister of the Arnaud de Nérac earlier in the century. The Albrets rose in importance there between 1130 and 1143, initially as its protectors, and one of the twelfth-century lords of Albret held the title of abbot and had built the town's castle. In all three towns they were working in relative harmony with the ecclesiastical authorities and also with the *prudhommes* by the turn of the century, when urban customs were conceded and they became partly self-governing.[67]

These towns were not the most important on the left bank, however. This honour goes to an ancient port, one also acquiring communal identity, Le Mas-d'Agenais. Mas was vitally important for securing the Agenais, both militarily and in terms of resources. Duties were levied there by the late twelfth-century, and its customs make little reference to any seigneurial over-lordship, the *consuls* and *jurats* holding extensive powers.[68] It was also to assert its autonomy, though no particular religious preference, in the next century, and thus the crusaders would pay it significant attention.

Some of the laity on both sides of the Garonne were influenced by and co-operated with abbeys in both Aquitaine and the Languedoc, most notably Benedictine La Réole and Grand-Sauve in Entre-deux-Mers, and Cistercian Grandselve in the Toulousain. However, the Garonne was a dividing line not least in terms of the scale of orthodox religious affinity, for religious enthusiasm

---

66 *Rotuli chartarum in Turri Londinensi*, I/1: (1199–1216), ed. T. D. Hardy, London 1837, 62; *RHF* xii. 420.
67 *HGL* viii. 1851, 1860.
68 *Chartes Agen*, nos xiv, xvi, xviii.

north of the river paled in contrast with that inspired by the Gascon saints revered to the south.

North of the Garonne the abbeys of Saint-Maurin and Sainte-Livrade received little patronage and Agen had waned as a centre of pilgrimage. With the exception of the Templar convent, founded at Agen in 1154–8 by Bishop Elie, and the priory of Clairac, established under Duke Richard's protection at Marmande, the region is notable for the lack of monastic activity in the latter half of the century. The Lot valley in particular was still something of a religious wasteland. South of the Garonne, however, religious houses, especially in the sphere of the Gascon church, continued to be patronised, established and protected by the nobility. As such, the influence of Condom grew and a daughter house of La Réole was built at Meilhan by the end of the twelfth century, very possibly by the Albrets, which served also as a parish church. The colonisation of new land by monks and associated peasantry was a feature of the Garonne valley and especially the left bank, with the establishment of *sauvetats* by the monasteries noted in chapter 1.[69]

There is little indication of the role played by the bishops in the promotion of monastic activity in this period but we do have an idea of the geographical extent of their personal influence. Since the time of Arnaud II, on the day on which a new bishop was consecrated he ascended his episcopal throne in the church of Saint-Caprais and Agenais nobles then carried him in it across town to Saint-Etienne. This honour was accorded to the lords of Clermont-Dessus, Madaillan, Boville and, at different points, of Fossat and Fumel. These lords were amongst the bishop's greatest vassals, owing homage for much of the property and revenues they collected from various Agenais churches. The lords of Fumel, Clermont, Fossat and Madaillan almost certainly held their titles and lands from him. The lord of Boville probably held Castillon likewise. In 1190 Bertrand of Fumel accompanied bishop Bertrand de Béceyras on crusade.[70]

We should note three significant things about these lords. First, their estates were spread throughout the portion of the Agenais lying north of the Garonne almost marking its furthest boundaries. Bearing in mind the influence of Madaillan at Sainte-Livrade, we see that the bishop had a very wide but thinly-spread geographical network of secular and orthodox influence in that region. Second, none of his vassals appear as part of the southern resistance in the Albigensian wars. Third, there is little evidence of the suzerain power of the bishop south of the river by this date, and the essentially Gascon lords there were to have differing responses to the crusade. Thus, although it is appealing to believe William of Tudela that in 1211 the army raised in the Agenais in support of the count of Toulouse consisted of 'the whole Agenais; no one

---

[69] Ch. Higounet, 'Les Bastides du sud-ouest', in *L'Information historique*, Paris 1946, 28–35, and 'Les Chemins Saint-Jacques', 211–13.

[70] Tholin, 'Notes sur la féodalité', *RA* xxiii. 50–1, 55–7; xxv. 146; xxvi. 74.

remained behind', the nobles of the Agenais were actually very divided over the issue of heresy once the crusade demanded that they take sides.[71]

The Cathar diocese of Agen

The earliest possible recorded incidence of Catharism in the Agenais was in 1114, when Robert of Arbrissel preached at Agen against an otherwise unidentified heresy.[72] However, although Bogomil influence may well have entered western Europe again by this date, there is certainly not enough information to connect this heresy to it. On the other hand, it would also seem to be rather early to be related to the teachings of Henry of Lausanne or Peter of Bruys. But in the 1140s the Bogomil-derived heresy was indeed gaining success in the west and may conceivably lie behind the identification, before 1150, of certain heretics, whom Abbot Hervé of Le Bourdieu at Déols (Indre) calls 'Agenais' and also 'Manichaean', who opposed marriage and the eating of meat. We know a little about the nature of two incidents in the Agenais, one at Gontaud on the Canaule and the other at Gavaudun on the river Lède, occurring in c. 1155–60. Their position, and a reference to St Bernard having preached against the latter, make it possible that they could have been related to the heresy of Henry of Lausanne. But the same reference to Bernard, who we are told also encountered 'Arians' at Toulouse, and Abbot Hervé's reference makes a connection with early Catharism also possible. In c. 1155 Agen's bishop Elie made an appeal to Abbot Pierre II de Didonie of La Grand-Sauve for aid in restoring the lapsed faith of the people of Gontaud. To encourage the abbot, he donated to the abbey the church of Saint-Pierre de Nogaret, near Gontaud, and informed him that Vital de Gontaud, presumably its lord, invited him to establish monks at the town, which the abbot did. The castle of Gavaudun, in contrast, was thought irredeemable and was attacked in around 1160 by the army of Bishop Jean d'Assida of Périgueux. These actions did not rid the region of the heresy however. Robert of Torigny refered to the Cathars of Toulouse as 'heretics who are called Agenais' in 1178 and at the end of the century Raoul Ardent described in some detail Cathar beliefs in the Agenais.[73] Thus the heresy was well established in the Agenais by 1200 (further evidence for this will be discussed below), and may even have reached it by the 1150s.

---

71 William of Tudela, *Chanson*, i. 208–9.

72 *Monumenta conventus tolosani*, ii. 3.

73 *PL* clv.2011 (Ardent), clxxxi.1426 (Hervé); GC ii. 911 (Gontaud); l'abbé Cirot, *Histoire de l'abbaye et congrégation de Notre-Dame de la Grande-Sauve, ordre de Saint-Benoît en Guienne*, Bordeaux 1844, ii. 90 (Elie); Robert of Torigny, in *Chronicles of Stephen, Henry and Richard*, iv. 279; M. Capul, 'Notes sur le Catharisme et la croisade des Albigeois en Agenais', *RA* xc (1964), 4–6; Duvernoy, *Catharisme*, ii. 206; Guignard, *Agenais*, 107–8. Migne and his sources place Raoul Ardent's homilies at around 1100, but he has since been shown to have lived around a century later: Ralph Ardens, *Speculum universale*, ed. Th.-J. Gründel, Munich 1961, 3; C. Thouzellier, *Catharisme et valdéisme en Languedoc à la fin du xiie et au début de xiiie siècle*, Paris 1966, 128–9; Dondaine, *Le Hiérarchie cathare*, AFP xx. 272–3.

Heretical labels and structures

Some observations should be made at this point about terminology used for labelling and identifying heretics in the sources. We need to be suspicious to some extent of the origins of all of it, for southern French dissidents whom we call Cathars typically just referred to themselves by such terms as 'good men' or Christians, just as heretics had done in the previous century. Whilst we might learn something of the heresy through the labels accorded it by the sources, we might as easily be led into some propagandist's trap. The term *texterant* is a case in point, being at the same time prejorative – weaving being a lowly occupation and a suspicious one, undertaken by itinerants in dark cellars – but also instructive, for historians have noted the possible association between the transmission of heresy and both the international cloth trade and the suitability of the weavers' working practices for the dissemination of radical ideas.[74]

The origin of the term 'Cathar' itself is unclear and continues to receive attention. Lambert dismisses Eckbert of Schönau's assertion that it was adopted by the Cologne heretics themselves not only because of its meaning, 'the pure', from the Greek *katharos*, but because it linked them to a fourth-century group of Manichees, the *Catharistae*. This does not seem quite as implausible to me, as it did not to Borst. Ekbert had a good knowledge of the twelfth-century sect and we rely on his account in many ways. It is not impossible that the heretics identified themselves in some way with the ancient sect just as their detractors did, misleadingly but with some cause, even though no actual line of descent seems likely. Certainly Eckbert's suggestion is more plausible than the suggestion by Alan of Lille that the term derived from an over-familiarity with cats.[75]

I have already suggested that the terms 'Arian' and 'Manichee' were not as ill-chosen as historians often assume, that they might indeed imply truly heretical understanding of, for example, the status of the Son in relation to the Father. These terms are used to describe Cathars in the twelfth and thirteenth centuries. Few doubt the presence of certain doctrines being recognised by them after about 1150, but when the terms are used earlier in the century we do encounter problems. The use of 'Arian' to describe heretics encountered by St Bernard might mean that they were dualist, if we apply my argument for the eleventh-century usage. But, as is the case in the eleventh century, we need more than a label to convince us. Abbot Hervé arguably used 'Manichee' in around 1150 to help us further understand the doctrine of heretics he also identifies for us geographically. But I find it difficult to envisage a strong Cathar presence by this time in the Agenais, unless we speculate that the earliest southern

---

[74] A summary of terms used to describe what we now call Cathars is given in *Heresies of the high Middle Ages*, 41–2. See also Borst, *Die Katharer*, 240–53, esp. p. 247. Criticism of historians' ready use of such labels is offered forcefully in Pegg, *Corruption of angels*, 17, and 'Historiographical essay', 192–4. Here I only deal with terms used in southern France. On weaving see Lambert *Cathars*, 43. Moore addresses the issue critically in *Origins*, esp. pp. 173–5, 194–5, 199–200, 238.

[75] Eckbert of Schönau, *PL* cxcv.16, 18; Alan of Lille, *PL* ccx.366; Lambert, *Cathars*, 43; Borst, *Die Katharer*, 240.

French converts of the sect identified at Cologne in mid-century were made in the county of Agen.

The designation 'Agenais', used by Hervé and by Robert of Torigny, attempts to be specific about the location of the heresy. In this it is like 'Albigensian' and 'Bulgari'. 'Albigensian' denotes a region in which Cathars were highly active and, because it fell into that sphere of especially rebellious and heretical authority which was not allied with the Catholic counts of Toulouse, it is not unnatural that respectable early thirteenth-century sources associated these two uncontrollable entities. Bulgari presumably reflects contemporary knowledge that Bulgaria was the birth place of the heresy.[76] But unlike these two terms, 'Agenais' does not refer to an infamous dualist centre. None the less, it must have some logic. Knowledge of the Anglo-Norman and Angevin sphere informed Robert of Torigny's world-view very centrally, and the label was possibly chosen to alert his readers to dissidence within that realm specifically.

Whilst the names used by heretics differed from those used by their enemies, this in itself should not make us doubt the validity of the evidence of the latter. The heretics naturally came to use only terms which implied that they were the 'true' or 'good' Christians, and in southern France they were also identified as such by their sympathisers. Thus we find in use terms of local significance and deference such as *bons omes* and *prodomes*.[77] Their enemies, however, surely sought not only to defame them but to identify them instructively; either with other sects, for example 'Manichees', or as distinct from them, thus labelling them regionally or so that they would not be confused with, most obviously, Waldensians. None the less, just as it is only from other supporting evidence, for example description of belief and practice, that we can be sure that 'Albigensians' were what we also call Cathars, it is not labels but other evidence that makes it likely that what was described as 'Agenais' was of the same variety. Aside from Abbot Hervé's use of 'Manichee', problematic not least because of its date, little in the sources composed before that of Raoul Ardent clearly connects the Agenais with the Cathar heresy. For this we must turn to sources relating to the east-west infiltration of Bogomilism in a wider geographical context.

In 1266/7 the Dominican inquisitor Anselm of Alessandria reported that Balkan dualists had inspired the establishment of French Cathar bishoprics, including one at Agen, between 1150 and 1200.[78] He is thought by most to be referring in particular to the foundation of new heretical sees at a Cathar council at Saint-Félix de Caraman in the Lauragais in 1167 or, more likely, in 1174x7. The evidence for this is a document published by Guillaume Besse in 1660,

---

[76] On 'Albigensian' and 'Bulgari' and sources employing the terms see again Borst, *Die Katharer*, 243, 248–9, and J.-L. Biget, ' "Les Albigeois": remarques sur une dénomination', in Zerner, *Inventer*, 219–56.

[77] See some interesting discussion in Arnold, *Inquisition and power*, 138–49. Arnold finds a closer correlation between the terms 'good man' and 'heretic' than does Pegg: *Corruption of angels*, passim. I consider him more convincing.

[78] Anselm of Alessandria, 'Tractatus de hereticis', 308–24 at p. 308.

apparently copied from portions of a thirteenth-century manuscript, later lost.[79] The most commonly accepted understanding of this very central chapter in the heresy of southern French Catharism is that a Bogomil leader, Nicetas, undertook a mission to convert the moderate dualists of western Europe to the absolute dualist *ordo* of Drugunthia to which he belonged, the culmination of which as far as the southern French were concerned was this council, to which most of Besse's document relates. In attendance were the Cathar bishops Mark of Lombardy, Robert de Spernone of 'France', and Sicard Cellerier of Albi. Three new bishops were elected and then consecrated by Nicetas; Gerald Mercier to Carcassonne, Bernard-Raymond to Toulouse and Raymond de Casalis to Agen. All present received the *consolamentum* from Nicetas, implicitly into his *ordo*.[80]

But this evidence is not uncontroversial. Dossat (amongst others) has argued that Besse's document was a forgery, on the basis that material within it did not reflect twelfth-century Catharism accurately, noting amongst other things that Besse had forged other materials.[81] A. Dondaine responded that the document correlated with related sources, including Anselm's *Tractatus*, which he made known for the first time.[82] Bernard Hamilton agrees that the document was genuine, and it is generally acknowledged that his article on the subject, on which the above version of events is based, 'supersedes earlier work'. He argues that Besse was not in a position to have forged the document; it reflects an understanding of the development of the heresy as only recently attained by scholars and certainly not exhibited anywhere else by Besse, and sections of the discourse attributed to Nicetas are most unlikely to have been composed by westerners of any century. Very importantly, he also makes sense of the document by relating its content to the context in which Besse claimed that the manuscript he was using itself purported to have been drawn up. At some remove from the mission of Nicetas itself, the manuscript was apparently a response to the renewed influence in the west of the continued schism between the absolute and moderate dualists in the east (this was to affect the Agenais centrally). Besse's incomplete manuscript thus represents portions of copies

---

[79] G. Besse, *Histoire des ducs, marquis et comtes de Narbonne*, Paris 1660, 483–6, cited in B. Hamilton, 'The Cathar council of Saint-Félix reconsidered', *AFP* xlviii (1978), 23–53, repr. in his *Monastic reform*, 23–53 n. 1. Besse's document is reproduced ibid. pp. 51–3 and in P. Jimenez, 'Relire la charte de Niquinta, II: Sens et portée de la charte', *Heresis* xxii (Dec. 1994) 1–28, at pp. 27–8. M. Lambert gives an overview of various emendations made to the text by its editors: *Cathars*, 47 n. 7.

[80] A good recent summary account of the nature and influence of the two varieties of dualism is given in Lambert, *Cathars*, 54–9.

[81] Y. Dossat, 'A Propos du concile cathare de Saint-Félix: les Milingues', *CF* iii (1968), 201–14; L. de Lacger, 'L'Albigeois pendant la crise de l'albigéisme', *Revue d'histoire ecclésiastique* xxix (1933), 272–315.

[82] A. Dondaine, 'Les Actes du concile albigeoise de Saint-Félix de Caraman: essai de critique d'authenticité d'un document médiéval', in *Miscellanea Giovanni Mercati*, v, Rome 1946, 324–55. See also F. Šanjek, 'Le Rassemblement hérétique de Saint-Félix de Caraman (1167) et les églises cathares au xiie siècle', *Revue d'histoire ecclésiastique* lxvii (1972), 767–99.

made in 1223 of three twelfth-century documents relating to Nicetas's mission. It is also Hamilton who makes the case for a date of 1174x77 for the mission and council, again usually accepted.[83] He has thus resolved the sort of problems about the source which Philippe Wolff argued rendered the issue of its authenticity irresolvable.[84]

We should note also that Besse's document in fact refers not to *ecclesia agenensis* but to *ecclesia aranensis*, i.e. the Val d'Aran in the Gascon county of Comminges. It is now generally agreed that this was a scribal error resulting from Besse's misreading of the source. This is on the basis of corroborating evidence for a heretical diocese of Agen, and also as a result of Dossat's still entirely sustainable assertion that the heresy did not make an impact west of the Garonne.[85]

However, the interpretation of the evidence contained in Besse's document is disputed as well as its authenticity. Duvernoy and Brenon consider that Nicetas was not so much concerned with the conversion of the Cathars from moderate dualism to the absolute *ordo* as simply with their structural organisation in descent from the eastern churches and the consequent validity of the *consolamenta* that their *perfecti* administered.[86] Pegg doubts the credibility of the Saint-Félix document, the general concept of an east–west transmission of doctrine and even connections between the different sects historians and medieval clergy collectively call 'Cathars'.[87]

These debates touch on the extent to which historians accept Bogomil influence on the nature of Catharism more generally. It does have to be admitted

---

83 Hamilton, 'Saint-Félix', esp. pp. 23–35, 43–51. See Lambert's *Cathars*, at pp. 46–7 n. 4, for the evaluation of Hamilton's work and the quotation. For the council more generally see Lambert's discussion at pp. 45–59: note that he finds 1167 the more convincing date (p. 47 n. 7). At pp. 46–9 and 54–8 Lambert gives a good account of Nicetas's broader mission in the west– he visited Lombardy as well as France – and a detailed summary of the relative positions concerning its significance. In his *Cathars* (pp. 71–3) M. Barber also accepts Hamilton's interpretation.

84 *Documents de l'histoire du Languedoc*, ed. P. Wolff, Toulouse 1969, 99–105.

85 Dossat, 'Catharisme en Gascogne', 150–3. See also his 'Comminges', 119–21, 125. See also Thouzellier, *Catharisme et Valdéisme*, 13–14; Šanjek, 'Le Rassemblement', 786–7; Hamilton, 'Saint-Félix', 35–6, 42; Barber, *Cathars*, 21. Lambert (*Cathars*, 46 n. 5) notes that *Agenensis* is still not accepted by all (see, for example, Jimenez, 'Charte de Niquinta', i. 15–20), although he accepts it himself (*Cathars*, 70). E. Peters also prefers Aran, and the date 1167 (*Heresy*, 121–3). See also J. B. Lataillade, 'Catharisme en Comminges, Couserans et Armagnac', *Revue de Comminges* lxxxvi (1973), 212–16.

86 J. Duvernoy, *Le Catharisme*, I: *La Religion des cathares*, Toulouse 1976, i. 105–7; Brenon, *Le Vrai Visage*, 109, 122–8 (cf. Lambert, *Cathars*, 46 n. 6). To be effective in removing the soul of the deceased from the physical realm this ceremony had to have been performed by a heretic whose own *consolamentum* proceeded from an unbroken line of *perfecti* who had died in a perfect state, an issue over which the Italian Cathars were currently in turmoil and which Nicetas hoped to settle by reconsoling the westerners.

87 Pegg, *Corruption of angels*, 16–19 n. 13 at pp. 145–6, and 'Historiographical essay', 185, 187, 191–2. See J. B. Russell, 'Interpretations of the origins of medieval heresy', *Medieval Studies* xxv (1963), 26–53, for another case against Bogomil origins.

that we have little direct evidence for the content of early Cathar belief, and this is not least the case for southern France. But the assertion that it was moderate dualist seems reasonably sound in the light of the evidence concerning Cathars in Cologne in the 1140s. Hamilton's interpretation, that a Bogomil mission of the 1170s saw the conversion of southern French Cathars from the moderate to absolute *ordo* as well as the establishment of a structured Cathar church, has persuaded most including, eventually, Moore, most difficult to convince of non-indigenous influence in many respects.[88] The evidence relating to the Cathars of the northern Languedoc in the twelfth century and into the 1220s, for belief, internal structure and the development of their Church and place within the broader Cathar movement, makes most sense when Hamilton's well reasoned interpretation is applied to it. As such his thesis centrally informs my own approach.

But Pegg's reservations about the evidence extend to the concept of any hierarchically structured dualist church or hierarchy in southern France. He does not find titles such as 'bishop' reflected in the reminiscences of the inquisition witnesses he has studied from the Lauragais and suspects the evidence relating to the Saint-Félix council of being 'at best' probably a mid thirteenth-century forgery.[89] However, not all of our evidence for an Agenais Cathar hierarchy comes from polemical sources or those whose origins are considered doubtful. An important Occitan noble, Raymond de Péreille, lord of the stronghold at Montségur and one of the Occitan nobles most knowledgeable about Cathar affairs, and most closely examined about them by the inquisition in the 1240s, gives us crucial evidence for the organisational structure of the Agenais hierarchy, as does the knight Bérengar de Lavelant, also present at the castle with the heretics. Elements of their testimony have caused scholars some problems, but these obstacles do not affect the substantial content of what we are told about the election of both a named Cathar bishop for the Agenais translated in the source as 'episcopus haereticorum in agennensi' and his 'filius maiorus', an appointed second and successor. These sources, de Péreille's in particular being one of the most important for understanding the upper echelons of Occitan Cathar society, both in terms of heretics and their supporters, are not as far as I know suspected of being other than a close account of oral testimony except in minor detail mentioned, and no further removed from the original than other depositions drawn into written Latin form through the inquisitorial filter.

---

[88] Moore, *Origins*, 205–7, esp. pp. 212–15 and n. 19, but compare his 'Nicétas, émissaire de Dragovitch, a-t-il traversé les Alpes?', AM lxxxv (1973), 85–90. D. Obolensky also finds Hamilton's interpretation sound: 'Papa Nicetas: a Byzantine dualist in the land of the Cathars', *Harvard Ukrainian Studies* vii (1983), 489–500, esp. p. 491. So does Barber, *Cathars*, 2, 7–8 n. 3, 21–2. Kienzle is convinced to the extent of referring to 'the Cathar counter-Church' (*Cistercians*, 3 and see p. 46) and to St Félix as 'an international Bogomil-Cathar council . . . to confirm the boundaries of four Cathar bishoprics', although she prefers Lambert's date. The most recent account of the establishment of a Cathar Church and hierarchy is in Barber, *Cathars*, 71–6.

[89] Pegg, *Corruption of angels*, 96, 130, and 'Historiographical essay', n. 14 at p. 187.

Furthermore, we find the same *filius maiorus* recollected in an unrelated source, the testimony of Arnaud de Villemur.[90]

None the less Pegg's approach challenges us to prove effectively the existence of a Cathar church. Although I think that his case has yet to be made really convincingly it forces us, for example, to consider that for the periods of its history when we have little or no evidence of an organised hierarchy for the Agenais, most obviously for most of the inquisitorial era itself, there possibly wasn't one. This seems as likely as the possibility that the names of Cathar leaders have been lost. Yet the latter case is also plausible. Not only are there few extant sources in which such information might have been recorded, but it may be, as Brenon and others suspect, that the core beliefs of the heretics and the organisational sphere of those who kept them alive and preserved them in their purest form were neither the aspects of the heresy which were most important to the ordinary believer nor what witnesses remembered or related. Indeed, from the evidence I have gathered it would appear that the most important Cathar of the northern Languedoc, Vigouroux de la Bacone, the *filius major* referred to above and named in non-inquisitorial sources on several occasions as 'bishop' of the Agenais heretics, is not called by these titles by witnesses of the region to which he apparently ministered, in spite of appearing in numerous of their testimonies.

Several other approaches taken in very recent works should be considered too. James Given addresses the ability of the inquisition to control behaviour, revealing a wealth of strategies employed by the individuals and communities of the Languedoc to resist the implications of appearing before its court. Given is able to produce his models of resistance using the relative wealth of documentation available for the 1275 to 1325 inquisitions in the southern, central and eastern Languedoc. Although it would be reading to much into the earlier sparse evidence for the north to apply his model consistently to the examples we have – he deals in the main with a period in which the inquisition as well as strong French authority were well established whereas in our period responses to it were only beginning to be explored – many of his conclusions must be considered universally applicable. These include forms of collective and individual resistance to the inquisitors, and many of the structural constraints which hindered its functions, and I shall address these models to some extent.[91]

Likewise asking 'how do we analyse the effects of power within the inquisitorial register?', John Arnold seeks to do more than steer a middle course between the extremes of trusting or dismissing inquisitorial documents as evidence for the lives and beliefs of deponents. He is able to discern much about the inquisition and its subjects without losing sight of the fact that we will never know as much about the latter as the former.[92] The problems encountered in this process

---

90 Doat xxii, fos 160v, 226v; xxiv, fos 43v–44v.
91 Given, *Inquisition*, 2–4 and esp. pp. 93–165 (resistance), 191–212 (constraints).
92 Arnold, *Inquisition and power*, esp. pp. 1–15, quotation at p. 8.

are again most pertinent to the later sources, for those of the 1240s are in general so formulaic that no one would be tempted to assert that they reveal 'the truth'. Yet they are all that we have for the northern Languedoc. Whilst we should indeed be wary of drawing a line, for example between those 'in' the heresy and those 'outside' of it,[93] it seems sensible to consider at least that many of the people whose deeds and beliefs the documents claim to record were involved in the sorts of activities which looked 'heretical' to the authorities, and that some of this activity was indeed concerned with Catharism.

The geography and population of the heretical diocese

The Cathars of the Agenais were, I suspect, nowhere near as numerous or significant as those of the heretical dioceses of Toulouse, Carcassonne and Albi. It is unlikely that this is simply a reflection of the fact that we have little documentation relating to the region. If it had been of greater significance, it might have been a target of the missions against the heresy initiated in 1198 by Innocent III and intensified in 1204. William of Tudela asserts that in 1209 the pope gave instructions to the crusade's convenor, Arnaud Aimery, abbot of Cîteaux, to 'destroy anyone who offers resistance, from Montpellier to Bordeaux'.[94] In spite of this rhetoric and a pre-crusade in the Agenais, it was clearly the region from Toulouse eastwards which was the pope's main concern.

It has been noted how difficult it is to establish exact boundaries of jurisdiction for the Catholic bishoprics of Agen and Cahors in the Middle Ages.[95] The task is even more difficult for the Cathar church. Whilst the Cathars of southern France followed the Bogomil and Italian dualist practice of naming their dioceses after Catholic bishoprics, and often followed the borders of Catholic dioceses for practical reasons, they did not always limit themselves to the exact shape of the orthodox structures. From the Saint-Félix document we know that the Catholic archdiocese of Narbonne and all the dioceses of the region of Catalonia were put under the authority of the Cathar bishop of Carcassonne, and that the Cathar bishop of Toulouse also had much of northern Spain under his wing. Nor were the Cathar bishops based in the towns after which the Catholic diocese were named, for the obvious practical reason that they contained the Catholic bishop and his servants, who had to be avoided.[96]

Thus it seems unlikely that we can reconstruct the Cathar diocese of the Agenais as it was conceived in the Saint-Félix document with any real accuracy and we would certainly be unwise to attempt to equate it closely with the boundary of its Catholic counterpart. We should instead discuss the Cathars of the Agenais most usefully by establishing as far as possible where they were actually situated and in what geographical context we can show them to have operated. As sources are few, especially for the period before the early thirteenth

93 Ibid. 120.
94 William of Tudela, *Chanson*, i. 18–19, 20–2.
95 E. Albe, *L'Hérésie albigeoise et l'Inquisition en Quercy*, Paris 1910, 27.
96 Hamilton, 'Saint-Félix', 36–8, 40–2, 52–3.

century, we have to extrapolate backwards cautiously from early references in sources such as those for the Albigensian Crusade and inquisition. From these we find no references to Cathars in that portion of the Agenais on the left bank of the Garonne. More surprisingly, we find no references to heretical centres in the Garonne towns themselves until much later. Instead, we find them concentrated in the valley of the Lot and using the Garonne apparently only for communication with the Cathars of Bas-Quercy, with whom they were probably most closely connected.

Heretics were present in Quercy relatively early but no Cathar diocese corresponds to the Catholic diocese of Cahors. This was perhaps a reflection of the uncertain political status of the region in the later twelfth-century when it was fought over and occupied variously by the duke of Aquitaine and the count of Toulouse. Duvernoy concludes that its Cathars must have been considered to have been under the authority of the Cathar bishop of Toulouse because the Cathars most active there after the start of the crusade were Guillaume de Caussade, heretic of south-eastern Quercy, and Vigouroux de la Bacone, Cathar bishop of the Agenais, both acting under the guidance of Guilhabert de Castres, the Cathar bishop of Toulouse.[97]

To this picture of activity in Bas-Quercy by heretics of the Toulousain we should also add Bernard de Lamothe, a very important member of the Cathar hierarchy in the years of the crusade, and, before the crusade, Arnaud Arrufat, *perfectus* of Verfeil, and Raymond Aymeric, Cathar deacon of Villemur. But their activities in the thirteenth century do not indicate a general Toulousain dominance of the Quercinois Cathars. In the first place, through his exceptional talents in the crisis of the war Guilhaert de Castres came to lead all the Cathars in the Languedoc in the mid-1220s, not just those in the heretical diocese of Toulouse.[98] Thus we should not infer that influence over Quercy had necessarily been the prerogative of his predecessors. Second, there is evidence of the heresy only in Bas-Quercy in the twelfth century. Thus the absence of a Cathar hierarchy in Quercy as a whole before the crusade should not concern us, for we only need to establish the orientation of the heretics of the Tarn-Aveyron-Garonne basin. Finally, although it should be noted in support of Duvernoy's theory that Bas-Quercy was part of the Catholic diocese of Toulouse and not of Cahors, this was evidently an inappropriate geographical demarcation even for the Catholic Church and was changed around a century later with the creation of the diocese of Montauban.[99]

The evidence does not point clearly to the dominance of any individual Cathar diocese over Bas-Quercy in the twelfth and early thirteenth century. If it was an extension of that of Toulouse, it seems strange that Bernard de Lamothe appears there in preference to two Cathar deacons of the northern Toulousain,

---

97 Duvernoy, *Catharisme*, ii. 230–4 esp. n. 86, 257–66 esp. pp. 264, 284.
98 Ibid. 265–6.
99 G. Passerat, 'Cathares en Bas-Quercy: entre l'église de l'Agenais et celle de l'Albigeoise', in *Europe et Occitainie: les pays cathares*, Carcassonne 1992, 151.

Pons Guilhabert and Arnaud de Cavelsaut. Both were based close to Bas-Quercy, at Verfeil and Villemur, but we find them in Bas-Quercy very infrequently.[100] The presence of Bernard de Lamothe is surely largely explained by the fact that he was actually a native of the region. Guillaume de Caussade, who had little to do with Bas-Quercy in any case, was most closely associated with the Cathar hierarchy of Albi which seems to have had little practical influence in Bas-Quercy at any point.[101]

The most important heretic of all to be found in Bas-Quercy was not from the Toulousain at all but was Vigouroux de la Bacone. Y. Dossat, the authority on Vigouroux, notes the extent to which he was active in Bas-Quercy, 'cette region qui devait naturellement relever de lui'. Bernard Guillemain has noted how easy communications were in the *Moyenne Garonne* for the heretics, and Georges Passerat that the heretics of Bas-Quercy and also Villemur had close associations with the *perfecti* of the Agenais.[102] It does not seem unreasonable to assert that the Cathars of the Agenais had a very strong influence, perhaps even the strongest, in Bas-Quercy from the start. Even though we have a good amount of evidence about Bas-Quercy at the start of the thirteenth century there is little indication that it contained an independently organised Cathar hierarchy of its own. It was the heretics of the Agenais and Villemur who were to decide how the northern Languedoc in general should respond to the first campaign of the crusade in 1209.

There is no evidence that Agen itself contained a heretical community until the 1240s. In spite of tensions between the town and its clergy its largest and most important families, for example the de la Casaihna and Peitavi, do not feature in the history of the heresy.[103] Indeed, this is the case for all the towns along the Garonne until we come to the junction of the river with the Lot. But in spite of the possibility that Cathars were at Gontaud in the 1150s and were at Tonneins by the 1220s, and the fact that the crusaders attacked both towns in 1209, we know nothing of the heretical life of this stretch of the Agenais Garonne around the turn of the century. In the pre-crusade period Cathar activity in the Agenais was concentrated instead along the Lot. The first heretics encountered by the Albigensian Crusade were at Casseneuil, at the junction of the Roman Périgueux-Agen road with the Lot. William of Tudela tells us that after the attack a youth rushed to Villemur and informed the townspeople that the crusaders were already striking camp.[104] Naturally the secular authorities of

100 Doat xxii, fos 5v–6r, 28v, 48v, 53v–54r, 54r, 54r–v; E. Griffe, *Le Languedoc cathare au temps de la croisade, 1209–29*, Paris 1973, 178; Roquebert, *L'Épopée*, iv. 168.

101 See Passerat, 'Cathares', 149–65. Passerat includes the heretics of Caussade amongst those of Bas-Quercy, and thus finds Albigeois influence in Bas-Quercy. I find Caussade to have been more closely associated with the other towns of the Avyeron on the eastern–Quercy/Albigeois border and think that it was regarded as part of the Cathar diocese of Albi.

102 Dossat, 'Un Évêque cathare', 628; Guillemain, 'Le Duché', 60; Passerat, 'Cathares', 149–65.

103 Names of important families of the town can be found in *Chartes Agen*, nos i, ii, iii.

104 William of Tudela, *Chanson*, i. 42–5. Duvernoy is surely wrong to attribute the burnings at

Villemur would need to know such news, and a natural response of the Agenais would be to send such a warning into the Toulousain. But why rush straight to Villemur, a town one hundred kilometres from Casseneuil and less easily accessible than Castelsarrasin, the more important seat of secular power in Bas-Quercy?

The action of the messenger perhaps indicates that Villemur was the next significant town in an organisational network, not of secular authority but of Catharism, and that the seat of the heretical bishops of the Agenais was Casseneuil. There is other evidence to support this. The attack on Casseneuil was in fact the culmination of this campaign of 1209, indicating that the curious first stage of the crusade was not as arbitrary or fruitless as is sometimes assumed. Peter des Vaux-de-Cernay says that the town was again full of heretics by 1214, indeed, that it was populated mostly by heretics. As a consequence it was besieged again in that year and again many Cathars were taken and burned. The same chronicler describes it not only as one of the most important centres of the heresy, but also as one of the oldest and most resistant to Christianity. Perhaps symbolically, after it fell in 1214 its revenues were granted to the Dominican convent at Prouillé, whose foundation had been the major spiritual initiative against heresy in the Languedoc.[105]

An explanation has been offered as to why the Agenais Lot was an important region for heretics. Aside from its obvious opportunities for transmitting the heresy using river traffic, the valley was forested heavily and its cliff and hillsides full of caves.[106] Long before the crusade and inquisition, security must surely have been a concern in the Agenais. It was an outpost of the heresy in an essentially orthodox duchy, and safety could not have been offered as easily by larger towns on the Garonne for they were more closely under the scrutiny of the officials of the dukes of Aquitaine. We can perhaps speculate as to why Casseneuil in particular might have become the most important centre after 1196. The town had excellent natural and man-made defences and Hugues de Rovinha was supported by his lord Raymond VI and was thus well placed to protect leading Cathars from his brother Bishop Arnaud. Indeed, it took an entire army to threaten the security of this Cathar stronghold in 1209, and then only temporarily.

The towns neighbouring Casseneuil, most notably Castelmoron-sur-Lot, Villeneuve and Pujols were to play an important role in the heresy in the thirteenth century and it is possible that there may have been houses of Cathars in them previously. However, Sainte-Livrade was and remained Catholic, and east of Villeneuve there is little evidence of heresy either in spite of efforts made to identify such centres in the Penne area in 1212 (although the family of the heretic Guillaume-Amanieu of Sainte-Livrade were land-holders in the Penne

---

Casseneuil to Gontaud and Tonneins: *Catharisme*, ii. 236. There seems to be no reason to doubt the evidence of William of Tudela.

105 Peter des Vaux-de-Cernay, *Histoire*, 198–9.

106 Capul, 'Notes', 10.

district by 1214).[107] In addition, there is almost no evidence of Catharism north of the Lot in the late twelfth century, even along the Lède where it had perhaps been established earlier at Gavaudun. The Agenais, in contrast with the other parts of the Languedoc, was thus probably of marginal importance as a heretical region by the turn of the century.

In contrast Bas-Quercy had several large towns containing heretical communities before the Albigensian Crusade. Here we see the truth of Barber's observations that there was no automatic relationship between towns and heresy: in the Agenais in this period, the most urbanised centres were the least heretical, whereas in Bas-Quercy almost the opposite is true. This begs further exploration into exactly what features made some towns in the south receptive to heresy. Yet just as there was a natural cultural association between Bas-Quercy and much of the Agenais, the same appears to have been true in confessional matters. It is interesting to note that the only surviving inquisitorial documents concerning trials at Agen relate not to the Agenais at all but mostly to the heretics of Bas-Quercy.[108]

Although the town of Villemur in the Toulousain was a Catholic archdeaconry of Toulouse and part of the same Cathar diocese, its heretical history is intertwined in this early period with that of Bas-Quercy, as noted by Michel Roquebert and Elie Griffe, and the Agenais. This was to continue well into the crusade. The assumption by its inhabitants that Villemur was to be attacked in 1209 is therefore understandable. If an army were to travel from the Agenais into the Toulousain it might well do so via this town in spite of the indirect route for it was a major centre of heresy with its own Cathar deacon, Raymond Aymeric. In the event, the Agenais crusade was called off after the fall of Casseneuil and Villemur escaped attack, but not before its inhabitants had abandoned their town in terror.[109]

Most of our evidence for the heretical community of Villemur in this period comes from the deposition of the *perfecta* Arnauda de Lamothe whose family were from Bas-Quercy. She and her sister Péronne were moved to Villemur from their home at Montauban around the turn of the century by arrangement between Raymond Aymeric and Arnauda's kinsman, the *perfectus* Bernard de Lamothe. At Villemur they lived as Cathar novices with other girls at the house

---

107 *Actes de Simon de Monfort*, 78. Cassany-Mazet claims a female heretic for the Penne area, Girauda of 'Lavaux': *Villeneuve*, 48. His source is the earliest history of the Agenais, the often unreliable J. Darnalt, *Remonstrance faicte en la cour de la sénéchausée d'Agenois . . . antiquités de l'Agenais*, Paris 1606, 72. Darnalt is clearly confusing Penne with Penne d'Albigeoise and his heretic, who is thrown down a well and covered with rocks by the crusaders, with Dame Girauda of Lavaur in the Albigeois, executed in 1211: William of Tudela, *Chanson*, i. 164–7, 172–3; Peter des Vaux-de-Cernay, *Histoire*, 89, 94.

108 For discussion of the heretics of Bas-Quercy and Villemur see especialy Roquebert, *L'Épopée*, i. 96–100, 241–2, 477, 527–8; iv. 179; E. Griffe, *Le Languedoc cathare de 1190 à 1210*, Paris 1971, esp. p. 89, and *Le Languedoc, 1209–29*, esp. p. 117; Duvernoy, *Catharisme*, ii. 268; Albe, *L'Hérésie en Quercy*, esp. p. 17.

109 William of Tudela, *Chanson*, i. 44–5.

of the *perfecta* Poncia where they were visited by Bernard in 1207/8 and hereticated whilst still young.[110] It was not long after this that the news of the attack on Casseneuil reached Villemur, and Arnauda tells us that Raymond Aymeric organised an evacuation into the Albigeois.[111]

The Lamothes were amongst the many minor nobles of Bas-Quercy. In origin I suspect they were lords of what is modern Lamothe-Capdeville, just north of Montauban on the Aveyron. Since 1203 Guillaume de Lamothe and his son Raymond had been under the protection of Count Raymond himself.[112] Arnauda's immediate family resided in Montauban itself, founded on the Tarn in 1144 by Count Alfonse-Jourdain of Toulouse and attaining much political independence in 1195.[113] There she and her sister spent their early childhood with her mother Austorgue and brother Arnaud, frequently accepting Cathars into their home and adoring them. The rest of the family remained in Bas-Quercy in 1209; a Hugues de Lamothe fought in the defence of Toulouse, and Lamothes were still in the area in the period of the inquisition.

It is at this point that we should perhaps note also a word of caution, sounded most recently by Arnold, that we should not talk of heretical families, for heresy did not follow automatically from being in a family that contained many *perfecti* or *credentes* (even if the latter were a clearly definable group, which they were not).[114] The evidence for the northern Languedoc contains many examples of divergent beliefs and allegiances within one family. None the less, although a few families were rent asunder by the issue as we shall see, many more extended a general tolerance to a variety of beliefs. Whilst the inquisition wrongly considered individuals within such groupings automatically tainted and suspect, we should not go too far the other way in assuming a naive eclecticism on the part of members of these families, for there is evidence of a good deal of debate and understanding of the relevant issues by ordinary people. Some families thus consciously allowed heresy to prosper. This discussion also applies to communities more widely. Whilst there are no towns for which we could assert 100 per cent orthodoxy or heresy, it is a central thesis of this book that patterns concerning adherence to one or the other do emerge, and that towns and villages chose whether to accept or reject heresy, that is to say to respond to them as a community, whatever the actual preferences of the individuals and families within them.

---

110 Pegg doubts that these specialised houses of novitiates really existed (*Corruption of angels*, 119) but I find the evidence for such at Villemur very convincing in the light of other depositions discussed in chapters 4 and 5 below.

111 Doat xxiii, fos 2v–49v, esp. fos 2v–5v.

112 *Layettes du trésor des chartes*, ed. A. Teulet and others, Paris 1863–1909, i. 710; William of Tudela, *Chanson*, ii. 299 n. 5. The toponyme de Lamothe (and de la Mothe, or de la Mota) is not uncommon throughout the Languedoc, but it seems likely that the many people called de Lamothe in Montauban and its immediate vicinity were of one family.

113 A. Ligou, G. Passerat and others, *Histoire de Montauban*, Toulouse 1992, 28–30; Barber, *Cathars*, 67.

114 Arnold, *Inquisition and power*, 118–19: and see pp. 149–52 for the importance of family connections to the heresy.

One such town was Castelsarrasin, dominating the Garonne below its junction with the Tarn. This administrative seat of Quercy for the counts of Toulouse was, by 1209, notorious for its support of the heresy and several of its leading families were implicated. Most important was the Grimoard: Pons Grimoard, a *credens* himself from around 1204, was later the seneschal of Quercy for the count of Toulouse. It was the elder generation of Pons's family that dominated the heretical life of the town before the crusade. His father Vital was a heretic who later lived at Moissac, and his mother Arnauda was a *credens*. One of the most important accounts we have is of a meeting in 1204 at their house at which many other heretics and *credentes* of the region were present. Pons's uncle Raymond Grimoard was the most important *credens* of Castelsarrasin and was later hereticated. Vital and Raymond's brother, Pierre Grimoard, was married to Na Berètges and fathered Raymond-Bernard Grimoard before also being hereticated.[115]

Amongst the inquisition's witnesses, Pons Grimoard's memory was one of the longest, and the other families of the town emerge only hazily in this early period. None the less we know that the Fabers of Pechermer, a suburb of Castelsarrasin situated on the Garonne road to Moissac were already very important socially and in terms of the heresy. Both of Guillaume Faber's parents were hereticated before death, as were many other family members, and the whole family had a good deal of contact with the Cathar hierarchy. Guillaume Faber married Bernarda de Ruptari, daughter of Guillaume-Arnaud de Ruptari, at an unknown date in the early decades of the thirteenth century.[116] Both the Fabers and the de Ruptaris were also related to the Audebert family, active in the heresy into the late crusading period.[117] Emerging also in the sources for this period, and important allies of the heretics in later years, were members of the Bressols family, especially Raymond and his nephews Aymeric and 'P'.[118]

We know a good deal also about the de Cavelsaut family into which the *credens* Na Pros, Pons Grimoard's cousin and the daughter of Raymond Grimoard, was married by the early years of the century. Pros and Johannes de Cavelsaut had a daughter, Raimunda, who had been hereticated by *c.* 1218. The couple were apparently married by the meeting of *c.* 1204, which Pros attended with Bertranda, wife of Johannes's brother Hugues, a *perfectus*, who was also present. Both the de Cavelsaut brothers and other family members were to continue in the heresy for several decades.[119]

---

115 Doat xxii, fos 34v, 38r, 40v (references to Pons before the crusade); 8v, 13v–14r, 15r–v, 16r–v, 18r, 19r–v, 20v–21r, 23v, 23v–24r (Vital and Arnauda); 4r–v, 15v–16r, 22v, 23r, 23v–24r, 34r–v, 36r, 37v (Raymond); 15r, 21r–v (Pierre); 16v, 23v–r (Raymond-Bernard). See chapter 5 below for the Berètges.
116 Ibid. fos 2r–v, 4r, 6r, 9v–10r, 11r, 15v–16r, 23r–v, 26r–v, 28v, 34r–v, 34v–35r, 35r, 35v–36r, 36r, 36v, 37r–v, 44v–45v.
117 Ibid. fos 9v–10r, 11r–v, 13v–14r, 20v–21r, 24r, 26r–v, 34r–v, 35v.
118 Ibid. fos 34r–v, 38r (Raymond); 4r–5r, 10r, 13v–14r, 18r, 34r–v, 36v, 37r–v (Aymeric); 13v–14r, 20v–1r, 35r–v ('P.').
119 Ibid. fos 7v, 9v–10r, 15v, 15v–16r, 17r–v, 18r, 19v–20r, 20r, 22r, 23r, 24v, 28v, 34r–v, 35v

Further north, on the Tarn-Garonne junction, the abbey town of Moissac was far more subject to actively Catholic influences than Castelsarrasin. Its protagonists in authority were the count of Toulouse and a series of dynamic and ambitious abbots. Both controlled secular rights in the town in a situation not dissimilar to that at Agen. The abbots were to prove active in promoting orthodoxy in the town and the abbey. None the less, they were only partially successful amongst the laity, and the heresy found a foothold at an early date in the instability and conflict between the count and the abbey. The important *perfectus* Raymond Imbert came from the town and had been hereticated before the crusade.[120] The seigneurial family of Moissac contained many *credentes* by c. 1224 and were possibly involved in the heresy before then.[121] The Falquet de Saint-Paul family were also influential *credentes*, many of whom aided the heretics throughout the wars.[122]

Finally, we should note the possibility that heretics sometimes found shelter in the rural abbey of Belleperche in this period. The eleventh-century foundation, on the Garonne south of Castelsarrasin, was influenced by Géraud de Sales and became Cistercian by the late twelfth century.[123] But we find that before the attention of the inquisition fell upon it *credentes* were being admitted there; B. d'Alegre de Borrel and Folquet, a *credens* of Moissac, entered the abbey as monks, and the latter lived there until the friars arrived in the region and he was forced to flee to Italy.[124] In the early 1240s Rostanh de Bressols led R. Stephani, a condemned heretic, to the abbey apparently expecting to find him shelter there, but this pair were met by an angry and frightened, brother Otto, who later recounted the story to local *credentes*.[125] The change in attitude at Belleperche was presumably the result of not only the presence of the inquisition but also legislation passed by the Cistercian order, first in 1218, against monks who sheltered heretics.[126]

It would appear therefore that before the crusade at least one abbey in Bas-Quercy had been infiltrated by heretical ideas and another, at Moissac, was at risk from the heretical urban community whose religious life it dominated only theoretically. The river towns of Bas-Quercy were well accustomed to heretics in the late twelfth century, probably including those from the more rural and castellan dominated region of the Agenais, who we know from more abundant evidence certainly travelled to and through Bas-Quercy in later years. Whatever its relationship to the Agenais or Toulousain Cathar hierarchy, its own *credentes*

(Pros); 15r–v, 16v, 19v–20r, 22r, 23v–24r, 34r–v, 36r, 37v (Johannes); 17r–v, 20r, 23r, 28r–v (Raimunda); 11r, 14r–v, 15r–v, 19v–20r, 21r–v, 21v, 28v, 34r–v, 35r, 37v, 38r (Hughes).

120 Ibid. xxiii, fo. 167v.

121 See chapters 4 and 5 below.

122 Doat xxi, fo. 294r–v; xxii, fos 6r, 36r–v.

123 GC xiii. 259; Mousnier, 'Implantations monastiques' (unpaginated).

124 Doat xxii, fo. 3r; *Documents pour servir à l'histoire de l'inquisition dans le Languedoc*, ed. C. Douais, 2nd edn, Paris 1977, 95.

125 Doat xxii, fo. 12r.

126 Kienzle, *Cistercians*, 171, 215.

and heretics were anything but peripheral to the heretical life, for some of the most significant examples of the discussion of dualist beliefs in popular circles come from this region, most notably from members of the Faber and Audebert families.[127] How these heretical towns fared in the coming wars and inquisition will be discussed in subsequent chapters.

To conclude, Guillemain implies that the Agenais, alone in Aquitaine, was home to heretics because it was 'disputée, entre l'influence toulousaine et l'influence bordelaise'.[128] This indeed provides an insight into the religious tolerance of the region, but not because the two powers were closely involved in the Agenais in the period during which Catharism was being implanted there. On the contrary, its importance to them was apparently primarily as a military buffer zone. It was built up in defensive terms by Duke Richard; Marmande defended the Bordelais from enemy activity along the Garonne, the loyalty of Agen was bought to secure its co-operation also, and we should not neglect the defensive as well as commercial significance of the bridge which the town intended to build, and Penne guaranteed Aquitainian interests in Quercy by its domination of the Lot. Aside from the probability that the dukes installed seneschals in the Agenais, there is little indication that they were interested in the immediate government of the region. Indeed, its economic potential pertained most immediately to the bishops and the towns. Thus higher lay authority was very distant in the Agenais under the Angevins. This changed under Raymond of Toulouse to an extent, but his seneschal Hugues d'Alfaro was no more interested in the persecution of heresy than were the count's officials in the Toulousain, and there is no evidence that the lethargic bishop Bertrand de Béceyras took action in spite of the papal initiative of 1198.

In the absence of activity by the highest authorities, heresy thrived in the more 'Languedocian' northern portion of the county in very similar conditions to those which favoured it in Bas-Quercy, the Toulousain and the counties to its south and east. Lordship was weak, legal hierarchy between families rarely in evidence, accountability to comital authority apparently voluntary and loyalty to the bishop existing only amongst a small orthodox section of the nobility. Minor castellanies in the Agenais could thus accept heretics into their protection with little fear of action from above. Whilst there is not enough evidence from any sources to indicate generalised female and peasant support for the heresy, the presence of Languedocian patterns of partible inheritance at all social levels, and the highly militarised and castle based culture and weak monastic life, make it possible that these characteristics of heretical adherence were also present along the Lot.

In contrast, Dossat's premise that Catharism did not establish itself beyond the Garonne holds true even for the Gascon Agenais, with its far more vibrant orthodox life. There is no evidence of the heresy even in the assertively independent port of Mas-d'Agenais. We have noted that the Garonne divided the

---

127 See Barber's discussion of popular belief: *Cathars*, 96–7.
128 Guillemain, 'Le Duché', 63.

region in linguistic terms. Whilst, as argued above, this was unlikely to have proved a barrier in itself, it reinforces the impression of cultural differences either side of the river. Thus the Agenais was far from being a coherent entity and was instead an almost accidental geographical construct, the result of two distinct influences: Gascon on the one hand, dominated by powerful secular lords who, like other Gascons, favoured orthodoxy; Languedocian on the other, and thus, either through genuine adherence or religious ambivalence, open to the Cathar heresy. The next few decades were to see the Agenais plunged into appalling warfare. Patterns of local partisanship in the fighting and its geographical orientation indicate that the orthodox authorities of France were well aware that the region was neither united in confessional terms nor in social solidarity.

4

The Agenais in the Albigensian Wars, 1207–1229

On 14 January 1208 Pierre de Castelnau, papal legate to the Midi charged with investigating the Cathar heresy, was murdered. Count Raymond VI of Toulouse was held by many to be responsible. Not only was the Languedoc a haven for heretics but their protectors had now murdered a servant of Christ's vicar. Arnaud Aimery, abbot of Cîteaux and papal legate to the Languedoc, was initially charged with organising and leading the crusade.[1] The pope advised him to target for recruitment Christians including those of Périgord, the Limousin and Poitou specifically.[2] Thus the main crusading army came

[1] This is necessarily the briefest of summaries of the crusade, designed to provide a chronological context for the impact of the crusade on the Agenais, Aquitaine and Quercy. There are two major contemporary literary sources for the crusade. The *Chanson de la croisade albigeoise*, is an Occitan poem by William of Tudela and his anonymous continuator. William was a cleric from Navarre based in the Languedoc under the patronage of Baldwin of Toulouse, the brother of Count Raymond VI of Toulouse. Whilst a staunch defender of orthodoxy, his writing reveals great empathy with the suffering of his adopted countrymen. He began the *Chanson* in 1210 and finished writing at *laisse* 132, when King Peter II of Aragon entered the war. The continuator, also orthodox, was much more of a southern partisan than William. There is a recent English translation (*The song of the Cathar wars*, trans. A. Shirley, Aldershot 1996). The second source is Peter des Vaux-de-Cernay's *Hystoria albigensis*. Peter was a northern French Cistercian, nephew of Guy des Vaux-de-Cernay, bishop of Carcassonne from June 1212; his account was probably the official record of the crusade commissioned by Rome. Peter was young and impressionable, fanatical about the justness of the crusade and an apologist for its excesses. His partisanship is so apparent, however, that his value as a source is not especially undermined by it. His Latin chronicle covers events until 1218. I have mainly used the French translation but the original Latin (*Hystoria albigensis*, ed. P. Guebin and H. Maisonneuve, Paris 1951) is referred to for its excellent footnotes. Since writing, an English translation has been published (*The history of the Albigensian Crusade*, ed. and English trans. W. A. Sibly and M. D. Sibly, Oxford 1998). Another important southern French source is the *Chronique* of William of Puylaurens, a southern notary who was later in the service of Raymond VII of Toulouse and of the inquisition. He was especially interested in the subject of heresy and his chronicle, written c. 1250, contains some important insights into the crusade, of which he probably had first hand experience: Y. Dossat, 'A Propos du chroniqueur Guillaume de Puylaurens', in his *Eglise et hérésie*, 47–52, and also 'Le Chroniqueur Guillaume de Puylaurens était-il chapelain de Raymond VII ou notaire de l'inquisition toulousaine?', ibid. 343–53. Finally, the anonymous *Histoire de la guerre des albigeoise* (RHF xix. 114–92; HGL viii. 1–205) is a later thirteenth-century work which follows Peter des Vaux-de-Cernay almost entirely, but occasionally contains interesting information from other sources. The most thorough secondary accounts of the crusade are in HGL viii and Roquebert, *L'Épopée*. See also that by M. Barber (*Cathars*, 120–40) for discussion of the actual relationship of crusading campaigns to the extirpation of heresy.

[2] William of Tudela, *Chanson*, i. 38–45.

from the whole length and breadth of the Auvergne, from Burgundy, from France, from the Limousin, from the whole world – north and south – Germans, Poitevins and Gascons, men from the Rouergue and Saintonge.[3]

It mustered in Lyon in June 1209 and approached the Languedoc via the Rhône valley, anticipating the confiscation of such lands as it could wrestle from the protectors of heretics. The excommunicate Raymond VI sought reconciliation with the Church as it approached, not only because of this army but because his lands in the Agenais had been attacked by an earlier expedition. Friendless amongst the clergy of the Languedoc, he sent into Gascony to request Archbishop Bernard of Auch and Montazin de Galard, abbot of Condom, to intervene on his behalf. This they did successfully in Rome, so that when the main crusade arrived Raymond had already, on 18–22 June, taken the cross and could not be attacked.[4] The lands of Viscount Raymond-Roger Trencavel in the eastern Languedoc were targeted instead.

Events until the settlement at the Fourth Lateran Council of 1215 can be summarised in four stages.[5] Aquitainians played a part in all of them, and on both sides. The first phase, from 1209 to 1211, was the brief expedition in the Agenais and the conquest of the Trencavel lands. In its early stages a courageous and skilful military leader quickly came to the fore, Simon, lord of Montfort in the Île de France, who was to dominate events in the Languedoc until his death in 1218. Gascons were involved in two of the sieges of this phase. Their soldiers, famous for lethal skill as *dardassiers*, were employed as defenders of Casseneuil in the Agenais in 1209.[6] In the ranks of the crusaders at Minerve in spring 1210 was a contingent of more respectable Gascons, recruited by Archbishop Bernard of Auch.[7] From August to November of that year these same soldiers were part of a Gascon contingent at the siege of Termes, of which Amanieu V d'Albret, son of the crusader of 1190, was also a member and a Gascon force he had recruited at Langon, near La Réole. Archbishop Guillaume II de Geniès of Bordeaux (1207–27) was also present.[8] At the siege of Minerve in June–July 1210 Gascons served under the crusader Guy de Lucy, and a contingent of Angevins were present.[9]

The second phase began when de Montfort and the legates again secured the excommunication of Raymond VI, early in 1211. Then the conquest of the Toulousain was achieved, with the exception of Toulouse itself, as was the submission of much of Quercy and the Agenais by late in the following year. At an unsuccessful siege of Toulouse by the crusade in June 1211 Gascons were

---

3   Ibid. i. 36–9 (*Song of the Cathar wars*, 17).
4   William of Tudela, *Chanson*, i. 30–1.
5   As they are in A. P. Evans, 'The Albigensian Crusade', in K. M. Setton and others (eds), *History of the crusades*, Philadelphia 1962, ii. 287.
6   See n. 16 below.
7   Peter des Vaux-de-Cernay, *Histoire*, i. 899.
8   William of Tudela, *Chanson*, i. 134–5.
9   Peter des Vaux-de-Cernay, *Histoire*, i. 155.

amongst the defenders. They included Count Bernard IV Comminges and his cousin Raimond-At de Castelbon of Couserans, who was killed.[10] In September an important double siege took place at Castelnaudary. Savary de Mauléon, King John of England's seneschal at Poitiers, appeared in the southern army at this point, arriving from Bergerac after being summoned by Raymond VI for a substantial reward.[11] During the subsequent battle at Castelnaudary the *routier* Martin Algaïs, John's seneschal for Gascony and Périgord, arrived to support the crusaders with twenty men, but then deserted.[12] Viscount Gaston VI of Béarn brought a force to aid the southerners at the same siege.[13] In the winter of 1211–12 the Agenais was attacked again and treacherous Gascons with local knowledge acted as guides to the northerners.[14] When Moissac was besieged in 1212, Gascons were amongst the crusader force repelling a sortie from the town.[15]

The third phase saw King Peter of Aragon, Catholic hero and victor of the battle of Las Navas de Tolosa against the Moors in the previous year, intervening on the southern side in 1213. His objective was to protect his brother-in-law Raymond VI and his Pyrennean vassals, whom he considered to have been unjustly demonised and threatened by the crusade. This intervention coincided with papal misgivings about the conduct of the crusade and moves by Innocent III to divert military activity toward the Holy Land. Ultimately, however, the pope was persuaded by the legates that Peter and his allies were in the wrong. The result was a decisive but horrific battle at Muret, gateway to Couserans and the Gascon Pyrenees, on 12 September 1213. It resulted in the decimation of the combined southern forces, probably many Gascons amongst them, and the death of King Peter.

The fourth phase, between the defeat at Muret and the Fourth Lateran Council of November 1215, saw the south no longer able to resist northern domination. De Montfort continued to assume secular powers throughout the Languedoc, with the approval of Prince Louis, son of Philip Augustus, in spite of a ruling by the pope that he should await the arbitration of the council.

---

[10] William of Tudela, *Chanson*, i. 192–3.
[11] Peter des Vaux-de-Cernay, *Histoire*, i. 105, 112; William of Tudela, *Chanson*, i. 219, 235; *HGL* vi. 368–70. For John's involvement in the crusade and that of his officials see C. Taylor, 'Pope Innocent III, John of England and the Albigensian Crusade (1209–1216)', in J. C. Moore (ed.), *Pope Innocent III and his world*, Aldershot 1999, 208–14. Peter des Vaux-de-Cernay calls de Mauléon a heretic but there is no actual evidence of such sympathies on his part. For his *vida* see *Biographies des troubadours*, ed. J. Boutière and A. H. Schutz, Toulouse 1950, 317–20.
[12] William of Tudela, *Chanson*, i. 226–9.
[13] Ibid. i. 208–11, 220–3; Peter des Vaux-de-Cernay, *Histoire*, i. 109.
[14] William of Tudela, *Chanson*, i. 254–7.
[15] Ibid. i. 269.

The crusaders and the Cathar diocese to 1215

At the time of the apparently minor campaign in the Agenais in 1209, the very first of the crusade, the county was governed for Raymond VI by Hugues d'Alfaro from Penne d'Agenais. William of Tudela's is the only source which gives us an account of its events.[16] His knowledge perhaps results from the fact that in the years 1198 to 1211 he was based near the Agenais, at Montauban.[17] The leaders and major recruiters of the campaign were Count Guy II of Auvergne and Archbishop Guillaume of Bordeaux. Their army was mainly drawn from the archdiocese of Bourges and included four of the most important nobles of central and upper Quercy, regions likewise outside the heretical sphere at this time. These were Bertrand II de Cardaillac, Bertrand de Gourdon, Ratier de Castelnau-Montratier, and Viscount Raymond III of Turenne.[18] Amongst the churchmen were Bishop Jean de Veira of Limoges and Bishop Guillaume de Cardaillac of Cahors (1208–34), who was the uncle of Bertrand de Cardaillac and a vassal of Raymond VI.[19] Absent, in spite of the crusading assembly at Agen itself in May, were the laity and most of the clergy of the Agenais, with the exception of Arnaud de Rovinha, bishop of Agen. Indeed, it was perhaps Arnaud, 'turbulent et fanatique' in his relations with the heretics and their supporters in his diocese, who instigated the campaign. His motive was not just concern for orthodoxy. He was personally in dispute with Raymond VI over their respective rights in the county, a matter he had apparently referred to Rome.[20]

Their army first destroyed Gontaud and sacked Tonneins, both towns which possibly had a heretical population (although no indication of this is given by William of Tudela). It is not known whether the latter attack was on Tonneins-Dessus, held by members of Bishop Arnaud's own family, or Tonneins-Dessous, held by the Ferréols. It is however quite possible that the bishop would attack heretical sympathisers amongst his own family, for the most important activity of this campaign was aimed at his brother Hugues, lord of Casseneuil, probably the seat of the Cathar diocese. There a major siege took place. The town was built on a rocky outcrop, the Pech-Neyrat, between the Lot and the Lède,

16 Ibid. i. 38–45.

17 *Dictionnaire de biographie française*, ed. J. Balteau and others, Paris 1989, xvii. 191–2.

18 'Documents de la maison de Turenne', 330–2. Raymond III was viscount from 1190 to 1191: ibid. 310, 325–6; Higounet, *Comminges*, 149. His Quercinois lands included Castelnau-Montratier, which he inherited from his mother (see chapter 3 above). It is unclear whether he held it from Raymond VI, from whom most Quercinois seigneuries were held: 'Documents de la maison de Turenne', 312, 330–2; Roquebert, *L'Épopée*, i. 239–40; ii. 110–13 and n. 7; *Dictionnaire de la noblesse*, xix. 256–7.

19 In 1211 Bishop Guillaume transferred this homage to Simon de Montfort: Doat cxx, fo. 3r; Albe, *L'Hérésie en Quercy*, 2. Bishop Jean's dates are uncertain but he was bishop after 1199 and before 1215: *Series episcoporum ecclesiae catholicae*, ed. P. B. Gams, 3rd edn, Leipzig 1931. There is a later edition of this latter volume (Graz 1957) to which I did not have access.

20 Cassany-Mazet, *Villeneuve*, 44 (quotation); Capul, 'Notes en Agenais', 7; Samazeuilh, *Histoire*, i. 229–30, 235.

natural barriers which were rendered almost insurmountable by the addition of a man-made ditch three hundred metres long, twenty-five metres wide and fifteen deep. This, built in the twelfth century, had been filled in and since re-excavated.[21] The well-equipped garrison was commanded by Séguin de Balenx, a member of a family of heretical sympathisers.

The outcome of the siege is curious. William of Tudela tells us that the town was well defended by the garrison and its Gascon recruits, but that it could have been taken had Count Guy not defied the archbishop and intervened in its favour. The reason for this, he tells us, is that Guy held property at the town. This sounds most unlikely. Another explanation is that the *quarantaine* was up and that recruits began to drift away.[22] It is also likely that the crusaders heard of Raymond VI's amnesty of mid-June, and the consequent illegality of their campaign. However, numerous heretics were apparently captured from the unconquered town and burned, the very first executions or, indeed, recorded encounters with heretics of the Albigensian Crusade. This led to the temporary evacuation of Villemur and probably to the view in Rome the following year that, although there were still heretics in the Agenais, their numbers had been greatly reduced.[23]

In 1211, when Raymond of Toulouse was again excommunicated, the Agenais declared for him. William of Tudela tells us that the people of Agen said they would go into exile into Gascony rather than be subjected to rule by foreigners. Raymond preferred them to fight, however, and they probably did so under the command of Hugues d'Alfaro, present with his brother Pierre Arcès in the ranks of the defenders of Toulouse that summer. Men from the Agenais and Bas-Quercy were also summoned by the count to the double siege at Castelnaudary that autumn. Around the same time, Raymond managed to force Bishop Arnaud from his see and seize all secular resources there for himself, including the comital powers pertaining to the bishop.[24]

In the following year the arrival of Guy de Montfort, brother of Simon, made possible the conquest of the lands and communication routes surrounding Toulouse. The capture of the Albigeoise Aveyron by the crusaders allowed them also to target the towns commanding the Lot and Garonne. In this context, and undoubtedly with the encouragement of its exiled bishop, the Agenais was again attacked. First the army approached the Lot via Montcuq. Its inhabitants, including the *bailli* Guiraud de Montfabès, fled on 1 June and took refuge at

---

[21] Peter des Vaux-de-Cernay, *Histoire*, 199. M. Roquebert discusses the problems that the re-excavated ditch posed to the crusaders only with reference to the 1214 siege: *L'Épopée*, ii. 279, 281. Given the similar difficulties faced by the crusaders of 1209, it would seem probable that the ditch had been re-dug by then.

[22] Guillemain, 'Le Duché', 60.

[23] Peter des Vaux-de-Cernay, *Histoire*, 127 n. 1.

[24] William of Tudela, *Chanson*, i. 146–53, 194–7, 205–37; Peter des Vaux-de-Cernay, *Histoire*, 104–14; *PL* ccxvi.836; Roquebert, *L'Épopée*, ii. 122; Labénazie, *Annales d'Agen*, 124; Samazeuilh, *Histoire*, i. 237. See also chapter 5 below.

Penne d'Agenais. Montcuq was put into the hands of the crusader Baldwin of Toulouse, the northern-raised half-brother of Raymond VI.[25]

The crusaders then amassed at Penne on Sunday 3 June and established two camps below the castle. But Penne had been well designed by Duke Richard and was almost impenetrable. It was also well provisioned, and Peter des Vaux-de-Cernay, who was present, says that d'Alfaro had hired the *routier* chief Bausan, four other captains and their 400 mercenaries to defend it. But the mere presence of the crusaders sent shock waves through the Agenais and the brave words of 1211 were forgotten. On 4 June, even before the siege was begun in earnest, de Montfort was received with honour by the town of Agen, and on the 17th, along the lines traditional to the town, he divided the *comitalia* between himself and the reinstated bishop.[26]

The besieging of Penne could now commence properly. It began on 6 June and continued throughout a hot month with neither side gaining the advantage. Indeed, the crusaders struggled to keep up their numbers as the *quarantaine* lapsed. In late June, however, due to the arrival of reinforcements from northern France, morale in the castle fell and d'Alfaro expelled its non-combatants. But continual bombarding of the castle still did not bring a result and de Montfort decided to begin the second phase of his conquest of the Agenais. He sent Robert Mauvoisin, who was ill but none the less zealous, to Marmande shortly after 17 July to engage Raymond VI's garrison. The town surrendered as the result of a mangonel bombardment and a northern garrison was installed.[27]

During June and July the nobles of the Agenais became as demoralised as the towns, and began to declare for the crusade's commander, receiving their lands back as fiefs. Amongst those who defected was possibly Hugues de Rovinha himself, for in 1214 he is described by Peter des Vaux-de-Cernay as breaking faith with de Montfort. On 25 July this mass defection, combined with a serious shortage of food and water at Penne and a lack of reinforcements from Raymond VI, led d'Alfaro to request that he and his garrison be allowed to surrender armed but unharmed. His timing was unfortunate for, unknown to him, another large group of crusaders had been about to desert the camp. As it was, the conditions were accepted. De Montfort put his own garrison in place and began to re-build this strategically important fortification.[28] Penne became his main base in the northern Languedoc, from which he would launch campaigns into Périgord and Bas-Quercy; he would later base there the first French *sénéchaussée* in the Languedoc.

Because the Agenais had submitted, almost without a fight, by late summer 1212, its inhabitants were not dispossessed. Unlike the landless *faidits* of the

---

25 Peter des Vaux-de-Cernay, *Histoire*, 127.

26 Ibid. 127–33. See also William of Tudela, *Chanson*, i. 254–61; Roquebert, *L'Épopée*, i. 370–1; and chapter 5 below.

27 Peter des Vaux-de-Cernay, *Histoire*, 130–2; Higounet, *Marmande*, 8.

28 Peter des Vaux-de-Cernay, *Histoire*, 129–32, 199. Labénazie states that Hugues transferred his homage in 1210 at the instigation of his brother the bishop: *Annales d'Agen*, 123.

Lauragais, Albigeoise and Trencavel lands, who had been conquered and their lands given to crusaders, and who were thus irrevocably opposed to the crusade, the loyalty of the Agenais lords was apparently taken for granted. The weakness of the Agenais resistance was not to last however. In truth, its lordships and towns were to change allegiance whenever it was necessary in order to avoid political subjection and the confiscation of their property or, indeed, whenever the dominant authority in their region looked like facing a reversal of fortune.

Thus it was that in 1214 confidence revived in the Agenais. The deciding factor was the intervention of an external power in the spring, but as early as February Hugues de Rovinha appears to have recovered his nerve. After the terrible defeat at Muret, of which d'Alfaro was one of the lucky southern survivors, the depression that had hit the Languedoc was somewhat alleviated by the capture and execution of the hated Baldwin of Toulouse, by that time lord of much of Quercy and the Albigeoise. The lord of Casseneuil, we are told, openly defied the crusade by sheltering his murderers.[29]

Then in April, whilst marching his army from La Rochelle to Poitou, King John of England took a detour via La Réole. De Montfort sensed the threat and on 13 April moved to Penne. His fears appear to have been justified. Marmande, the next major town up river from La Réole, surrendered to John, who garrisoned it heavily with his own men and placed in charge his seneschal for Gascony, Geoffrey de Neville. This began a wave of defections in the Agenais. The castle of Montpezat-d'Agenais, across the river from Castelmoron on a plain dominating the Lot, became a rallying point for the Agenais rebels. Le Mas d'Agenais also defected and the crusaders attempted in vain to win it back, hampered by an armed flotilla of barges from La Réole. But events went de Montfort's way again when John left the region and the Marmande garrison was isolated. The crusaders destroyed Montpezat d'Agenais, which was abandoned as they approached, and made for Marmande. At first the townspeople refused entry to the crusade but after a short siege fled by boat to La Réole. Geoffrey de Neville and his garrison were granted safe conduct after surrendering and de Montfort refortified and garrisoned Marmande himself.[30]

---

[29] Peter des Vaux-de-Cernay, *Histoire*, 199; Roquebert, *L'Épopée*, ii. 199, 278.

[30] Peter des Vaux-de-Cernay, *Histoire*, 197–202; *HGL* vi. 446; Roquebert, *L'Épopée*, ii. 257–8. De Neville evidently replaced Martin Algaïs as seneschal for Gascony after he was killed: Taylor, 'Pope Innocent III', 210–12 esp. n. 40. The identification of Montpezat has caused historians some problems. Peter des Vaux-de-Cernay was with the army and is clear that the castle in question was in the diocese of Agen (*Histoire*, 197–8). However Devic and Vaissète identified it as Montpezat-de-Quercy and the archivist G. Tholin follows them (*HGL* vi. 445; 'Notes sur la féodalité', *RA* xxvi. 71–2). The chronicler says that de Montfort destroyed castles in Quercy and moved for Marmande destroying Montpezat *en route*. We know from another source that he was near Montcuq on 12 June (see n. 47 below). Tholin's objection rests on his own assumption that if Montpezat were the Agenais castle this meant an unlikely detour back to Montcuq before reaching Marmande. However, the route given by the chronicler is Castelnau-Montratier, Mondenard, Montpezat, Marmande, then back up the Lot to Casseneuil. It is perfectly possible that de Montfort was at Montcuq on 12 June between

Now he could turn his attention to the rebels and murderers at Casseneuil, described at this time by Pierre des Vaux-de-Cernay, in his typical polemic, as 'one of the most important centres of heresy and one of the oldest, whose inhab-itants were in the majority heretics, thieves and traitors'.[31] On 28 June the crusaders established a fortified camp, known subsequently as the Château de Montfort, on one of the hillsides overlooking the town. They began bombarding the walls and houses with a catapult and organising for reinforcements. This was to be a long and protracted siege. To the fascination of Peter des Vaux-de-Cernay it involved the use of specialist siege technology as the besiegers attempted to span the man-made ditch joining the Lot and the Lède to the east of the town. During the night of Sunday 17 August a constructed causeway at last reached the opposite bank and the crusaders, under cover, were able to begin demolishing the barbicans. The defenders sensed defeat and the merce-naries in the town charged out on horseback and escaped. On the following day Casseneuil was stormed and burned, and its heretics and other inhabitants massacred.[32]

This time the loyalty of the conquered region was not taken for granted. De Montfort appointed Philip de Landreville, a knight of the Île-de-France, as his seneschal for the Agenais, presumably based at Penne, and Pierre de Voisin was installed as his marshal. By late August the Agenais nobility had done homage to the crusade's commander, promising to demolish their castles, and recognised the authority of his officials. As part of this process Hugues de Rovinha was apparently deprived of Casseneuil, or at least its revenues, for de Landreville granted them to Dominic Guzman.[33] De Montfort returned briefly to the Agenais later in the same year to ensure that destruction of fortifications was actually taking place, and to receive at Penne the homage of the *quercinois* lord Raymond de Montaut for lands he held in the Agenais.[34] De Montfort certainly anticipated that he would be confirmed in possession of the Agenais at the Lateran council scheduled for the following year.

Quercy was also a target in the wars. After the second excommunication of Raymond of Toulouse in 1210 his lands there were again very vulnerable. Bishop Guillaume of Cahors, the crusader of 1209, was active again in the army from early February 1211 and transferred his homage for Cahors from Count Raymond to de Montfort on 20 June, and later in the year to King Philip. He was working in alliance with Abbot Raymond du Proët of Moissac, Raymond VI's

---

visiting Mondenard and Montpezat-d'Agenais. It is a logical route, allowing the crusaders to join the river at Penne.

31 Peter des Vaux-de-Cernay, *Histoire*, 198–9.

32 Ibid. 198–202.

33 Roquebert, *L'Épopée*, ii. 277–84, 358; HGL vi. 465; viii. 677; M. H. Vicaire, *Saint Dominique et ses frères: évangile ou croisade?*, Paris 1967, 81, and *Histoire de Saint Dominique*, Paris 1957, i. 322 n. 247.

34 Peter des Vaux-de-Cernay, *Histoire*, 204; Doat lxxv, fo. 53r; HGL vi. 448; Roquebert, *L'Épopée*, ii. 290.

rival for secular authority in the abbey town, who was in the camp from spring 1211.[35]

A good many nobles of central and upper Quercy also transferred their homage that same summer.[36] Never having received the heresy themselves, they saw no reason to lose their lands to the northerners by resisting the invasion. Thus, in the retinue of Baldwin of Toulouse we find the viscount of Monclar-de-Quercy and the *quercinois* Hugues de Breil, and they were joined by an unidentified 'Raymond de Périgord'.[37] Peter des Vaux-de-Cernay tells us that other lords of Quercy sent Bishop Guillaume to the siege of Toulouse to offer their submission, although William of Tudela sees the surrender of Quercy as resulting from pressure applied by Arnaud Aimery. Whatever the case, in August 1211 de Montfort received at Cahors the promised homages of the most important lords of Quercy, the crusaders of 1209: Bertrand de Cardaillac, Bertrand de Gourdon and Ratier de Castelnau-Montratier, and in addition that of Raymond of Turenne.[38]

The following year de Montfort began rewarding his allies in the northern Languedoc and punishing those whom he considered traitors. Activity also took place in Périgord, very likely at the instigation of its count, Archembaud II (he was with the army at points between 1212 and 1214 and probably looked to use its presence to extend his rather nominal authority in the county).[39] When the siege of Penne ended in late July 1212, de Montfort moved just across the Agenais border with Périgord to the castle of the traitor Martin Algaïs at Biron. The occupants of the castle soon sought to negotiate for their safety. De Montfort suspected that this adversary, for whom he appears to have developed a special dislike, had a secret escape route and suggested that the garrison hand over their commander in exchange for their freedom. This they did. Algaïs was cruelly executed and his castle granted to the *quercinois* Arnaud de Montaigu, a recent recruit to the crusade who had provided much needed reinforcements at Penne.[40]

De Montfort returned briefly to Penne and then, on 6 August, via Montcuq to Bas-Quercy. Its conquest was essential if he was to benefit from his easily won domination of the northern Languedoc by having access to it from the Toulousain. Its towns understood the special position they occupied both strategically, dominating the river system of the northern Languedoc, and psychologically, in support of the still resilient people of Toulouse. The first town to be attacked was Moissac. It was not as strategically important as Montauban, which

[35] *HGL* viii. 160, 611–12. See also Dutton, 'Aspects', 42.
[36] Canon 27 of the 1179 Lateran Council allowed a Catholic lord to renounce his oath to a protector of heretics: Roquebert, *L'Épopée*, ii. 138.
[37] William of Tudela, *Chanson*, i. 176; Roquebert, *L'Épopée*, i. 480, 503.
[38] Peter des Vaux-de-Cernay, *Histoire*, 101 and n. 4; William of Tudela, *Chanson*, i. 202–3; Roquebert, *L'Épopée*, i. 428–30; ii. 111 n. 8.
[39] Guillemain, 'Le Duché', 66. Archembaud of Périgord performed homage to Philip Augustus in 1211: Dutton, 'Aspects', 42–3.
[40] William of Tudela, *Chanson*, i. 256–61; Peter des Vaux-de-Cernay, *Histoire*, 113, 132.

was garrisoned by a son of the count of Foix, or Castelsarrassin, garrisoned by Guiraud de Pépieux. It was more vulnerable, however, and its fall would be a great blow to the other towns.

In the disputes between Raymond VI and the monks, the people of Moissac typically sided with the count. Earlier in the year it had expelled the abbot and he was imprisoned at Montauban. Now the town supported the count and also its heretics, and was aided by a mercenary garrison supplied by Count Raymond. The crusaders reached it on 14 August. The ensuing siege consisted of frequent sorties and offensives in which the town initially had the upper hand. However, soldiers from Montauban unsuccessfully attacked a crusader party and were captured by Baldwin of Toulouse and the *quercinois* lords Armand de Mondenard and Hugues de Breil. To demoralise Moissac, they were held as prisoners in the camp outside. In September, the arrival of northern reinforcements enabled the crusaders to encircle the town at last, and a series of offensives and counter-offensives ensued in which it became apparent that the town could eventually be overwhelmed.[41]

At this crucial point the garrison at Castelsarrassin deserted and its people sent a delegation to the crusaders offering their surrender. This was accepted and the town was given to Guillaume de Contres. The people of Moissac were by now on the verge of surrender themselves but the mercenary garrison, which faced certain death if not on the winning side, wanted to hold out. The *routiers* were betrayed by the townspeople as a condition of their own safety when they opened the gates to de Montfort on 8 September, and were indeed executed. On 14 September the abbot, accustomed to sharing the lay rights and responsibilities at Moissac with the count of Toulouse, acknowledged de Montfort in this secular capacity.[42] However, Bas-Quercy was not quite lost. It was too late in the season to besiege Montauban, an even better defended and more resilient town, and so the success of the crusade in the Agenais and Quercy did not lead to the fall of Toulouse. None the less, de Montfort had seriously reduced Toulousain influence along the Lot and the Garonne in Quercy and the Agenais by late summer 1212.

As for the lords of central and upper Quercy who capitulated so readily, it has been noted that few are to be found at any point actually engaged in combat on behalf of the crusade.[43] The reality of northern domination was not only frightening but sickening to even the Catholics of the region, and many were to change sides again. It was in this context that Baldwin of Toulouse was murdered, during a peace under which the Languedoc had been placed after Muret. On 17 February 1214 after a journey through the Agenais he went to bed in the castle of Lolmie, whose lords had done homage to him as lord of Montcuq,

---

41 William of Tudela, *Chanson*, i. 261–77; Peter des Vaux-de-Cernay, *Histoire*, 134–7; Sumption, *Albigensian Crusade*, 151–3; Roquebert, *L'Épopée*, i. 477–81. For the abbot's incarceration see also Roquebert, *L'Épopée*, ii. 122, and *PL* ccxvi.836
42 *HGL* viii. 621; AD, Lot, F 125. See also chapter 3 above.
43 Roquebert, *L'Épopée*, i. 503.

ten kilometres to the south, which he had also just visited. The treacherous castellans alerted two other *quercinois* lords to his presence. One was Bertrand de Mondenard, a kinsman of Armand de Mondenard, the crusader of 1212 and vassal of de Montfort. The other was a Montfortist vassal in his own right, Ratier de Castelnau-Montratier, the crusader of 1209. Both were now secretly southern partisans. During the night they and their men were let into the castle and seized the unsuspecting Baldwin from bed. They took him to Montcuq, where he agreed to dismiss his garrison and hand the town over to the southerners, and then to Montauban where he was executed. As a direct result the confidence of the southerners was temporarily revived.[44]

This was not enough to defeat the crusade, however. Raymond submitted to the legate Peter of Benevento and the Languedoc was placed under a peace until the anticipated arbitration in Rome of 1215.[45] In spite of this crusader forces remained in the northern Languedoc in summer 1214. De Montfort justified this defiance of papal wishes by enlisting the support of another legate, Robert de Courçon, charged not with duties in the Languedoc but with recruiting throughout France for a planned crusade to the east. However he was with the army for many of its manoeuvres from April 1214 and it was with his blessing that de Montfort launched a campaign to punish the rebellious *quercinois*, especially Ratier de Castelnau-Montratier and the family of Mondenard. These rebels were under the protection of Hughes de Rovinha at Casseneuil, but their own castles were taken in the first two weeks of June.[46] It was now that de Montfort moved for Montpezat d'Agenais, pausing near-by Montcuq on 12 June to receive the submission of the *quercinois* Déodat de Barasc, lord of Béduer and Lissac, who was forced to agree to destroy his own castles.[47]

After taking Casseneuil in late August, de Montfort decided to attack a stretch of the Dordogne in southern Périgord. This followed information received by the crusade that several of its castles harboured enemies of the peace and of the faith, that is to say, *routiers* and heretics. Domme and Montfort, although well fortified, were abandoned before the crusaders arrived. Neighbouring Castelnaud-Brétenoux was also deserted and from it the crusaders organised a successful siege of the castle of a robber chief Gaillard de Beynac.[48]

Aspects of this crusade in Périgord are puzzling. I have argued that there was no Cathar enclave there in the twelfth century, and there is likewise no substantial evidence that there were any there by the early thirteenth. In fact the crusade's real target was the *routier* Bernard de Cazenac, lord of Domme, Cazenac and Montfort, who fled before it arrived. He and his wife Hélis of

---

[44] Peter des Vaux-de-Cernay, *Histoire*, 189–92; William of Puylaurens, *Chronique*, 92–3; William of Tudela, *Chanson*, ii. 276; Albe, *L'Hérésie en Quercy*, 4.

[45] *RHF* xix. 210.

[46] Roquebert, *L'Épopée*, ii. 269–76, 287.

[47] Peter des Vaux-de-Cernay, *Histoire*, 197–8; *Actes de Simon de Montfort*, 8; William of Tudela, *Chanson*, iii. 303 n. 6; Roquebert, *L'Épopée*, ii. 269–76, 287.

[48] Peter des Vaux-de-Cernay, *Histoire*, 202–5. The original editors and not Peter des Vaux-de-Cernay identify Beynac's lord (*Hystoria*, ii. 228 n. 5). See also *HGL* vi. 448–51.

Montfort were, according to Peter des Vaux-de-Cernay, already notorious in the crusader camp for their barbarous exploits. After their castles were taken, the chronicler says that crusaders visiting the nearby abbey of Sarlat saw 150 horribly mutilated victims of the couple. However, although he was with the army at this time, he does not claim to have seen this for himself, and nor does he name those who did. In addition he alludes to atrocities which he does not even attempt to describe let alone to verify, except to say that they constituted less than 'one thousandth part of the evil crimes committed by this tyrant and his wife'. These accounts are suspicious not least because there is no corroborating evidence from sources composed locally, for instance by the abbeys of Sarlat or Cadouin.[49]

It has often been observed that the chronicler's portrayal of de Cazenac is in stark contrast with that of the anonymous *Chanson* author who describes him in 1218, when he came to aid the besieged Toulouse, as a

> Pus adreit cavalier, per complida lauzor,
> Qu'el a sen e larueza e cor d'emperador
> E governa Paratge e capdela Valor.[50]

In addition, de Cazenac cannot be shown to have either favoured the heretics or defied crusaders by the time he was attacked, although he did both in later years. It seems that he was perhaps no worse than any other *routier* and that, unlike many others employed by both parties in these wars, had done little to justify a campaign that distracted the crusade from more obviously important targets. How can we account for this diversion?

Perhaps the explanation lies in the fact that Périgord was part of Aquitaine. Even though John's control there was weak and he does not appear to have received homage for its lands, nor to have replaced his dead seneschal Martin Algaïs, very few of its land-holders were the vassals of the enemies of the Church in the Languedoc. Given evidence offered below that the Albigensian wars were not distinct from the wars between the kings of France and England, we might speculate that this attack on the Périgord/Quercy border was intended as a warning to John. That is, were it not for de Cazenac's own protest that the crusaders should leave him in peace because he had been the only lord in Périgord to take the side of the French king against that of England.[51] Unlike Martin Algaïs, therefore, the *routier* de Cazenac was not an ally of the duke of Aquitaine. Nor can we assert that the count of Périgord encouraged the crusade, as he may have done against Algaïs, in order to strengthen his own hand in his

---

[49] Peter des Vaux-de-Cernay, *Histoire*, 203 (quotation translated in Peter des Vaux-de-Cernay, *History* at p. 238). Nothing is noted in *Chartier du monastère de Sarlat*, ed. G. Marnier, *BSHAP* xi (1884) or in the *Cartulaire de l'abbaye de Cadouin*, ed. J.-M. Maubourgnet, Cahors 1926. See also Taylor, 'Innocent III', 213–14.

[50] William of Tudela, *Chanson*, iii. 138–9.

[51] An incident dating back some twenty years: Peter des Vaux-de Cernay, *Hystoria*, 228 n. 5.

county, for there is no evidence of his presence in the army at this particular time and he does not appeared to have benefited from the expedition.

A possible source for the stories which so maligned the couple is the Benedictine abbey of Sarlat, six kilometres to the north of Montfort, where the victims of the *routier* and his wife were supposedly seen. Its abbot, Élie de Vignon, was an ally of the crusade and was in the camp at Domme on 12 September, where he submitted the abbey and the town of La Roque-Gageac into de Montfort's protection.[52] It is possible that his emissaries took the stories of the de Cazenacs' 'victims' to the crusader camp in the first place, despite the lack of reference to this in the abbey's surviving records.

If the explanation for the attack can be found by looking at who was newly in the camp at the time the stories first emerged, we have a more likely candidate for their origin. If Peter des Vaux-de-Cernay places the reports in the correct chronological framework, they began to reach the crusaders around 14 June at Casseneuil when Raymond of Turenne performed homage to de Montfort and promised the service of ten knights and ten sergeants to be deployed in the dioceses of Agen, Cahors and Rodez.[53] He remained in the army after Casseneuil and, at the point when de Cazenac's property was taken from him, this loyal Catholic was firmly in favour with the crusade's commander. In addition, and this cannot have been incidental, he had a legal claim to the castle of Montfort, for Viscount Raymond II had, at an uncertain date, married Hélis de Castelnau, heiress of the castle of Montfort and mother of de Cazenac's wife of the same name. In September at Domme, in the presence also of Abbot Elie, Turenne was invested with the confiscated Montfort, all the lands of de Cazenac and the other lands and castles captured in the area.[54]

We might think that the viscount considered that he deserved a return for all his crusading activity in previous years, both in the Languedoc and at Las Navas de Tolosa (notwithstanding a brief conscientious defection to the Aragonese party in 1213).[55] We should also remember that one of his predecessors had been Henry II's representative against heresy in the Languedoc. However, the accusations I level at the viscount of Turenne cannot be made with any great certainty. This is the case not least because the nature and paucity of early documentation for the house of Turenne make it very difficult even to identify the viscount of 1214. Indeed, historians are considerably confused as to whether or not he was the same as the crusader of 1209, Raymond III, who became de Montfort's vassal

---

[52] *Actes de Simon de Montfort*, 87; Doat lxxv, fos 57r–58v; Escande, *Périgord*, 95–6.
[53] AD, Lot, F 125; Doat lxxv, fos 51r–52r. Through his marriage to Hélis of Montfort (see chapter 3 above) Viscount Raymond II had acquired Castelnau-Brétenoux, north-east of Saint-Céré. He was very probably the vassal of the count of Toulouse for this, and also for the viscounty of Brassac, near Castres, and Salignac in southern Périgord, for in 1236 Viscount Raymond IV did homage for these possessions to Raymond VII of Toulouse saying that his predecessors had held them of the count's predecessors: 'Documents de la maison de Turenne', 309–12, 325–6; Roquebert, *L'Épopée*, ii. 294, 350, and see chapter 5 below.
[54] *Actes de Simon de Montfort*, 82, 88, 89a, 288; Doat lxxv, fos 55r–56v.
[55] HGL vi. 383; Roquebert, *L'Épopée*, ii. 52.

in 1211. DeVic and Vaisète are prepared only to concede that there were two viscounts between 1178 and 1236. Roquebert says that Raymond III was viscount until some point in 1214. However Higounet is certain that Raymond III was viscount from 1191 to 1212, and that Raymond IV was viscount 1212–43.[56]

If we are dealing with Raymond III alone we must see him as a confused character, committing himself fervently at different times to both sides, for 1213 was not the only year in which he switched sides because he believed the crusaders were not the party of God: in 1218 he was to contribute to an army being raised to restore Toulouse to Raymond VI and his son. True, many southerners who had declared for the crusade later defected, not least when Peter of Aragon, the hero of Las Navas de Tolosa, took their part. But very few of them threw themselves into fighting on both sides with the fervour apparently exhibited by Raymond III. And few turned against their siblings in the process: Raymond III would have been the brother of Hélis of Montfort.

If, however, Raymond III died in 1212 as Higounet suggests, the scenario is rather different. Raymond IV would have been the viscount of Turenne at Muret, and he would not have been alone there amongst the perfectly orthodox Catholic southerners. When the southern cause appeared to have been lost in midsummer 1214, not least because the rebellious northern Languedoc was on the point of collapse, he performed homage to de Montfort as his father had done and attached himself firmly to that camp. Indeed, he used his influence to extend crusader authority across the Dordogne into Périgord, with the consent of abbot Elie, and at the same time added to the holdings of his viscounty.

Yet, whether or not Higounet's dates are correct, this portrait of an opportunist viscount is still incomplete. Its major imperfection is the fact that the southern army in question was in 1218 being raised by de Cazenac himself. If the brother-in-law of the *faidit* had deliberately dispossessed his own family, an alliance between them seems unlikely, although possible as part of the dire necessities of the war. On the other hand, if the viscount was merely the passive recipient of Montfortist favour, an alliance with Hélis and her husband, reassured that their castles were at least still in the hands of their own southern family, seems more understandable. However, in the latter case, unless the extent of de Cazenac's crimes was in fact not exaggerated by the chronicler, the catalyst for the expedition of 1214 in Périgord still remains somewhat obscure.

The same cannot be said for the expeditions which penetrated far into Gascony, whose clear objectives were to deprive the Languedoc of the support of Béarn and Comminges in particular, and to do this by dispossessing Gascon lords who opposed the army of God and rewarding crusading families with the territory they conquered. This was justified initially by the false assertion that heresy was rife in the mountains and that the lords there supported it. However those same Gascon lords eventually began to intervene militarily in the Languedoc against the crusade, outraged by the fate of their fellow Occitans. It thus became strategically imperative to the crusaders to control the Gascon Toulousain.

---

56 *HGL* vi. 1023; Roquebert, *L'Épopée*, ii. 111 n. 8; Higounet, *Comminges*, i. 149.

The process by which the Gascons were dispossessed, eventually condoned in Rome, was made all the easier by two local factors. First, not only were the rights of the duke of Aquitaine rather nominal south of the Bordelais as we have seen, but in the period in question he was more concerned with the defence and extension of his power north of the Dordogne. Although, as I will show below, John did make a minor response to such infringements of his rights, he simply did not have the resources to prioritise the defence of the Gascon towns and nobility who, experience taught him, would almost certainly prove ungrateful. Second, the really powerful overlord of the Gascon Pyrenees, King Peter II of Aragon, whose familial connections within the Languedoc were actually strengthened in the first two years of the crusade, was successfully demonised and then eliminated by the crusaders in the summer of 1213.

As we have seen, some Gascon nobles, most notably Amanieu V d'Albret, involved themselves on the side of the crusade from the start. Significantly, Viscount Roger II of Couserans defected from the southern party, performing homage to the crusade's commander in April 1211.[57] Although he was a kinsman and vassal of the counts of Comminges and Foix, his lands were most immediately vulnerable to whoever controlled the Toulousain.

More typical of the Gascon response to the war was that of Bernard IV of Comminges and his son-in-law Gaston VI of Béarn. On 17 December 1210 Pope Innocent had instructed these lords to co-operate with de Montfort.[58] The command had little effect. Gascons were not unwilling to commit themselves in a holy war, for they had crusaded in the Holy Land as we have seen, and in summer 1212, whilst the Albigensian Crusade was attacking the Agenais, the archbishop of Bordeaux, the count of Astarac and hundreds of Gascon knights, not to mention many Aquitainians from north of the Dordogne, journeyed across the Pyrenees to fight the Almohads under the leadership of Peter of Aragon. However their identity, like that of the lords of the Languedoc, was rooted in the love of independence from foreign authority, not least that originating in northern France. Thus, although in the very early stages of the crusade Catholic Gascons found their loyalties divided and did not commit themselves to either side, this ended when the crusade threatened Gascony and its allies. Bernard of Comminges went to the aid of the southerners during the 1211 siege of Toulouse and at the battle of Saint-Martin-la-Lande, and his support continued the following year. Gaston of Béarn joined forces with the counts of Toulouse and Foix at Castelnaudary in 1211. He apparently journeyed to Penne d'Agenais in summer 1212 to negotiate with the crusaders, but the submission they had hoped for was not forthcoming and he returned to the south still their enemy. Subsequently both lords were excommunicated.[59]

Another factor prompting the invasion of Gascony was that on 15 April 1211

---

[57] HGL viii. 608; Roquebert, L'Épopée, i. 389, 454.
[58] HGL viii. 601; PL ccxvi.356.
[59] William of Tudela, Chanson, i. 186–9, 222–3; Peter des Vaux-de-Cernay, Histoire, 105, 118; Higounet, Comminges, i. 92–3; Roquebert, L'Épopée, i. 476.

Innocent III had written to Archbishop Bernard of Auch demanding his resignation. This was not least because his only voluntary intervention in the
crusade had been in defence of Raymond VI in 1209 (his mobilisation of Gascon
crusaders 1210 took place only after the pope had commanded him to recruit
them). Bernard would not resign, and in 1214 he was finally deposed. In 1212 he
was therefore regarded amongst those failed clerics of southern France who,
through neglect and indifference, hindered the imposition of orthodoxy.[60]

Thus the two major lords of the Gascon Pyrenees had abetted the protectors
of heretics and had no credible ally in the Church to intervene in their defence.
Indeed, bishops Garsie of Comminges and Navarre of Couserans were adamant
that de Montfort invade 'heretical' Comminges, which would in turn make
easier an attack on Béarn, whose viscount was notoriously anti-clerical. In order
to isolate the Toulousain and Gascon parties from each other, Muret was occupied in late 1212. Within a short time many lesser nobles of Comminges,
Couserans and Béarn surrendered to de Montfort. He himself entered Saint-
Gaudens, which capitulated in spite of good relations with its lord Roger of
Couserans (this troubled lord had denounced his new crusading allies and
rejoined the southerners, but in 1211 was again brought to heel by de Montfort).
William of Tudela, who was not with the crusaders at this time, tells us that they
also conquered lands pertaining to Béarn, l'Isle-Jourdain and everything as far as
Oloron, although this seems unlikely and is verified by no other sources.[61]
Indeed, crusader control of Comminges was actually only nominal by the end of
this campaign.

This was to change the following year. In the winter of 1212–13 Peter of
Aragon intervened in support of his Catholic vassals, demanding the return of
the Pyrenees to southern authority. He was denied by pro-Montfortist clerics at
the Council of Lavaur in January 1213. The direct result of this was that on 27
January, along with important figures in the Languedoc, Gaston of Béarn and
Bernard of Comminges performed homage to Peter for their lands, including
even Marsan and Gabardan held by Béarn in central Gascony. This was done
with the express understanding that if these lords were to fall foul of the Church
decisively, Peter would take control of their lands and guarantee orthodoxy
within them. In June the crusader presence in Comminges was accordingly
strengthened. De Montfort's son Amaury was knighted and enfeoffed with the
conquered lands there, which were garrisoned by a new crusading force, meeting
serious resistance only at Rochefort, near Saliés-de-Sarlat in Comminges, which
they were forced to besiege. The battle of Muret was by now probably inevitable.
It had become so not least because of the failure of the papacy to rule decisively
on the matter of who should hold the invaded Gascon territories: in March,
Innocent III had denounced the crusaders for their illegal excess, then in May

60 PL ccxvi.408; William of Tudela, Chanson, i. 30–1 and nn. 1, 2; Peter des Vaux-de-Cernay,
Histoire, 67; Dossat, 'Comminges', 123.
61 Peter des Vaux-de-Cernay, Histoire, 138–40; William of Tudela, Chanson, i. 278–81;
Roquebert, L'Épopée, i. 487–9; Higounet, Comminges, i. 93–4.

was persuaded that it was Peter and the Pyrenean lords under his protection who threatened peace and orthodoxy. And so, although de Montfort and his son were not actually granted the Gascon counties by the pope, they could not be recovered by the south without battle.[62]

The forces of Aragon, Toulouse, Foix and Comminges began to besiege Muret on 10 September. A smaller, but militarily superior crusader army arrived from Fanjeaux to relieve the siege and battle ensued on the 12th, before the arrival of Béarnaise troops under Guillaume-Raymond de Moncade, brother of the viscount and King Peter's seneschal for Catalonia. The southern forces were decimated and de Montfort was able to take even firmer control of the south-west of the Toulousain/Gascon frontier. Count Raymond could now only hope that his title would be confirmed in Rome the following year. In April 1214, therefore, he submitted, along with other southerners including the count of Comminges, to the legate Peter of Benevento, who was under instruction from the pope to institute a peace in the Languedoc until its possession could be determined in 1215.[63]

An Anglo-French context for the crusade, to 1214

The attempts made by Pope Innocent III to persuade a royal figure to involve himself in a crusade in southern France are well known. From 1204 to 1208 he consistently called for a truce between Philip of France and John of England so that their efforts could be put into such a venture. The circumstances of the troubled relationship between John and Rome from the years 1205–13 cannot be rehearsed here in any detail, but the dispute over his refusal to accept Stephen Langton as archbishop of Canterbury is a factor which stood in the way of his co-operation in the crusade. Indeed, he was excommunicated on 8 November 1209.[64] In addition, there is little evidence that John showed much

---

[62] Peter des Vaux-de-Cernay, Histoire, 145–72; PL ccxvi.739–41, 743–4, 836, 839–40, 848, 849, 852; Roquebert, L'Épopée, ii. 61–2, 82–5, 99–102; Higounet, Comminges, i. 94–5; Dossat, 'Catharisme', 153–4; Sumption, Albigensian Crusade, 156–63.

[63] Peter des Vaux-de-Cernay, Histoire, 173–84; RHF xix. 210; HGL viii. 643; Roquebert, L'Épopée, ii. 259–64.

[64] PL ccxv.355–7, 501–3, 1360, 1545; Letters of Pope Innocent III (1198–1216) concerning England and Wales, ed. C. R. Cheney and M. G. Cheney, Oxford 1967, 37–156, 272–3; RHF xix. 500; C. R. Cheney, Innocent III and England, Stuttgart 1979, 147–54, 293, 298–325; H. Tillmann, Pope Innocent III, trans. W. Sax, Amsterdam–New York–London 1980, 79–85, 230; B. Bolton, 'Philip Augustus and John: two sons in Innocent III's vineyard?', in D. Wood (ed.), The Church and sovereignty (SCH subsidia ix, 1991), esp. pp. 113–26; D. Knowles, 'The Canterbury election of 1205–6', EHR liii (1938), 211–20; W. L. Warren, King John, 3rd edn, New Haven–London 1997, 154–73, 206–17; Turner, King John, 147, 154–66; S. Painter, The reign of King John, Baltimore 1949, 151–203. Claire Dutton has noted that the pope asked Philip of France to intervene in the Languedoc as early as 1201: Vetera monumenta slavorum meridionalium, i, ed. A. Theiner, Rome 1863, 222, cited in 'Aspects', at p. 28. See Taylor, 'Innocent III', 205–22, for John's involvement in an international context.

interest in affairs in the Languedoc on the eve of the crusade. And yet how could he have been indifferent to his position as overlord of the count of Toulouse for the Agenais?

King John's involvement

Anglo-Toulousain relations shed a good deal of light on John's attitude. Although the recovery of Normandy and Anjou was most pressing, and his actions were informed by concern about his worsening position with regard to Rome, John did not remain passive with regard to the crusade for long. There is evidence between 1209 and 1215 that he was attempting to undermine the French position in the south. This activity cannot be explained simply by his overlordship of Gascony, for his lack of activity and diplomacy concerning the region south of the Garonne indicates that it was not his immediate concern. But it does make sense viewed in the context of his political interest in the Languedoc and his war with Philip Augustus. John's aim was to improve the position of his Toulousain kin, and thereby his own. His involvement is somewhat obscured, however, by his relationship with the pope: unwillingness to draw papal attention to his anti-crusade activity meant that most of his involvement was semi-covert and its objective thus not immediately clear. But, as will also be shown, the French crusaders were far from oblivious to the enemy in Aquitaine.

Perhaps surprisingly, there is no evidence of a reaction on John's part to the crusade of 1209 in the Agenais, held of him by Raymond VI. In 1211 there is somewhat unsatisfactory circumstantial evidence for his involvement, for it was in this phase that his officials Savary de Mauléon and Martin Algaïs undertook anti-crusade activities, although there is nothing to suggest that they did so on his behalf, and Algaïs originally supported the northerners. We can, however, see the Anglo-Toulousain alliance being realised in the affairs of the Languedoc in subsequent years. It was certainly thought by the crusaders that John was involved, for the Council of Lavaur in January 1213 denounced Raymond for putting his faith in him and also made reference to the involvement of Savary de Mauléon.[65] In early May, when the crusaders were attempting to secure their position at Muret, they were faced with the untimely defection of a significant contingent led by the Walloon Alard II de Strépy. De Strépy was a vassal of John and had apparently received a message from him in late April. Historians have speculated that this was the reason for his departure.[66]

There is concrete administrative evidence that John was exchanging embassies with the southerners. Count Raymond had a Provençal official, Vital, at John's court from late 1212 to at least 7 April 1213, when he was making preparations to return home. Vital had replaced another ambassador, Robin, and was himself replaced by envoys from Raymond and also Peter of Aragon, whose

65 PL ccxiii.836–8.
66 Peter des Vaux-de-Cernay, Histoire, 164; Hystoria, ii. 113 and n. 1; Roquebert, L'Épopée, ii. 149; Taylor, 'Innocent III', 208–9 n. 23.

expenses John paid from 14 to 20 April.[67] They were surely sent in an attempt to involve John in the Aragonese/Toulousain alliance of 1213. John himself had an ambassador, a Cistercian monk, at the Aragonese court between 14 April and 8 May.[68] On 8 July he again sent embassies to both Peter and Raymond, this time travelling in an armed ship.[69] On 17 August he sent two more envoys to the southerners with letters of accreditation, one of whom was Geoffrey de Neville.[70]

After Muret, Raymond was denied the revenues and resources required for a counter-offensive. Several sources tell us that he and the young Raymond fled to England where they sought refuge and aid from John.[71] Ralph of Coggeshall tells us that the count did homage to his brother-in-law. Perhaps this was simply a renewal of the homage to Richard of 1196 for the Agenais, but it could also have been a revival of that of 1173 for Toulouse. This is certainly implied by the chronicler, who notes that Raymond's position was so weak that Toulouse itself was all he in fact held at this point. We are also told that he received 1,000 marks from John. Apparently this money was raised as part of a levy of 22,000 livres on the Cistercian order imposed because of their support for the crusade.[72] The money was granted on 15 December 1213 at Reading and 16 January 1214 at Winchester, the second grant being arranged by Geoffrey de Neville.[73] The two Raymonds were then expelled from England by the papal legate, Bishop Nicholas of Tusculum.[74]

In 1214 John involved himself directly against the crusade. Since February, whilst preparing to engage the French in Poitou, he had been based at La Rochelle, and from there he took his army to La Réole, remaining there from 13 to 16 April. As we have seen, his proximity caused the crusader garrison at Marmande to surrender, and on 15 April he sent down-river a force under Geoffrey de Neville. Support for de Neville was not forthcoming, however, and in June the crusade was able to begin to reoccupy the Agenais. The crusaders also believed John to have promised support for the town of Casseneuil, besieged from 28 June, although this did not arrive either.[75]

---

67 *Rotuli litterarum clausarum*, ed. T. D. Hardy, London 1833–44, ii. 126; *Documents illustrative of English history of the thirteenth and fourteenth centuries*, ed. H. Cole, London 1844, 258–9; Peter des Vaux-de-Cernay, *Hystoria*, ii. 113–14 n. 5

68 Peter des Vaux-de-Cernay, *Hystoria*, ii. 113–14 n. 5; *Documents illustrative of English history*, 262.

69 *Rot. lit. claus.*, i. 164; Peter des Vaux-de-Cernay, *Hystoria*, ii. 134 n. 2.

70 Peter des Vaux-de-Cernay, *Hystoria*, ii. 134 n. 2; *Foedera, conventiones, litterae . . . publica*, ed. T. Rymer and others, London 1704–34, i. 175.

71 William of Tudela, *Chanson*, ii. 40–1; *Annales prioratus de Dunstaplia*, in *Annales monastici*, ii. 39; *Annales monasterii de Waverleia*, ibid. iii. 280.

72 Ralph of Coggeshall, *Chronicon anglicanum*, ed. J. Stephenson (RS, 1875), 164, 168.

73 *Rot. lit. pat.*, i. 106, 108. John's itinerary gives us the location of the court (unpaginated in T. D. Hardy, A *description of the patent rolls*, London 1835).

74 *Annales Waverleia*, 280.

75 John's itinerary in *Description of patent rolls*; Peter de Vaux-de-Cernay, *Histoire*, 198–202; *HGL* vi. 446.

John's continued neglect of the Agenais from June into July was prompted by several factors. Most obviously, on 2 July his army was routed by the French royal army in Poitou. In addition, his activity with regard to the crusade had been noticed by the papal legate Robert de Courçon, who had been with the crusaders in April, but had left to preside over the Council of Bordeaux of 25 June. To this he had summoned John, who failed to appear.[76] The legate evidently pursued him further, this time successfully, for in a letter of 6 July John promised neutrality in relation to the dioceses of Agen and Cahors.[77] In addition the legate sent 20,000 *sous* to de Montfort for the war effort in John's name, although the money did not come from John's own coffers.[78] At some point later in July, de Courçon travelled a short distance down-river from the siege at Casseneuil to the abbey at Sainte-Livrade, all the more friendly since one of the lords of the town, Pons Amanieu had done homage to de Montfort in April at Penne, receiving the property of his heretical relative Guillaume in return (see chapter 3). There the legate issued a charter granting to de Montfort rights to the conquered lands of the Agenais, Quercy, Albigeois and the county of Rodez.[79] It was in this context that the nobility of the Agenais did homage to the crusader in late August 1214.

But the legate's activity was apparently undertaken without reference to Rome or to Peter of Benevento, the official papal representative in the Languedoc, who was at this point in Spain. De Courçon had embarked on this course of action in December 1212 when the Council of Montpellier, which he had convened, unofficially elected de Montfort as count of Toulouse and recommended him to the pope.[80] A letter was then sent from the papal *curia*, on 18 January 1213, to the same churchmen in which it was pointed out that John, as Duke Richard's successor, was owed homage for Jeanne's dowry lands from whoever held them. The pope also made it clear that no decisions regarding possession of lands in the Languedoc would be taken until the Lateran Council.[81]

In the light of this, de Courçon's activity requires explanation. It is likely that he perceived that John's actions, by strengthening the southern hand and thus perpetuating the war, touched upon the success of the planned crusade to the Holy Land. Like the pope, he saw conflict in Europe as a major obstacle to its

---

76 *Concilia*, xxii. 931–4; Rymer's *Foedera*, i. 186–7; Peter de Vaux-de-Cernay, *Hystoria*, ii. 216–17 n. 1; M. Dickson and C. Dickson, 'Le Cardinal Robert de Courson: sa vie', *Archives d'histoire doctrinale et littéraire du moyen âge* ix (1934), 85–116, 141; J. Baldwin, *Masters, princes and merchants: the social views of Peter the Chantor and his circle*, Princeton 1970, i, esp. pp. 19–25; ii. 7–15.

77 Rymer's *Foedera*, i. 188.

78 In August John ordered that the money paid to de Montfort be recouped from the townspeople of La Réole and paid back to the archbishop of Bordeaux who, by implication, had supplied it: *Rot. lit. claus.*, ii. 171; Peter de Vaux-de-Caernay, *Hystoria*, ii. 216–17 n. 1.

79 *Actes de Simon de Montfort*, 85; *HGL* vi. 451; viii. 653–5.

80 *Concilia*, xxii. 936–7; Dickson and Dickson, 'Le Cardinal', 101.

81 *PL* ccxvi.739; Roquebert, *L'Épopée*, ii. 64; Sumption, *Albigensian Crusade*, 177.

success and between September 1213 and 1215 he attempted to arbitrate between John and Philip Augustus. Thus in the summer of 1214 he involved himself in the Agenais. It is certain that he played a constructive and diplomatic role in securing the peace between the kings of France and England in the period immediately after Bouvines.[82] Indeed, he was able to achieve this by first weakening John's hand in the Languedoc. However, whilst the legate undoubtedly felt duty bound to continue the anti-heretical work of his absent colleague Peter of Benevento, he had neither his tact nor his knowledge of the situation.[83] Having neutralised John with regard to the Agenais and Quercy, he initiated a crusade into other lands pertaining to the duchy of Aquitaine. In this way he almost managed to provoke another military response by John: during the siege of Casseneuil, perhaps between 20 and 25 July, Peter des Vaux-de-Cernay tells us that John was at Périgueux receiving refugee soldiers who had fled the re-conquered Agenais (which, we are told made him the object of scandal and compromised his reputation). The chronicler is clear that John's actions were prompted by a desire to relieve the Agenais and thereby avenge his nephew, dispossessed of his mother's dowry.[84] This was not John's plan, however, for his presence in Périgord could never constitute more than a threat. He was wiser than to actually engage the army of God directly, and by the time it attacked Périgord he had retreated to the Atlantic to nurse the many wounds his ambition had sustained that summer.

King John and Philip Augustus, 1209–14

By the start of the crusade in 1209 all parties could have anticipated that the wars of John and Philip might also have implications for the south. Indeed, in May 1208 the French king had quarrelled with Raymond VI because of a visit he made to Otto of Brunswick, enemy of Philip and ally of John.[85] If John wished to intervene in the Languedoc in his own interests and those of the house of Saint-Gilles, his activity in this context must be understood in relation to his major concern in these years, his war against the king of France. In the early stages of the crusade, it would have suited John well if Philip had joined its ranks. To have his enemy fighting on two fronts could only increase John's chances of success in Normandy and Anjou. Indeed, in spring 1213 Philip and Prince Louis had to choose between intervention in the Languedoc and a planned invasion of England.[86]

---

82 Dickson and Dickson, 'Le Cardinal', 105–8; Baldwin, *Masters*, i. 21–2.

83 He was noted for lack of diplomacy in other situations: H. Mayer, *The crusades*, trans. J. Gillingham, Oxford 1972, 206.

84 Peter des Vaux-de-Cernay, *Histoire*, 199–200. John's presence at Périgueux is not attested by charters and does not appear in his itinerary, although its silence about his location between these dates makes it quite feasible. See also *Hystoria* ii. 215–16 n. 4; *HGL* vi. 446–8.

85 *HGL* vi. 271.

86 News that the papacy had suspended the crusade had not reached Paris, whilst the pope had declared the excommunicate John's throne vacant. In the event, the French navy was destroyed by the count of Flanders: Warren, *King John*, 202–5.

But John, in a sense, was also fighting on two fronts, strategically improbable as this seems to modern historians. His visit to La Réole and capture of Marmande has caused the most confusion. M. Roquebert asks 'allait-il s'engager dans l'affaire albigeoise?', and is inclined to answer negatively, pointing to the difficulty of choosing conflict on both the Gascon and Poitevin borders. K. Norgate assumed that John's manoeuvres from La Rochelle in April 1214 were part of the wars in the north of France, designed 'to baffle Philip and to ascertain the extent of his own resources in the South'. Even Charles Higounet does not explain the presence of John's garrison in the Agenais. W. L. Warren has added that 'the chroniclers are not at all clear about John's operations from La Rochelle'.[87]

J. Gillingham at least makes a connection between John's manoeuvres and the crusade. M. Roquebert does suggest that John considered something of a show-down with the crusaders, perhaps even at the request of his brother-in-law, and J. Sumption follows him in this. But none see any deliberate strategy here, only vain posturing.[88] Yet from an Agenais perspective, it appears quite simply that 'Jean-sans-Terre s'était rendu en vain en 1214 dans l'Agenais pour le secourir'.[89] And, whilst it may be true that Anglo-Norman chroniclers are unclear what was going on, those of the Albigensian Crusade are far from ambiguous. The war's main apologist states that John's activity was in opposition to the crusade and in defence of his family interests in the Agenais, and that Geoffrey de Neville raised his banner at Marmande to defy the crusaders. From a French perspective, William the Breton makes a direct connection between the wars of John and Philip and the power struggle in the Languedoc, saying that Bouvines was fought against the allies and defenders of the Albigensian heretics.[90]

Thus it seems that John was indeed active on two fronts, in fact in two wars, as part of the same strategy. Having lost the northern territories of the Angevin empire since 1204 he was now hedging his bets. He was in danger of losing Poitou, but by early 1214 had secured the homage of the counts of Toulouse for their county and for the Agenais. If they succeeded in their own battle against the northern French he would have access to an Occitan empire comprising Gascony, the Agenais and the Toulousain. This could occur whether or not he managed to secure Poitou and recover Normandy, even though these were his most immediate concerns and those to which he devoted most of his resources. In garrisoning Marmande John was a self-interested overlord acting in defence of his vassal Raymond VI.

---

87 Roquebert, L'Épopée, ii. 257–8; K. Norgate, John Lackland, London 1902, 198; Higounet, Marmande, 8; Warren, King John, 218 and see p. 219. C. Dutton takes more or less the same view as Norgate: 'Aspects', 46–7, 55–8.

88 J. Gillingham, The Angevin empire, London 1984, 78; Roquebert, L'Épopée, ii. 258; Sumption, Albigensian Crusade, 176.

89 Cassany-Mazet, Villeneuve, 54.

90 Peter des Vaux-de-Cernay, Histoire, 194, 198–9; William the Breton, Philippide, in Oeuvres de Rigord et de Guillaume le Breton, ed. H. F. Delaborde, Paris 1882–5, ii. 229.

And yet he never sought actual confrontation with the crusaders. As a strategic priority this would have proved foolish, weakening him both militarily, before marching his army to Poitou, and politically, in terms of his relationship with Rome. Indeed, it may be important to note that it was de Neville's standard, not that of John, which appeared on the tower at Marmande. Therefore he did not linger on the borders of the Agenais, let alone enter it in person, but took his army north into Poitou after causing the defection of the Garonne towns. John was in fact reminding the French both in the north and in the Languedoc of his claims in the south, recently renewed as a result of the homages received from Raymond and his son. Indeed, 'Geoffrey de Neuville . . . avait ostensiblement arboré sa bannière au sommet du donjon, comme pour rappeler aux Croisés que la bastide que Richard Coeur-de-Lion avait fondée trente ans plus tôt, était toujours de mouvance anglaise'.[91] There is no more convincing context for the stationing of a garrison at Marmande under one of his most important officials than that John intended, if able, to hold it for himself or his vassals and in-laws.

John's enemies take the cross.

Moreover, John had many personal enemies who took part in the crusade, disinclining him further towards it. The most significant amongst these was of course the Montfortist faction. De Montfort had been heir to the earldom of Leicester, and although in the early years of the century John had dispossessed English nobles who also held lands in France, he continued to use his Leicester title until at least 1217.[92] However from 1204 he had moved very firmly into the French sphere, and from 1209 his territorial ambition, that of his wife's family the Montmorencys, and at least the eldest two of the couple's three sons Amaury, Guy and Simon, were inseparable from the success of the crusade.[93]

Three more of John's enemies had also taken the cross. Hugh de Lacy, co-lord of Meath, had been aided in his ambition in Ireland by John and given the newly created earldom of Ulster in 1204, but had since fallen from royal favour and been dispossessed. Once joining the crusade, he evidently remained close to de Montfort. Also in the camp was William des Roches. He had supported Arthur in 1199, been briefly reconciled with John in 1200, and rebelled in 1202. By 1209 he was one of the most important allies of the French king in the conquered Anjou and Poitou. In 1211 the crusaders were also joined by Walter Langton, brother of Archbishop Stephen. He was captured on the borderlands of Foix and exchanged for southern prisoners.[94] Thus John's political enemies were conquering and gaining the lands of his vassals and, in the case of de Montfort in the Agenais, were usurping his authority where he was the acknowledged suzerain.

---

[91] Roquebert, L'Épopée, ii. 277.
[92] Doat cxxv, fos 110r–112v. Amaury de Montfort used it from 1220 (fos 139r–140r).
[93] For more detailed discussion of the involvement of John's other enemies, sources for them and some problems with the evidence see Taylor, 'Pope Innocent', 216–18.
[94] William of Tudela, Chanson, i. 92–3; ii. 282–4; Peter des Vaux-de-Cernay, Histoire, 39, 102–3.

John and Pope Innocent III

When the crusade began England had been under an interdict for almost a year because of John's refusal to accept Stephen Langton as archbishop of Canterbury.[95] If John ever considered promising support for the crusade in order to win again the favour of Rome, this would not have been straightforward. In addition, the lands of Raymond VI were protected by the Church from June 1209 to 1211, and so John would have had to send troops down the Rhône to join the attack on the lands of the Trencavel viscounts of Béziers. This was unthinkable, for it would have subjected his army to the authority of the French, not least to de Montfort. In any case, in reality John was less than distraught about the excommunication. When he did begin to consider involvement in the Languedoc it was from political not religious motives.

From the summer of 1212 his position was very difficult. He faced a baronial conspiracy in England and the Dunstable annalist indicates that the rebels wanted to put Simon de Montfort himself on the throne.[96] Rumours were also circulating that the pope was about to release John's vassals from their fealty. At the same time in Europe a papal, Capetian and Hohenstaufen alliance was emerging.[97] John had no choice but to make his peace with the pope and on 15 May 1213 surrendered to him the realms of England and Ireland, receiving them back as fiefs and promising to take part in the proposed Fifth Crusade.[98]

Suddenly his relationship with Rome changed. Innocent treated him as though he believed the change of heart to be entirely genuine. He warned the barons and the clergy of England against any actions that would undermine John and withdrew his support for the planned Capetian invasion.[99] However, before and after John's submission, even during the days in which it took place, there is evidence that the king was considering intervention in the Languedoc. On 13–15 May, that is to say while negotiating his own surrender to Rome with the papal *nuncio* Pandulf, he was exchanging ambassadors with Raymond of Toulouse and King Peter of Aragon. John had great financial problems in 1213.[100] These limited but did not rule out aid, for he gave readily enough later that winter. But he could in no way be seen to be helping Count Raymond in the spring. His own embassy to the southerners in August surely confirmed that, as a new vassal of Rome, he could not give them the support he would undoubtedly have liked to give and which could have proved decisive at Muret.

By the winter of 1213/14 John did feel able to act, if covertly. The financial help he gave at this time to his Toulousain kin was relatively discreet, although

---

95   Since 24 March 1208: *PL* ccxv.1422–3.

96   *Annales Dunstaplia*, iii. 33. This source dates the rebellion to 1210, however. See also J. C. Holt, *Magna Carta*, 2nd edn, Cambridge 1992, 226.

97   Turner, *King John*, 166–7.

98   *Rot. chart.*, I/1, 195; *Regesta pontificum romanorum inde ab a. post Christum natum 1198 ad a. 1304*, ed. A. Potthast, Berlin 1957, i, no. 4776; Roger of Wendover, *Flores*, i. 145; J. Sayers, *Innocent III: leader of Europe, 1198–1216*, London–New York 1994, 72, 80, 84–6.

99   *Regesta pontificum romanorum, 1198–1304*, nos 4774–5, 4777.

100   Turner, *King John*, 171–2.

the legate Nicholas of Tusculum suggested that an extended stay by the Toulousains would not be wise. Likewise, John's motive in intervening in the Agenais in the spring was concealed from many by his war against Philip. But Robert de Courçon saw what was happening. The legate has been called 'le docile instrument des ambitions de Montfort'. This charge, like the complaints of contemporary chroniclers at his interference in French ecclesiastical affairs, has a 'myopic quality' when his actions are contextualised by his concern for reform and orthodoxy.[101] Weakness of character was not behind de Courçon's encouragement of the attack on Périgord in 1214, during the Peace under which the Languedoc had been placed.[102] Like the pope, the legate was a believer in the war that could impose peace and papal authority. Where they differed was that the legate wanted to settle affairs in the Languedoc, not suspend them.[103] Unlike the pope, he wished this war to continue over the summer of 1214 in order to put de Montfort in as strong a position as possible. John and the house of Saint-Gilles were forced to wait until the autumn of 1215 for the fate of the Agenais and the Toulousain to be decided. In the meantime, John had to maintain his good relationship with the pope if his own opinion on the matter was to be taken into consideration.

It has to be said that the rebellion of the English barons in 1215 could only help John in this matter. In March and April the pope had written to them stating that they must show loyalty to the king, not least because on 4 March John finally took the cross and promised to aid the Holy Land. The pope also wrote to various English churchmen expressing his surprise that so few of them were helping the king against the barons. On 24 August he denounced and annulled Magna Carta and ordered the barons to withdraw it. By the autumn John's secular enemies had been excommunicated, Stephen Langton had been suspended and the papal vassal was very much in favour at Rome.[104]

In addition, John's enemies in France were not all thought well of at the papal *curia* by this time, for in spring 1215 de Montfort had declared himself count of Toulouse against the pope's wishes and Prince Louis had accepted his homage for the county. Montauban was the last significant town in the Languedoc to hold out. In June it too submitted and there on 8 June de Montfort received the submission of two Agenais lords, Itier de Villebroy and Guiraud Cabrols. Also in June, Géraud, count of Armagnac and Fézensac and viscount of Fézensaguet did homage de Montfort for his lands in Gascony, excepting those which he held from the archbishop of Auch, in return for Mauvezin in Bigorre. Although Géraud had never performed homage directly to John, the duke's authority was not taken into consideration, as had been the case also in the

---

101 *Annales Waverleia*, 275–7; Roquebert, *L'Épopée*, ii. 296 (quotation); J. M. Powell, *Anatomy of a crusade, 1213–1221*, Philadelphia 1986, 35–6 (quotation).
102 See Sumption, *Albigensian Crusade*, 172–8; Roquebert, *L'Épopée*, ii. 256–9, 285–9.
103 Dutton, 'Aspects', 98–105, 187.
104 *Letters of Innocent III*, 167–70, 272–3, 1026; *Regesta pontificum romanorum, 1198–1304*, i, nos 4990–1; *Concilia*, xxii. 1070, 1076; Matthew Paris, *Chronica majora*, ii. 633–4; Warren, *King John*, 224–45; Holt, *Magna Carta*, 196.

Pyrenees and Agenais. Indeed, the crusade's commander entered Gascony again and on 25 September at Condom he enfeoffed Eudes de Montaut with Gramont in Lomagne.[105] Southern France was not the place that Pope Innocent had intended it to be on the eve of the Fourth Lateran Council.

And yet the Montfortist grip on lands in which John had an interest did not go entirely unchallenged. In late September he learned that Bernard de Cazenac had recovered Castelnaud, which dominated the junction of the Dordogne and the Céon. The crusaders besieged it successfully, although de Cazenac again escaped.[106] The defiance of this *routier* was the last serious resistance to de Montfort's authority before he sent his brother Guy to represent him at Rome.

The Fourth Lateran Council, November 1215[107]

Crusader sources tell us that before the council Count Raymond had sent his son to England again to take advice from his uncle John.[108] John was apparently furious at the threat to the family lands. He paid for the young Raymond's transport and sent letters of recommendation for the Toulousains to be delivered to the pope.[109] It is clear that further strategies were worked out for the council in order to give the son, if not his father, a chance of asserting his rights to Toulouse and also the Agenais. We are told that the young Raymond made a

105 *HGL* viii. 665; *Actes de Simon de Montfort*, 107, 115; 'Acte de reddition à Simon de Montfort de deux seigneurs de l'Agenais', ed. M. R. Mazieres, *Mémoires de la Société des arts et sciences de Carcassonne* iv/6 (1970), 99–100; Peter des Vaux-de Cernay, *Histoire*, 215; Roquebert, *L'Épopée*, ii. 297–344, esp. p. 338.

106 Peter des Vaux-de Cernay, *Histoire*, 215; Escande, *Périgord*, 95–6.

107 For the canons of the Fourth Lateran Council see *Concilia*, xxii. 953–1086, esp. pp. 1069–70 for the business regarding Toulouse and the Agenais. For commentary see William of Tudela, *Chanson*, ii. 40–89; Peter des Vaux-de Cernay, *Histoire*, 215–17; anon., *Histoire*, 160–3. The account from the Giessen codex is also very important: S. Kuttner and A. García y García, 'A new eyewitness account of the Fourth Lateran Council', *Traditio* xx (1964), 124–5, lines 44–59 and commentary at pp. 138–43. The latter account is regarded by Kuttner and García y García as a reliable source for the sentence passed. Although it lacks the background knowledge of that of the anonymous *Chanson* author or of Peter des Vaux-de-Cernay, both of whom were also present, it is comparatively less partisan in tone. The papal judgement on the matter was also published in a bull of 14 December 1215: *Regesta pontificum romanorum*, 1198–1304, i, no. 5009.

108 William of Tudela, *Chanson*, ii. 40–1 and n. 3; William of Puylaurens, *Chronique*, 98–9; anon., *Histoire*, 156.

109 Anon., *Histoire*, 156. This is the only source to give us detailed information about John's response to his nephew's visit in 1215. The reference in the anonymous source is perhaps derived from the *Chanson* author's claim that the English churchmen carried a letter from John (*Chanson*, ii. 76–7). According to this source the young Raymond then went to meet his father in Rome. The anonymous *Chanson* author and William of Puylaurens tell us that the young Raymond travelled from England to rejoin his father in Provence, having crossed the Languedoc with great difficulty and in secret in the company of Arnaud Topina, a prominent citizen of Agen: *Chanson*, ii. 41 n. 3; William of Puylaurens, *Chronique*, 98–9.

favourable impression on the pope, not least because of the eighteen year-old's illustrious lineage.[110]

To help his case, John himself had sent two trusted advocates, the Cistercian Hugh, abbot of Beaulieu in Hampshire, and Walter Gray, bishop of Worcester, who was to be elevated to the archiepiscopal see of York at the council. On 14 November Gray presented the case for Saint-Gilles in legal terms: the Agenais was the dowry of the young Raymond's dead mother Jeanne and therefore his to inherit, even if the pope judged the lands of his father forfeit. This was apparently because in 1196 the marriage contract had stipulated that if Jeanne died and in the case of the *mort civile* of Raymond, which would be the case if the council condemned him, her entire dowry would pass to her heir. The bishop argued that this agreement had been confirmed by Rome. Therefore, even if the judgement went against Raymond VI and granted Toulouse to de Montfort, there was no basis for preventing Jeanne's son from taking possession of the Agenais. The pope made it known that this case on behalf of the young Raymond was indeed valid. Things were going well. Hugh of Beaulieu then presented the pope with letters from John, a vassal who loved his lord 'with an ever constant heart', pleading clemency on behalf of his nephew with regard also to the lands of Toulouse.[111] The pope also agreed that it would be unjust to deny the young Raymond his Toulousain inheritance, even if it were to be taken from his father.

However the bishops of the Languedoc voiced their outrage at the pope's liberality towards the Toulousains, and they were supported by the new archbishop of Auch, Garsias de l'Ort (1214/5–1225), who acted very differently over the issue to his predecessor. The *Chanson* author tells us that these bishops followed the harassed pope into the Lateran gardens, where he had retired to think the matter over, and threatened rebellion. The pontiff then returned to the council and announced his decision: all the conquered territories, not least the Toulousain and the Agenais, were to go to de Montfort. He even included the unconquered towns of Toulouse and Montauban. In compensation, at least according to the *Chanson*, he declared that the lands were not necessarily permanently lost to the young Raymond. He suggested that de Montfort should guard his undeserved prize well, saying 'let him keep it if he can, for if any of it is taken from him I will not help him to get it back'.[112] Thus the county of Toulouse and the Agenais were granted to de Montfort, as a fief of the French king.[113]

Accounts excuse this apparent miscarriage of justice by emphasising that the pope was unable to carry the council with him, so strong was the feeling against

[110] William of Tudela, *Chanson*, ii. 42–3; iii. 262–3.

[111] Ibid. ii. 76–7. For English interests at the council see Taylor, 'Innocent III', 222–7.

[112] William of Tudela, *Chanson*, ii. 78–9, and see pp. 58–61. Only the traditional family lands of Saint-Gilles of which the crusaders were not actually in possession were given to the young Raymond; the most important of these was the marquisate of Provence.

[113] Not as a fief of Rome as de Montfort had wished: Kuttner and García y García, 'Eyewitness account', lines 54–5 and commentary at pp. 142–3.

the house of Saint-Gilles and for de Montfort, amongst the French bishops especially.[114] We are told that the pontiff was forced to act very much against his will. But Innocent III was a great pragmatist. What he wanted for the Languedoc was stable orthodox rule. He also wanted the kings of France and England to go on crusade to the Holy Land. These things were only possible with the Languedoc, France and England at peace. In recognising the justice of the young Raymond's claim, he understood what lay behind the support from England. The house of Saint-Gilles was firmly in John's pocket. John, having lost his lands in northern and central France, had his eyes on an Occitan empire, with the allod of Gascony as its cornerstone. Since 1213 he had been binding Raymond VI and especially the young Raymond ever more closely to him. The pair had become dependent on him financially and had performed homage to him for the Agenais and perhaps Toulouse, assuming they could recover them with his help.

John has thus been portrayed as one of the vultures represented at the Fourth Lateran, picking over the bones of the forfeited lands of the Languedoc, his ambassadors sent there to press for his personal claim to the Agenais.[115] But this is not the strategy that he pursued through his envoys at Rome, and there is little indication that the astute pope thought John to be purely self-serving in the matter. None the less, Innocent knew that John had submitted to his authority in 1213 pragmatically, from a position of weakness. It is not in fact the case that since John's submission in 1213 the pope 'regarded his new vassal with the same unrealistic indulgence that he had shown before the Canterbury crisis'.[116] He understood John's motives only too well, for in late 1213, after his homage, he had warned him against any further disobedience and persecution of the Church.[117] The possession by Saint-Gilles of the Languedoc, still infested with heresy, would pose an on-going threat to orthodoxy and thus a diversion from the reconquest of the Holy Land. In addition, John's personal ambition in the Languedoc meant perpetual war in France. The pope would not allow his vassal to go down that road and, in the context of his concern for peace and orthodoxy probably felt he had little choice but to depose Raymond VI formally and even disinherit his son.

Yet having denied John's wishes for southern France, the pope continued to support his vassal in England against the barons and Capetian invasion until his own death on 21 May the following year.[118] Unknown both to him and to John, who died himself after a long illness in late 1216 during an invasion of England by Prince Louis, the wars in the Languedoc were not at an end.

---

114 For example, the pope 'could not control the self-interest of those who had already made the south of France a battle-ground': Cheney, *Innocent III*, 396.
115 Sumption, *Albigensian Crusade*, 179.
116 Turner, *King John*, 170.
117 *Selected letters of Pope Innocent III, concerning England (1198–1216)*, ed. and trans. C. R. Cheney and W. H. Semple, London 1953, 169–70.
118 Matthew Paris, *Chronica majora*, ii. 654–7; *Selected letters of Innocent III*, 172–7.

Rebellion and a return to war, 1216–29

In the fighting which marked a revival of confidence in the Languedoc, the towns and nobility of the Agenais and the Gascon Pyrenees had a limited but important role. Like the rest of Occitania under northern rule, they faced a dire choice when things began to go the way of Saint-Gilles again after the death of Simon de Montfort in 1218. From that point onwards the less powerful sought to attach themselves to masters who would neither destroy them nor be themselves destroyed, leaving their allies helpless again. The fate of the people of the Agenais was once again played out in the context of the developing territorial power of the Capetian state and the claims of the Plantagenet king of England to western France. It makes most sense to describe their fortunes in the broad chronological framework of the Albigensian wars and diplomacy between the Fourth Lateran Council and the 1229 Peace of Paris, and to allude along the way to the influence of Henry III of England and his rivals in France. The fate of the people of Quercy once again affected the towns, nobles and heretics of the Agenais. The story of the lords of the Gascon Pyrenees is described in less detail, as it has been thoroughly explored elsewhere.[119]

1216–25: the defeat of the crusade

After the settlement of the Fourth Lateran Council de Montfort could not afford to wear his new title complacently because Count Raymond and his son soon began to organise again against him. On 11 May 1216, for example, the consuls of Agen were told to raise an army to be commanded by Guillaume-Arnaud de Tantalon, Raymond's titular seneschal in the Agenais.[120] The young Raymond had won back Beaucaire in the eastern Languedoc by August and his father moved to raise an army in Aragon. However, Guy de Montfort, Simon's brother, had arrived with an army in June, which Hugh de Lacy joined.[121] This was used to strengthen control of the Gascon Pyrenees. In April 1214 Gaston de Béarn had died and the viscounty was now held by his brother, Guillaume-Raymond de Moncade. Gaston's daughter Petronilla, heiress to the county of Bigorre, was married to Nuño Sanchez of the Aragonese royal family. In November 1216 the archbishop of Auch forcibly divorced the couple at the request of the de Montforts and Petronilla was married to Simon's son Guy. This was met with fury in Aragon where Raymond VI was recruiting. Sanchez and Moncade resisted for a time at Lourdes, but the possession of Bigorre and occupation of stretches of the Pyrennean Garonne by the crusaders was a great blow for the southerners.[122]

---

[119] See *HGL* vi. and, more analytically, Roquebert, *L'Épopée*, iii, and Higounet, *Comminges*, i. Good summaries exist in Sumption, *Albigensian Crusade*, 119–225, and Evans, 'Albigensian Crusade', 307–24.

[120] *Chartes Agen*, no. vi.

[121] William of Tudela, *Chanson*, ii. 121; Peter des Vaux-de-Cernay, *Histoire*, 218–19.

[122] Ibid. ii. 256–7; *HGL* vi. 149; Higounet, *Comminges*, i. 100–2 (and see pp. 108–16 for the succession to Bigorre after Guy's death in 1226); Dossat, 'Comminges', 120–1.

However, Raymond's attempts to raise a new army were very successful and on 13 September 1217 it entered and re-occupied Toulouse. By the time the crusaders began to besiege the town it also contained contingents led by Bernard of Comminges and his family and by Bertrand-Jourdain de l'Isle, son-in-law of Count Raymond. During the course of the siege, which lasted until the death of de Montfort on 25 June 1218, many other Gascons arrived including Arnaud de Lomagne, Roger de Montaut and Arzieu Montesquiou de l'Armagnac.[123] *Faidits* from the Agenais arrived, commanded by Hugues d'Alfaro and Guillaume-Arnaud de Tantalon, amongst them Guillaume Amanieu of Sainte-Livrade, dispossessed for heresy, and Bertrand and Guitard de Marmande. From Quercy the besieged included Bernard de Montaigu, probably a kinsman of Arnaud de Montaigu, the crusader of 1211, who was soon to change sides himself. Also in evidence in the town were Hugues de Lamothe, Déodat de Barasc, who had defected from the Montfortist party, and Araimfré de Montpezat.[124]

Bernard de Cazenac set about raising an army from Quercy and Périgord with the help of defectors from the northern side including Viscount Raymond of Turenne, Arnaud de Montaigu and the co-lords of Gourdon.[125] In the winter, Philip de Landreville, de Montfort's seneschal for the Agenais, took hostages at Montauban to attempt to neutralise this threat. A force from Toulouse joined the townspeople in an attempt to free them, but the French held the town. De Cazenac was more successful and entered Toulouse with his reinforcements around Easter 1218. With him was the Gascon viscount Vezian of Lomagne, who also held Auvillars in the Agenais, and whose son Espan was amongst the besieged.[126]

Archbishop Garsias of Auch was asked to aid the crusaders during this siege of Toulouse. He was especially involved in advising de Montfort how to ensure his access to Gascony, by building a new town dominating the westward route out. Walter Langton was again present, in a force recruited by Alice de Montfort, involving himself in strategic decisions regarding the suburb of Saint-Cyprien. Hugh de Lacy was also in the camp.[127] Interestingly, an Agenais noble was apparently also in the besieging army, Anissant de Caumont, lord of Saint-Barthélmy and son of Nompar de Caumont.[128] However, amongst the besiegers were also less enthusiastic Gascons, obliged to be present by their previous submissions, who apparently rejoiced when things were going the way of the Toulousains. Amongst them was probably Géraud, count of Armagnac,

---

123 William of Tudela, *Chanson*, iii. 120–1; Roquebert, *L'Épopée*, iii. 95–6, 99–123.
124 William of Tudela, *Chanson*, iii. 302–3, 308–13; Roquebert, *L'Épopée*, ii. 275; Barrère, *Histoire*, i. 363.
125 The pope wrote to these lords on 13 January 1218 requiring them to cease aiding the enemies of the crusade: *RHF* xix. 648.
126 William of Tudela, *Chanson*, iii. 60–1, 138–41, 308–9.
127 Ibid. ii. 202–3, 292–5; iii. 22–3, 36–7, 74–7, 84–5, 106–7, 122–5; 172–3, 188–9.
128 Barrère, *Histoire*, i. 204. The source for this is uncited, but his presence seems possible because Nompar and Bégon de Caumont witnessed the homage of Étienne de Ferréol to Amaury de Montfort on 8 October (see n. 134 below).

and a group of Gascons sent as security for the co-operation of Bernard-Jourdain de l'Isle, who had threatened to defect.[129]

De Montfort's son Amaury was elected to lead the crusade after his father's death and the raising of the siege of Toulouse, but he had little of his predecessor's success. Soon, Bernard of Comminges was able to re-occupy his county, chasing the crusaders along the Garonne and into Astarac where they were surprised and defeated in battle. Aiding Bernard were non-Commingeois Gascons. Some, such as Espan de Lomagne, Roger de Montaut and Raymond-At d'Aspet, had involved themselves previously against the crusade in the Languedoc, but others such as Bernard de Marestaing of l'Isle Jourdain were involved against the northerners for the first time. Other southerners defeated the crusaders, with whom Hugh de Lacy was again present, at Baziège in early 1219. This army included Bernard of Comminges, Bertrand Jourdain de l'Isle, Hugues d'Alfaro and Hugues de Lamothe of Montauban.[130]

In part because Amaury was able to secure Moissac and control much of Bas-Quercy, the Agenais was divided in its response to the revival. Count Raymond and Amaury de Montfort both entered the region in the autumn of 1218 to win its co-operation. Many important towns elected to declare for Raymond. These included Clairac, Marmande, Aiguillon and also Condom, which had been garrisoned from an unknown date. The French garrisons of the latter three towns were massacred in the process.[131] Pons Amanieu of Sainte-Livrade, who had benefited from his relative Guillaume Amanieu's dispossession for heresy, now defected to the southern side.[132] But these defections did not include Agen itself, where the bishop's party had been in the ascendancy since his return in 1217.[133] Etienne de Ferréol of Tonneins also became an ally of the crusade. He was enfeoffed at Gontaud with Montastruc, which had easily succumbed to the crusaders, on 8 October.[134]

The most famous event in this period was a protracted and terrible siege of the rebels at Marmande, which Amaury undertook from December 1218 and whose course again reflects the broader conflict between the Plantagenets and Capetians and their respective allies. Marmande had learned how important its strategical position was, between English Gascony and whoever controlled the Toulousain, and it had prepared accordingly with Gascon allies. The town's defence was thus led by Count Centulle of Astarac, son-in-law of Bernard of Comminges and part of the crusader army himself until he defected in 1218, and

---

129 William of Tudela, *Chanson*, iii. 24–5.
130 Ibid. iii. 236–51, 262–5; *HGL* vi. 529.
131 Roquebert, *L'Épopée*, iii. 150; Barrère, *Histoire*, i. 364. In the late winter of 1221 Moissac was easily re-taken, having been left ungarrisoned by Amaury de Montfort.
132 William of Tudela, *Chanson*, ii. 298–9 n. 3; iii. 256–7 incl. n. 1.
133 Ibid. iii. 234–5; Roquebert, *L'Épopée*, iii. 59, 145; Samazeuilh, *Histoire*, i. 259–60.
134 At the same time Pons Amanieu was forbidden from entering Montastruc because of his treachery, although his connection with Montastruc is unclear: *Actes de Simon de Montfort*, 168; Rocquebert, *L'Épopée*, iii. 150; Samazeuilh, *Histoire*, 158, 274.

Guillaume-Arnaud de Tantalon.[135] Vézian and Espan de Lomagne were amongst the southerners, as were a *quercinois* force including Aramfré Montpezat, and the recently dispossessed Agenais lord Gaston de Gontaud. Also inside was Arnaud de Blanquefort, probably of an Agenais seigneury north of Fumel, Guillaume Amanieu, *credens* and *faidit* of Sainte-Livrade, and his brother Pons.[136]

During the siege Raymond sent embassies both to Paris, to plead for recognition as count of Toulouse, and to England, to alarm the court that a crusader force being raised by Prince Louis might invade Gascony and take it from the minor Henry III.[137] This seemed all the more likely because Geoffrey de Neville reported that Elie Ridel was apparently in danger of losing lands in Bergerac to Louis's army. Louis arrived at Marmande in June and was met by William des Roches whose contingent had travelled via Bordeaux down the Garonne, almost resulting in the surrender of La Réole. The terrified people of Marmande did submit, and its inhabitants – men, women and children, probably several thousand people – were ruthlessly massacred. Almost certainly amongst them were the tragically reconciled Amanieus, for the only known survivors were Centulle of Astarac and Guillaume-Arnaud de Tantalon.[138]

Aquitainians were again amongst the crusaders. They included a Jean de Lomagne and Amanieu V d'Albret, who was placed in charge of the fallen town and thus increased his family's influence in the Agenais considerably. Part of the crusader army was led by Bishop Pons of Saintes, who had argued that Centulle should be put to death with the rest of the townsfolk. Archbishop Garsias, however, took the southern part for once, arguing that the count and his men, people of his own archdiocese, should be spared, as they were not heretics. He was supported by William des Roches, whose argument that Centulle should be traded for the crusader Foucaud de Berzy, imprisoned at Toulouse, won the day.[139]

---

135 William of Tudela, *Chanson*, iii. 252–61, 282–91; Roquebert, *L'Épopée*, iii. 164. Centulle was a vassal of Simon de Montfort, and his ambassador at Saint-Lizier in 1216, where he obtained the homages of Tinhos, lord of Castillon-en-Couserans, and his two sons. He performed homage to Raymond VI in 1218: *Actes de Simon de Montfort*, 138; Dossat, 'Comminges', 123–4. Before the treaty of 1229 he made his peace with the king and anticipated receiving control of the Agenais from him. The Treaty of Paris gave it to Raymond, and Centulle received compensation: *HGL* viii. 895–6.

136 William of Tudela, *Chanson*, ii. 298–9, iii. 139 n. 5, 256–7 incl. n. 1; *Actes de Simon de Montfort*, 168; Roquebert, *L'Épopée*, iii. 153.

137 *Diplomatic documents preserved in the Public Records Office, 1101–1272*, ed. P. Chaplais, London 1964, 34; Sumption, *Albigensian Crusade*, 203; D. Carpenter, *The minority of Henry III*, London 1990, 153. The French were using as justification the argument that the lands in France that had pertained to Henry's father were forfeit since 1204. However it is noted that the status of Gascony as an allod is not recorded anywhere in diplomatic documents relating to the regency: Carpenter, *Henry III*, n. 1; cf. Chaplais, 'Le Traité'.

138 William of Tudela, *Chanson*, iii. 252–61, 282–91; *Diplomatic documents*, 38, 48–50; Carpenter, *Minority*, 153–4; Roquebert, *L'Épopée*, iii. 161, 164.

139 William of Tudela, *Chanson*, iii. 255, 282–3, 286–7, 288–9, 290–1; William of Puylaurens, *Chronique*, 112–13, although the chronicler neglects to mention the massacre that accompa-

There can be no question of the crusaders believing that the entire town of Marmande was heretical. Like the massacre at Béziers in 1209, this attack was intended to induce panic in the Languedoc and result in its submission, especially that of Toulouse, after only a limited campaign. In this objective Louis was unsuccessful; he was forced to besiege Toulouse from 17 June to 1 August, ultimately unsuccessfully. We learn from the *Chanson*, which ends during this siege, that Hugues de Lamothe was again amongst its defenders with fellow *quercinois* Déodat and Arnaud de Barasc. Guillaume-Arnaud de Tantalon and Hugues d'Alfaro were also present, as were Bernard de Comminges and two of his cousins, Espan de Lomagne and the brothers Bertrand-Jourdain and Bernard-Jourdain de l'Isle, the latter having evidently left the crusaders. Bernard de Marestaing and Roger de Montaut, fully committed to the southern cause since the crusaders invaded their Gascon homeland, guarded the barbican called *Pertus*.[140]

After the defeat of Marmande furious arguments erupted within Agen. The city had been increasingly Montfortist since 1212 and especially since 1217, but by 1221 was none the less still divided. It almost admitted Amaury's soldiers, but eventually it was Raymond who won the town over, promising amnesty for the Montfortists, a large southern garrison and further privileges.[141] By spring 1222 Amaury's position throughout the Languedoc was untenable because most of the lands of the Midi were again in southern hands. He was persuaded by the legate Romanus of St Angelo to submit to Capetian ambition and hand his few possessions in the Languedoc, and his titular comital title, to the French crown. In addition, Pope Honorius III offered King Philip financial inducements to send a force to make his claim on Toulouse real. Yet Philip still refused to crusade. His motives are unclear, but he probably feared making more enemies in southern France to add to those in Poitou and Gascony. In addition, the death of Raymond VI in August 1222 meant that the highly popular and capable young Raymond was the one now facing dispossession, a prospect unjust and provocative enough in 1215 to have induced large-scale rebellion.[142] Thus Amaury, left to shift for himself, was forced to surrender virtually all of his southern property, including Penne d'Agenais, with his few other possessions protected by a truce. When this elapsed in March 1224 the Toulousains reoccupied the rest.

This was a month before a truce between Prince Louis and Henry III was also due to elapse. The pope had been urging its renewal in order to allow Louis to crusade in the south. The English also wanted the truce, to preserve Gascony and what remained to them of Poitou. But they also feared the crusade, which threatened Plantagenet claims to the overlordship of Toulouse, which were

nied the sparing of these two nobles; Marquette, 'Les Albret', 308; Roquebert, *L'Épopée*, iii. 145, 151–5, 163–6, 172.

140 William of Tudela, *Chanson*, iii. 302–17.

141 *HGL* viii. 748–9, 753–55; *Chartes Agen*, nos xii, xiii; Roquebert, *L'Épopée*, iii. 207–8.

142 Sumption, *Albigensian Crusade*, 205–6; Higounet, *Comminges*, i. 103.

asserted again in this context. Louis, brilliantly, saw his chance; he both raised an army to invade the Languedoc and rejected the truce, leaving open the opportunity of a later invasion of Poitou. However the primary interests of both the English and Capetians were thwarted when Raymond and the pope were temporarily reconciled. Louis turned his army instead against Poitou. By mid-July it was lost and, but for the defiant stance taken by Bordeaux and Bayonne, Gascony too might have fallen.[143]

Still Louis looked to extend French influence to the Midi, which would make the conquest of Gascony yet possible. With the help of the pro-Capetian legate Romanus, he was able to persuade Amaury to cede his inherited claims in the Languedoc to him in 1225, by which time he was king of France. A royal crusade was declared. As a pre-requisite to this, Raymond VII was excommunicated by the legate and a truce imposed on the English. But the allies had already antici-pated this outcome and had made a secret pact that summer. Henry had sent his brother Richard of Cornwall to aid the defence of Gascony and to keep an army ready there to help the Languedoc. Thus, when the royal crusade mustered at Bourges in May 1226 it looked as though the war would at last involve a king of England openly. But at the last minute Henry's opposition was neutralised by three factors: a warning from Pope Honorius in late April threatening Henry with excommunication if he interfered, Richard of Cornwall's assessment that English help would not be needed in any case, and an astrologer's prophetic opinion that Louis would die as a result of the crusade.[144]

1226–9: the victory of the Capetians

In June 1226 the royal army, including the Poitevins Hugh of Lusignan and Savari de Mauléon, marched down the Rhône, and Raymond was left to his own devices.[145] Some allies, including the town of Agen, remained loyal. Indeed, an even stronger and mutually beneficial alliance had been struck between Raymond and the people of Agen on 21 or 22 May of that year, referring to the fact that the two parties would make common cause against the crusade and the king of France.[146] However Louis took Avignon after a three-month siege and, rather than face invasion again, the desperately war-weary Languedoc

---

143 *Diplomatic documents*, 136–7, 139; Sumption, *Albigensian Crusade*, 210–12; Carpenter, *Minority*, 344, 349, 355, 358, 370–5; Roquebert, *L'Épopée*, iii. 234, 283–4; Higounet, Renouard and others, *Histoire de Bordeaux*, iii. 41–5.

144 Rymer's *Foedera*, i. 277, 281; Ch. Petit-Dutaillis, *Étude sur la vie et le règne de Louis VIII*, Paris 1894, 518–20; Evans, 'Albigensian Crusade', 316; Carpenter, *Minority*, 375–8; Roquebert, *L'Épopée*, iii. 286–7, 317–18; *HGL* vi. 602–3; Sumption, *Albigensian Crusade*, 212–16.

145 Hugh had allied with Louis as a pre-requisite to the conquest of Poitou. Savari de Mauléon had defected from the English side in 1225, when Poitou was lost, and was placed in charge of La Rochelle by Louis: Roquebert, *L'Épopée*, iii. 303, 336, 349; Sumption, *Albigensian Crusade*, 216.

146 *Chartes Agen*, no. xvii; *HGL* viii. 835–6; Sumption, *Albigensian Crusade*, 217; Roquebert, *L'Épopée*, iii. 324–5. Roquebert (ibid.) notes the importance of this: the last royal military intervention in the Languedoc had been an expedition into the Agenais.

submitted, with the exception of Toulouse. Bertrand de Gourdon had regretted his defection to the southern party in 1218 and performed homage to de Montfort again on 25 May. In 1226 he was forced to further clarify his position by submitting to Louis.[147] Even Bernard V of Comminges, count since his father's death in February 1225, made his peace with Louis at Avignon in late summer 1226.[148]

The death of Louis on the return journey to Paris briefly raised southern hopes over the winter of 1226–7. Étienne de Ferréol defected to the south, although he was soon killed in fighting.[149] Some Agenais towns returned to the southern party and defied Louis's deputy Humbert of Beaujeu (whose predicament was made worse by the diversion of French forces into Poitou in response to a rebellion by Hugh of Lusignan). A campaign in 1228 managed to secure more towns for the south, including Castelsarrasin, and when it was taken it was given to Bernard de Cazenac. But the regency of Louis's queen, Blanche of Castille, was a strong one and royal enemies in the south as well as the north, including rebel barons encouraged by Henry III, were forced into submission. With relative stability in the north Raymond had to sue for peace and, in Paris on 12 April 1229, in exchange for the lifting of his excommunication, he formally submitted.[150]

The terms of the Treaty of Paris were punitive indeed for the house of Saint-Gilles.[151] Gregory IX had succeeded Honorius in 1227, and he gave the legate Romanus the power to exact numerous concessions. They included a promise to aid the Church in rooting out heresy, although there is no evidence that Raymond had any religious qualms about complying with this. In order to preclude any chance of further rebellion, the walls of various castles and towns were to be destroyed, including Casseneuil, Pujols, Agen and Auvillars in the Agenais, and Montcuq and the towns of Bas-Quercy. Raymond lost many lands in the Languedoc and was obliged to perform homage for the others to the French crown. In one act this ended centuries of political independence for the counts of Toulouse and deprived the king of England of overlordship of the Agenais, acknowledged through homage in 1214 and recognised by Innocent III in the letter sent to the bishops of the Languedoc in 1213. But most appalling of all to the southerners was the betrothal of Louis's son Alphonse to Jeanne of Toulouse, Raymond's heir. Jeanne had already been promised to a son of Hugh of Lusignan in 1224 when Raymond, apparently panicked by his uncertain status, had chosen to hedge his bets by making an alliance with an enemy of Henry III. This betrothal was forcibly ended by Romanus. Intrinsic to this part

[147] Doat cliii, fo. 93r–v, and *Layettes*, ii. 1760 (for 1218); *HGL* viii. 704–6, and Roquebert, *L'Épopée*, iii. 305 (for 1226).

[148] Higounet, *Comminges*, i. 111–12; Roquebert, *L'Épopée*, iii. 262, 335–6, 350.

[149] William of Puylarens, 132–3.

[150] Ibid; Doat xxii, fo. 9v; Roquebert, *L'Épopée*, iii. 366–7; Samazeuilh, *Histoire*, 158, 274; Sumption, *Albigensian Crusade*, 222–3.

[151] The articles of the treaty are contained in *HGL* viii. 878–94, and in Roquebert, *L'Épopée*, iii. 386–414.

of the agreement was the stipulation that Raymond's lands would be inherited by Alphonse, through Jeanne, if Raymond had no male heir, and in the case of Toulouse this would happen even if Raymond did have a son.[152] Thus only the lands in the eastern Languedoc and Provence would remain to the house of Saint-Gilles after Raymond's death. However, until that time, he would live as count of Toulouse and hold the lands pertaining to that title, an opportunity which neither he nor the Languedoc, utterly exhausted by two decades of warfare, could refuse.

The English were no position to undermine the Franco-papal party either. During the minority of Henry III, and into the 1220s, England was strongly influenced by the papal legates Guala and Bishop Pandulf of Norwich. The papal agenda they worked to was remarkably similar to that at the start of the century: the limiting of the Anglo-French conflict, which they did by protecting English interests and thus deterring French aggression, and the organisation of a crusade to recover the Holy Places. Therefore, aside from a few periods of conflict in 1224–7, England and France were bound by truces which would have been undermined by overt aid to Toulouse. In addition, English hopes of regaining control in Poitou had been irrevocably shattered by a successful French invasion during the summer of 1224, and also by an alliance with the Lusignan party, now including Henry's mother Isabella of Angoulême. Blanche of France, as regent for her son Louis IX, managed not only to save the Capetian line at this vulnerable time but also seriously to weaken the position of Richard of Cornwall, brother of the English king, sent to secure Gascony. Indeed, if anything, it was the English who needed Toulousain help in this period. Lusignans, no more loyal as vassals of Capetian Poitou than they had been of the Plantagenets, continued in their support of Saint-Gilles into the 1240s. But the English shrank from crossing the papacy. Apart from hoping that a Toulousain alliances with James I of Aragon and the Emperor Frederick II might restore the Languedoc to its former independence, Henry III had to be content with limiting his interest in southern France to the allod of Gascony.[153]

Various political features of the local lordships give a context to the transition between the state of affairs in 1209 and that of 1249. First, we should note patterns in the motives and allegiances of the lords and towns of Quercy. The townspeople of Bas-Quercy, for example, were amongst the bravest of the crusade, submitting to the north only when resistance was hopeless. Cahors, by contrast, features scarcely at all. Because of its pro-crusader stance it was most typically a place of peace. Most interesting though, is the shift of allegiance witnessed amongst the lordships of central and Haut-Quercy. In the 1209–11 period especially, we see them hurry to declare their support for the crusade. And why not? To do otherwise would have meant losing their lands when they had never been heretical. Thus their political support sprang from their religious

---

152 *Chronicon turonense*, in *RHF* xviii. 307, 314; Evans, 'Albigensian Crusade', 316.
153 A good summary of these developments can be found in M. Powicke, *The thirteenth century, 1216–1307*, 2nd edn, Oxford 1962, 80–103.

allegiance, and in this they followed their bishop. But in 1214 and most especially from 1217–18 they began responding negatively to the humiliations inflicted on the Languedoc, a state of affairs to which they had contributed by their early collaboration. The defection of the lords of Mondenard, Lolmie and Castelnau-Montratier in the former year, and those of Gourdon, Montaigu and Barasc from the time of the second siege of Toulouse, did not happen as part of a general revival in southern confidence but were in fact a major cause of it. In chapter 5 we will see that this shift in loyalty affected another change, one of confessional indifference and even allegiance to the heresy, most notably on the part of Bertrand de Gourdon who, by the end of the crusade of 1226, was leading a double life as a vassal of the French crown and protector of the most notorious heretics.

In the Agenais, in contrast, we can discern no clear pattern of allegiance or identity. Indeed, the Albigensian wars, although their impact is neglected in the work of both Bisson and Clémens, show most clearly the deep complexities of the identity, or rather identities, of the region. It was not divided between Catholic and heretic any more than the rest of the Languedoc was, for the Catholic Agenais lords of Albret, Lomagne, Sainte-Livrade and townspeople of Agen found themselves on different sides. The Gascon Agenais, south of the river and Catholic to the core, was not entirely pro-crusade, nor was the Languedocian Agenais entirely opposed to it. For whilst Albret collaborated, Condom, whose orthodoxy was never in question, massacred its northern occupiers. Whilst Sainte-Livrade was home to the crusaders, other towns on the Lot resisted. Indeed, as we have seen, the Catholics of Agen were themselves in dispute about which side to take throughout much of the crusade, and the same is surely true for less well documented towns. Nor did 'heretical' towns of the Lot resist or suffer more than the 'Catholics' of the Garonne: witness the frequent horrors experienced at both Marmande and Casseneuil. We find several Agenais lords apparently acting as allies of the crusade, for example Anissant de Caumont, and some, like Hughes de Rovinha, forced to submit and probably to perform homage to de Montfort. Etienne de Ferréol, on the other hand, appears to have embraced the crusader cause for a time and been one of that handful of trustworthy southerners placed in charge of the property of their dispossessed countrymen. Thus no simple model of loyalty or identity can be demonstrated in the period 1209–29. Each town and lordship appears to have shifted for itself and, where it could, judged its own chances of success by the fate of its neighbours. The lord of Albret alone appears to have remained firmly northern in his allegiance, and in 1219 managed to extend his territory to the right bank of the Garonne as a direct result. As with the Aquitainians Savari de Mauléon, the Lusignans and the viscounts of Turenne, there were factors more worldly and immediately pressing than religious doctrine behind his allegiance.[154]

Although Catholic Gascony was itself very divided in its initial response to

---

[154] B. Guillemain suggests that from the start d'Albret wanted to use the crusade to pursue his interests in the Agenais, which conflicted with those of the count of Toulouse: 'Le Duché', 61.

the crusade, most of it remaining passive and unwilling to stand in the way of the army of God, the Albrets contrast starkly with the reaction of the vast majority of Gascons when the duchy itself was actually invaded. But Gascons did not only fight in their own defence on their own soil. We see, most notable amongst many, the lords of Comminges, Béarn and Astarac active in the Languedoc as part of a strategic plan for a generalised Occitan resistance. Indeed, although Gascony and its English masters were still to play a part in the affairs of Toulouse after 1229, it was perhaps fortunate for the duchy that the French contented themselves with the prize of the Languedoc for the time being. Had they wished to make moves to invade Gascony again, they had been provided with many excuses for doing so.

5

The Cathar Diocese of the Agenais, 1207–1249

We now turn our attention to the fate and fortunes of the populations, heretical and otherwise, of the towns, castles and villages of the Cathar diocese of the Agenais on the eve of the crusade, during the wars and in the period of the inquisition.

The Cathar diocese during the crusade

The Cathar bishop Vigouroux de la Bacone

After the initial foundation of the Cathar bishopric of the Agenais in the 1170s and the appointment of Raymond de Casalis as its bishop, there is no record of any other heretical bishop there until the early 1220s. Whilst it is true of Vigouroux de la Bacone that 'il émerge de la demi-obscurité qui, en général, enveloppe les représentants de l'albigéisme', inquisitorial sources in particular are not lacking in references to him. Yves Dossat identified Vigouroux's origins. The name Bacone is Gascon-Toulousain, specifically from l'Isle Jourdain, between Auch and Toulouse, which pertained to the house of Saint-Gilles. Dossat proposes that the name Vigouroux is a family name from the region of the forest of la Bacona. It should also be noted that a hamlet bearing the name Vigouroux lies three kilometres due south of modern Casseneuil, the town which we suspect was the seat of the Cathar bishopric of the Agenais. Dossat has also given us 1233 as the date of his death.[1]

But a problem presents itself when we attempt to trace the career of Vigouroux as bishop of the heretics of the Agenais.[2] When questioned in 1244 after the fall of his castle of Montségur, seigneur Raymond de Péreille told the inquisitors that fifteen years or so earlier, i.e. in about 1229, the fortress had been the site of an important ceremony. The Cathar bishop of Toulouse, Guilhabert de Castres, had ordained one 'Tento', about whom nothing else is known, as Cathar bishop of the Agenais and that Vigouroux de la Bacone had been made

---

[1] Y. Dossat, 'Un Évêque cathare originaire de l'Agenais: Vigouroux de la Bacone', in his *Église et hérésie.* at p. 623. See also Griffe, *Le Languedoc, 1209–29*, 176–7, and Duvernoy, *Catharisme*, ii. 264.

[2] This is discussed in Dossat, 'Un Évêque cathare', 633–9; Hamilton, 'Saint-Felix', 45–9; Roquebert, *L'Épopée*, i. 99; iii. 162–4.

his *filius major*.[3] The account is problematic because two other sources say that Vigouroux was already Cathar bishop of the Agenais by 1223 at the latest. First, 1222/3 is the date attributed to the *Liber contra manicheos*, written by the Waldensian convert Durand de Osca, in which Vigouroux is designated bishop of the Agenais.[4] Second, the papal legate Conrad von Urach, cardinal bishop of Porto, an ally of the crusade in the Languedoc since 1217, stated in 1223 that a certain Barthélémy of Carcassonne had been sent into the Agenais by a new 'pope' of the Cathars, a heresiarch in Bosnia, in order to achieve the resignation of the Cathar bishop *Vigorosus de Bathona* and that after he had convinced Vigouroux to resign, at a Cathar council at Pujols, just south of Villeneuve-sur-Lot, the latter retired to the Toulousain and Barthélémy took over the running of his church.[5]

It seems unlikely that Vigouroux had been made *filius major* of the Agenais after he had been made its bishop. Dossat concludes that the Doat scribe was mistaken in transcribing Raymond de Péreille's statement that Vigouroux was ordained *filius major* fifteen or so years before 1244, and that the lord of Montségur must have given a much earlier date, before 1223. He supports this with the fact that the events de Péreille describes immediately before this account took place closer to thirty years previously.[6] He points also to possible problems with the dating of another eye-witness account of the Cathar hierarchy at Montségur, which he says are mistakes by the inquisition scribe contained in the testimony of Bérenger de Lavelant.[7] This witness says that he saw Guilhabert de Castres, his *filius major* Bernard de Lamothe and *filius minor* Jean Cambiaire, and also Hugues de la Bacone, *filius major hereticorum Agenensium*, Pons Guilhabert, heretical deacon of Villemur, and Bishop Tento when they came in about 1232 to suggest that the castle act as a special refuge for the leaders of the heretical church. In other words, whether or not he was ordained bishop before 1223 or in 1229, by about 1232 he is again called *filius major*. Dossat suggests that just as the inquisition's scribe must have mistakenly written *Hugonis* instead of *Vigorosus*, he also wrote the wrong date, and that a more likely one for the event is 1219, further evidence that Tento's episcopacy preceded that of Vigouroux.[8]

---

3 Doat xxii, fo. 226v. Each Cathar bishop had both a *filius major* and a *filius minor*. Typically the former would become bishop on the old bishop's death, and the *filius minor* would then become *filius major*.

4 *Une Somme anti-cathare, le* Liber contra manicheos *de Durand de Huesca*, ed. C. Thouzellier, Louvain 1964, esp. pp. 36–8 for the dating, and pp. 76–8 for the reference to *Vigorosi de Bachona*.

5 The manuscript is discussed in Dossat, 'Un Évêque cathare', 635–7. Good texts exist in *Thesaurus novus anecdotorum*, i. 901–3, and *Concilia*, xxii. 1201, 1204–6. There is a translation of the relevant section in *Christian dualist heresies*, 264. See also Duvernoy, *Catharisme*, ii. 70–1, 263. Barthélémy was in all probability Barthélémy de Nalauretta, or Lauressa, known to have had houses at Laure and at Montoulieu, both in Aude and near Carcassonne, between 1220 and 1227: Duvernoy, *Catharisme*, ii. 264; Dossat, 'Un Évêque cathare', 637–9.

6 Dossat, 'Un Évêque cathare', 633–4.

7 Doat xxiv, fos 43v–44v.

8 Dossat, 'Un Évêque cathare', 634–5.

This is one way of resolving the mystery, but concentrating on the dating of evidence ignores the significance of the content of the legate's testimony. Bernard Hamilton is certain both that Vigouroux was a bishop before he was *filius major* and that the dates given in Raymond de Péreille and Béréngar de Lavelant's testimonies are correct. This thesis rests on evidence for a schism amongst the Cathar churches of the Languedoc. Dossat himself has noted of dualists that 'la validité des ordinations faisant souvent l'object de contestations'.[9] The issue was one of great importance. Unless heretication was performed by a heretic who had led 'a good life', i.e. was in a perfected state at the time of death, a convert's own *consolamentum* was invalid, and the Bogomil church had experienced a schism before *c.* 1150 between absolute and moderate dualists, essentially between the churches of Drugunthia and Bulgaria. In the 1170s the absolute dualist Bogomils had converted the heretics in France to their faith. By as early as around 1180 the Cathar church of 'France' was already in schism with the southern absolutists, having reverted to the moderate *ordo* of Bulgaria, and at about that time part of the Lombard church, the church of Bagnolo, was also in schism with the Lombard Albanenses, who remained absolutist.[10]

B. Hamilton takes Conrad von Urach's statement as evidence that this schism had spread into the Languedoc by the early 1220s: in the context of the lessening of crusader control of the region and the weakened state of the Cathars, the moderates attempted to take control of the southern French churches, and Vigouroux was himself converted and reconsoled into the moderate *ordo*. This schism was apparently very short-lived, for we hear little else concerning it after 1223, and it has been noted that Barthélémy of Carcassonne was typically to be found back in Laure and Montolieu from about 1225 to 1227, not in the Agenais. What took place in 1229 at Montségur, therefore, was Vigouroux's *reconsolamentum* in the absolute *ordo*, made possible through the able diplomacy of Guilhabert de Castres, whose position as Cathar bishop of Toulouse made him head of all the Languedocian churches, as he set about reviving the absolutist church in southern France.[11] Tento, it would appear, was a little known compromise candidate for the bishopric of the Agenais, and the deposed Vigouroux de la Bacone, as *filius major*, was set to reclaim his diocese in due course.

An important piece of evidence for this theory is the context in which the 1223 copy of the Saint-Felix document used by Guillaume Besse was written. Describing the establishment of the Cathar churches of southern France in the 1170s, it was copied from the original on 14 August 1223 for Peter Isarn, Cathar bishop of Carcassonne, by his *filius minor* Peter Pollan. The document used and partially transcribed by Besse was in three parts: a history of the elections and ordinations of Cathar bishops at Saint-Felix, a sermon by Nicetas to the Cathars of Toulouse delivered on a different date and a description of the boundaries of

---

9   Hamilton, 'Saint-Felix', 47; Dossat, 'Un Évêque cathare', 633.
10 *Christian dualist heresies*, 250–3; Hamilton, 'Saint-Felix', 32–3, 45; Moore, 'Nicétas', 85–90.
11 Hamilton, 'Saint-Felix', 43–9. See also Duvernoy, *Catharisme*, ii. 264.

the heretical dioceses of Toulouse and Carcassonne drawn up before the history. Peter Pollan brought these sources together in 1223, the context being the revival of the Cathar churches in the Languedoc in this period when the crusade appeared to have failed, and, most important for our understanding of the career of Vigouroux de la Bacone, the threat of a resurgence of moderate dualism, for it was only one month before this that Conrad von Urach had described the activities of Barthélémy of Carcassonne in the Agenais noted above.[12]

This theory is very convincing and receives further support from the fact that inquisition witness Arnaud de Villemur describes Vigouroux as *filius major* when stating that he preached at Queille in *c.* 1232.[13] In addition, on one occasion Vigouroux was turned away from the seigneurial castle of Gourdon by one of its heretical co-lords, Bertrand. Although we cannot date this incident, 1223 is likely for we hear that the heretic had *in societate sua* Barthélémy de Carcassonne and that Bertrand refused to welcome him either.[14] If so it seems likely that this journey to the isolated but important community at Gourdon was undertaken in the context of the meeting at Pujols at which Vigouroux had been converted. It seems possible that Bertrand was making a distinction between the two types of heresy. If the attempted conversion of the community at Gourdon to moderate dualism was unsuccessful, better luck was apparently had at Montcuq, on the boundary between the Agenais and central Quercy, for we hear that the *credens* Durand Pairet of Montcuq, heavily implicated in heretical affairs, admitted to having been in Laure at the house of Barthélémy de Carcassonne where he assisted at an important gathering of seventy heretics.[15]

It is possible to place references to Vigouroux de la Bacone in many locations throughout the Languedoc into the chronology of a career as outlined above. As suggested in chapter 3, the Cathars of the Agenais were closely involved with the heretics of Bas-Quercy, and Vigouroux spent a good deal of time there. At least twice in 1213 he was at Raymond Grimoard's house in Castelsarrasin, as testified by Pons Grimoard, who on one occasion was himself given the kiss of Peace by the heretic.[16] The same witness also places him and his *socius* at Moissac in about 1213 at the home of Falquet de Saint-Paul.[17] A Cathar *perfectus* typically travelled with a long-standing companion, but although we hear of Vigouroux's *socius* several times he is never named in the documentation (a pattern which Arnold notes as typical). Guillaume Faber de Pechermer also encountered Vigouroux at Castelsarrasin *c.* 1218 in the home of the Campairan family.[18]

Vigouroux was in the Agenais at Castelmoron, where Dossat has shown that

---

12 Hamilton, 'Saint-Felix', 26–8, 42, 51–3; Barber, *Cathars*, 72.
13 Doat xxii, fo. 160v.
14 Doat xxi, fo. 186v. See pp. 253–4, 256 below for heresy at Gourdon.
15 Doat xxii, fos 220v–221r. See also Dossat, 'Un Évêque cathare', 638.
16 Doat xxii, fos 36r–v, 40v–41v (for the latter see also Griffe, *Le Languedoc, 1209–29*, 176–7).
17 Doat xxii, fo. 36r–v.
18 Ibid. 4v; Dossat, 'Un Évêque cathare', 629; Griffe, *Le Languedoc, 1209–29*, 176; Arnold, *Inquisition and power*, 139.

property was in his name, in about 1220, when the knight Guillaume de Castillon visited him and his *socius*.[19] Another mention of his home was made by Bertrand de Rupe de Monteruguo at his trial at Montcuq in 1241, although we are not given its location.[20] Vigouroux did not spend much time in Quercy or the Agenais between 1223 and 1228, as we might expect from the contents of Conrad d'Urach's letter. None the less, Othon de Beretges, *bailli* for Raymond VII at Moissac and Montcuq, was accused of failing to apprehend the heretic in spite of seeing him on at least three occasions at Castelsarrasin in *c.* 1224; twice at the house of Arnaud de Bressols with his *socius* and also at the home of the Pechermers.[21]

In 1228, by which time the schism was certainly over, Castelsarrasin was retaken by Raymond VII. It should not surprise us to find Vigouroux de la Bacone active in the newly optimistic Bas-Quercy. Guiraud Guallard stated in 1243 that he had seen him on three occasions around 1228: at Moissac on the quayside, about to be led into a house of Guillaume Faber and twice at the home of Arnaud de Bressols at Castelsarrasin, once with Bernard de Lamothe. On each occasion he was in the company of the most important families of heretical supporters in Bas-Quercy.[22] Vigouroux, still only a *perfectus* again in 1228, was very possibly reasserting himself in the region in the context of the work of Guilhabert de Castres to re-establish absolute dualism throughout the Languedoc.

We have a handful of other references to the heretic which are non-specific about dates, but which probably relate either to before 1223 or to 1228. Na Berètges of Castelsarrasin testified that he was in the house she shared with her husband Othon.[23] Two other accounts are from Moissac; Na Aurimunda heard him preach and Na Cuidalz de Goire offered him hospitality and 'adored' him (the customary way for *credentes* to acknowledge the status of *perfecti*).[24] We also have an account of Vigouroux from outside Bas-Quercy in this period at a Cathar meeting at Toulouse in *c.* 1228.[25]

We have accounts of Vigouroux in central Quercy, in the area around

---

[19] Bibliothèque de Toulouse, MS 609, 109v, cited in Dossat, 'Un Évêque cathare', 625 n. 5, and in Duvernoy, *Catharisme*, ii. 264. MS 609 is a copy made in the second half of the thirteenth century of part of the inquisitorial record compiled by Bernard de Caux and Jean de Saint-Pierre of their enquiry into heresy in the Lauragais. It is studied in detail in Pegg, *Corruption of angels*, with an excellent account (pp. 20–7) of the process by which the manuscript and original were made.

[20] Doat xxx, fo. 219r–v.

[21] Doat xxii, fos 44v–45r. See also Griffe, *Le Languedoc, 1209–29*, 176; Albe, *L'Hérésie en Quercy*, 10; Duvernoy, *Catharisme*, ii. 265.

[22] Doat xxii, fos 13v–14r, 14r–v, 16r–v, 20v, 21v. The inquisitors apparently found this witness's evidence problematic. Two of the above references are repeated accounts of the same event but with different dates ascribed. In addition, he says that Vigouroux was again at Castelsarrassin in *c.* 1235 (fos 19r–v), although it seems most likely that he was dead by then.

[23] Doat xxii, fo. 43r.

[24] Doat xxi, fos 290r–v, 295r–v.

[25] Doat xxiv, fo. 2v.

Montcuq, seen by people who were questioned there in the 1240s. None of these indicate dates. They may relate to his period of allegiance to the moderate *ordo*, for there is other evidence for such activity at Montcuq as we have seen. However, this would contradict Conrad d'Urach's statement that he had retired to the Toulousain, so they may be rare records of his activity after being re-ordained *filius major*. One of Montcuq's Cathar sympathisers, Bertrand de Rupe, was well acquainted with Vigouroux, sending heretics to his home, perhaps at Castelmoron, and meeting him at Moissac to escort him through Quercy.[26] Another witness, François Clergue, escorted Vigouroux and his *socius* specifically around the Montcuq area, once from *La Costa* to *Prinhac*, and put his own property at the heretics' disposal whilst they were there.[27] He also took him wine, bread, fruit and oil on behalf of a *credens* Guillelmassa and held for a time a book and also money, which he gave to Guillaume de Bausfan at the heretic's request.[28] Vigouroux and his *socius* were also welcomed into the home of Geralda and Gausbert de la Costa to preach, perhaps led there by François Clergue, and Gausbert d'Arcmei of Montcuq was introduced to Vigouroux via a messenger.[29]

Guiraud Guallard places the heretic again in Bas-Quercy in and around *c.* 1231, although this sighting, like another for the same year, may be wrongly dated.[30] In 1232 the heretical see of Agen was deemed to be too dangerous and Tento and Vigouroux moved to Montségur under the protection of its lord.[31] This was no doubt as a result of the adherence of Count Raymond VII to the Peace of Paris, which involved action against the Cathars with the destruction of the most important towns and fortresses in the Agenais, leaving its heretics very vulnerable. This is not the last we hear of Vigouroux, however. At some point, probably in the early 1230s soon after his removal to Montségur, he was active in the lands of Toulouse and Foix; at Calmont, Dun and Montgiscard.[32] Although there are anomalies in the dating of these sightings, it seems likely that they all refer to the same preaching tour, as they describe similar events and involved some of the same people. Dossat agrees that 1230–1 is a likely date for the sightings, given Vigouroux's removal to Montségur and likely death in 1233.[33] In addition, of course, Arnaud de Villemur heard him preach at Queille, near Mirepoix, in about 1232.[34] Pierre-Guillaume d'Arvinha was at the same meeting and involved in providing the heretic and his *socius* with hospitality, for which he was rewarded with the gift of a hat.[35]

---

26 Doat xxi, fo. 219r–v.
27 Ibid. fos 219v–220r.
28 Ibid.
29 Ibid. fos 222r, 225r–226v.
30 Doat xxii, fo. 18v, and see n. 22 above.
31 Doat xxiv, fos 43v–44v.
32 Doat xxii, fos 153r–v, 221v–222r (and see Dossat, 'Un Évêque cathare', 631 and n. 7).
33 Dossat, 'Un Évêque cathare', 630–1.
34 Doat xii, fo. 160v.
35 Doat xxiv, fos 242r–243v.

It has been stated that Vigouroux was still active perhaps as late as 1236.[36] But it seems more likely that he died in 1233, when Aubri des Trois-Fontaines reports that the 'magnus princeps hereticorum Vigorosus de Baconi' was burned, along with other heretics, at Toulouse, perhaps at the instigation of Raymond VII.[37] He is referred to in this source as a heretical bishop, however. This implies that he had been consecrated as the successor to his bishop, Tento, during the lifetime of the latter, as was common.[38] He was possibly executed following the arrest of important Cathars in 1232 at Montségur, whilst Tento was still bishop.[39]

The changing geography of the Cathar diocese of the Agenais

The lack of inquisitorial sources for the Agenais makes it impossible to gain an accurate picture of the heresy there during the period of the crusade. However, it would seem from secular and crusading sources that there were still heretics in the region soon after the crusade in the Agenais of 1209 and that the crisis no more permanently traumatised the heretics of the region than it did those of Villemur or Bas-Quercy.

Little if any action was taken against heresy along the Garonne in this period. The crusading dynamism of Arnaud de Rovinha makes it unlikely that this was the result of neglect, and it seems more probable that Catharism was still relatively weak along the river and that the heretical presence at its towns was limited to through-traffic.[40] In contrast, we have far more evidence for the heresy and for heretically sympathetic families along the Lot and also for Tonneins, at the meandering confluence of the two rivers.

We know a little about the heretical life at Casseneuil during the crusade, mostly about another member of the family of its defender Seguin de Balenx. Inquisitorial sessions in Quercy reveal that on unspecified occasions at Casseneuil Hartemanda de Balenx had been the close associate of the heretics. She had listened to them preaching, adored them, and believed them to be good men and to be saved. She gave them bread, wine, cider, fish and cakes, had one time sent blankets to them at a house where they were staying and had also eaten with them and shared bread which they had blessed. Most important, she was responsible for escorting them in their journeys through the Agenais, taking them at least once from *Pradasol*, which she says lay near Casseneuil, and to a place she calls *Colorsach*. Although some members of her family remained at

---

[36] Lea, *Inquisition*, ii. 22–3; Borst, *Die Katharer*, 234–5. See also discussion of Guiraud de Guallard's testimony at n. 22 above.

[37] Aubri de Trois-Fontaines, *Chronicon*, ed. P. Scheffer–Boichorst, MGH SS xxiii. 931. Yves Dossat agrees with this date and makes the link with Raymond VII's persecution of heretics: 'Un Évêque cathare', 631–2.

[38] Hamilton, 'Saint-Felix', 48; Duvernoy, *Catharisme*, i. 238.

[39] As argued by Dossat ('Un Évêque cathare', 632–3) based on William of Puylaurens's account of an arrest of leading heretics in the mountains: William of Puylaurens, *Chronique*, 154–5; Doat xxiv, fo. 46r–v.

[40] See, for example, Doat xxi, fo. 239v.

Casseneuil, Hartemanda moved to the Gourdon region where she was found to be a *credens* and given a sentence, the severity of which perhaps indicates the significance attached by the inquisitors to her activities.[41] Of the lord of Casseneuil, Hugues de Rovinha, we hear little after his town fell in 1214, although in 1218, presumably as a *faidit*, he witnessed an agreement, underwritten by his brother Bishop Arnaud, regarding a debt owed by Philippe de Landreville, de Montfort's seneschal for the Agenais, to several townspeople of Agen in 1218.[42]

I have offered evidence that Casseneuil was the seat of the Cathar diocese in the Agenais by 1209. However in 1212, after the fall of Penne, much of the Agenais was occupied by northern soldiers, forcing the submission of Hugues de Rovinha. This meant that the town and its Cathars were saved from outside intervention for another two years, but the town fell in 1214 and its heretics were burned. After this, it is not possible to establish the continuation of heretical activity there. Indeed, the transferral of the revenues of Casseneuil to Prouille after 1214 implies the ongoing presence of Catholic authority. If it was still the seat of the Cathar bishop, it was so only in theory.

We have however noted the close association of Vigouroux de la Bacone with Castelmoron-sur-Lot in the 1220s, where he owned property and received *credentes*. He was not the only heretic there in the period of the crusade, for many other people had their property confiscated by the inquisition before 1237.[43] We also have a reference to a heretic Gairaldus *de Castelmeiran* who stayed at the home of Pierre de Noye at Castelsarrasin *en route* to Moissac, probably in the 1220s.[44] In addition, we should note that the town did not receive the attention of the crusade. I suggest, therefore, that Castelmoron may have been the centre of the Cathar diocese under Vigouroux, but that heretical operations from there were more covert and successful than they had been under the unfortunate Casseneuil.

We know that heretics were still welcome at Tonneins in this period, for the witnesses 'B.' del Loc, Isarn Pontonier and 'B.' Nauta admitted that they had ferried them there along the Garonne from their own town of Moissac.[45] It is unclear whether the evidence refers to the de Rovinha's town of Tonneins-Dessus or the Ferréol's Tonneins-Dessous, as we have little other evidence about either town in this period after the attack of 1209. We do know a little of their seigneurial families. We have noted that Étiénne de Ferréol of Tonneins-Dessous was one of the many Agenais lords to be involved on both sides in the crusade. It seems likely that Raymond-Bernard de Rovinha of Tonneins-Dessus

---

41 Ibid. fo. 216r. Hartemanda was sent to Saint-Gilles, to Compostella, to Saint-Sauveur, Saint-Denis and Canterbury and instructed to spend three years in the Holy Land. It is one of the most severe sentences passed against a repentant *credens* in Quercy.

42 *Chartes Agen*, no. ix.

43 Archives nationales, JJ 24B, 63r–v, cited in Dossat, 'Un Évêque cathare', 624. See also p. 253 below.

44 Doat xxii, fos 27v–28r.

45 Doat xxi, fos 293r, 305r.

fell foul of the crusade at some point, for as part of the armistice of 1224 he was promised back property taken from him. A restoration was in part initiated by his kinsman Bishop Arnaud.[46] The de Rovinhas remained at Tonneins and at Casseneuil into the period of the inquisition and beyond. However we learn little of any further involvement in the religious conflicts which beset the Agenais.

Finally, we know that there was a Cathar council at Pujols in 1223; so was there also a heretical community there? Bernard Hamilton says that Conrad von Urach's evidence suggests that the Cathar see was being administered from there under the absolute dualists.[47] However, we only have evidence of the triumph of the moderate *ordo* at Pujols. Because we lack other references to heresy there in the period of the crusade I suggest that the town was chosen for the council in part for practicality. It was a fortified hill top town and easily accessible to heretics in the Agenais, being situated on the Roman route from Périgueux to Agen and close to the Lot.[48] If my suspicion that there was no significant Cathar presence at Pujols is correct, the town was also neutral territory for this conference. In addition, I think there is another reference to the Pujols council. The *credens* 'B.' Raimos told the inquisition that he was hired to accompany a Cathar to Pujols. He does not say when, but tells us the *perfectus* was attending a large gathering of heretics taking place there.[49]

Of the heretical life of Bas-Quercy and its borderland with the Toulousain, inquisitorial records reveal much more. Villemur, as we know, was evacuated in 1209 but was again settled by Cathars and their supporters.[50] So much so that we are told that by about 1213 its hundred or so inhabitants were virtually all either heretics or *credentes*.[51] Just as the evidence of Arnaude de Lamothe shows the link between the heretical community at Villemur and those of Bas-Quercy before 1209, that of the witness Bernarda Targuier, originally of Castelsarrasin, does so for the period after. Bernarda and her sister Guillelma were raised as *credentes* and were sent to Villemur where they lived at a house of heretics run by Na Unauda, wife of Arnaud Calvera. They were hereticated there c. 1213 and Bernarda then lived at Corbarieu, just south of Montauban on the road to Villemur, for four months. She was later reconciled to the Church by Bishop Fulk of Toulouse, after which she married the *credens* Pons Gran of Castelsarrasin and moved back to her native town.[52]

---

46 *HGL* viii. 779–80.
47 *Christian dualist heresies*, 264; Hamilton, 'Saint-Felix', 47–8.
48 For the military potential of Pujols see Tholin 'Notes sur la féodalité', *RA* xxv. 147–8, and 'Causeries', 517–28.
49 Doat xxi, fo. 286r.
50 Griffe describes the heresy at Villemur in this period (*Le Languedoc, 1209–29*, 178–80) but very much in terms of a continuation of heretical practice from 1209 onwards: *Le Languedoc, 1190–1210*, 89; *Le Languedoc, 1209–29*, 178. The evidence of Arnaude de Lamothe, the patterns of recruitment of female heretics in the town (see p. 234 below) and William of Tudela's evidence for 1209 would seem to disprove continuity.
51 Doat xxii, fo. 2r–v.
52 Ibid. fos 1v–3r, 15v–16r, 22r–v, 23r, 41v–42r.

Bernarda's evidence about Unauda Calvera reminds us also of Arnauda de Lamothe's reminiscences of the youthful community of female charges at the *perfecta* Poncia's just a few years earlier. I think we should consider Unauda's house for women around 1213 as a replacement for that formerly run by Poncia for, although the two were almost contemporary, we know that the Cathars of Villemur, and presumably Poncia with them, had fled in 1209. Thus we should see the heretication of Bernarda and her sister in 1213 as part of a process by which the hundred or so inhabitants of Villemur, perhaps a mixture of new settlers and returnees, attempted to revive the heresy in the dark days of the crusade. This they apparently did in part by recruiting children from Castelsarrasin. A visit by Unauda and her *socia* to Bas-Quercy to meet important heretical families, and visits by others between 1218 and 1226, may have played a part in this.[53]

However, at the same time as its heretical strength grew again, the town of Villemur began to reorientate itself into its more natural Toulousain context. Villemur and its families always had as much of a Toulousain as a Quercinois orientation, but this change occurred most immediately in the context of the marriage of lord Arnaud Razigot of Villemur to Na Comptor of Saverdun in the early years of the century.[54] Other heretical families of the Villemur region which were associated with Arnaud Razigot likewise became more southern in orientation, and thus after 1220 we find few remaining connections between the heretics of Villemur and Bas-Quercy.[55]

The survival of Catharism in Bas-Quercy is most impressive, given not only the weakening of links with the Toulousain but also the fall of Moissac and the submission of Castelsarrasin in 1212, not liberated until 1228, and the transferral of the remaining autonomous town, Montauban, to de Montfort by Innocent III in 1215. At Castelsarrasin in 1212, as at Casseneuil, recognition of crusader authority meant the avoidance of property confiscation by the northerners, and thus the survival of the heresy in private homes. Indeed, from the wealth of documentation for Castelsarrasin we can see that the heretics still had quite a high profile in the town in spite, presumably, of the presence of crusaders at points during these sixteen years and even of a northern garrison at times.[56] One explanation for this is that the crusaders apparently failed to govern Quercy very closely. Apparently neither side had a seneschal for the region in place for much of the 1220–30 period.[57] Whatever the reason, Castelsarrasin was the most important heretical community in Bas-Quercy.

Pons Grimoard and his wife Arnauda could be called the 'first couple' of

---

53 Ibid. fos 3r, 9v–10r, 23r, 27v–28r.
54 See Roquebert, *L'Épopée*, ii. 351–2, 365–6; iii, esp. pp. 156–7, 170–4; iv. 110, 122.
55 I disagree with Griffe here (*Le Languedoc, 1209–29*, 178–9). See, for example, evidence relating to the Helias family (Doat xxii, fos 52r–57v), to lesser families of Villemur (fos 46v–52r, 53v–54r, 54r–55r, 56r, 58r–v, 59r, 62v, 63r), and to the lords of Tauriac (fos 49v, 52r, 58r–v, 59v–60r, 61v, 62v, 62v–63r, 64v.)
56 As suggested in Griffe, *Le Languedoc, 1209–29*, 175.
57 See AD Lot F 97, 98, 104, 105.

Castelsarrasin. Arnauda attended heretical gatherings until at least 1228. Pons was important to the heretical community not least as Count Raymond's seneschal for Quercy, from 1234. It was more likely in this capacity rather than in his heretical one that he met with the *faidit* Bernard de Cazenac of Périgord at Castelsarrasin in 1228, when the latter took control of the town for Raymond VII, although the account points to the heretical sympathies of both by this time. We also have information about many other Grimoard family members, some of whom were mentioned in chapter 3. Raymond Grimoard, Pons's uncle, was an active supporter of the heretics for years and was himself hereticated in 1213 at Corbarieu in the company of other *credentes* of Castelsarrasin. He met other heretics, including Bernard de Lamothe, in 1218, but was reconciled to the Catholic Church sometime after this. The *perfectus* Pierre Grimoard was still adhering to the faith around 1218, as was his son Raymond-Bernard. We do not hear of either of them again, and Na Berètges, wife of Pierre and Raymond-Bernard's mother, is mentioned after that date without her immediate kin.[58]

Pons Grimoard's cousin Pros, married to Johannes de Cavelsaut, became one of the most active female *credentes* in the community, attending heretical meetings throughout the period of the crusade both at her father's house and very frequently at Guillaume Faber's. As early as about 1218 she had female heretics at her own house behind the market place at Castelsarrasin. They included Unauda, the *perfecta* of Villemur, and Pros's own hereticated daughter Raimunda. Also in attendance at this time were Pros's servant Passiona and friend Petrona de Cahors.[59] The Cavelsauts belonged to a major family of Cathar sympathisers. Four members, Hugh, Guillaume, Pons and Bernard are identified as *perfecti* in inquisitorial documents referring to the later years of the crusade. Bernard is not referred to as hereticated by 1213 when he, Pros and Bertranda, wife of Hugh, were at a large heretical meeting in Castelsarrasin, but Pons and Bernard, whom I suspect were brothers, were both hereticated by 1218, in which year Guiraud Guallard saw them preaching to the rest of their family in an upper room at Johannes de Cavelsaut's. The pair are mentioned almost always together up to c. 1225. Hugh de Cavelsaut was *credens* by around 1213 when he and Johannes de Cavelsaut attended the heretication of Raymond Grimoard, and was still so in 1225 when he was at the Fabers with Bernard de Lamothe. He was hereticated by 1228, just before he died.[60]

Another family related to the Grimoards by marriage was that of Na Berètges,

---

[58] Doat xxii, fos 9v–10r, 15r–16r, 21v, 22v, 23r, 23v–24r, 37v, 43r. Griffe suggests that the heretication of Vital away from home was the result of the occupation of Castelsarrasin mentioned above (*Le Languedoc, 1209–29*, 175), but Corbarieu does appear to have been a significant centre in its own right (see p. 233 above). See also Passerat, 'Cathares', 155–6.

[59] For references de Raimunda de Cavelsaut see Doat xxii, fos 17r–v, 19v–20r, 20r, 23r, 23v, 24v, 28r–v. For the other women see fos 9v–10r, 15r–16r, 22v, 23r.

[60] Ibid. fos 11r, 14r, 15r–v, 19v–20r, 21r–v, 21v, 28v, 34r–v, 35r, 37r, 38r (Hugh); fos 4r, 15r–v, 22v, 37r, 40r (Guillaume); fos 6r, 17r, 19v–20r, 22v, 24r, 24v, 35v (Bernard); fos 4r–v, 15r, 17r, 19v–20r, 22v, 24r, 24v, 58v–59r, and Griffe, *Le Languedoc, 1209–29*, 177 (Pons).

wife of the heretic Pierre Grimoard, both important *credentes*. Jordan de Berètges appears to have been the most actively heretical family member, discussing theological issues on several occasions. Featuring regularly in depositions is Othon de Berètges, Na Berètges's brother and Raymond VII's *bailli* for Moissac who failed to apprehend Vigouroux de la Bacone in about 1224.[61] We also have information about the Gran family into which Bernarda Targuier married after being reconverted to the Catholic faith. We hear from the knight Guiraud Guallard that she and Pons Gran had two sons, one of them called Guillaume, who, intriguingly, were apparently both in England by 1243.[62]

The Fabers of the Castelsarrasin suburb of Pechermer were by now a mixture of heretics, *credentes* and Catholics. Guillaume Faber de Pechermer was the head of the family by 1222 at the latest and heretics, not least Vigouroux de la Bacone and Bernard de Lamothe, were reported at the house by inquisition witnesses throughout the 1220s as well as at his property at Moissac, where Vigouroux was welcomed in 1228. Guillaume had at least three siblings. His brother Arnaud was possibly a heretic by the time of the crusade and ran a household by 1213. His sister Geralda was a *credens* and was at one of the meetings with Bernard de Lamothe at Guillaume's house, as was his other sister Guillelma, although Guillelma was apparently fervently Catholic and never adored the heretics.[63] Guillaume Faber's wife Bernarda was also a loyal Catholic, according to her husband.[64]

The de Bressols family of Castelsarrasin also remained central to the heretical life of Bas-Quercy.[65] Almost all family members of whom we know were *credentes* and were at Arnaud de Bressols's house in around 1224 and 1228 with Vigouroux de la Bacone. They include Aimeric de Bressols and two brothers Arnaud and 'P.' Much evidence again comes from Guiraud Guallard, who admitted having attempted to protect the family when previously questioned by Guillaume Arnaud in the 1230s because they had helped him so much in his own heretical faith.[66] Arnaud appears to have been the head of the family, owning the house and a vineyard, and associated often with other family leaders, Guillaume Faber de Pechermer and Pons Grimoard in the 1220s. We also know that Aimeric travelled to Toulouse on heretical business in *c.* 1219 with

---

61 Doat xxii, fos 4v–5r, 5v–6r, 10r, 37r–v (Jordan); fos 13v–14r, 20v–21r, 43r, 45r (Othon).
62 Ibid. fos 15v, 22v–23r.
63 Ibid. fos 2r, 11r–v, 16r–v, 17r, 23r, 23v, 28v, 36r, 44r (Arnaud); fos 34v–35r, 47r–v (Geralda); fos 9v–10r, 17r (Bernarda).
64 We also know of another family member, Raymond, who had heretics and leading believers at his house in about 1226 (ibid. 16v). For references to other family members see fos 14r–v, 18r, 19r–v (Na Grazida); fos 11r, 11v–12r, 13v–14r, 40v (Rostanh); fos 34r–v, 38r ('P.' and Aimeric). The insistence of some witnesses that family members were not sympathetic to the heretics is another aspect of the evidence to which we could cautiously apply one of Given's models of collective resistance, that of giving the inquisitors information that would protect family or community members.
65 They may also have had a branch at Montpezat-de-Quercy, for a certain Bernarda, wife of 'B. de Brazolz', was convicted there in 1242: ibid. fo. 307v.
66 Ibid. fo. 81r.

Guillaume Faber de Pechermer and Raymond-Guillaume de Berètges, and that he influenced Pons Grimoard's decision to remain faithful to the heretics.[67]

The inquisition at Moissac revealed heretical activity by a huge number of families in the town over the preceding decades, although almost all of it is very hard to date accurately. The most significant is that of the seigneurial family. Around 1224 the lady of Moissac and her daughter Na Ondrada entertained Bernard de Lamothe, and Ondrada's two sons Bertrand and Arnaud-Guillaume also adored him.[68] The Saint-Paul family of Moissac continued in the heresy and Pons Grimoard was at a meeting at their house in c. 1213 at which Vigouroux de la Bacone was present.[69] We have also seen that Vital Grimoard, Guillaume Faber de Pechermer and Othon de Berètges formed a connection between the communities at Castelsarrasin and Moissac, the former two owning property used for lodging heretics and holding meetings, and the latter living at Castelsarrasin whilst being Raymond VI's *bailli* for Moissac.[70] Much of this evidence again comes from Guiraud Guallard, something of an acolyte of Vital Grimoard.[71]

The most sizeable community of female heretics in Bas-Quercy would appear to have been at Montauban. The *perfecta* Joanna d'Auvione was at the centre of activity. She was supported with food by Raimunda Salinera and she and her heretical associates were received, fed and adored at the homes of a Fabrissa and Guillelma de Sapiac, the latter of whom told the inquisition that she had been a *perfecta* of the town herself, had been reconciled by the bishop of Cahors, but had lapsed to the status of *credens*. Fais de Sapiac also told the inquisitors that she knew of many male and female heretics in the town. Another woman, Petronilla, had been hereticated twenty years prior to her deposition of 1241 and had lived as a *perfecta* for three years, but had escaped punishment because she had been reconciled by Bishop Fulk of Toulouse.[72]

Near the town to the south, as noted, Corbarieu was an important Cathar site. To the north, just as before 1209, the de Lamothe family were still heretical, implied essentially by their activity in later decades. During the crusade Hugues, fought in the army of Raymond VI in 1217–19.[73] Another, Géraud, apparently the brother of Bernard de Lamothe, was also a heretic and spent time in Lombardy.[74]

---

[67] Ibid. fos 2r–v, 4v–5r, 8r, 10r, 11r, 18r, 19r–v, 20r–v, 31r–v, 45r–v; HGL viii. 1147 (Arnaud de Bressols); Doat xxii, fos 20v–21r, 35r–v ('P.'); fos 4r–5r, 10r, 18r, 35r–v, 36v, 37r–v (Aimeric); fos 20v–21r (Guillaume and Vital).
[68] Doat xxiii, fo. 266r.
[69] Doat xxii, fo. 36r–v.
[70] Ibid. fos 16r–v, 23b.
[71] Ibid. fo. 18r.
[72] Doat xxi, fos 240r–242r, 244v, 268r–v.
[73] William of Tudela, *Chanson*, ii. 298–9; iii. 86–7, 92–3, 262–3, 308–9.
[74] Toulouse, MS 609, fos 43r, 45r, cited in Roquebert, *L'Épopée*, iii. 364.

The start of the revival

Much of the above evidence, relating as it does to secret meetings with heretics and their covert accommodation, shows that although the heresy was in no way destroyed by the crusade its adherents were made wary. Indeed, with the exception of a community to be discussed next, the heretics of the northern Languedoc did not attempt to spread the heresy further until the crusader presence lessened. Thus we find that the efforts of Guilhabert de Castres in the 1220s really came to fruition in our region only after the Peace of 1229. This change and the reasons for it will be discussed below with the inquisitorial evidence that reveals it. First, it remains to examine briefly its precursors, the influence of the seigneurial family of Gourdon, of a peripatetic member of the Cathar hierarchy at work in Bas-Quercy and most immediately to identify the earliest heretical activity in central Quercy.[75]

Montcuq had suffered much in the previous decades. It lies where the Agenais meets central Quercy, above the river valley of the Barguelonne, quite easily accessible from the Garonne at modern Lamagistere. That is to say, it would have represented an ideal point of entry into the central Quercy area by heretical missionaries with support in the Agenais, as had perhaps been proved by the moderates in about 1223 when a *credens* of Montcuq was apparently supporting their cause and another was at work in the home town of Barthélémy de Carcassonne. It is possible that Vigouroux de la Bacone's many visits to Montcuq relate to before 1228 and to his moderate period. In addition, another believer, Guillaume Varrers, interviewed at Montcuq, stated that as well as receiving heretics in his own home he too had been active in Aude, escorting heretics from Montolieu to Toulouse. This witness also sounds like someone who might have been influenced by the schism; not only was he connected with Barthélémy of Carcassonne's Montolieu but he admitted to having given the nature of his faith careful consideration, wavering at times between different beliefs, being hereticated himself, although into what *ordo* we do not know, and being educated enough to make use of a heretical book with which he was presented at this ceremony.[76] It thus appears that a moderate enclave of sorts may have formed at Montcuq.

On the other hand, other families of the area had heretical sympathies almost certainly with the absolute *ordo*. Jeanne de Lolmie, later convicted at Montauban from where there is no evidence of the moderate *ordo*, was probably of the Lolmie family of Montcuq implicated in the murder of Baldwin of Toulouse, and

---

75 Roquebert explains the expansion of the heresy into central and upper Quercy in terms of evacuations of the Toulousain during the fighting: *L'Épopée*, i. 96–9. I feel that this is not the whole picture. Quercy, especially between Cahors and Bas-Quercy, was attacked and occupied many times and was no safe haven. The evidence indicates that the southern partisans north of the river Tarn were not heretical supporters until later. In fact heretics are not mentioned there in the period before 1229 except at Montcuq.

76 Doat xxi, fos 220r–221v. For literacy amongst the Cathars, including discussion of this and other heretics of our region, see P. Biller, 'The Cathars of the Languedoc and written materials', in Biller and Hudson, *Heresy and literacy*, 61–82, esp. pp. 77–8.

Othon de Berètges, *bailli* also for Montcuq by the 1220s, was a known absolutist *credens*. Indeed, in heretical terms this town was quite eclectic by 1229, for we find much support for Waldensians, including mention of a debate between adherents of that sect and Cathars.[77] However, a path was being paved for a more concerted effort to implant Catharism in the Montcuq region.

Until their lands and those of their neighbours were terrorised by the crusade, the seigneurial family of Gourdon was amongst those actively Catholic families of Quercy. Géraud de Gourdon was a member of the cathedral clergy at Cahors.[78] As we have seen, Bertrand de Gourdon crusaded in 1209 and made and renewed his homage to the de Montforts in 1211, 1217 and also in 1218. However, in the latter year he was criticised by Rome for aiding the southern army. By the time he was forced to submit to the royal crusade, in 1226, he was not only a southern partisan but was also tolerant of the heresy, if not a *credens* himself, for he allowed Cathars to preach in Gourdon and even to establish a community in his town. He was involved enough with the heresy apparently to take sides in the heretical schism of 1223. By 1229 the town of Gourdon contained the major heretical community in Haut-Quercy, and when the Peace was signed many of its *perfecti* left the town for safety accompanied by *credentes*.[79]

Where did they go? We might speculate that the exodus was more constructive than mere flight. The Gourdon heretics were perhaps proselytising in other Quercinois towns where they would be protected, for by about 1229 we can establish seigneurial links between the leading family of Gourdon and towns in central Quercy in which the inquisitors were later to find heretical communities. This evidence is extensive. In 1241 at Sauveterre, lying between Castelnau-Montratier and Montcuq, a Guiraud de Gourdon admitted that he had previously received heretics on his property where he was blessed by them, adored them and listened to them preach.[80] This is very likely the same Guiraud de Gourdon who in 1230 had ceded to Raymond VII property not only at Sauveterre but at three other locations – significantly at Montcuq, twenty-seven kilometres to the south at Mondenard, and also at *Montemaccistum* – and who held land at Montaigu, ten kilometres west of Montcuq, which he had also ceded to the count by 1248.[81] In 1241 a Fortanier de Gourdon was also associated with Mondenard.[82] Thus we find that the family had influence both in Gourdon, where it had already encouraged the heretics, and in central Quercy before 1229, specifically in and around Montcuq where Cathars had been working to implant the heresy. And the testimonies of Hartemanda de Balenx,

---

[77] Doat xxi, fos 217v–19r, 221v–222v, 225v.
[78] Albe, *L'Hérésie en Quercy*, 19.
[79] Doat xxi, fos 189r, 199r, 201v; Duvernoy, *Catharisme*, 268.
[80] Doat xxi, fos 226v–277r. Giraud de Gourdon is not to be confused with the *perfectus* of the same name, whose title relates to the Gourdon estate at Caraman, of which town he was Cathar deacon: Duvernoy, *Catharisme*, ii. 260; Griffe, *Le Languedoc, 1209–29*, 177 and n. 13.
[81] *HGL* viii. 1957, 2004.
[82] AD, Lot, F 126, 428.

Pierre de Penne and P. de Casseneuil indicate that *credentes* of the Lot valley in the Agenais were in touch with those at Gourdon and also Montcuq.

Turning our attention back to Bas-Quercy, amongst those most responsible for maintaining the influence of the heresy there was Bernard de Lamothe, originally a *perfectus* of Montauban, then Cathar deacon of Lanta from *c.* 1223, and by *c.* 1225/6 *filius major* of Guilhabert de Castres at Toulouse.[83] Few witnesses recall Bernard's activity in the early years of the crusade, although his relative Arnauda recalled that in *c.* 1214 he was at Montauban with his *socius* Guillaume Solier and family members.[84] In fact, although the Lamothes remained at Montauban, there are few accounts of the heretic or his *socius* in that town, and apart from Arnauda few attribute dates to the encounters.[85] He was however preaching at Corbarieu at some time around 1213–15 according to Bernarda Targuier.[86]

The heretic was apparently more closely associated with the community of Castelsarrasin, especially in the years 1218–19. There he and his *socius* met heretical and secular leaders, most notably Raymond and Vital Grimoard, also Johannes, Pons, Pros and Raimunda de Cavelsaut and Unauda of Villemur on one of her visits to the town. Such meetings were a mixture of closed conferences and public preaching in private homes. On one occasion he debated with two Catholic priests. We also have an account of the heretic and his *socius* with Vigouroux de la Bacone at Castelsarrasin at the home of minor *credentes* the Campeirans in *c.* 1218.[87]

When the life of the heretical church in the Languedoc began to revive in the central 1220s under Guilhabert de Castres, Bernard de Lamothe was instrumental in his plans.[88] Amongst this work was activity in Bas-Quercy, again specifically at Castelsarrasin and its *environs*. In *c.* 1223 and *c.* 1225 he was visiting and preaching at the Faber household in Pechermer, at Na Pros de Cavelsaut's in *c.* 1223, and visited minor families of believers, most notably the Sanches, on occasions between 1223 and 1228. Accounts also refer to meetings at Castelsarrasin between Bernard de Lamothe and Bernard de Cazenac hosted by Pons Grimoard, who attests that they happened *c.* 1225. 1228 would appear to be the real turning-point in the revival of the church in Bas-Quercy after the occupation, a process naturally at its most dynamic after the recapture of Castelsarrasin in that year. It should not surprise us to find Bernard de Lamothe at Castelsarrasin around that time: at the Faber household with de Cazenac

---

83 It has been suggested by Griffe that originally he may have been from Moissac, although I am not sure what the evidence is for this: *Le Languedoc, 1209–29*, 175–7. For his activity elsewhere in the Languedoc see Roquebert, *L'Épopée*, i. 241; iv. 113–14; Griffe, *Le Languedoc, 1209–29*, 163, 165, 181, 184, 187 and 204; and Duvernoy, *Catharisme*, i. 261–2.

84 Doat xxiii, fo. 7r.

85 See Doat xxi, fos 233r, 278v, in the latter of which Guillaume Solier is alone.

86 Doat xxii, fo. 2v.

87 Ibid. fos 4r–v, 16v, 23r, 23v–24r, 28v, 36v; Griffe, *Le Languedoc, 1209–29*, 177.

88 For his activity in around 1223–6 as Guilhabert de Castres's envoy see sources cited at p. 226 above and also Hamilton, 'Saint-Felix', 49–51.

again, now lord of the town as appointed by the count, at the home of Arnaud de Bressols, close to its hospital, and preaching to many of the town's leading families at a meeting also attended by Guillaume Salomon, Cathar deacon of Toulouse. The last account of Bernard de Lamothe in Bas-Quercy is in c. 1231, the year before his death, being entertained again in the home of Arnaud de Bressols.[89]

The heretical societies by the Peace of 1229

It is clear that many important families were involved in the heresy and that, being politically powerful and having material resources, they were at the forefront of both its defence and promotion. These families of our region are not well documented dynasties. For example, the de Rovinhas of Tonneins-Dessus, by 1229 probably dispossessed of Casseneuil, emerge from near total obscurity largely through the written documentation of other secular and religious parties and not from their own administrative, territorial or religious initiatives (although in the case of Bishop Arnaud this may have as much to do with the destruction of the diocesan archive). Such families none the less appear to have dominated their towns in the Agenais, with families like the Balenx in their service. However, unlike the nobles more loyal to the bishops, the lords of Casseneuil and Tonneins were not in practice beholden to the bishop-count of Agen as a result of his limited comital authority. Elsewhere in the countryside other castellans, of whom there are even fewer records, operated apparently independently of higher authority until they allied against the crusade or submitted to it, when they are mentioned in administrative and chronicle sources.

Bas-Quercy is even less clearly hierarchical and even more 'Languedocian', in that a meaningful distinction between noble and non-noble is almost impossible. The clearest picture of social composition comes from Castelsarrasin. Aside from the Grimoards, implicated in the political life of the south more widely and constituting the heretical aristocracy of their town, the Faber family of Pechermer and the de Bressols, de Berètges and de Cavelsauts emerge as the most important families because they were landowners. It was on their property that heretics were most frequently protected and in whose houses they most commonly preached. However a middle range of related families, including the Targuiers, Audeberts, Mazelers, Grans, Campeirans and Sanches, do not appear to have operated in a significantly different religious sphere. Not least, from the association of the Sanches with Bernard de Lamothe and the Campeirans with Vigouroux de la Bacone it seems that hosting heretical meetings usually fell to

---

[89] Doat xxii, fos 4v–5r, 9v–10r, 13v–14r, 14v, 15v–16r, 19v, 20r–v, 20v–21r, 21r–v, 21v, 22r–v, 23v–24r, 35r, 36r–v, 45r–v; xxiii, fo. 265r; Griffe, *Le Languedoc, 1209–29*, 177; Passerat, 'Cathares', 160. See also Doat xxii. 15v–16r for a meeting at Castelsarrasin with another set of important heretics, not from the Bas-Quercy region. They are Saturninum, Pons Dairos and Pons Guilhabert. The meeting is not dated, however, and so it is difficult to know what significance to attach to it.

the more major families because they had larger and more suitable property rather than because they especially dominated religious life. The *perfecti* were in principle blind to social status, and in practice were fed and accommodated by a cross-section of *credentes*. Having said this, it is frequently the leading families who are to be found in conference – rather than simply in religious practice or sharing meals – with leading heretics. It would appear, predictably, that the politically and economically powerful and better connected families were most relied on in the strategical plans of the heretics in their times of crisis and renewal.

The less important families, with more limited geographical and political connections, emerge from the history of early thirteenth-century southern France only because of the relatively socially inclusive nature of inquisitorial documents. They were called upon and often paid, both directly by the heretics and by the powerful protectors of heretics, to act as guides, boatmen and messengers, and to provide and carry food to heretics in hiding. They thus had a specific economic relationship to the heresy, but appear no less devoted to it than its wealthy benefactors. More of these lesser *credentes* will be identified below, in the context of a summary look at the heretical life of the region until the end of our period.

The Peace of Paris and the inquisition

The Languedoc saw relative peace after 1229 for over a decade. Then in 1241 Raymond VII rebelled again, supported, amongst others, by Count Roger-Bernard of Foix and the Aquitainians Hugh of La Marche and Viscount Arnaud Othon of Lomagne, whose family held Auvillars in the Agenais, and other lords and nobles of the Agenais, those loyal to the Catholic Church and otherwise. However, the alliance was short lived, for Raymond was forced to besiege the count of Foix at Penne d'Agenais, the last conflict of the Albigensian wars in the Agenais, and to fight a battle against the royal army which he lost. Another truce was agreed in consultation with Rome and the allies submitted to the crown in June 1242. In addition, on 28 May that year at Avignonet, the inquisitors Guillaume-Arnaud and Etienne de Narbonne had been murdered, sparking off another short-lived insurrection in the Languedoc. Heavily implicated in the murder was Raymond VII's *bailli* for Castelsarrassin, Raymond d'Alfaro, son of the count's illegitimate half-sister Guillelmette and Hugh d'Alfaro, Raymond VI's seneschal for the Agenais and now the governor of Avignonet. Although the murder went effectively unpunished and Count Raymond's lands were placed under Roman protection in 1245, he had been unsuccessful, either through force against France or by appeals to the pontiff in 1243, in getting the terms of the Peace of Paris overturned. Raymond VII died on 27 September 1249 without producing a son, and so the Toulousain and Agenais passed to Jeanne and Alphonse, count of Poitiers since 1241, in spite of protest also by Henry III of England. Under Jeanne and Alphonse the Agenais was at peace and was to experience relative prosperity; Raymond d'Alfaro was rehabilitated and became seneschal for the Agenais, which was from then on administered through division into fifteen *bailliages*, and many of its towns received charters and existing charters were renewed.[90]

But the town of Agen itself had in fact been steadily improving its position throughout the first half of the century. It had won protection for its loyalty and concessions with regard to franchises, collection of duties and elections of magistrates from Raymond VI in 1212, and confirmation of its customs, as well as amnesty resulting from its action in the war, from both Amaury de Montfort and Raymond VI in 1221, and from Raymond VII in 1226. In 1242 the commune, whilst providing an army for the count's war with France as it was obliged to do, also persuaded Raymond VII to pay for the rebuilding of its own ramparts. In March 1243 Agen conformed to a general submission to the French crown by the towns of the Languedoc, but this time too was able to negotiate relative autonomy in terms of economic and judicial affairs, which was confirmed by Alphonse as count of Toulouse.[91]

During the upheavals of the first half of the thirteenth century the towns of the Garonne ensured their economic survival with agreements to act in mutual accord and protection, also in conjunction with towns in Bas-Quercy.[92] As Charles Higounet has shown, we can tell much about the social composition and prosperity of the towns at this time from the lists of *consuls* who took oaths to the crown in 1243. We learn, for example, that after the execution of its inhabitants in 1219 Marmande received an influx of recent immigrants from as close as Tonneins and Pujols to as far away as Périgord and the Toulousain. Artisan, notarial, merchant and bourgeois families were now amongst Marmande's population of probably well over 1,000, 248 families being listed.[93]

The bishops of Agen did not fare as well in the Peace as did the towns and were further marginalised politically and economically. In the first instance this was brought about by the count. On 18 April 1217, in the church of Saint-Caprais, Bishop Arnaud was forced to divide the *comitalia* with Simon de Montfort as count of Toulouse. In practice, this meant that the responsibility for the maintenance of public order in the county – i.e. control of the region – was to be shared between them, as were the proceeds of justice at Agen, the bishop's

---

[90] Sources for the general history of the Agenais from 1229 into the early 1250s include *HGL* vi, esp. pp. 543, 586–808, 753–5; viii. 1087, 1113–15, 1153–7, 1261, 1854; *Layettes*, ii. 1777, 3045, 3048, 3166, 3169, 3171; William of Puylaurens, *Chronique*, 166–9. See also Samazeuilh, *Histoire*, 274–94; Guignard, *Histoire*, 107–29; Baumont, Burias and others, *Histoire d'Agen*, 51–76; Bisson, 'General court', 1–19; Ducom, 'Essai', i. 205–6, 211–14, 263, 272, 287; Lea, *Inquisition*, ii. 35–41; Duvernoy, *Catharisme*, ii. 281–6; Sumption, *Albigensian Crusade*, 237–8. Raymond d'Alfaro was a hostage during the 1229 negotiations in Paris: *HGL* viii. 893.
[91] *Chartes Agen*, nos x–xiii; Doat cxvii, fos 219r–221v; *Enquêtes administratives d'Alphonse de Poitiers*, 64–70; *HGL* viii. 1952, 1955; Ourliac, 'Coutumes', 243–4; Ducom, 'Essai', i. 205–11, 265–7; ii. 231–2. For the submissions of 1243 see *HGL* viii. 1118–20.
[92] *Chartes Agen*, nos xiv–xviii, xxxi.
[93] *HGL* viii. 1118–20; Higounet, *Marmande*, 8–9; Ricaud, *Marmande*, 36.

half to be held of de Montfort as a fief. The right to mint was also now only held in fief. In short, only the bishop's ecclesiastical powers and privileges in the diocese were not undermined by the new count.[94] In 1224 and 1228 he was forced into similar agreements with Raymond VII, and the comital rights of the bishop had been almost entirely eroded by the end of our period. He was also undermined by the *consuls* of the commune of Agen, who ceased to perform homage to him and, significantly, he was excluded from either participating in or convening the *cour d'Agenais*.[95]

Although the *cour* was in existence in 1212 and operated in the 1220s, the earliest curial session for which records survive was in 1232, and it would seem to be after the Peace of Paris that it operated regularly.[96] By the mid-1230s it was very powerful, controlling some rights to minting, public order and justice.[97] In fact, the powers of the bishops, held since 1217 only as a fief from the count of Toulouse, were taken from them by the counts and granted to the *cour*.[98] For example, the bishop's right to mint *Arnaudines* did not even include the ability to change the weight and composition of coins by 1232, when bishop Géraud II (1231–2) had to gain permission to do so from the *cour*. In 1234 Bishop Raoul de Pins (1233–5) had to promise the *cour* that he would leave the coinage unchanged and allow the townspeople of the Agenais to chose themselves how to regulate the economy.[99]

We must ask ourselves why the counts were empowering the people of the Agenais at the expense of the bishop. The explanation may lie in what I suspect were the real origins of the *cour*. I feel certain that the role of the crusade has been under-estimated in providing a context for its creation. Indeed, Simon de Montfort could have been its original architect, not the dukes of Aquitaine or the house of Saint-Gilles as Bisson and Clémens argue. The earliest evidence pointing to this is the first mention of the *cour*, in 1212. At Pamiers, in the presence of churchmen including the bishop of Agen and the archbishop of Bordeaux, de Montfort issued general customs for the lands he had conquered. At the same gathering, he dealt with a dispute between the inhabitants of Condom and their abbot. The plaintiffs, the people of Condom, were given leave to appeal 'ad curiam Agennensem'.[100] It was in the same year that de Montfort felt it prudent to recognise the traditional powers of the reinstated Bishop Arnaud and to divide the *comitalia* with him. Yet they must have seemed anomalous to a baron of the Ile de France and an obstacle to his own control and exploitation of the region. The crucial event was therefore probably on 14 May

94 Doat cxvii, fos 217r–218v; GC ii. 431–2; *HGL* vi. 502–3; *Coutume d'Agen*, 156, 169.
95 *HGL* vi. 586; Ducom, 'Essai', esp. i. 206–7, 294–321; Samazeuilh, *Histoire*, 259, 270; *Coutume d'Agen*, 157–60; Bisson, 'General court', 6.
96 *Chartes Agen*, nos xiv, xxxi, xxxii; *Coutume d'Agen*, esp. pp. 28, 30 and item 3; Clémens, 'Cour', 73. See also discussion in chapter 3 above.
97 Ducom, 'Essai', i. 199–213, 298ff.; ii. 229–30.
98 Clémens, 'Cour', 73–5.
99 *Chartes Agen*, no. xxiv; *HGL* viii. 303; Ducom, 'Essai', i. 299–307.
100 *HGL* vi. 396–7; Clémens, 'Cour', 72; Samazeuilh, *Agenais*, 187.

1217, the forced surrender by Bishop Arnaud of the powers which the *cour* later held, and their partial return to him by de Montfort as count of Toulouse in the form of a fief. Thus the bishop had to renounce his right to control the *comitalia* and accept that he held it conditionally and even temporarily, for 'the *pariage* of 1217 created a new situation and gave new rights to the count [and marked] the decline of the privileges of the bishop'.[101] The creation of the *cour* appears to have been the brain-child of the highest secular authority in the Agenais in this period, and did not have its origins in its local traditions after all. It was apparently conceived of in or just before 1212, and the necessary powers needed to make it a viable gift to the people of the Agenais acquired in 1217.

I suggest that it was the logical institutional conclusion to the problem of authority in the Agenais which had emerged over the preceding centuries. The crusader occupation of the region during the years 1209–17 had revealed the difficulty of governing this sprawling, divided and politically fickle land. Garrisoning the Agenais had only had limited effect in securing its co-operation and was never a stable solution for the French. Arnaud de Rovinha had never proved himself an able politician or commander, was understandably hated after 1209, and was not well suited to execute secular authority in this crucial but volatile region on behalf of de Montfort. The best government for the Agenais, de Montfort perhaps realised, was neither a clerical nor an alien one but the people of the Agenais themselves, made loyal through the granting of self-governing powers and privileges. And what better powers to grant them than the secular authority held by the loathed Bishop Arnaud?

Further indication that de Montfort and no previous authority was the engineer of the *cour* lies in the fact that on 11 May 1217, only three days before the bishop's homage to de Montfort, Raymond of Saint-Gilles wrote to 'honoratis et karissimis amicis sui [sic] maiori et consulibus et omnibus aliis probis hominibus Agenni' to support a rising against the bishop and other clergy of the Agenais. He does not mention the *cour*, the logical context in which this rebellion would happen had he recognised the *cour* himself.[102]

This is not to say that the *cour* became an institution in 1217. Its development was certainly disrupted by de Montfort's death the following year and there is little indication of its activity in the next decade or so. But whatever its exact origins, documentation shows that it was regularly convened by the count and his representatives from the 1230s.[103] Perhaps Raymond VII understood the political vision of the crusade's leader and sought to implement it. The *cour* certainly served the needs of future counts of Agen and Toulouse, including their need to have the region willingly accept their authority. On the one hand, the voluntary centralisation of judicial and military organisation made it easier for first Raymond VII and then the crown to draw the towns, villages and nobles

---

101 Ducom, 'Essai', i. 265.

102 *Chartes Agen*, no. vii.

103 See Bisson, 'General court', esp. pp. 3–20, in which the sources for the *cour* mentioned above are also discussed, with different conclusions.

of the Agenais into oaths of loyalty and military service: the general army was summoned by a single command in 1241, oaths were taken to the two parties via summonses from Raymond in 1241 and then by Louis IX's representative in 1243, and by the time of its convocation by Alphonse in 1249 the *cour* was a body with royal approval.[104] On the other hand, as a relatively united body militarily indispensable to the defence of comital lands, it ensured a degree of autonomy for its nobles as well as concessions for its towns. For example, it seems likely that Raymond VII had to get approval from the *cour* for levies on the towns of the Garonne to pay off his debts and improve communications just as the bishop needed its approval to alter coinage.[105]

This latter point should not imply that the bishop had lost all support amongst the nobility. The leading vassals of bishops Géraud II, Raoul de Pins, Arnaud IV de Galard (1235–45), Pierre de Reims (1245–8) and Guillaume II (1248–63/4) were still the lords of Boville, Clermont-Dessus, Fossat and Madaillan and Fumel. These remained loyal during the Albigensian wars and beyond. But as before the wars, the native lords of the region were still relatively minor and were overshadowed by the powerful Catholic Gascon lords Amanieu VI d'Albret and the viscounts of Lomagne. These held Agenais fiefs of the counts of Toulouse on the left bank of the Garonne, at Meilhan and Auvillars respectively, and attended the *cour* in respect of other Agenais possessions, but still do not appear closely associated with the bishops of Agen.[106]

The actively rebellious lords of the Agenais acted pragmatically in the shifts of political power of the 1240s. In May 1242 Guillaume Ferréol of Tonneins-Dessous, Amanieu d'Albret and other lords did homage to the count. However, as result of the southern defeat those same lords did homage to the crown in 1243, as did Bernard de Balenx of Casseneuil, Arnaud de Montaigu, Raimond de Pujols, Gaston and Vidal de Gontaud and Arnaud de Montpezat, and also Bernard, Aimery, Hugues and Autinier de Rovinha (lords of Tonneins-Dessus and, interestingly, also Auterive and again of the de-fortified Casseneuil, presumably returned to the family in 1229).[107]

If the political position of the Catholic bishop was weak with regard to the laity, especially after 1228, so was that of its clergy and religious. As a group they were excluded from the *cour d'Agenais* until 1271.[108] Few records of donations or

---

104 *HGL* viii. 1118–20 (and see also 1952); *Layettes*, iii. 3833; Bisson, 'General court', esp. pp. 2–3, 6, 18–20, 30.

105 *Chartes Agen*, nos xxxii, xxxiii; Bisson, 'General court', 39; Higounet, *Marmande*, 11.

106 Marquette, 'Albret', 304–9; Guignard, *Histoire*, 126; Tholin, 'Notes sur la féodalité', *RA* xxiii. 50; iv. 68–71. See confirmations of the Albret possession in *HGL* viii. 1860, 1977. The viscounts of Lomagne held Auvillars since 1215 at the latest, when Viscount Veszian made concessions and donations to Grandselve with the approval of his sons Odo and Espan at Agen, and they were confirmed as fief-holders by Raymond VII in 1249 (*HGL* viii. 1854). Viscount Arnaud-Othon appears to have been alienated from the *cour* by the same year: *HGL* viii. 2005.

107 *HGL* viii. 1119; Guignard, *Histoire*, 119.

108 Bisson, 'General court', 14.

foundations exist for the period and those that took place affected the Catholic left bank of the Garonne.[109] Count Raymond alienated other churchmen too. There was a priory at Mas-d'Agenais by 1224, and in 1235 its prior appealed to Rome against the seizure of seigneurial rights in the town by the count, which Raymond only returned under duress as part of the truce of 1242.[110] Raymond's relationship with the local clergy improved a little in the year of his death, 1249, in which he very successfully attacked heresy in the town, as described below, and the *Couvent de Paris*, or *Les Jacobins*, was founded, a process presided over and fostered by the inquisitor Bernard de Caux, a native of the Agenais.[111]

The inquisitors in the Agenais and Quercy

The medieval inquisition, initiated with the purpose of discovering and prosecuting heretics and their believers and supporters, was staffed initially by the Dominicans. From its activities in the heretical diocese of the Agenais we learn much about the extent and nature of Cathar activity there over the preceding decades and also gain a picture of the geographical spread and strength of the heresy in the 1230s and 1240s.[112]

Pierre Seilan and Guillaume Arnaud were named as inquisitors for the Catholic dioceses of Cahors and Toulouse in 1231 and began their enquiry in 1233, interviewing suspects in Quercy until 1239 aided by Guillaume Pelhisson, the major chronicler of this early period of the inquisition in the south of France. Many of the heretics summoned by the inquisition in Bas-Quercy were originally unmasked by the *perfectus* Raymond Gros, convicted at Toulouse in 1237.[113] In 1241 Pierre Seilan was still continuing this work at Montauban. Then for the years 1241–2 we have evidence of 724 sentences passed by a peripatetic court sitting at Gourdon, Montcuq, Sauveterre, Beaucaire, Montauban, Moissac, Montpezat, Montaut and Castelnau-Montratier. Little of this evidence is

---

[109] For example to Nomdieu: AD, Lot-et-Garonne, E supplt. 2745 (II.1), 1–3.

[110] *HGL* viii. 1856; Guignard, *Histoire*, 118.

[111] Doat cxvii, fos 222r–223v. See Douais, *Frères prêcheurs*, 282–5; Baumont, Burias and others, *Histoire d'Agen*, 68–71; Verger and others, *Agen*, 47. See also Y. Dossat, 'Une Figure d'inquisiteur, Bernard de Caux', *CF* vi (1971), 253–72 at p. 269, and 'L'Inquisiteur Bernard de Caux et l'Agenais', in his *Église et hérésie*, 75–9, esp. pp. 78–9.

[112] The inquisitorial processes in the region under discussion have been very thoroughly examined in the works used in the following summary. For sources see especially fonds Doat (as cited); *Documents de l'inquisition*, esp. nos vi–xxii, cxliv–clxvi, ccx–ccxxiii; *Layettes*, iii. 3877; *HGL* vi. 57–8; vii, *ordonnance* 419; viii. 1313–14; *Chronique de Guillaume Pelhisson (1229–1244)*, ed. and trans. J. Duvernoy, Paris 1994, esp. pp. 13–42. For analysis see Dossat, 'Une Figure', and 'L'Inquisiteur'; Lea, *Inquisition*, ii, esp. pp. 16–39; B. Hamilton, *The medieval inquisition*, London 1981, esp. pp. 61–5; Albe, *L'Hérésie en Quercy*; Duvernoy, *Catharisme*, ii. 267–73, 353–5; M. Roquebert, *Les Cathares de la chute de Montségur aux derniers bûchers, 1244–1329*, Paris 1998, 115–26, and *L'Épopée*, vi. 327–50, 357, 379–81, 391–2, 396–7; Passerat, 'Cathares', esp. pp. 152–5; Barber, *Cathars*, 144–64. Recent works examining how inquisitorial evidence should be assessed are Pegg, *Corruption of angels*; Arnold, *Inquisition and power*; and Given, *Inquisition*.

[113] Lea thinks that it may have been Raymond Gros who led the inquisitors to Vigouroux de la Bacone: *Inquisition*, ii. 21–3.

detailed or investigative, being hurriedly gathered during a period of grace in which the townspeople were allowed to come forward voluntarily. The inquisitors Bernard de Caux and Jean de Saint-Pierre were then active in the dioceses of Agen and Cahors from 1243 to 1245. The evidence they amassed is the most detailed and useful for studying the heretics of the region, for lengthy statements survive from trials at Agen, Bas-Quercy and Cahors. Unfortunately little of this information relates directly to the Agenais, or to the Cahorsin for that matter, for the heretics tried were almost all of Bas-Quercy and the northern Toulousain.

From the outset Raymond VII was not happy to accept the authority of the Dominicans in his lands. When Othon de Berètges, his *bailli* at Moissac and Montcuq, was tried in 1244 we learn from his testimony that he was instructed by the count to obstruct the inquisitors in the 1230s, disputing their judicial authority and forbidding anyone convicted from accepting their penance.[114] The pope was eager to keep the peace as well as to eradicate heresy. Thus in 1235 Pierre Seilan was removed from the Toulousain and confined to operations in Quercy and between 1238 and 1241 Pope Gregory IX suspended the inquisition at comital insistence. Bishop Arnaud IV de Galard of Agen supported Raymond's objections to Bernard de Caux, and the Languedocian inquisition as a whole was removed from the control of the mendicants by Innocent IV in 1248 and put under that of Bishop Guillaume II of Agen.[115]

This is not to say that the count was sympathetic to the heresy. A condition of his peace with the church in 1229 had been his co-operation in undermining the heresy and this intent was reaffirmed on 2 May 1233.[116] The count in fact showed every sign of wanting to continue this policy, but on his own terms, not those of the Dominicans. Thus Pons Grimoard's successor, Arnaud de Tantalon, seneschal for the Agenais under Raymond VI, was co-operative with the Catholic authorities on Raymond VII's behalf, enacting the confiscations at Castelmoron in 1237. Raymond himself agreed to launch the first attack on the castle stronghold of Montségur in the Pyrenees in 1241, and many soldiers from his lands, including the Agenais and Quercy, were recruited into the royal armies which besieged the fortress in 1243–4.[117] When suing for peace in 1242 he agreed to extirpate heresy in his own lands in the presence of Bishop Arnaud, and in 1243 initiated an inquisition under his own control in the dioceses of Agen and Cahors, staffed by clergy of his own choosing, to the satisfaction and with the support of Arnaud.[118] The not insignificant scale of this inquisition is indicated by later documents relating to it. It continued into the second half of

---

114 Doat xxii, fos 45v–46r.

115 *Spicilegium*, iv. 265; Dossat, 'Une Figure', 266–8, and 'L'Inquisiteur', 75. The exact reason for the pope's acquiescence in 1238 is not known but it seems most probable that he feared an alliance between Raymond VI and the Emperor Frederick II: Hamilton, *Inquisition*, 62.

116 *HGL* viii. 884. He had also co-operated with the Cistercians in the matter of revenue raised in the Agenais since 1231: ibid. 1961, item cxxvii.

117 *Spicilegium*, iii. 621.

118 Doat xxxi, fo. 40r–v; *HGL* vi. 737–8; viii. 1088–9; Samazeuilh, *Agenais*, 281–2; Guignard, *Agenais*, 119; Dossat, 'L'Inquisiteur', 75.

the decade, a letter of 1248 from Innocent IV to Agen's new bishop, Pierre of Reims, indicating that he wished the bishop to support the count's offensive against the still flourishing heresy in the town.[119] Although this comital-episcopal inquisition was probably far from routinely active, its most dramatic act showed that Raymond was as fervent as the inquisitors about destroying the heresy and that he could do it without their help: William of Puylaurens reports the burning of eighty relapsed *credentes* at a spot nearby Agen called *Béoulaygues* in 1249.[120]

The heretical diocese from 1229

We find from inquisitorial documents, both mendicant and comital, that the geographical scope of Catharism in the region under discussion had significantly changed by end of the 1240s. In the Agenais it survived along the Lot and apparently increased along the Garonne. The community at Gourdon, whose members left the town in 1229, perhaps to preach in central Quercy, was refounded by the 1240s. The heretics of Bas-Quercy increased in confidence after 1228. Finally, partly as a result of these other factors, absolute dualism expanded successfully into central Quercy for the first time.

If depositions made at Agen are uninformative about the heretics and believers of the region, those collected as a result of the capture of Montségur in 1244 are likewise uninformative about the existence or whereabouts of a Cathar hierarchy from the Agenais.[121] Tento and Vigouroux, we have heard, had removed themselves there in 1232, but we hear little more of them or even whether a hierarchy for the Agenais existed after the early 1230s. But from sources other than inquisitorial depositions it is possible to identify many heretics who lived in the Agenais in the years leading up to 1249 and beyond.[122] Under Raymond VII the properties of Elie Auque, Colombe Denovar, Guillaume Astorg, Guillaume Engas and Guillaume de Toulouse were confiscated, all at unknown locations in the Agenais.[123] Two of those burnt at Agen in 1249 may have been Vital d'Artigues and Guiraude de Lamegia, for they were certainly executed at some time by order of Raymond VII at Agen.[124] Another was possibly Elie d'Aigrefeuille, inhabitant of Agen in 1227, whose possessions were later granted to Sicard d'Alaman, which we know about because in 1253

---

[119] *HGL* viii. 1240–1. For discussion of this in the context of the strategy of Pope Innocent IV in dealing with tensions between the bishop of Agen and the inquisitors see Roquebert, *Les Cathares, 1244–1329*, 182–5, 169, 182–6, 196–7, 205–7.

[120] William of Puylarens, *Chronique*, 184–5; *HGL* viii. 1981; Hamilton, *Inquisition*, 65; Guillemain, 'Le Duché', 59.

[121] This is noted in Lea, *Inquisition*, ii. 40–1. Capul suggests that the famous *perfectus* Jean Cambiaire became *filius major* for the Agenais after Vigouroux according to the deposition of Raymond de Pereille ('Notes', 11) but I think this is a misreading of the source.

[122] See also Dossat, 'Catharisme', and 'L'Inquisiteur', esp. p. 78.

[123] BN, MS lat. 9019, fo. 35.

[124] *Layettes*, iv. 5600, and AD, Lot, F 121 9r (Vital); AN, JJ 24B, 66v (Guiraude), cited in Dossat, 'Catharisme', 161.

he compensated Elie's wife Marie de Lacassagne for the portion representing her dowry.[125] Heretics apparently still even lived at Agen after 1249. They included Arnaud Pairol, Guillaume Baudès and the brothers Elie and Gaucelm de Clèves.[126]

At Marmande Gaillarde Marty also had his possessions confiscated by Raymond VII.[127] There is evidence that heretics were again at Gontaud in the period, for in 1253 Guiraude, wife of Stephen Dealas of the town, recovered possessions which had been confiscated earlier from her heretical husband.[128] In 1289 Pierre Badouin of Gontaud regained possessions earlier confiscated by Bernard de Caux.[129] Bernard Gasc of Gontaud was apparently in contact with heretics of the Languedoc who had fled to Lombardy in fear of the inquisition.[130] Vital d'Artigues, burnt at Agen, was originally from the town.[131] Finally, in 1270 Marie d'Anduze – countess of Périgord and viscountess of Lomagne, through which she gained her interests in the Agenais – held property seized earlier from heretics of Gontaud and nearby Hautefeuille and Fauillet.[132]

We learn a little more of the activities of the Tonneins families in this period. In 1242 a Raymond-Guillaume de Tonneins – possibly of the Ferréol as these names were popular with them – was involved in the insurrection following Avignonet.[133] In the same year Guillaume 'de Ferréol', co-lord of Tonneins-Dessous and Grateloup, who had rights in other towns including Gontaud, fought with fifty men-at-arms at Taillebourg for Henry III and also witnessed various documents relating to the Anglo-Toulousain alliance of that period, including in 1239 a treaty between Gaston de Gontaud and Elie Rudel of Bergerac.[134] We know that he had probably tolerated the heresy for in 1270 he complained to the Alphonsin officials of loss of revenues resulting from the condemnation of some of his men for the heresy.[135] Another inhabitant of the region, Étienne Bouc, was condemned sometime before 1269.[136] The de Rovinha family appear to have become associated with viscounts of Lomagne by 1243, for in the same year an Arnaud 'de Roviniano' and his brother Gaston de Lomagne are listed as the men of the count of Toulouse.[137] In 1251 Hugues and

---

125 *Un Cartulaire et divers actes des Alaman*, ed. E. Cabié and E. Mazens, Toulouse 1882, 18, cited in Dossat, 'L'Inquisiteur', 77. See also his 'Catharisme', 163, 166.

126 AN, JJ 24b, 64r–v, cited in Dossat, 'Catharisme', 166–7; *Correspondance administrative d'Alphonse de Poitiers*, i. 455, 93.

127 AN, JJ 24B, 61v–62r, cited in Dossat, 'L'Inquisiteur', 77, and 'Catharisme', 162.

128 *Chartes Agen*, no. xlix; Dossat, 'L'Inquisiteur', 77.

129 *Rôles gascons*, ed. C. Bémont, Bordeaux, 1885–1906, ii. 355–6.

130 Doat xxvi. fo. 2v (Duvernoy, *Catharisme*, ii. 308). Flight is discussed by Given as one of his models of individual resistance to the inquisition.

131 Dossat, 'Catharisme', 162–3.

132 G. Tholin, 'Documents relatifs à l'Agenais', AHGi xxxv (1900), 12–14.

133 Doat xxiv, fo. 155v.

134 AD, Lot, F 105; Lagarde, *Notes historiques*, 38; Dossat, 'Catharisme', 163 n. 99.

135 *Enquêtes d'Alphonse de Poitiers*, 338.

136 *Correspondance d'Alphonse de Poitiers*, ii. 236.

137 HGL viii. 1264.

Bernard de Rovinha appear amongst the witnesses of the homage of Arnaud-Othon de Lomagne to Alphonse of Poitiers at Agen.[138]

The valley of the Lot, especially Castelmoron, was still the main Agenais foyer of heresy. From the same charter of 1269 by which Dossat identifies Vigouroux de la Bacone with Castelmoron we know of ten other people whose property, confiscated by Raymond VII because of their heresy, was bought by a Raimond Talon of that town in 1237. They are Elie Bertrand, Ponce de Serment, Vigouroux du Bosc del Comte, Gaillarde and Seignoret de Faget, Pierre Aym, Raimond Isarn, Bernarde Brunet, Audiarde del Polenc and Bernis de Mirepoix.[139] A Bertrand, father of Bertrand and Savari de Castelmoron, also had his goods confiscated.[140] A *credens* Hugues de Castelmoron held land not only in this town but at neighbouring Casseneuil and Sainte-Livrade.[141]

Whilst the heretical community at Casseneuil had clearly been decimated, we still find the Balenx family amongst the Agenais *credentes*. A Raimond-Bernard de Balenx, who had been amongst the lords of the Agenais taking oaths to King Louis in 1243 and who witnessed a letter of Raymond VII to Arnaud Othon, viscount of Lomagne in 1249, had his Casseneuil property confiscated because of his belief in the 1240s.[142] Another heretic of the town was Arnaud Bertin.[143]

A heretic burnt before 1257, called Pons Vigouroux, held property at Sainte-Livrade, near which lies the hamlet also bearing the name Vigouroux.[144] The heresy was still strong at Villeneuve-sur-Lot in the years leading up to the inquisition, encountered there by Adémar Einard as he told the inquisitors at Gourdon in 1241.[145] Gausbert de Clusel told the inquisitors at Moissac that he had taken heretics to Monflanquin, our only reference to heretics in this town between the Lot and Gourdon.[146]

Although I have suggested that Pujols perhaps did not have a heretical community by 1223 this changed later on, for in 1270 the *consuls* of neighbouring Villeneuve wanted to use stones from the homes of the condemned for new building works.[147] At Penne d'Agenais Raymond VII also undertook confiscations, but later returned some confiscated goods to the heirs of the

---

138 Ibid. viii. 1291.
139 AN, JJ 24b, 63r–v, cited in Dossat, 'Un Évêque', 624, 'L'Inquisiteur', 77–8, and 'Catharisme', 164.
140 *Correspondance d'Alphonse de Poitiers*, ii. 1511.
141 AN, JJ 24b, 68v, cited in Dossat, 'Catharisme', 164.
142 HGL viii. 1119, 1254; *Enquêtes d'Alphonse de Poitiers*, 245 and n. 7; Duvernoy, *Catharisme*, 302.
143 Dossat, 'Catharisme', 164.
144 In 1270 it yielded a revenue of 15 *livres* which Alphonse de Poitiers used to found a chapel: AD, Lot, F 111, 9r; Dossat, 'Catharisme', 164–5.
145 Doat xxi, fo. 205v.
146 Doat xxi, fos 293r–294r. This reference is undated but it is likely that it refers to this period of expansion.
147 *Enquêtes d'Alphonse de Poitiers*, 312; Dossat, 'Catharisme', 165.

condemned.[148] In documentation relating to the affair, we learn that members of the Nouaillac, Marty and Pelicier families were implicated in the heresy, the latter possibly members of the important family of the same name at Agen.[149]

Information for Bas-Quercy originates not only in the area but also from trials in Toulouse, Agen and Cahors, and it indicates the survival of the heresy well beyond 1229. Pons Grimoard, Raymond VII's seneschal for Quercy, first admitted his activity and belief to Guillaume Arnand on 29 March 1235. His case provides the earliest surviving inquisitorial document, a letter of penitence, dated the following year. After Castelsarrasin was retaken in 1228 he and Othon de Berètges the *bailli* for Moissac and Montcuq, played what must have been an important supporting role in the revival of the heresy and its extension into central and upper Quercy. Pons was said to be frequently in the company of important *perfecti*. Charged specifically with allowing the *perfectus* Guillaume de Caussade to escape from his custody at *Loseler* – also known then as Beaucaire, and as modern Lauzerte – he was sentenced to make four pilgrimages.[150] This penance had been completed by 1244 when Pons and Othon gave statements to the inquisitors. Here we see an example of what Given describes as the use of inquisitorial documentation as 'instruments . . . not only of knowledge but of coercion'. Pons's letter was not only a record of what had been admitted to and renounced, but proof that he understood fully the implications of his lapse back into heresy. He was now completely at the mercy of his accusers. The power this gave the friars enabled them not only to punish but to exert a great hold over him, perhaps to further manipulate him by creating some distance between him and the communal solidarity which led this powerful individual to protect other people. We should suspect such subsequent intrigue because whilst Pons, certainly guilty, was dismissed, Othon was convicted of having let Vigouroux de la Bacone escape from his custody in the 1220s.[151]

Another *credens* who continued to run risks on behalf of the heretics in this difficult period was Guillaume Faber, harbouring the *perfectus* Raymond Imbert of Moissac and receiving a one hundred *livres* fine for allowing him to escape.[152] The women of Castelsarrasin also continued in the heresy. Arnanda Grimoard, Pons's wife, was present in the town in 1244 when she was implicated by the testimony of Na Berètges.[153] Na Pros de Cavelsaut continued to defy the Catholic authorities as late as 1233–9. In addition to hosting various heretical meetings attended by both sexes, her house was still home to her heretic daughter Raimunda and used as a covert lodging for other *perfectae*, for whose protection and service she worked closely with other local *credentes*, most notably her servant Passiona and her friends Aurimunda de Serra and Petrona de Cahors,

---

148 Dossat, 'Catharisme', 165–6.
149 AN, JJ 1031 A, 11, cited in Dossat, 'L'Inquisiteur', 78.
150 The letter is copied in Doat xxii, fos 38v–40r; his evidence is to be found at fos 32–44. See also *HGL* viii. 1016; Roquebert, *L'Épopée*, iv. 254–7; Albe, *L'Hérésie en Quercy*, 10, 20.
151 Doat xxii, fos 32–45; Given, *Inquisition*, esp. pp. 39, 169.
152 Doat xxii, fo. 8r; Roquebert, *L'Épopée*, iv. 179.
153 Doat xxii, fos 42v–44r.

and also the latter's son and daughter.[154] One of the latest accounts of these women together is at the meeting with Vigouroux de la Bacone in 1228 or the early 1230s.[155] Aurimunda was hereticated herself on the point of death in about 1240, at which time she was still keeping the company of Petrona and Pros.[156]

One of the most important trials associated with the town was in 1243, part of investigation into the murders at Avignonet the previous year. Jean Vital told that shortly after the murders the heretic Stephen Mazeler arrived in Castel-sarrasin where Guillaume Audebert had initiated a celebration, along with Guillaume Faber de Pechermer and Pons de Montmirat. Guillaume Audebert sang Stephen *sirventes*, songs with satirical lyrics, in this case including a grisly description of the death of the friars.[157]

At Montauban we find less detailed evidence, but still gain a picture of a strong heretical presence, for in the week before Ascension 1241 254 people were convicted, eighty-five of them women.[158] Raimond d'Archa told of how as a boy his heretical mother used him as a messenger and errand runner for her and her associates.[159] Jeanne de Lolmie, possibly originally of Montcuq, was also condemned.[160] In 1244 Arnauda de Lamothe, having returned to her native town after years of evading the authorities, made her famous deposition. Also still in the locality were other de Lamothes; a Guillaume Bernard, who had adored heretics with his mother, and a 'B.' de Lamothe, both convicted as *credentes*.[161] The heresy continued in the town into the 1250s.[162]

Although the inquisition appears to have effectively undermined the heretical presence in the monastery of Belleperche, a heretical community remained in the abbey town of Moissac. In 1234–9 210 people were burned and in Ascension week 1241 the inquisition convicted ninety-nine people, including forty-three women.[163] However, some heretics of Moissac were amongst those who fled for Lombardy, including Raymond Imbert, who had narrowly escaped capture on the property of Guillaume Faber de Pechermer in 1239.[164] Of those who remained we learn that the Falquet de Saint-Paul family were still very influential in the heretical life of the town.[165] Gourdon was the first heretical

[154] Ibid. fos 7v, 17r–v, 17v, 20r, 24v, 28v.
[155] Ibid. fo. 19r–v.
[156] Ibid. fos 17v, 25r.
[157] Ibid. fos 11r–v. See P. Bec, *Nouvelle Anthologie de la lyrique occitane du moyen âge*, 2nd edn, Poitiers 1970, 122–3; Duvernoy, *Catharisme*, ii. 281.
[158] Doat xxi, fos 229–82. See also Albe, *L'Hérésie en Quercy*, 17. Many were also involved with the Waldensian heresy.
[159] Doat xxi, fo. 289r–v.
[160] AD, Lot, F 106; Albe, *L'Hérésie en Quercy*, 17 n. 2.
[161] Doat xxi, fo. 233r–v.
[162] AD, Haute-Garonne, MS lat. 202, 106 (H. Blaquière and Y. Dossat, 'Confessions inédites de catharisme quercinois', CF iii. 264–6).
[163] Doat xxi, fos 282v–306r; AD, Lot, F 106.
[164] Doat xxii, fo. 8r; xxv, fo. 298r; Duvernoy, *Catharisme*, 304; Roquebert, *L'Épopée*, iv. 179.
[165] Doat xxi, fos 291–5; xxii, fo. 18v; Albe, *L'Hérésie en Quercy*, 17; Roquebert, *L'Épopée*, iv. 237–8, 254, 257, 258–9, 276.

centre in the northern Languedoc to be targeted by the inquisition, during Advent week 1241 and again in the following year.[166] Bertrand de Gourdon, the crusader, admitted having received heretics, although his son Fortanier appears to have been the most active Cathar sympathiser.[167] Just as Bertrand had changed political sides, in 1241 Guillaume de Gourdon, as co-lord of Gourdon and lord of Salviac in Périgord, did homage to Raymond VII but transferred his loyalty to the French king the following year.[168] Fortanier de Gourdon remained a vassal of Raymond VII at least until 1244.[169]

That the extent of the heresy in the Gourdon area was great is evident from the passing of 219 sentences against all sections of the urban and rural population, including a priest.[170] We also find there the *credens* 'P.' de Casseneuil who had given leeks and scallions to the heretics and who had also been entrusted with a heretical book from which he had read.[171] The presence of heretical sympathisers originating in the Agenais in one of the newer heretical centres in Quercy was possibly far from coincidental, as we shall see.

The inquisition in central Quercy took place in Lent 1242.[172] By this time the process of heretical conversion, begun at Montcuq, had been very successful, for eighty-four people were convicted. The family of Saint-Genies – Guaillard, Bernard, Bertrand and his wife Na Finas – and Guillaume, lord of the manse at Laborda, were amongst its most important *credentes*.[173] We also find more *émigrés* from the Agenais, Hartemanda Balenx, discussed above, and also a Pierre de Penna. He associated extensively with Cathars and, along with the examples from Bas-Quercy noted above, gives us one of the fullest accounts of heretical theology to be found in the Quercy documentation.[174] If, as I believe, the conversion of Montcuq took place through its connections with Gourdon, the Agenais and Bas-Quercy, it seems not unreasonable to speculate that his name might refer to nearby Penne d'Agenais rather than Penne d'Albigeoise. As E. Albe has also noted, testimonies from Montcuq often refer to families from the region lying between the two towns.[175]

At Sauveterre, where both Cathars and Waldensians had been preaching openly, lying between Montcuq and Castelnau-Montratier, the inquisition convicted five people, amongst them its lord Guiraud, also of Gourdon.[176] Immediately after this seven people were convicted at Beaucaire. Most of them were part of a community established by the *perfectus* Guillaume de Caussade,

---

166 See also Albe, *L'Hérésie en Quercy*, 12–39.
167 Doat xxi, fos 186r–v, 195r–v, 197r, 199v–200r.
168 AD, Lot, F 98; HGL vi. 735–6, 1242; viii. 1119, 1980.
169 AD, Lot, F 123.
170 Doat xxi, fo. 199r–v.
171 Ibid. fos 194r, 202v–203r.
172 These inquisitorial documents are also contained in AD, Lot, F 106.
173 Doat xxi, fos 214r, 222r, 226r–v.
174 Ibid. fo. 217r–v.
175 Albe, *L'Hérésie en Quercy*, 14 and nn. 11–13.
176 Doat xxi, fos 227v–8r; Dossat, 'L'Inquisiteur', 75; Albe, *L'Hérésie en Quercy*, 15.

possibly Cathar deacon of Quercy, under the protection of the castellan, probably also called Guillaume. Guillaume de Caussade had left his family's estates
in eastern Quercy for the heretical life by 1233, in which year Pons Grimoard
saw him and his *socius* at the home of 'P.' de Belfort in Beaucaire, but he was
possibly newly arrived there then, for Pons says that 'P.' did not know them to be
heretics.[177]

The inquisitors then convicted twenty-two people at Montpezat-de-Quercy.
The town had been a focus of support for the southern party during the crusade
and, when captured and occupied by the crusaders, its *faidits*, notably Aramfré de
Montpezat of its seigneurial family, had continued to act against the the de
Montforts from other bases. Étienne de Montpezat made a donation to the
southern cause in 1224 of almost all his possessions. After the Peace of 1229
Bertrand de Montpezat and Geralda, wife of 'G. A.' de Montpezat, supported the
heretics, although we hear no more of Aramfré. Members of the Cabanolas
family were also important *credentes*, providing Cathars with money.[178] The
inquisitor Pierre Seilan then travelled to Montaut, where Arnaud de Rupe, who
had read a heretical book, and a landowner 'S.' Sobressen were amongst those
convicted.[179]

In spite of the important role played in the crusade by its castellan Ratier de
Castelnau, the seigneurial family of Castelnau-Montratier, sometimes called
Castelnau-Hélene, do not emerge as fervently Catholic, not apparently contin-
uing the pattern of family donations to Beaulieu-en-Rouergue of earlier
generations.[180] The town under their governorship yielded eleven convictions.
Amongst the most interesting activity there was that of heretical doctors.
Guillaume de la Mota was cured of an illness by one. Petronilla de Fabrica had
them cure her son, and then her husband, perhaps in payment, did work for them.
One of the most extensively implicated *credentes* was a woman, Bigordana.[181]

Though the evidence from central Quercy is not at all detailed it is possible to

---

177 Doat xxii, fos 37r, 41r, 219r–v, 228r–9v. For the possible identity of the castellan see fos
226v–7r. See also Duvernoy, *Catharisme*, ii. 264 n. 43, 284–5 and n. 35, where the case for
Guillaume de Caussade's status as deacon is made. See also Albe, *L'Hérésie en Quercy*, 15–16.
Caussade itself was a heretical centre into the 1250s (ibid. *pièce justificative*, no. i.40, and
Blaquière and Dossat, 'Confessions inédites', 259–98). G. Passerat places the community of
Beaucaire under the jurisdiction of the Cathar bishop of Albi ('Cathares', esp. pp. 149–50).
Certainly there is a strong case for an overlap of influence there but, as noted in chapter 3
above for Bas-Quercy, I do not think it is possible, or especially useful, to see the heretics of
Quercy under the rigid jurisdiction of any one Cathar diocese. Both Pons Grimoard, as seneschal, and the inquisitors certainly related to Beaucaire in a Quercinois context.
178 Doat xxi, fos 306r–308v; *HGL* vi. 583–4. For convictions in central Quercy see also Albe,
L'Hérésie en Quercy, 16.
179 Doat xxi, fos 309–10.
180 For which see AD, Lot, F 365.
181 Doat xxi, fos 310r–12v. There is another reference to a heretical doctor in Quercy, one
'W. R.', who had treated Pons Grimoard, who in turn seems to have attempted to protect him
from the inquisitors: Doat xxii, fo. 42r. On Cathar doctors see also W. Wakefield, 'Heretics as
physicians in the thirteenth century', *Speculum* lvii (1982), 328–31; Arnold, *Inquisition and
power*, 135–6; and Pegg, *Corruption of angels*, 106–7.

make some assertions about the way in which the heresy was transmitted there. It seems that it spread into the region after the Peace of Paris – although slightly earlier in the case of Montcuq – from Gourdon in the north, from the Agenais Lot, from Bas-Quercy and from eastern Quercy, within the sphere of the Cathar church of Albi. Just as it may well have been the case that conversions in and around Montcuq and at Sauveterre took place with the active support of the lords of Gourdon associated with those towns, it is possible that the spread of heresy to Castelnau-Montratier happened likewise, for its seigneurial family also made alliances with Gourdon.[182] We can safely assume that the political connections made by Othon de Berètges between the *bailliages* of Moissac and Montcuq either facilitated transmission to the latter town or at least encouraged its tolerance by the Montcuq authorities. The presence of a heretical member of the Lolmie family of Montcuq at Montauban, noted above, may also have been part of this process. Not least, we have seen evidence from both before and after 1229 to suggest that first Vigouroux de la Bacone and then Agenais heretical sympathisers were in central Quercy and connected with Gourdon.

Why the spread of the heresy into central Quercy did not continue into the Cahorsain itself or north-eastern Quercy can probably be explained in part by the more Catholic orientation of those regions. Two key figures were responsible for maintaining their orthodoxy. Bishop Guillaume de Cardaillac not only crusaded against centres of heresy but took initiatives to prevent Catharism ever entering Cahors, founding a Dominican convent there in 1226. He was also one of the initiators of an organisation based at Rocamadour, the remit of which was the detection of heretical subversion within monastic houses. The other architect of this movement was Viscount Raymond IV of Turenne, whose family numbered Rocamadour amongst the numerous abbeys over which it had an influence. If the viscount had reservations about the crusade, he clearly had none about the need to assert orthodoxy in north-eastern Quercy, of which his family were amongst the most important lords and into which he brought the influence of the Catholic Limousin.[183]

That such action was still necessary is illustrated by the continuation of patterns of infiltration of religious houses by heretics in lower, central and upper Quercy. Such attempts by Cathars were now being challenged by the monks and the perpetrators reported to the inquisition, as at Belleperche. None the less, when the inquisition visited Montpezat in 1241 Raymonda de Mazerac, prioress of the Augustinian monastery of Lativia near Castelnau-Montratier, was discov-

---

182 AD, Lot, F 365, 366.
183 Albe, *L'Hérésie en Quercy*, 1–6. Our Lady of Rocamadour was a dependency of Tulle and closely connected to Obazine in the Limousin with which the viscounts were associated: *Miracles of Our Lady of Rocamadour*, 63–4, 66. A later twelfth-century bishop of Cahors was of the Escorailles family of the northern Limousin, also closely associated with the major foundations in that county (ibid. 69–90). The context for the compilation of a collection of miracles at the abbey in the 1170s in itself attests to the relative vibrancy of the orthodox faith in this region, and Marcus Bull speculates convincingly yet cautiously (pp. 65–6) that its composition may have had some connection with the fight against heresy even in that early period.

ered to have been a heretic for four or five years.[184] Near to Gourdon the towns of Linars contained an ostensibly Catholic convent in which the heresy was firmly implanted and protected by its lord Ranulphe de Golesme and other members of the family, lords of Milhac, until they were discovered.[185]

Thus, although the Cathars in Quercy survived the crusade and even increased in number in its aftermath in some areas to the south and west of Cahors, the combined efforts of orthodox laymen such as the viscount of Turenne and Raymond VII and the bishop of Cahors and the inquisition were successful finally in exposing and extirpating the heresy in Quercy, for we hear of few further incidents after the mid-1240s.[186] There is evidence that in the 1260s the leading families of Castelsarassin were actively Catholic and making concessions to Grandselve.[187]

In contrast, Bishop Arnaud de Rovinha of Agen, full of crusading zeal and anger at the protectors of heretics in the Agenais, lacked the vision of his colleague at Cahors. Only towards the end of our period did the bishops of Agen work with the count of Toulouse and the Dominicans to establish coherent organisations for the detection and eradication of heresy, and also the elimination of the causes of the heresy through the promotion of a more dynamic religious life.

In about 1250 Rainier Sacconi estimated that the Cathar church of Agen had been all but destroyed.[188] But his propaganda does not describe very well what was actually occurring in the region. From 1252 Alphonse of Poitiers's officials, most notably Jacques Dubois, were still dealing with heretics, and new excommunications and confiscations were enacted into the 1270s, including at Agen itself and in the towns of the Lot.[189] They included the confiscation of income from the oven at Casseneuil from a heretic Hugues of Castelmoron, and its transference in around 1270 to count Archembaud of Périgord, new husband of Marie d'Anduze who received property at Gontaud at the same time.[190] Heretics appear to have remained also at Tonneins at least until 1264, when Arnaud de Tremoleto of the town had his goods confiscated.[191] There is possibly evidence of an important Cathar in the Agenais as late as c. 1310, for the register of the inquisitor Jacques Fournier notes a Raimond de Castlenau of the Agenais, otherwise known as Raimond de Toulouse, who, afraid of capture, sent his nephews to

---

184 Doat xxi, fo. 307a.
185 Doat xxi, fos 188r–v, 193v, 211v; Duvernoy, *Catharisme*, i. 208; ii. 258; Bordes, *Périgord*, 87–8.
186 A handful of heretics were also discovered by the inquisition in western Quercy in the 1270s: Albe, *L'Hérésie en Quercy*, 23.
187 *HGL* viii. 1869.
188 Rainerius Sacconi, 'Summa', 70; Lea, *Inquisition*, ii. 49.
189 For example *HGL* vii, *ordonnance* 420; *Correspondance d'Alphonse de Poitiers*, i. 493; ii. 1513; *Enquêtes d'Alphonse de Poitiers*, 245; Dossat, 'Catharisme', 166–7; Capul, 'Notes', 13.
190 *Correspondance d'Alphonse de Poitiers*, ii. 2118, and see p. 250 above.
191 *Enquêtes d'Alphonse de Poitiers*, 338 and n. 6; *Correspondance d'Alphonse de Poitiers*, i. 440; Dossat, 'Catharisme', 163; Capul, 'Notes', 7, 13.

Catalonia, entrusting to them 16,000 gold florins.[192] Although the heresy was surviving in a debased form in the Pyrenees by this date, the isolated nature of this account, not to mention the unbelievably large amount of money involved, make me reluctant to concede that there were still significant numbers of Cathars active in the Agenais. I am inclined to think that by about 1280 the inquisition had undermined the security of the heretical faith where the crusade had not, and that the more pastorally dynamic Catholicism of the friars served to fill the void left by the exiled and executed *perfecti* in the Agenais and Quercy as it did throughout most of the Languedoc.

Postscript: the Agenais from 1249 to 1279

Before making more general conclusions about the subject of dualism in Aquitaine, I should like to draw together some themes relating to the society of the Agenais and its place in the power struggles in the Midi. I have argued that Rainier Sacconi was perhaps over-confident in his assertion that the heretical diocese of Agen had been destroyed by *c.* 1250. None the less, what heresy survived was sparser and probably less coherently structured than in previous decades. Perhaps it was more the survival of a habit or an ingrained tendency than a dynamic Church. Alternatively, whereas adherence to the heresy and to the heretics was once second nature, the inquisition had made even the slightest acquaintance with them a serious offence, destroying a significant amount of the social basis of their support in the fickle Agenais.[193] Certainly there now existed a stronger and more active adherence to Catholicism there than had hitherto been the case. This is expressed particularly through the forceful work of local Dominicans from 1249 at Agen and by friars minor at Marmande, where the Couvent des Cordeliers was established in 1265.[194] By *c.* 1255 Agen was even deemed a suitable place for pilgrimage for repentant heretics.[195] At some point in the thirteenth century a very ancient church of Agen, which had apparently been destroyed by Vikings, was rebuilt as the chapel of Notre-Dame du Bourg.[196] It strikes me that the Catholic revival mid-century might offer a likely context for this. The Dominican convent at Agen was to be the burial place of the native-born inquisitor Bernard de Caux, at his own request, when he died on 26 November 1252. In 1281 his body was translated to allow for building work and

---

192 Register of Jacques Fournier (1318–25), MS Vatican reg. lat. 4030, ii. 59, 484, cited in Duvernoy, *Catharisme*, ii. 326, 351.
193 See discussion on this issue in Pegg, *Corruption of angels*, 125, 131.
194 Ricaud, *Marmande*, 8, 43.
195 Bishop Bartholemew of Cahors (1250–73) gave letters of remission to a heretical woman from Moissac, N. Affalx, who made such a pilgrimage as part of her sentence: Albe, *L'Hérésie en Quercy*, 21, and *pièce justificative*, no. iv.43. I have not observed it on penitential itineraries before this date.
196 Verger and others, *Agen*, 45.

found, according to Bernard Gui, to be almost intact, a miracle met with great enthusiasm by the people of Agen.[197]

But if the Agenais became more fervently Catholic from mid-century, it was less than willing to submit to French rule. In 1249, when Raymond VII died, Alphonsin officials summoned the *cour d'Agenais* but could not persuade its representatives, especially those of Agen itself, to swear allegiance to their new lord. The *cour* argued, amongst other things, that the Agenais belonged to Jeanne of Toulouse, as the granddaughter of Jeanne of England whose dowry the county had been, not to her husband Alphonse. They also pointed out that the region had come to expect a certain amount of self-government. This, says Bisson, was the Agenais expressing itself as a political community. However we should note that when the officials approached the people of Penne and Marmande separately they agreed to swear, and that Agen itself soon did likewise.[198] Alphonse and Jeanne died within a few days of each other in August 1271 and Toulouse passed to Philip III of France. On this occasion the Agenais did homage to its new lord along with Quercy and the Toulousain.[199]

We should also conclude the examination of the place of the Agenais within the broader conflicts taking place in south-western France.[200] The intervention of the French in 1229 sounded the death knell in the Languedoc for the house of Saint-Gilles and for English influence there. Count Raymond attempted to negate the terms of the Peace of Paris, and he was aided by Henry III, who engaged the French in Poitou in 1230 and again in 1241 when Alphonse was invested with Poitou by his brother King Louis IX of France. But Henry's humiliating defeat meant that Poitou too was irretrievably lost.

From 1249, when Raymond died and Toulouse and the Agenais passed to the French crown, authority in the Midi would be contested between the rulers of France, England, Aragon and Castile. But the failure to recover Poitou and the loss of Toulouse and the Agenais to the French was not the only cause for concern for the English in southern France. Gascony was granted in 1249 to Henry's son Edward as an appanage, but dissent there was mounting. It was aimed primarily at the English representative at Bordeaux, Simon de Montfort, third son of the crusader and governor of Gascony from 1248 to 1252. Amongst

---

[197] Bernard Gui, *De fundatione et prioribus conventuum provinciarum tolosanae et provinciae ordinis praedicatorum*, ed. P. A. Armagier, Rome 1961, 109–11.

[198] Philip, treasurer of Saint-Hilaire de Poitou, wrote to Alphonse, whose chaplain he was, of the problems he had encountered in the Agenais. The letter is published in E. Boutaric, *Saint-Louis et Alphonse de Poitiers*, Paris 1870, 69–77 (cited in Roquebert, *Les Cathares, 1244–1329*, 199–202). See also Guignard, *Histoire*, 119, 125–6; Samazeuilh, *Histoire*, 159, 284–7; and Bisson, 'General court', 19–20.

[199] Published as *Saisimentum comitatus tholosani*, ed. Y. Dossat, Paris 1966.

[200] Except where otherwise cited this summary of political events is taken from J. R. Maddicott, *Simon de Montfort*, Cambridge 1994, 107–24; Powicke, *Henry III*, i. 221–3, 231–4; J. P. Trabut-Cussac, *L'Administration anglaise en Gascogne sous Henry III et Edward I, de 1254 à 1307*, Paris–Geneva, pp. xxvi–xli, 18–21, 59–61. An interesting account of French administration from the mid-1200s, from the point of view of the operations of the inquisition, is provided in Given, *Inquisition*, 16–22.

the Gascons' objections to his rule were their claims, which proved partially justified, that he would be as ruthless and avaricious as his father had been in the Languedoc.[201] From the late 1240s Archbishop Gerard de Malemort, factions in Bordeaux and major Gascon lords, most important amongst them Gaston de Béarn, allied against England with the kings of Navarre, Aragon and Castile, the latter still claiming Gascony as Princess Eleanor's dowry.[202]

By late 1254 Gascony was at last secured and its most immediate and enduring enemies, Alfonso of Castile and Gaston de Béarn, had been reconciled with the English. However, the proximity of French power to the north and east of Aquitaine meant that the crown would always face the threat of rebellions and alliances between Gascon rebels and the Capetians or Castilians. This situation played an important part in encouraging the English towards a settlement with France over the issue of authority with regard both to Gascony and the Agenais. Truces between the two kings were agreed until 1259 and in that year, through the Treaty of Paris, Henry III renounced his claim to Normandy, Anjou and Poitou and offered homage for Gascony. It was also agreed that if Jeanne of Toulouse died childless the Agenais would revert to the English.[203] This latter provision was amongst the few English gains in 1259. The clause technically became active in 1271, although the English did not receive the Agenais until 1279, through the Treaty of Amiens. Thus the county of Agen, whose ownership had been disputed since the early Middle Ages, became English, for as long as the kings of England could hold Gascony.

---

201 Simon was the third son of de Montfort and Alice de Montmorency and was probably with them at various points during the Albigensian Crusade. For a time he was constable of France for the regent Queen Blanche but, after receiving back his family's lands in Leicestershire from the English crown, by 1231, he was dismissed. Thus the de Montfort family moved back into the English sphere. His role in Gascony and the baronial rebellions in England is well documented. See Maddicott, *Simon de Montfort*, esp. pp. 3–9 for his early life and p. 110 for the criticism of the Gascons.
202 Roger of Wendover, *Flores*, 355–86; Ellis, 'Gaston de Béarn', 398.
203 Roger of Wendover, *Flores*, 440; Matthew Paris, *Chronica majora*, iv. 225, 477–82, 506; v. 509–10. The allodial status of Gascony would be raised as an issue again by English lawyers during the Hundred Years War.

Conclusion

In part I of this book it was argued that accounts of religious heresy in early eleventh-century Aquitaine may well have been describing dualism. Reading them in the context of what we know about Aquitainian society and eastern-European dualism in the millennial period make this hypothesis as plausible as the case for a purely indigenous surfacing of religious dissent. A plausible sequence may be constructed thus.

Aquitaine in the period from the 990s to the 1030s was, to generalise, a society experiencing great social upheaval. Land in the countryside fell into private hands, essentially those of the castellans. Those dominating the new rural order did not consider themselves accountable to public authority. This was the case especially with regard to their treatment of the peasantry, increasingly enserfed from this period, and the monasteries, which they theoretically protected but in practice menaced. The abbeys and bishops reacted against this with appeals to the duke for protection, at the same time voicing the complaints of the poor about their plight. The poor grew disillusioned with the resultant movement, the Peace of God, and to an extent with saints' cults for, at the end of the day, their situation worsened in this period rather than was ameliorated. They were greatly in need of explanations for and relief from their oppression. In the same period some people at least were made aware, through contacts with churchmen and monks, of the apocalyptic significance of the period and events through which they were living.

Around the same time, in the Balkans, Bogomil heretics were meeting western pilgrims travelling east to Jerusalem, some of whom were affected by the tendencies I have described above. Bogomils had already successfully infiltrated Orthodox monasteries and declared their intention to spread their belief throughout Christendom. It seems plausible that they and/or their converts concealed themselves within the body of foreign traffic travelling east to west and were able to enter western monasteries and cathedral chapters and to spread their ideas amongst the Aquitainian populace. Thus they attempted to provide an explanation for evil and human suffering in this period when such issues were at the forefront of the minds of Aquitainians. Some sources insist these heretics were 'Manichees' and from another part of the world, and although the former claim, being clearly anachronistic, appears to discredit them it is difficult to envisage another way in which they could have usefully labelled what they encountered. It is their impulse to categorise with which we really take issue, but this does not mean that there were not significant similarities between some of what they saw and the other features of the category in which they wished to place it.

I have argued that this case can be made using the Aquitainian and Balkan evidence alone. However, when what I believe to be the equally compelling evidence of dualism in other western sources is taken into account, we seem to have a picture of organised Bogomil missions to the west more widely over a period of several decades.

Dualist heresy in the west seems to have died out by the second half of the eleventh century. This was perhaps as a result of the passing of the millennial era, but more significantly of the weakened contact between east and west and the growth of clerical and monastic reform. The combination of reformed monasticism and an actively orthodox secular elite in Aquitaine also goes some way to providing an explanation of why dualism could not gain a foothold in most of the duchy in the twelfth century: the authorities proved able to channel and contain religious dissent.

Dualism possibly re-emerged in the west around the time of the earliest crusades, but certainly by the 1140s, as Catharism. The evidence suggests that dualists may have been present in the Agenais, more Languedocian in orientation than most of Aquitaine, even in the 1150s. Certainly by the 1170s they were present in such numbers as to warrant the establishment of a Cathar diocese there. Although we lack the wealth of sources available for Catharism in other parts of the Languedoc, we can tell that the Lot valley was the major foyer of heresy in the Agenais, whilst the Garonne towns and the Gascon Agenais remained essentially orthodox.

The region did not respond uniformly to the heresy because it was not politically or culturally homogenous. Indeed, it seems that the creation of the *cour d'Agenais* was an attempt by the crusaders to encourage stability in a region where it was lacking, rather than being a Plantagenet or Toulousain response to an inherent sense of regional identity. In one of the most extreme examples of discord in the region, we find that two members of the same family, Hughues de Rovinha, lord of Casseneuil, and Bishop Arnaud of Agen, his brother, were amongst the leading protagonists in the religious and military conflict, on different sides.

It was probably Casseneuil that was the seat of the first Cathar bishopric in the Agenais, and chronicle evidence attests to its importance. In 1214 it fell to the crusaders, and from that time we find most heretical activity at Castelmoron-sur-Lot, as revealed by secular documentation. Certainly we find most references to Vigouroux de la Bacone, Cathar bishop of the Agenais in the 1220s, at Castelmoron. Vigouroux was involved in a schism between absolute and moderate dualists which originated in the Balkans. We have no evidence of a Cathar hierarchy for the Agenais after the early 1230s, and if it existed it was probably in hiding at Montségur. However, the inquisitors found heretics in the region into the 1240s, Raymond VII discovered and executed heretics in the Agenais until his death in 1249, and Capetian administrative records continue to refer to heretics identified in the Agenais even into the 1270s. These heretical communities were still concentrated along the Lot but we learn that by the late 1240s there were also heretics in towns on the Garonne.

Although the Agenais towns attacked in 1209, in a crusade which I suspect was largely initiated by Bishop Arnaud of Agen, were home to many heretics, the geographical spread of the heresy was not the major factor determining the operations of the Albigensian Crusade in this region. Military considerations are more in evidence, as the French sought to eliminate resistance to their control of the Garonne and to enforce the lasting allegiance of the fickle Agenais towns and lords. For much of the crusade, such authorities as submitted to the French were left largely in peace. Ironically, therefore, it was when castellans like Hughues de Rovinha chose to do homage to the crusade's leaders, which he did in 1212, thus keeping their castles and towns, that they were of most use to the heretics. These needed secure places in which to ride out the war, which they found at Casseneuil in 1212, and new centres in which to establish heretical enclaves when the crusader presence lessened, which they did at Castelmoron and in Quercy from the 1220s. It was in such places that the inquisitors discovered them.

However, a rising number of heretics were identified along the Agenais Garonne, after the inquisition had left the region, most notably those executed in 1249 but also into the 1270s. This is harder to account for as the river towns, always relatively orthodox, could not have been considered a safe haven for heretics under Raymond VII, the inquisitor Bernard de Caux, or bishops Arnaud IV and Guillaume II. Perhaps the relapsed *credentes* burned at Agen by Raymond VII in 1249 had first been identified by his extensive inquest of 1243 or by that of the Dominicans, and had since chosen to defy the orthodox religious authority. The absence of detailed inquisitorial records will always leave such *lacunae* in our understanding of the transmission of heresy in the Agenais.

The heretics of the Agenais were also very closely involved with those of Bas-Quercy. It seems that from there with the help of Vigouroux de la Bacone and Raymond VII's heretical officials Pons Grimoard and Othon de Berètges, and from the heretical towns of the Agenais Lot with the help of the Cathar converts of Gourdon, new centres of heresy were established in central and Haut-Quercy in the later years of the crusade.

We have seen also that the Albigensian Crusade was not only a war between France and the Languedoc. The rulers of Gascony and Aquitaine had had a tense relationship with the counts of Toulouse since the early Middle Ages and rights to Toulouse and the Agenais had long been contested between them. The Plantagenet dynasty managed to resolve this conflict by drawing the Toulousains into relationships of dependency, most effectively since 1196. The Albigensian Crusade obstructed King John as he attempted to increase this influence in the Languedoc. Crusade leaders were unashamed about attacking the Aquitainian frontier from Périgord to the Pyrenees, exploiting the fact that the papacy was less than well-informed by its legates about the geographical spread of the heresy. John aided and supported Toulouse and used his position as over-lord of the Agenais to dislodge the crusader presence as far west as Marmande in 1214. He considered greater intervention in the conflict on behalf of his Occitan kinsmen and vassals, but was restrained by his need to contain the more immediate French threat to Poitou and by his vulnerable position with regard to Rome.

Other Aquitainians also took sides in the conflict, for the duchy was no more united in response to the crusade than was the Agenais. Some acted in defence of Occitan independence, some in defence of that same orthodoxy which shaped the Aquitainian resistance to heresy, and others with a view to establishing themselves territorially in a newly Catholic Languedoc. Entirely absent in the motivation of Aquitainians was the protection of heretics. And by the late 1240s, and certainly by 1279 when the Agenais was returned to the English, we find the Agenais nobles and townspeople to be as actively Catholic as those of the Plantagenet authorities under whose rule they again found themselves.

APPENDIX 1

Genealogies

1. The dukes of Aquitaine (simplified genealogy)

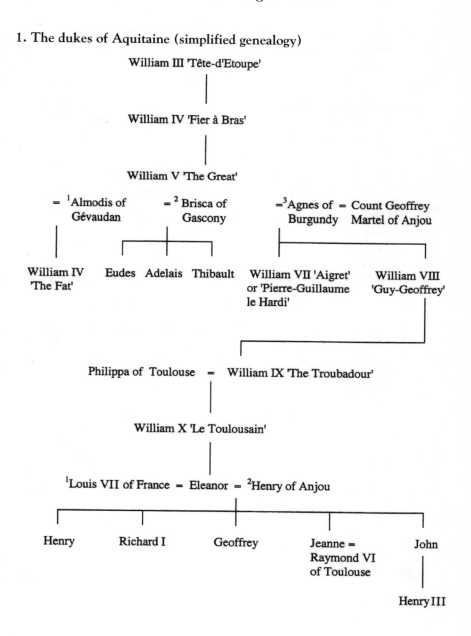

2. The Gascon ducal family (simplified genealogy stressing secular titles)

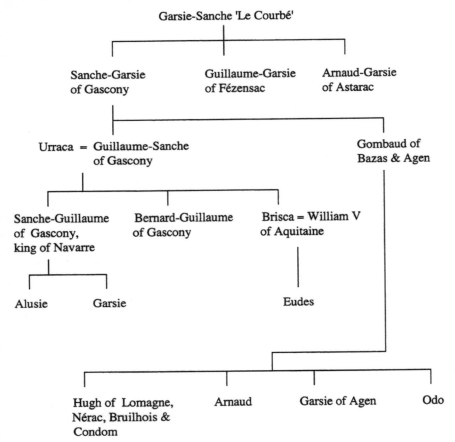

3. The counts of Toulouse/Agen and Toulouse (simplified genealogies)

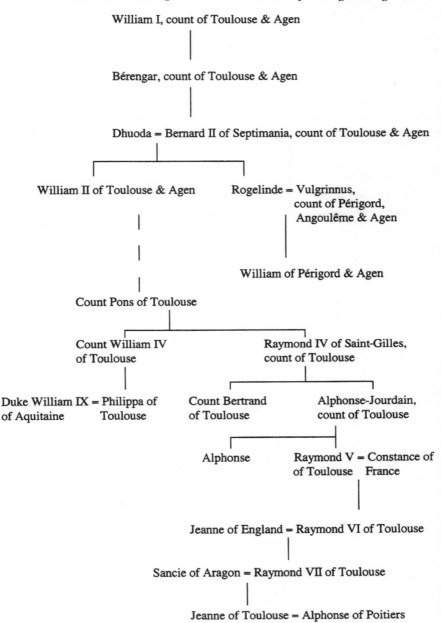

William I, count of Toulouse & Agen

Bérengar, count of Toulouse & Agen

Dhuoda = Bernard II of Septimania, count of Toulouse & Agen

William II of Toulouse & Agen

Rogelinde = Vulgrinnus,
count of Périgord,
Angoulême & Agen

William of Périgord & Agen

Count Pons of Toulouse

Count William IV
of Toulouse

Raymond IV of Saint-Gilles,
count of Toulouse

Duke William IX = Philippa of
of Aquitaine   Toulouse

Count Bertrand
of Toulouse

Alphonse-Jourdain,
count of Toulouse

Alphonse

Raymond V = Constance of
of Toulouse   France

Jeanne of England = Raymond VI of Toulouse

Sancie of Aragon = Raymond VII of Toulouse

Jeanne of Toulouse = Alphonse of Poitiers

APPENDIX 2

Maps

1. Aquitaine and the Languedoc within France, c. 1154

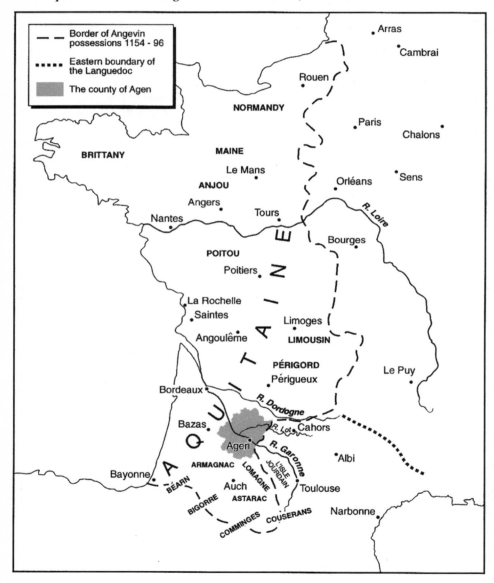

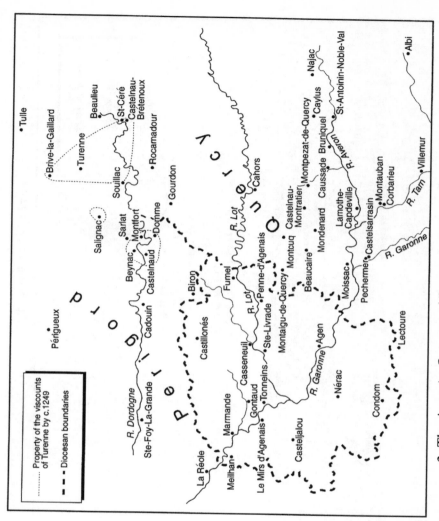

2. The Agenais, Quercy and Périgord, eleventh–thirteenth centuries

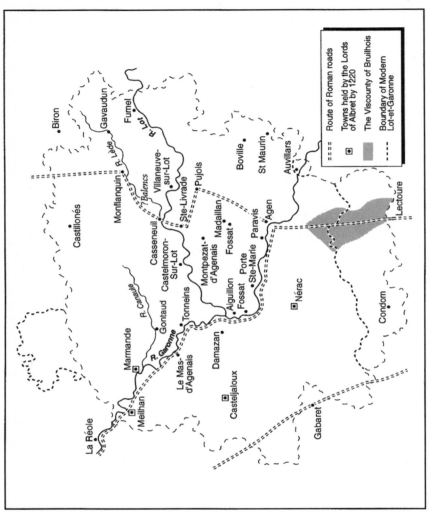

3. The Agenais by c. 1249

Bibliography

Unpublished primary sources

Agen, Archives Départementales du Lot-et-Garonne
Série AA Secular acts etc. relating to the commune of Agen, 1197–1789: MS AA4
Série E Supplt. Secular and clerical acts etc. relating to arrondissements of Agen,
  Nérac, Marmande and Villeneuve: MSS 195, 327, 665, 690–1, 1077–8, 1178,
  1859, 1917, 2745, 2906, 3043, 3416, 3481, 3663, 3794
Série G Parishes and regular clergy: MS 8

Berlin, Staatsbibliothek
MS Lat. Phillipps 1664, 1r–170v

Bordeaux, Archives Départementales de la Gironde
Série E Supplt. Secular and clerical acts etc. relating to arrondissements of La Réole,
  Monségur and Libourne: MSS 2770–4, 2906–7, 3247, 3968–9, 4771
Série G Relating to archdiocese of Bordeaux: MSS 334–6

Bordeaux, Bibliothèque Municipale
MS 745, fos 16r–v Cartulaire de Bigorre: eleventh-century homage of viscount
  Centulle of Béarn and count of Bigorre to King Alfonso of Aragon
MSS 769–70 Grand cartulaire de la Sauve-Majeure

Cahors, Archives Communales
Archives municipales de Cahors MSS chartes nos 9, 13, 29, 31–3, 36–42

Cahors, Archives Départementales du Lot
Série F Nineteenth-century copies of documents relating to families, abbeys, secular
  clergy and secular administration and inquisition: cahiers nos 97–106, 111–12,
  119, 121, 125–6, 129, 146, 163, 171, 175–7, 189, 191, 198–200, 204, 218–19,
  260–4, 268, 308, 318, 341, 346, 349–53, 365–6, 367–70, 377–8, 388, 401,
  423–30, 450, 455–6, 469, 499, 501–2, 513

Paris, Bibliothèque Nationale de France
MSS lat. fonds Doat. esp. xxi–xxv Inquests into heresy in the Languedoc
MS lat. 1745, fo. 31r Letter of Héribert
MS lat. 2469 Sermons of Adémar of Chabannes
MS lat. 5652 Charter naming members of the Gascon ducal family
MS lat. 5926, fos 1–141 Gamma version of Adémar of Chabannes's chronicle
MS lat. 9019, fos 35r–v Act of Raymond VII of Toulouse against heretics
MSS lat. 12763–8, esp. fos 223v–224v Charter of Hugh of Lusignan c. 1073–8/9
MS lat. 18363 Cartulary of the abbey of Solignac
MS nouv. acq. lat. 1560 Cartulary of the abbey of Obazine

271

Published primary sources

Acta sanctorum, ed. J. Bolland and others, Brussels–Antwerp–Paris 1965 (repr. of 1643– edn)

Acta synodi atrebatensis in manicheos, PL cxlii

'Acte de reddition à Simon de Montfort de deux seigneurs de l'Agenais', ed. M. R. Mazières, *Mémoires de la Société des arts et sciences de Carcassonne* iv/6 (1970), 99–100

Actus pontificum cenomannis in urbie degentium, ed. G. Busson and A. Ledru, Le Mans 1901

Adémar of Chabannes, *Chronicon*, ed. J. Chavanon, Paris 1897

——— Sermones, *PL* cxli.115–24

Ademari Cabannensis Chronicon, ed. P. Bourgain, R. Landes and G. Pons, Turnhout 1999

Adso of Montier-en-Der, 'Libellus de Antichristo', in *The play of AntiChrist*, ed. and trans. J. Wright, Toronto 1967, 100–10

Aimon, *Vita S. Abbonis abbatis floriancensis*, PL cxxxix.375–414

Albert of Aix, *Historia hierosolymitana*, RHC Occ., iv

Andrew of Fleury, *Vita Gauzlini abbatis floriencis monasterii*, ed. R.-H. Bautier and G. Labory, Paris 1969

Anna Comnena, *Alexiad*, trans. E. R. A. Sewter, Harmondsworth 1969

Annales engolismenses, MGH, SS iv

Annales lemovicensis, MGH, SS ii

Annales monastici, ed. H. R. Luard (RS, 1864–9)

Annales ordinis Sancti Benedicti, ed. J. Mabillon, Paris 1703–39

Annales prioratus de Dunstaplia, in *Annales monastici*, ii. 39

Annales rodenses, MGH, SS xvi

Anselm of Alessandria, 'Tractatus de hereticis', in Dondaine, *La Hiérarchie cathare*, AFP xx. 308–24

Anselm of Liège, *Gesta pontificum leodiensium*, MGH, SS vii

Archives municipales d'Agen: chartes première série (1189–1328), ed. A. Magen and G. Tholin, Villeneuve-sur-Lot 1876

Aubri de Trois-Fontaines, *Chronicon*, ed. P. Scheffer-Boichorst, MGH, SS xxiii

Augustine, *De actis cum Felice manichaeo*, PL xlii.519–52

——— *De civitate dei*, CCL xl

——— *Confessionum*, PL xxxii

——— *The confessions*, trans. R. S. Pine-Coffin, Harmondsworth 1961

——— *Contra Adimantum manichaei disciplum*, PL xlii.129–72

——— *Contra epistolam manichaei*, PL xlii.173–206

——— *Contra Faustum manichaeum*, PL xlii.207–518

——— *Contra Secundinum manichaeum*, PL xlii.577–638

——— *De duabus animabus contra manichaeos: acta contra Fortunatum manichaeum*, PL xlii.93–112

——— *De Genesi ad litteram imperfectus liber*, PL xxxiv.219–484

——— *De Genesi contra manichaeos*, PL xxxiii.171–219

——— *De haeresibus*, CCL xlvi. 290–345

——— *De libero arbitrio*, PL xxxii.1221–310

——— *De moribus ecclesiae catholicae et de moribus manichaeorum*, PL xxxii.1310–76

——— *De natura boni contra manichaeos*, PL xlii.551–72

———— *De utilitate credendi*, PL xlii.63–92
———— *De vera religione*, PL xxxiv.122–69
Bec, P., *Nouvelle Anthologie de la lyrique occitane du moyen âge*, 2nd edn, Poitiers 1970
Benedict of Peterborough, *Gesta Regis Henrici Secundi*, ed. W. Stubbs (RS, 1867)
Bernard Gui, *Practica inquisitionis heretice pravitatis*, ed. C. Douais, Paris 1886
———— *De fundatione et prioribus conventuum provinciarum tolosanae et provinciae ordinis praedicatorum*, ed. P. A. Armagier, Rome 1961
Biographies des troubadours, ed. J. Boutière and A. H. Schutz, Toulouse 1950
Book of Saint Foy, ed. and trans. P. Sheingorn, Philadelphia 1995
Cartulaire de l'abbaye de Beaulieu en Limousin, ed. M. Deloche, Paris 1859
Cartulaire de l'abbaye de Cadouin, ed. J.-M. Maubourgnet, Cahors 1926
Cartulaire de l'abbaye cardinale de la Trinité de Vendôme, ed. C. Métais, Vannes 1893–1904
Cartulaire de l'abbaye de Cellefrouin, ed. E. Brayer, BPH, 1940–1,
Cartulaire de l'abbaye de Condom, in *Spicilegium*, ii
Cartulaire de l'abbaye de Conques en Rouergue, ed. G. Desjardins, Paris 1879
Cartulaire de l'abbaye royale de Notre-Dame de Saintes de l'ordre de Saint Benoît, ed. Th. Grasilier, Niort 1871
Cartulaire de l'abbaye de Sainte-Croix de Bordeaux, ed. P. Ducaunnès-Duval, *AHGi*, xxvii (1892)
Cartulaire de l'abbaye de Saint-Cybard d'Angoulême, ed. P. Lefranq, Angoulême 1930
Cartulaire de l'abbaye Saint-Jean de Sorde, ed. P. Raymond, Pau 1873
Cartulaire de l'abbaye d'Uzerche (de Xe au XIVe siècles), ed. J.-B. Champéval, Tulle 1901
Cartulaire de l'abbaye de Vigeois en Limousin (954–1167), ed. M. de Montégut, Limoges 1907
Cartulaire de l'église collégiale de Saint-Seurin de Bordeaux, ed. A. Brutails, Bordeaux 1897
Cartulaire du prieuré de Saint-Pierre de La Réole, ed. C. Grellet-Balguerie, *AHGi* v (1864)
Cartulaires du Bas-Poitou, ed. P. Marchegay, Les Roches-Baritaud 1877
Cartulaires du chapitre de l'église métropolitaine Sainte-Marie d'Auch (Cartulaires noir et blanc), ed. C. La Cave La Plagne-Barris, *AHGi* ii/3, ii/4 (1899) (cited as i and ii)
Catalogue des actes de Simon et Amaury de Montfort, ed. A. Molinier, Paris 1874
'Charte de Pierre, évêque de Limoges, administrateur de l'évêché de Périgueux de l'an 1101', ed. G. Babinet de Rencogne, *BSHAP* lv (1928), 156–60
'Chartes de l'abbaye de Nouaillé de 678 à 1200', ed. P. Monsabert, *AHP* xlix (1936)
Chartes et documents pour servir à l'histoire de l'abbaye de Charroux, ed. P. de Monsabert, *AHP* xxxix (1910)
Chartes et documents pour servir à l'histoire de l'abbaye de Saint-Maixent, ed. A. Richard, *AHP* xvi, xviii (1886)
Chartes de Fontevrauld concernant l'Aunis et La Rochelle, ed. P. Marchegay, Paris 1858
Chartier du monastère de Sarlat, ed. G. Marnier, *BSHAP* xi (1884)
Christian dualist heresies in the Byzantine world, c. 650–1405, ed., trans. and annotations B. Hamilton and J. Hamilton, Manchester–New York 1998
Chronicles of the reigns of Stephen, Henry II and Richard I, ed. R. Howlett (RS, 1884–9)
Chronicon aquitanicum, MGH, SS ii
Chronicon turonense, in *RHF* xviii

Chronique dite Saintongeaise, ed. A. de Mandach, Tübingen 1970

Chronique de Saint-Maixent, 751–1140, ed. and trans. J. Verdon, Paris 1979

Chroniques ecclésiastiques du diocèse d'Auch, ed. L. C. de Brugèles, Toulouse 1746

Chroniques des églises d'Anjou, ed. P. Marchegay and E. Mabille, Paris 1899

Chroniques de Saint-Martial de Limoges, ed. H. Duplès-Agier, Paris 1874

Concilia, ed. J. Mansi, Graz, 1960–1 (repr. of *Sacrorum conciliorum nova et amplissima collectio*, Venice 1759–98)

'Conventum inter Guillemum aquitanorum comes et Hugonem Chiliarchum', ed. J. Martindale, *EHR* lxxxiv (1969), 528–48

Conventum (vers 1030): un précurseur aquitain des premières épopées, ed., trans. and intro. G. Beech, Y. Chauvin and G. Pons, Geneva 1995

Correspondance administrative d'Alphonse de Poitiers, ed. A. Molinier, Paris 1894–1900

Cosmas the Priest, *Traité contre les Bogomiles*, ed. and trans. H. C. Peuch and A. Vaillant, Paris 1945

Councils and synods, I: A.D. 871–1204, ed. D. Whitelock, M. Brett and C. N. L. Brooke, Oxford 1981

Coutume d'Agen, ed. H. Tropamer, Bordeaux 1911

'Coutumes d'Agenais', ed. P. Ourliac, *AM* lxxiv (1962), 241–53

Coutumes de l'Agenais, I: Les Coutumes du groupe Marmande: Marmande, Caumont, Gontaud, Tonneins-Dessous, La Sauvetat-du-Dropt, ed. P. Ourliac and M. Gilles, Montpellier 1976

'Coutumes de La Réole', ed. P. Imbart de la Tour, *Annales de la Faculté des lettres de Bordeaux* (1893), 221–63; (1894), 99–119

Coutumes, privilèges et franchises de la ville d'Agen, ed. A. Moullie, Agen 1850

De antiquis legibus liber . . . cronica maiorum et vicecomitum londoniarum, 1188–1274, ed. T. Stapleton, London 1846

Diplomatic documents preserved in the Public Record Office, 1101–1272, ed. P. Chaplais, London 1964

Documents de l'histore du Languedoc, ed. P. Wolff, Toulouse 1969

Documents illustrative of English history in the thirteenth and fourteenth centuries, ed. H. Cole, London 1884

Documents pour l'histoire de l'église de Saint-Hilaire de Poitiers (768–1300), ed. L. Rédet, *Memoires de la Société des antiquaires de l'ouest* xiv (1847); xv (1852)

Documents pour servir à l'histoire de l'abbaye de Saint-Croix de Poitiers, ed. P. de Monsabert, *Revue Mabillon* ix, x (1913–14)

Documents pour servir à l'histoire de l'inquisition dans le Languedoc, 2nd edn, ed. C. Douais, Paris 1977

'Documents relatifs à l'histoire de la maison de Turenne', ed. A. Vaissiere, *Bulletin de la Société historique et archéologique de la Corrèze* vii (1885), 310–402

Dhuoda, *Manuel pour mon fils*, ed. and trans. P. Riché, 2nd edn, Paris 1991

Enquêtes administratives d'Alphonse de Poitiers, arrêts de son parlement tenu à Toulouse et textes annexes, 1249–71, ed. P. F. Fournier and P. Guébin, Paris 1959

Euthymius Zigabenus, *Panoplia dogmatica*, in *Patrologiae series Graeco-Latina*, cxxviii–cxxxi

Ex anonimi chronici . . . ab initio mundi ad annum MCLX, in *RHF* xii. 118–21

Foedera, conventiones, litterae . . . publica, ed. T. Rymer and others, London 1704–34

Fulbert of Chartres, *The letters and poems*, ed. F. Behrends, Oxford 1976

Fulcher of Chartres, *A history of the expedition to Jerusalem, 1095–1127*, ed. and trans. H. S. Fink and F. R. Ryan, Knoxville, Tenn. 1969

Gallia christiana in provincias ecclesiasticas distributa, ed. D. Sainte-Marthe and others, Paris 1744–1877

The Gascon register, ed. G. P. Cuttino, London 1975–6

Geoffrey of Vigeois, *Chronica*, in *Nova bibliothecae manuscriptorum . . . collectio*, ed. P. Labbé, Paris 1657, ii. 279–342

Gerard of Cambrai, 'Acta synodi atrebatensis', *PL* cxlii.1269–312

Gervais of Canterbury, *Opera historica*, ed. W. Stubbs (RS, 1879–80)

Gesta episcoporum Cameracensium, ed. L. C. Bethmann, MGH, SS vii. 393–510

Gesta francorum et aliorum hierosolimitanorum, ed. R. Hill, London 1962

Gesta treverorum: additamentum et continuatio prima xx, MGH, SS viii

The golden legend of Jacobus de Voragine, trans. W. G. Ryan, Princeton, NJ 1993

Gratian, *The treatise on law (Decretum DD. 1–20)*, trans. A. Thompson and J. Gordley, Washington, DC 1993

Guibert of Nogent, *Gesta dei per francos*, in *RHC Occ.*, iv
———— *Histoire de sa vie (1053–1124)*, ed. G. Bourgin, Paris 1907

Le Guide du pèlerin de Saint-Jacques de Compostelle, ed. and trans. J. Vielliard, 3rd edn, Mâcon 1963

Heresies of the high Middle Ages, ed., trans. and annot. W. L. Wakefield and A. P. Evans, New York 1991

Herrman of Reichenau in MGH, SS v. 130.

Histoire de la guerre des albigeois, in *RHF* xix; *HGL* viii

Histoire générale de Languedoc, ed. C. de Vic and J. Vaissète, rev. A. Molinier, Toulouse 1872–1904

Histoires des conciles, trans. C. J. Héfele and H. Leclerc, Paris 1907–73

Historia pontificum et comitum engolismensis, ed. J. Boussard, Paris 1957

Inventaire des archives municipales de Cahors, ed. E. Albe, i/1, Cahors 1998

Jerome, *De antichristo in Danielem*, CCL xlviii

Julius Caesar, *The gallic wars*, ed. and trans. T. E. Page, Cambridge, Mass. 1952

Landulphi senioris mediolanensis historiae libri quatuor ii.27, in *Rerum italicarum scriptores*, ed. L. A. Muratori, Bologna 1900, iv/2, 67–9

Layettes du trésor des chartes, ed. A. Teulet and others, Paris 1863–1909

Letters of Pope Innocent III (1198–1216) concerning England and Wales, ed. C. R. Cheney and M. G. Cheney, Oxford 1967

Liber apologeticus, PL cxxxix

Liber miraculorum Sancti Fidis, ed. L Robertini, Spoleto 1994

Le Livre d'Agenais, ed. G. P. Cuttino, Toulouse 1956

Livre des coutumes de Bordeaux, ed. K. Barckhausen, Bordeaux 1890

Matthew Paris, *Chronica majora*, ed. H. R. Luard (RS, 1872–83)
———— *Historia anglorum*, ed. F. H. Madden (RS, 1866–9)

Les Miracles de Nôtre-Dame de Roc-Amadour au XIIe siècle, ed. and trans. E. Albe (with new introduction and notes by J. Rocacher), 2nd edn, Toulouse 1997

The miracles of Our Lady of Rocamadour, ed., trans and intro. M. Bull, Woodbridge 1999

Monumenta conventus tolosani ordinis fratrum praedicatorum, ed. J. J. Percin, Toulouse 1693

Nova bibliothecae manuscriptorum . . . collectio, ed. P. Labbé, Paris 1657

Odo of Deuil, *De profectione Ludovici VII in orientem*, ed. V. G. Berry, New York 1948

Orderic Vitalis, *Ecclesiastical history*, ed. and trans. M. Chibnall, Oxford 1969–80

Patrologiae cursus completus, series Graeco-Latina, ed. J.-P. Migne, Paris 1857–66

Patrologiae cursus completus, series Latina, ed. J. P. Migne and continuators, Paris 1852–1904; 4 vols, index and 5 vols supplementum 1958–74

Paul of Chartres, *Gesta synodi aurelianensis*, in *RHF* x. 536–9

Peter of Sicily, *Historia manichaeorum qui et pauliciani dicuntur, Travaux et mémoires* v (1970)

Peter des Vaux-de-Cernay, *Hystoria albigensis*, ed. P. Guebin and E. Lyon, Paris 1926–30

———— *Histoire albigeoise*, ed. and French trans. P. Guebin and H. Maisonneuve, Paris 1951

———— *The history of the Albigensian Crusade*, ed. and English trans. W. A. Sibly and M. D. Sibly, Oxford 1998

Peter the Venerable, *Tractatus contra petrobrusianos*, ed. J. V. Fearns, *Corpus Christianorum, Continuatio Mediaevalis*, x, Turnhout 1968

Poéme au Roi Robert, ed. C. Carozzi, Paris 1979

Rainerius Sacconi, 'Summa de catharis et pauberibus de Lugduno', in 'Un Traité néo-manichéen du XIIIe siècle: *Le liber du duobus principiis*, suivi d'un fragment de rituel cathare', ed. A. Dondaine, Rome 1939, 64–78

Ralph Ardens, *Speculum universale*, ed. Th.-J. Gründel, Munich 1961

Ralph of Coggeshall, *Chronicon anglicanum*, ed. J. Stephenson (RS, 1875)

———— *Chronicon anglicanum*, MGH, SS xxvii (1885)

Raymond d'Aguilers, *Historia francorum qui ceperunt Iherusalem*, trans. J. H. Hill and L. L. Hill, Philadelphia 1968

Recueil des actes d'Henri II, roi d'Angleterre, concernant les provinces françaises et les affaires de France, ed. L. Delisle and E. Berger, Paris 1916–27

Recueil des actes de Philippe Auguste, ed. H.-F. Delaborde and Ch. Petit-Dutaillis and others, Paris 1916–79

Recueil des historiens des croisades: historiens occidentaux, Paris 1844–95

Recueil des historiens des Gaules et de la France, ed. M. Bouquet, rev. L. Delisle, Paris 1738–1904

Regesta Honorii Papae III, ed. P. Pressutti, repr. Hildesheim 1978

Regesta pontificum romanorum ab condita ecclesia ad annum post Christum natum 1198, ed. P. Jaffé and others, 2nd edn, Leipzig 1885–8

Regesta pontificum romanorum inde ab a. post Christum natum 1198 ad a. 1304, ed. A. Potthast, Berlin 1957

Das Register Gregors VII, ed. E. Caspar, Berlin 1920–3

Das Register Innocenz III, ed. O. Hageneder and others, Graz 1968–

Rerum italicarum scriptores, ed. L. A. Muratori, Bologna 1900

Robert of Torigny, in *Chronicles of Stephen, Henry and Richard*, iv.

Rodulfus Glaber, *The five books of the histories*, ed. and trans. J. France and N. Bulst, Oxford 1989

Roger of Hoveden, *Chronica*, ed. W. Stubbs (RS, 1868–71)

Roger of Wendover, *Flores historiarum*, ed. R. G. Hewlett (RS, 1886–9)

Rôles gascons, ed. Ch. Bémont, Bordeaux 1885–1906

Rotuli chartarum in Turri Londinensi, I/1: (1199–1216), ed. T. D. Hardy, London 1837

Rotuli litterarum clausarum, ed. T. D. Hardy, London 1833–44

Rotuli litterarum patentium, i, ed. T. D. Hardy, London 1835

Saisimentum comitatus tholosani, ed. Y. Dossat, Paris 1966

Select charters from the beginning to 1307, ed. W. Stubbs, 9th edn, Oxford 1913

Selected letters of Pope Innocent III, concerning England (1198–1216), ed. and trans. C. R. Cheney and W. H. Semple, London 1953

Une Somme anti-cathare, le Liber contra manicheos de Durand de Huesca, ed. C. Thouzellier, Louvain 1964

The song of the Cathar wars, trans. J. Shirley, Aldershot 1996

Spicilegium, ed. L. d'Achery, Paris 1723

Suger, abbot of Saint-Denis, *Vita Ludovici Grossi*, ed. A. Molinier, Paris 1887

Theophylact, patriarch of Constantinople, 'Letter to Tsar Peter I of Bulgaria', in V. N. Sharenkoff, *A study of Manichaeism in Bulgaria with special reference to the Bogomils*, New York 1927, 63–5

Thesaurus novus anecdotorum, ed. E. Martène and U. Durand, Paris 1717, repr. New York 1968

Vetera analecta, ed. J. Mabillon, Paris 1723

Vie de Saint Léonard solitaire en Limousin: ses miracles et son culte, trans. and annot. F. l'abbé Arbellot, Paris 1863

Vita of St Leonard of Noblat, *AS* iii

Vita of St Symeon the Hermit, *AS* vi

Vitae of St Bernard of Clairvaux, *PL* clxxxii–clxxxv

Walter Map, *De nugis curialium*, ed. T. Wright, London 1850

William the Breton, 'Philippide', and 'Chronique', in *Oeuvres de Rigord et de Guillaume le Breton*, ed. H. F. Delaborde, Paris 1882–5

William of Jumièges, *Gesta normannorum ducum*, ed. A. Duchesne, Paris 1619

William of Malmesbury, *De gestis pontificum*, ed. N. E. S. A Hamilton (RS, 1870)
———— *De gestis regum anglorum*, ed. W. Stubbs (RS, 1887–9)

William of Newburgh, in *Chronicles of Stephen, Henry and Richard*, i, ii.

William of Poitiers, *Gesta Willelmi*, ed. R. Foreville, Paris 1952

William of Puylaurens, *Chronique*, ed. J. Duvernoy, 2nd edn, Toulouse 1997

William of Tudela and continuator, *La Chanson de la croisade albigeoise*, ed. and French trans. E. Martin-Chabot, Paris 1960–72

William of Tyre, *Historia rerum in partibus transmarinis gestarum*, in *RHC Occ.*, i

Works of reference

Atlas of the crusades, ed J. Riley-Smith, London 1991

Atlas de la France de l'an mil, ed. M. Parisse and J. Leuridan, Paris 1994

Burias, J., *Guide des archives du Lot-et-Garonne*, Agen 1972

Bibliographie généalogique, héraldique et nobiliaire de la France: dès origines à nos jours, ed. G. Saffroy, Paris 1968–88

Dictionnaire de biographie française, ed. J. Balteau and others, Paris 1989

Dictionnaire de la noblesse, 3rd edn, ed. A. de la Chenaye-Desbois and others (1868–76), repr. Paris 1969

Hardy, T. D., *A description of the patent rolls*, London 1835 (including King John's itinerary, unpaginated)

Knowles, D. and others, *The heads of religious houses, England and Wales*, Cambridge 1972

Reuter, T. and G. Silagi (eds), *Wortkonkordanz zum Decretum Gratiani*, MGH, 1990

Saint-Sand, le comte de, *Généalogies périgordines*, 2nd edn, Bergerac 1914
Séguy, J., *Atlas linguistique et ethnographique de la Gascogne*, Toulouse 1954–6
Series episcoporum ecclesiae catholicae, ed. P. B. Gams, Leipzig 1931
Strayer, J. (ed.), *Dictionary of the Middle Ages*, New York 1982–9

Secondary sources

Albe, E., *Les Marchands de Cahors à Londres au XIIIe siècle*, Cahors 1908
────── *L'Hérésie albigeoise et l'inquisition en Quercy*, Paris 1910
Andrieu, J., *Histoire de l'Agenais*, Marseille 1976
Angold, M., *The Byzantine empire, 1025–1204*, London–New York 1984
────── *Church and society in Byzantium under the Comneni, 1081–1261*, London 1995
Arbellot, l'abbé F., *Les Chevaliers limousins à la première croisade (1096–1102)*, Paris 1881
Arbellot, M., *Vie de Saint Léonard Solitaire en Limousin: ses miracles et son culte*, Paris 1863
Arnold, J., *Inquisition and power: Catharism and the confessing subject in the medieval Languedoc*, Philadelphia 2001
Asad, T., 'Medieval heresy: an anthropological view', *Social History* xi (1986), 345–62
Aubrun, M., 'Le Prieur Geoffrey de Vigeois et sa chronique', *Revue Mabillon* lviii (1974), 313–26
────── *L'Ancien Diocèse de Limoges dès origines au milieu du XIe siècle*, Clermont-Ferrand 1981
────── *La Paroisse en France, des origines au xve siècle*, Paris 1986
Auzias, L., *L'Aquitaine carolingienne, 778–982*, Paris–Toulouse 1937
Bachrach, B. S., 'A study in feudal politics: relations between Fulk Nerra and William the Great, 995–1030', *Viator* vii (1976), 111–22
────── 'Towards a reappraisal of William the Great, duke of Aquitaine (995–1030)', *JMH* v (1979), 11–21
────── 'The pilgrimages of Fulk Nerra, count of the Angevins, 987–1040', in T. F. X. Noble and J. J. Contreni (eds), *Religion, culture and society in the early Middle Ages: studies in honour of Richard Sullivan*, Kalamazoo 1987, 205–17
────── *Fulk Nerra, the neo-Roman consul, 970–1040*, Berkeley, Ca. 1993
────── *The anatomy of a little war*, San Francisco–Oxford 1994
Baldwin, J. W., *Masters, princes and merchants: the social views of Peter the Chantor and his circle*, Princeton, NJ 1970
Barber, M., *The Cathars: dualist heretics in the Languedoc in the high Middle Ages*, Harlow 2000
Barrère, l'abbé J., *Histoire religieuse et monumentale du diocèse d'Agen depuis les temps les plus reculés jusqu'à nos jours*, Agen 1855–6
Barrière, B., 'Les Abbayes issues de l'érémitisme', *CF* xxi (1986), 71–105
────── 'The Cistercian convent of Coyroux in the twelfth and thirteenth centuries', *Gesta* xxxii (1992), 76–82
Barthélemy, D., *L'Ordre seigneurial, XIe–XIIe siècle*, Paris 1990
────── 'La Mutation de l'an mille, a-t-elle en lieu?', *Annales* xlvii (1992) 767–77

———— 'Sur les Traces du comte Bouchard: dominations châtelaines à Vendôme et en France vers l'an mil', in Parisse and Barral I Altet, *Le Roi de France*, 99–110

———— *La Société dans le comté de Vendôme de l'an mil au XIVe siècle*, Paris 1993

———— *La Mutation de l'an mille, a-t-elle en lieu? Servage et chevalerie dans la France des Xe et XIe siècles*, Paris 1997

———— 'Le Paix de Dieu dans son contexte', *Cahiers de civilisation médiévale* xl (1997), 3–35

———— *L'An mil et la Paix de Dieu: la France chrétienne et féodale, 980–1060*, Paris 1999

———— 'La Milice de Bourges et sa défaite du 18 janvier 1038', in J. Paviot and J. Berger (eds), *Guerre, pouvoir et noblesse au moyen âge*, Paris 2000, 71–81

Baumont, S., J. Burias and others, *Histoire d'Agen*, Toulouse 1991

Bautier, R.-H., *The economic development of medieval Europe*, trans. H. Karolyi, London 1971

———— 'L'Hérésie d'Orléans et le mouvement intellectuel au début du XIe siècle', in *Actes du 95e congrès national des societés savantes: Reims*, Paris 1975, 63–88

Bayless, M., *Parody in the Middle Ages: the Latin tradition*, Michigan 1996

Bec, P., *Les Interférences linguistiques entre Gascon et Languedocien dans les parlers du Comminges et Couserans*, Paris 1968

Becquet, J., 'La Mort d'un évêque de Périgueux à la première croisade: Reynaud de Thiviers', *BSHAP* lxxxvii (1960), 66–9

———— 'Chanoines réguliers en Limousin au XIIe siècle: sanctuaires régularisés et dépendances étrangères', *BSAHL* ci (1974), 67–111

———— 'Collégiales et sanctuaires de chanoines séculiers en Limousin aux Xe–XIIe siècles', *BSAHL* ciii (1976), 76–106

———— 'Les Évêques de Limoges aux Xe, XIe et XIIe siècles', *BSAHL* cv (1978), 79–104; cvi (1979), 85–114

Beech, G. T., *A rural society in medieval France: the Gâtine of Poitou in the 11th and 12th centuries*, Baltimore 1964

Bémont, Ch., 'Les Institutions municipales de Bordeaux au moyen âge: la mairie et la jurade', *Revue historique* cxxiii (1916), unpaginated

Bienvenu, J. M., *L'Étonnant fondateur de Fontevraud, Robert d'Arbrissel*, Paris 1981

Biget, J.-L., ' "Les Albigeois": remarques sur une dénomination', in Zerner, *Inventer*, 219–56

Biller, P., 'The Cathars of the Languedoc and written materials', in Biller and Hudson, *Heresy and literacy*, 61–82

———— 'William of Newburgh and the Cathar mission to England', in D. Wood (ed.), *Life and thought in the northern Church, c. 1100–c. 1700* (Studies in Church History, subsidia xii, 1999), 11–30

———— and A. Hudson (eds), *Heresy and literacy, 1000–1530*, Cambridge 1994

Biron, R., *Précis d'histoire religieuse des anciens diocèses de Bordeaux et de Bazas*, Bordeaux 1925

Bisson, T. N., *Assemblies and representation in Languedoc in the thirteenth century*, Princeton 1964

———— 'The general court of the Agenais in the thirteenth century', in Bisson, *Medieval France*, 3–30

———— 'The organised peace in southern France and Catalonia, c. 1140–1233', in Bisson, *Medieval France*, 215–36

———— *Medieval France and her Pyrenean neighbours*, London–Ronceverte 1989

———— 'The feudal revolution', *Past and Present* cxlii (1994), 6–42

Bladé, J. F. de, 'Notice sur le vicomté de Bézaume, comté de Bénauge, vicomtés de Bruilhois et d'Arvilars et le pays de Villandraut et de Cayran', *RA* lxxviii (1877), unpaginated

———— *La Vasconie cispyrénéan jusqu'à la mort de Dagobert Ier*, Le Puy 1891

———— 'Géographie politique de sud-ouest de la Gaule franque au temps des rois d'Aquitaine', *RA* (1895), 47–63, 114–25, 193–213

———— 'Les Origines du duché de Gascogne', *RSASAA* ii/13 (1897), unpaginated

Blaquiere, H. and Y. Dossat, 'Confessions inédites de catharisme quercinois', *CF* iii. 259–98

Bloch, M., *Feudal society*, trans. L. A. Manyon, 2nd English edn, London–New York 1989

Bois, G., *La Mutation de l'an mille: Lournand, village mâconnaise de l'antiquité au féodalisme*, Paris 1989

———— *The transformation of the year 1000: the village of Lournand from antiquity to feudalism*, trans. J. Birrell, Manchester 1992

Boissonade, P., 'Les Premiers Croisades françaises en Espagne: normands, gascons, aquitains and bourguignons (1018–32)', *Bulletin hispanique* xxxvi (1934), 5–28

Bolton, B., 'Philip Augustus and John: two sons in Innocent III's vineyard?', in D. Wood (ed.), *The Church and sovereignty* (SCH subsidia ix, 1991), 113–34

Bonde, S., *Fortress churches of Languedoc: architecture, religion and conflict in the high Middle Ages*, Cambridge 1994

Bonnaud-Delamere, R., 'Légende des associations de la Paix', *BPH* (1936–7), 47–65

———— 'Fondment des institutions de paix au XIe siècle', *Mélanges Louis Halphen*, Paris 1951

———— 'Les Institutions de paix en Aquitaine au XIe siècle', *Recueils de la Société Jean Bodin* xiv (1961), 147–52

Bonnassie, P., *La Catalogne du milieu du Xe siècle à la fin du XIe: croissance et mutations d'une société*, Toulouse 1975–6

———— 'Survie et extinction du régime esclavagiste dans l'occident du haut moyen âge, IVe–XIe siècle', *CCM* xxviii (1985), 307–43

———— *Le Catalogne au tournant de l'an mil: croissance et mutations d'une société*, Paris 1990

———— *From slavery to feudalism in south-western Europe*, Cambridge 1991

———— 'L'Espace toulousain', in Zimmerman, *Les Sociétés méridionales*, 107–45

———— 'Les Paysans du royaume franc au temps d'Hugues Capet et Robert le Pieux (987–1031)', in Parisse and Barral I Altet, *Le Roi de France*, 117–29

———— and R. Landes, 'Une Nouvelle Hérésie est née dans la monde', in Zimmerman, *Les Sociétés méridionales*, 435–59

Bonner, G., *St Augustine of Hippo: life and controversies*, 2nd edn, Norwich 1986

Bordes, M. and others, *Histoire de la Gascogne, dès origines à nos jours*, Roanne 1982

Bordes, R., *En Périgord: l'hérésie cathare*, Eglise Neuve d'Issac–Castelnaud-la-Chapelle 1996

Borst, A., *Die Katharer*, MGH, SS xii, Stuttgart 1953

Boudon de Saint-Amans, J.-F., *Histoire ancienne et moderne du département de Lot-et-Garonne depuis l'an 56 avant Jésus-Christ, jusqu'en 1814*, i, Agen 1836

Bournazel, E., 'Mémoire et parenté: le problème de la continuité dans la noblesse de l'an mil', in Parisse and Barral I Altet, *Le Roi de France*, 111–16

Bounoure, G., 'La Lettre d'Héribert sur les hérétiques périgourdins', *BSHAP* cxx (1993), 61–72

Bourin, M., *Villages médiévale en Bas Languedoc: genèse d'une sociabilité (Xe–XIVe siècles)*, Paris 1987

Bourin-Derruau, M., *Villages et communautés villageoises en Languedoc: l'example du Biterrois (Xe–XIVe siècle)*, Paris 1987

Boussard, J., *Le Gouvernement d'Henri II Plantagenêt*, Paris 1956

Boutruche, R., *Une Société provinciale en lutte contre le régime féodale: l'alleu en Bordelais et en Bazadais du XIe au XVIIIe siècle*, Rodez 1943

—— *Seigneurie et féodalité*, Paris 1959

Brenon, A., *Le Vrai Visage du catharisme*, Portet-sur-Garonne 1988

—— *Les Femmes cathares*, Paris 1992

—— 'Les Hérésies de l'an mil: nouvelles perspectives sur les origines du catharisme', *Hérésis* xxiv (1995), 21–36

Breuils, A., *Saint Austinde archevêque d'Auch (1000–1068) et la Gascogne au XIe siècle*, Auch 1895

Brooke, C., 'Heresy and religious sentiment: 1000–1250', *Bulletin of the Institute of Historical Research* (1968), 115–38, repr. in his *Medieval Church and society*, London 1971, 139–61

Brown, E. A. R., 'The tyranny of a construct: feudalism and historians of medieval Europe', *American Historical Review* lxxix (1974), 1063–88, repr. in L. K. Little and B. H. Rosenwein (eds), *Debating the Middle Ages: issues and readings*, Oxford 1998, 148–69

Brown, P., *The cult of saints: its rise and function in Latin Christianity*, Chicago 1981

Browning, R., *Bulgaria and the Byzantine empire*, London 1975

Bull, M., *Knightly piety and the lay response to the First Crusade: the Limousin and Gascony c. 970–1130*, Oxford 1993

Burias, J., 'La Guerre des albigeois et l'administration d'Alphonse de Poitiers', in Baumont, Burias and others, *Histoire d'Agen*, 51–76

Callahan, D. F., 'The sermons of Adémar of Chabannes and the cult of St Martial of Limoges', *RB* lxxxvi (1976), 251–95

—— 'Adémar de Chabannes et la paix de dieu', *AM* lxxxix (1977), 21–43

—— 'William the Great and the monasteries of Aquitaine', *Studia Monastica* xix (1977), 321–42

—— 'Adémar of Chabannes, apocalypticism and the peace council of Limoges of 1031', *RB* ci (1991), 32–49

—— 'The peace of God and the cult of the saints in Aquitaine in the tenth and eleventh centuries', in Head and Landes, *Peace of God*, 80–103

Capul, M., 'Notes sur le catharisme et la croisade des albigeois en Agenais', *RA* xc (1964), 3–14

Carpenter, D., *The minority of Henry III*, London 1990

Cassany-Mazet, A., *Annales de Villeneuve-sur-Lot et de son arrondissement*, Agen 1846

Caubet, J., *Histoire de Tonneins dès origines à 1870*, Tonneins n.d

Chaplais, P., 'Le Traité de Paris de 1259 et l'inféodation de la Gascogne allodiale', *MA* lxi (1955), 121–37

Chaytor, H. J., *Savaric de Mauléon, baron of troubadours*, Cambridge 1939

Cheney, C. R., *Innocent III and England*, Stuttgart 1979

—— *The papacy and England*, Aldershot 1982

Cheyette, F., 'Suum cuique tribuere', *French Historical Studies* vi (1970), 287–99

Cirot, l'*abbé*, *Histoire de l'abbaye et congrégation de Notre-Dame de la Grande-Sauve, ordre de Saint-Benoît, en Guienne*, Bordeaux 1844

Clémens, J., 'Les Oscidates campestres', *RA* cvii (1980), 91–6

———— 'L'Espace coutumier d'Agen au moyen âge', *RA* cix (1982), 3–19

———— 'La Coutume d'Agen au XIVe siècle', *RA* cxiii (1986), 303–11

———— 'Les Origines de la cour générale de l'Agenais', *Actes du 110e congrès national des sociétés savantes: Montpellier* (section d'histoire médiévale et de philologie, iii), Paris 1986, 69–80

———— 'La Maison de Béarn et les Plantagenêts dans la diocèse d'Agen durant la seconde moitié du XIIe siècle', in Desplat, *Terre et hommes du sud*, 201–12

Cohn, N., *The pursuit of the millennium*, 3rd edn, London 1990

Collins, R., *The Basques*, Oxford 1986

Congar, Y., 'Arriana haeresis comme désignation du néo-manichéisme au xiie siècle', *Revue des sciences philosophiques et théologique* xliii (1959), 449–61

Cowdrey, H. E. J., 'The peace and truce of God in the eleventh century', *Past and Present* xlvi (1970), 42–67

Crozet, R., *Villes d'entre Loire et Gironde*, Paris 1949, 39–78

Cursente, B., *Les Castelnaux de Gascogne médiévale*, Bordeaux 1980

———— 'L'Evêché de Gascogne et ses evêques (977–1059)', in *Actes du 104e congrès national des sociétés savantes: Bordeaux* (section philologique et historique, ii), Paris 1981, 131–44

———— 'Le Gascogne', in Zimmerman, *Les Société méridionales*, 257–93

———— 'Une Affaire de non-hérésie en Gascogne, en l'année 1208', in Zerner, *Inventer*, 257–62

———— *Des Maisons et des hommes: la Gascogne médiévale (XIe–XVe siècle)*, Toulouse 1998

Darnalt, J., *Remonstrance faicte en la cour de la seneschaucée d'Agenois . . . antiquités de l'Agenais*, Paris 1606

Davids, A. (ed.), *The Empress Theophano: Byzantium and the west at the turn of the first millennium*, Cambridge 1995

Debord, A., 'Castrum et castellum chez Adémar de Chabannes', *Archéologie médiévale* ix (1979), 97–113

———— *La Société laïque dans les pays de la Charente: Xe–XIIe siècles*, Paris 1984

———— 'The castellan revolution and the peace of God in Aquitaine', in Head and Landes, *Peace of God*, 165–83

———— *Aristocratie et pouvoir: le rôle du château dans la France médiévale*, Paris 2000

Deffontaines, P., *Les Hommes et leur travaux dans les pays de la moyenne Garonne (Agenais et Bas Quercy)*, Lille 1932

Degert, A., 'L'Evêché de Gascogne', *Revue de Gascogne* (1900), 5–23

Delarun, J., 'Robert d'Arbrissel et les femmes', *Annales* xxxix (1984), 1140–60

———— *Robert d'Arbrissel, fondateur de Fontevraud*, Paris 1986

Delort, R. (ed.), *La France de l'an mil*, Paris 1990

Delrieu, J. B., 'Les Puits de Richard-Coeur-de-Lion à Penne', *RA* i (1874), 181–9

Delvit, P. and others, *Garonne: de la rivière à l'homme*, Toulouse 1998

Desplat, C. (ed.), *Terre et hommes du sud: hommage à Pierre Tucoo-Chala*, Pau 1992

Devailly, G., *Le Berry du Xe siècle au milieu du XIIIe*, Paris–The Hague 1973

Dickson, M. and C. Dickson, 'Le Cardinal Robert de Courson: sa vie', *Archives d'histoire doctrinale et littéraire du moyen âge* ix (1934), 53–142

Dondaine, A., 'Les Actes du concile albigeoise de Saint-Félix de Caraman: essai de critique d'authenticité d'un document médiéval', in *Miscellanea Giovanni Mercati*, v, Rome 1946, 324–55.

—— *Le Hiérarchie cathare en Italie*, AFP xix (1949), 282–312; xx (1950), 234–324

—— 'L'Origine de l'hérésie médiévale: à propos d'un livre récent', *Rivista di storia della chiesa in Italia* vi (1952), 47–78

Dossat, Y., 'Catharisme et Comminges', in Dossat, *Église et hérésie*, 117–28

—— 'Catharisme en Gascogne', in Dossat, *Église et hérésie*, 149–68

—— 'Le Chroniqueur Guillaume de Puylaurens était-il chapelain de Raymond VII ou notaire de l'inquisition toulousaine?', in Dossat, *Église et hérésie*, 343–53

—— *Église et hérésie en France au XIIIe siècle*, London 1982

—— 'Un Évêque cathare originaire de l'Agenais: Vigouroux de la Bacone', in Dossat, *Église et hérésie*, 623–39

—— 'Une Figure d'inquisiteur, Bernard de Caux', CF vi (1971), 253–72

—— 'L'Inquisiteur Bernard de Caux et l'Agenais', in Dossat, *Église et hérésie*, 75–9

—— 'A Propos du chroniqueur Guillaume de Puylaurens', in Dossat, *Église et héresie*, 47–52

—— 'A Propos du concile cathare de Saint-Félix: les Milingues', CF iii (1968), 201–14

—— 'Les Restitutions de dîmes dans le diocèse d'Agen pendant l'épiscopat de Guillaume II (1247–63)', in Dossat, *Église et hérésie*, 549–64

Douais, C., *Les Frères prêcheurs en Gascogne au xiiie et xiv siècles*, Paris–Auch 1885

Drinkwater, J. F., *Roman Gaul*, London 1983

Duby, G., *Hommes et structures du môyen âge: recueil d'articles*, Paris 1963

—— *Rural economy and country life in the medieval west*, trans. C. Postan, London 1968

—— *La Société au XIe et XIIe siècle dans la région mâconnaise*, 2nd edn, Paris 1971

—— *Hommes et structures du môyen âge*, Paris 1973

—— *The early growth of the european economy*, trans. H. B. Clarke, Ithaca–New York 1974

—— *The chivalrous society*, trans. M. Postan, London 1977

—— *Medieval marriage*, trans. E. Forster, Baltimore 1978

—— *The three orders: feudal society imagined*, trans. A. Goldhammer, Chicago 1982

—— *The legend of Bouvines*, trans. C. Thanyi, Cambridge 1990

—— *France in the Middle Ages, 987–1460*, trans. J. Vale, Oxford 1991

Ducom, A, 'Essai sur l'histoire et l'organisation de la commune d'Agen jusqu'au traité de Brétigny (1360)', RSASAA ii/11 (1889), 161–322; ii/12 (1891–3), 133–234 (cited as i and ii respectively)

Duhamel-Amado, C., 'Les Pouvoirs et les parents autour de Béziers (980–1100)', in *Cadres de vie et société dans le Midi médiéval: hommage à Charles Higounet*, AM cii (1990), 309–17

Dunbabin, J., *France in the making: 843–1180*, Oxford 1985

Duvernoy, J., *Le Catharisme*, I: *La Religion des cathares*, Toulouse 1976

—— *Le Catharisme*, II: *L'Histoire des cathares*, Toulouse 1979

—— 'Le Problème des origines du catharisme', in J. Duvernoy, *Cathare, vaudois et béguines, dissidents du pays d'Oc*, Toulouse 1994, 39–52

Ebersolt, J., *Orient et occident: recherches sur les influences byzantines et orientales en France avant et pendant les croisades*, 2nd edn, Paris 1954

Edouard, J., *Fontevrault et ses monuments*, Paris 1873–4

Edwards, P., *Heresy and authority in medieval Europe*, Philadelphia 1980

Emmerson, R. K., *AntiChrist in the Middle Ages*, Seattle 1981

────── and B. McGinn (eds), *The Apocalypse in the Middle Ages*, Ithaca–London 1992

Erdmann, C., *The origins of the idea of crusade*, trans. M. W. Baldwin and W. Goffart, Princeton, NJ 1977 (first German edn 1935)

Escande, J. J., *Histoire de Sarlat*, Sarlat 1903

────── *Histoire de Périgord*, 2nd edn, Sarlat 1955

Esquieu, M. and others, *Agenais occitan, 1050–1978*, Villeneuve-sur-Lot 1978

Evans, A. P., 'The Albigensian crusade', in K. M. Setton and others, *History of the crusades*, Philadelphia 1962, ii. 277–324

Faucher, J., 'Contribution à l'histoire de la vicomté de Turenne', *BSHAP* lx (1938), 61–94

Favreau, R., *Histoire de Poitiers*, Toulouse 1985

────── 'Les Débuts de la ville de Loudun', *Bulletin de la Société des antiquaires de l'ouest* v (1988), 165–82

Faye, M., 'Notice sur le monastère de Montazai, de l'ordre de Fontevrauld', *Mémoires de la Société des antiquaires de l'ouest* xx (1853), 89–128

Fearns, J. V., 'Peter von Bruis und die religiöse Bewegung des 12 Jahrhunderts', *Archiv für Kulturgeschichte* xlviii (1966), 311–35

Fichtenau, H., *Heretics and scholars in the high Middle Ages, 1000–1200*, trans. D. A. Kaiser, Pennsylvania 1998

Focillon, H., *L'An mil*, Paris 1984

Fossier, R., 'Les Mouvements populaires en occident au XIe siècle', in *Académie des Inscriptions et Belles-Lettres: comptes rendus des séances de l'année 1971*, Paris 1972, 257–69

────── *Peasant life in the medieval west*, trans. J. Vale, Oxford 1988

Fouracre, P. and R. A. Gerberding, *Late Merovingian France: history and hagiography, 640–720*, Manchester 1996

Frassetto, M., 'Heresy, celibacy, and reform in the sermons of Adémar of Chabannes', in Frassetto, *Medieval purity*, 131–48

────── 'Reaction and reform: reception of heresy in Arras and Aquitaine in the early eleventh century', *Catholic Historical Review* lxxxiii (1997), 385–400

────── 'The sermons of Adémar of Chabannes and the letter of Héribert: new sources concerning the origins of medieval heresy', *Revue bénédictine* cix (1999), 324–40

────── 'The writings of Adémar of Chabannes, the Peace of 994, and the "Terrors of the Year 1000" ', *JMH* xxvii (2001), 241–55

────── (ed.), *Medieval purity and piety: essays on medieval clerical celibacy and religious reform*, New York–London 1988

Freedman, P., *The origins of peasant servitude in medieval Catalonia*, Cambridge 1991

────── *Images of the medieval peasant*, Stamford 1999

Garrouste, M. and J. P. Trabut-Cussac, *Penne d'Agenais, son histoire*, Villeneuve-sur-Lot 1961

Gaussin, P.-R., 'Y a-t-il eu une politique monastique de Plantagenêt', *CCM* xxix (1986), 83–94

Geary, P. J., *Before France and Germany*, Oxford 1988

Génicot, L., 'L'Érémitisme du XIe siècle dans son contexte économique et social', *Atti della settimana internazionale di studio Mendola* vii (1974), 374–402

Gibson, M. T. and J. Nelson (eds), *Charles the Bald: court and kingdom*, Aldershot 1990

Gillingham, J., *The Angevin empire*, London 1984

——— *Richard I*, 2nd edn, London 1989

——— 'Adémar of Chabannes and the history of Aquitaine in the reign of Charles the Bald', in M. T. Gibson and J. Nelson (eds), *Charles the Bald*, Oxford 1981, 3–14

Girard, R. P., 'Les Dominicans à Agen', *RA* xc (1964), 105–13

Given, J., *Inquisition and medieval society: power, discipline and resistance in Languedoc*, Ithaca–London 1997

Goetz, H.-W., 'Le Paix de dieu en France autour de l'an mil: fondements et objectifs, diffusion et participants', in Parisse and Barral I Altet, *Le Roi de France*, 131–45

Grégoire, H., 'Autor des pauliciens', *Byzantion* xi (1936), 610–14

Griffe, E., *Les Débuts de l'adventure cathare en Languedoc*, Paris 1969

——— *Le Languedoc cathare, 1190 à 1210*, Paris 1971

——— *Le Languedoc cathare au temps de la croisade, 1209–1229*, Paris 1973

——— *Le Languedoc cathare et l'inquisition, 1229–1329*, Paris 1989

Grundmann, H., *Religious movements in the Middle Ages*, trans. S. Rowan, Notre Dame 1995 (trans. of *Religiöse Bewegungen*, 2nd edn, Hildesheim 1961)

Guenée, B., *Histoire et culture historique dans l'occident médiévale*, Paris 1981

Guerreau, A., review of Bois, *La Mutation*, MA xcvi (1990), 519–37

Guignard, M., *Histoire de l'Agenais, dès origines au XV siècle*, Agen 1941

Guillemain, B., *Le Diocèse de Bordeaux*, Paris 1974

——— 'Les Origines des évêques en France au XIe et XIIe siècles', in *Le instituzioni ecclesiastiche della 'societas christiana' dei secoli XI–XII* (Miscellanea del Centro di Studi Medioevali, 7), Milan 1974, 374–407

——— 'Le Choix des évêques en Aquitaine XIIIe–XVe siècles', in *Actes du 104e congrès des sociétés savantes: Bordeaux* (*Section de philologie et d'histoire jusqu'à 1610*, ii), Paris 1981, 47–58

——— 'Le Duché d'Aquitaine hors du Catharisme', *CF* xx (1985), 57–71

Guiter, H., 'Limites linguistiques dans la région bordelaise', in *Études sur la Gascogne au moyen âge*, xi, Paris 1981, 59–67

Hajdu, R., 'Castles, castellans and the structure of politics in Poitou, 1152–1271', *JMH* iv (1978), 27–53

Hallam, E., 'Henry II as a founder of monasteries', *Journal of Ecclesiastical History* xxviii (1977), 113–32

——— *Capetian France, 987–1328*, London 1980

Hamilton, B., 'The Albigensian Crusade', in Hamilton, *Monastic reform*, 1–40

——— 'The Armenian Church and the papacy', in Hamilton, *Monastic reform*, 61–87

——— 'The Cathar council of Saint Félix reconsidered', in Hamilton, *Monastic reform*, 23–53

——— 'The city of Rome and eastern churches in the tenth century', in Hamilton, *Monastic reform*, 5–26

——— *Monastic reform, Catharism and the crusades (900–1300)*, London 1979

——— 'The origins of the dualist church of Drugunthia', in Hamilton, *Monastic reform*, 115–24

——— *The medieval inquisition*, London 1981

———— 'Wisdom from the east: the reception by the Cathars of eastern dualist texts', in Biller and Hudson, *Heresy and literacy*, 38–60

———— and P. A. McNulty, '*Orientale lumen et magistra latinitatis*: Greek influences of western monasticism (900–1100)', in Hamilton, *Monastic reform*, 181–216

Head, T. and R. Landes (eds), *The Peace of God: social violence and religious response in France around the year 1000*, Ithaca–London 1992

Higounet, Ch., 'Les Bastides du sud-ouest', in *L'Information historique*, Paris 1946, 28–35.

———— 'Bastides et frontières', MA iv (1948), 113–31

———— *Le Comté de Comminges de ses origines à son annexion à la couronne*, Toulouse–Paris 1949

———— *Le Développement urbain et le rôle de Marmande au moyen-âge*, Agen 1952

———— *Mouvements de populations dans le Midi de France du XIe–XVe siècle*, Paris 1953

———— *Bordeaux pendant le moyen âge*, Bordeaux 1963

———— 'Les Chemins Saint-Jacques et les sauvetés de Gascogne', in Higounet, *Paysages et villages neufs*, 207–14

———— 'Nouvelle approche sur les bastides du sud-ouest aquitain', in Higounet, *Paysages et villages neufs*, 347–54

———— *Paysages et villages neufs de moyen-âge; receuil d'articles de Ch. Higounet*, Bordeaux 1975

———— 'En Bordelais: *principes castella tenentes*', in P. Contamine (ed.), *La Noblesse au moyen âge, 11e–15e siècles*, Paris 1976, 97–104

———— 'A Propos de la fondation du prieuré de La Réole', *Actes du millénaire de la fondation du Priéure de La Réole*, Bordeaux 1980, 8–11

———— and J.-B. Marquette, 'Les Origines de l'abbaye de Saint-Sever, révision critique', in *Saint-Sever: millénaire de l'abbaye*, Poitou 1986

———— Y. Renouard and others, *Histoire de Bordeaux*, Bordeaux 1962–5

———— and others, *Histoire de l'Aquitaine*, Toulouse 1971

Higounet-Nadal, A., *Histoire de Périgueux*, Toulouse 1983

Hill, J. H. and L. L. Hill, *Raymond IV count of Toulouse*, Westport, Conn. 1980

Hilton, R., *Bond men made free*, London 1988

Holt, J. C., 'Aliénor d'Aquitaine, Jean sans Terre et la succession de 1199', CCM xxix (1986), 95–100

———— *Magna Carta*, 2nd edn, Cambridge 1992

Humbert-Vicaire, M., 'L'Action de St Dominique sur la vie régulière des femmes en Languedoc', CF xxiii, 219–40

Hutchinson, C. A., *The hermit monks of Grandmont*, Kalamazoo, Mich. 1989

Imbart de la Tour, P., *Les Élections épiscopales dans l'église de France du IXe au XIIe siècle*, Paris 1891

———— *Les Paroisses rurales du IVe au XIe siècles*, 2nd edn, Paris 1979

Iogna-Prat, D., 'Continence et virginité dans la conception clunisienne de l'ordre du monde autour de l'an mil', *Académie des inscriptions et belles-lettres; comptes rendu*, Paris 1985, 127–46

———— 'L'Argumentation défensive: de la polémique grégorienne au *Contra petrobrusianos* de Pierre le Vénérable (1140)', in Zerner, *Inventer*, 87–118

James, E., *The Franks*, Oxford 1988

Jaurgain, J. de, *La Vasconie*, Pau 1898–1902

Jeanroy, A., *La Poésie lyrique des troubadours*, Toulouse 1935

Jimenez, P., 'Relire la charte de Niquinta, I: Origine et problématique de la charte', *Heresis* xxii (June 1994), 1–26

—— 'Relire la charte de Niquinta, II: Sens et portée de la charte', *Heresis* xxii (Dec. 1994), 1–28

Jones, M. C. E., review of Barthélemy, *La Mutation*, *Times Literary Supplement*, 6 Mar. 1988, 26

Kienzle, B. M., *Cistercians, heresy and crusade in Occitania, 1145–1229*, York 2001

Knowles, D., 'The Canterbury election of 1205–6', *EHR* liii (1938), 211–20

Kuttner, S. and A. García y García, 'A new eyewitness account of the Fourth Lateran Council', *Traditio* xx (1964), 115–78

Labénazie, B., *Annales d'Agen*, Agen–Paris 1886 (repr. of eighteenth-century edn)

Lacoste, J., 'Le Château de Nérac', *RA* iv (1877), 193–8

Lagarde, A., *Notes historiques sur la ville de Tonneins*, Agen 1882

Lagarde, L. F., *Recherches historiques sur la ville et les anciennes baronnies de Tonneins*, Agen 1833

Lambert, M. D., *Medieval heresy: popular movements from Bogomil to Hus*, London 1977

—— *Medieval heresy: popular movements from the Gregorian Reform to the Reformation*, 2nd edn, Oxford 1992

—— *The Cathars*, Oxford 1998

Landes, R., 'The dynamics of heresy and reform in Limoges: a study of popular participation in the Peace of God (994–1033)', *Historical Reflections/ Reflexions historiques* xiv (1987), 487–503

—— 'Lest the millennium be fulfilled: apocalyptic expectation and the pattern of western chronology, 100–800', in Verbeke, Verhelst and Welkenhuysen, *Eschatology*, 137–211

—— 'L'Accession des capétiens: une reconsidération des sources', in D. Iogna-Prat and J.-C. Picard (eds), *Religion et culture autour de l'an mil: royaume capétien et Lotharingie*, Paris 1990

—— 'Between the aristocracy and heresy: popular participation in the Limousin Peace of God, 994–1033', in Head and Landes, *Peace of God*, 184–218

—— 'Millenarismus absconditus', *MA* xcviii (1992), 355–77

—— 'Sur les traces du millennium: la via negativa', *MA* xcix (1993), 1–26

—— *Relics, apocalypse and the deceits of history: Adémar of Chabannes, 989–1034*, Cambridge Mass.–London 1995

Lataillade, J. B., 'Catharisme en Comminges, Couserans et Armagnac', *Revue de Comminges* lxxxvi (1973), 212–16

Lauwers, M., '*Dicunt vivorum beneficia nihil prodesse defunctis*: histoire d'un thème polemique', in Zerner, *Inventer*, 157–92

Lauzun, P., 'Les Hôpitaux de la ville d'Agen', *RA* xix (1892) 200–91

Lea, H. C., *A history of the inquisition in the Middle Ages* (1888), repr. New York 1955

Le Jan, R., *Familles et pouvoir dans le monde franc (VIIe–Xe siècle)*, Paris 1995

Lekai, L. J., *The Cistercians*, Kent, Ohio 1977

Lemarignier, J.-F., 'La Dislocation du *pagus* et le problème des *consuetudines*', *Mélanges Louis Halphen*, Paris 1951, 401–10

—— *Le Gouvernement royal au premiers temps Capétiens (987–1108)*, Paris 1965

—— J.-F. Gaudemet and G. Mollat, 'Les Institutions ecclésiastiques en France de la fin du Xe au milieu du XIIe siècle', in F. Lot and R. Fawtier (eds), *Histoire des institutions français au moyen âge*, Paris 1957–62, iii. 1–139

———— and others, 'Political and monastic structures in France at the end of the tenth and the beginning of the eleventh century', in F. L. Cheyette (ed.), *Lordship and community in medieval Europe*, New York 1975, 100–27

Lewis, A. R., *The development of southern French and Catalan society, 718–1050*, Austin, Texas 1965

Lewis, P. A., 'Mortgages in the Bazadais and Bordelais', *Viator* x (1979), 23–38

Leyser, H., *Hermits and the new monasticism: a study of religious communities in western Europe, 1000–1150*, London 1984

Lieu, S. N. C., *Manichaeism in the later Roman empire and medieval China: a historical survey*, Manchester 1985

Ligou, A., G. Passerat and others, *Histoire de Montauban*, Toulouse 1992

Limouzin-Lamothe, R., *La Commune de Toulouse, 1120–1230*, New York 1954

Little, L. K. and B. H. Rosenwein (eds), *Debating the Middle Ages: issues and readings*, Oxford 1998

Lobrichon, G., 'The chiaroscuro of heresy: early eleventh-century Aquitaine as seen from Auxerre', trans. P. Buc, in Head and Landes, *Peace of God*, 80–103

———— *La Religion des laïcs en occident, XIe–XVe siècles*, Paris 1994

———— 'Arras, 1025, ou le vrai procès d'une fausse accusation', in Zerner, *Inventer*, 67–85

Lodge, E., *Gascony under English rule*, London 1926

Luchaire, A., *Innocent III*, Paris 1905–8

McGinn, B., 'Apocalypticism in the Middle Ages: an historiographical sketch', *Medieval Studies* xxxvii (1975), 252–86

———— *Visions of the end: apocalyptic traditions in the Middle Ages*, New York 1979

Mackay, A., *Spain in the Middle Ages*, London 1977

Mackinney, L.C., 'The people and public opinion in the eleventh-century peace movement', *Speculum* v (1930), 181–206

McNamara, J. A., 'Victims of progress: women and the twelfth century', in K. Glente and L. Winther-Jensen (eds), *Female power in the Middle Ages*, Copenhagen 1989, 26–37

Maddicott, J. R., *Simon de Montfort*, Cambridge 1994

Magnou-Nortier, E., 'Fidélité et féodalité méridionales d'après les serments de fidélité, Xe–début XIIe siècle', *AM* lxxx (1968), 457–84

———— *Foi et fidélité: recherche sur l'évolution des liens personnels chez les francs du VIIe au IXe siècle*, Toulouse 1976

———— 'Formes féminines de vie consacrée dans les pays du Midi jusqu'au début du XIIe siècle', *CF* xxiii (1988), 193–216

———— 'The enemies of the Peace: reflections on a vocabulary, 500–1100', in Head and Landes, *Peace of God*, 58–79

Marca, P. de, *Histoire de Béarn*, 2nd edn, Pau 1894

Marquette, J.-B., 'Les Albret en Agenais (XIe siècle–1366)', *RA* xcviii (1972), 301–11

Marsac, M., 'La Châtellenie et les seigneurs de Moncuq', *Bulletin de la Société historique et archéologique du Périgord* xcviii (1971), 89–98

Martindale, J., 'Succession and politics in the romance speaking world, c. 1000–1140', in M. C. E. Jones and M. Vales (eds), *England and her neighbours, 1066–1453: essays in honour of Pierre Chaplais*, London–Ronceverte 1989, 19–41

———— 'Peace and war in early eleventh-century Aquitaine', in C. Harper-Bill and

R. Harvey (eds), *Ideals and practice of medieval knighthood*, iv, Woodbridge 1992, 147–76

—— 'His special friend? The settlement of disputes and political power in the kingdom of the French: tenth to mid-twelfth century', *TRHS* vi (1995), 21–59

Mayer, H., *The crusades*, trans. J. Gillingham, Oxford 1972

Micheau, J., 'Le Développement topographique de Saintes au moyen âge', *BPH* (1961), 24–36

da Milano, Ilarino, 'Le eresie populari del secolo XI nell'Europa occidentale', *Studi Gregoriani* ii (1947), 43–89

Monfar y Sors, D. Diego, *Historia de los condes de Urgel*, i, in *Collección de documentos inéditos del archivo general de la corona de Aragón*, ed. D. Próspero de Bofarull y Mascaró, ix, Barcelona 1853

Monluzun, J. J., *Histoire de la Gascogne depuis les temps les plus reculés jusqu'à nos jours*, Auch 1846–50

Monoyer, J., *Essais d'histoire et d'archéologie*, II: *Les Villages de Houdeng, Goenies, Strépy*, 2nd edn, Mons 1875

Moore, R. I., *The birth of popular heresy*, London 1969

—— 'Nicétas, émissaire de Dragovitch, a-t-il traversé les Alpes?', *AM* lxxxv (1973), 85–90

—— 'Saint Bernard's mission to the Languedoc in 1145', *Bulletin of the Institute of Historical Research* xlvii (1974), 1–10

—— *The origins of european dissent*, London 1977

—— 'Family, community and cult on the eve of the Gregorian reform', *TRHS* 5th ser. xxx (1980), 49–69

—— 'Duby's eleventh century', *History* lxix (1984), 36–49

—— *The formation of a persecuting society*, Oxford 1987

—— 'Postscript: the Peace of God and the social revolution', in Head and Landes, *Peace of God*, 308–26

—— 'Literacy and the making of heresy, c. 1000–1150', in Biller and Hudson, *Heresy and literacy*, 19–37

—— 'Postface', in Zerner, *Inventer*, 263–9

—— 'Property, marriage, and the eleventh-century revolution: a context for early medieval communism', in Frassetto, *Purity*, 179–208

—— *The first european revolution, c. 970–1215*, Oxford 2000

Morghen, R., *Medioevo cristiano*, Bari 1951

Mouillé, A., 'Le Comté d'Agenais au Xe siècle: Gombaud et son épiscopat', *RSASAA* ii (1875), 136–70

Mousnier, M., 'Grandselve et la société de son temps', *CF* xxi (1986), 107–26

—— 'Implantations monastiques et encadrement des populations en Gascogne toulousaine dans la première moitié du XIIe siècle', in *Crises et réformes grégorienne à la préréforme*, Paris 1991, unpaginated

—— *La Gascogne Toulousaine au XIe–XIIe siècles*, Toulouse 1997

Mundy, J. H., *Liberty and political power in Toulouse, 1050–1250*, New York 1954

Mussot-Goulard, R., *Les Princes de Gascogne (768–1070)*, Lectoure–Marseden 1982

—— 'La Gascogne', in Zimmerman, *Les Sociétés méridionales*, 295–326

—— 'Remarques sur les textes relatifs à la fondation du monastère de Saint-Orens à Auch', in Desplat, *Terre et hommes du sud*, 79–82

Musy, J., 'Movements populaires et hérésies au xie siècle en France', *Revue historique* ccliii (1975), 33–76

Nelson, J., 'Society, theodicy and the origins of heresy', in D. Baker (ed.), Schism, heresy and religious protest (SCH ix, 1972), 65–77
—— Charles the Bald, London 1992
—— 'Dispute settlement in Carolingian west Francia', in Nelson, Frankish world, 51–74
—— The Frankish world, 750–900, London 1996
—— 'Ninth-century knighthood: the evidence of Nithard', in Nelson, Frankish world, 75–87
Norgate, K., John Lackland, London 1902
Noulens, J., Maisons historiques de Gascogne, Guienne, Béarn, Languedoc et Périgord, Paris 1865–6
Obolensky, D., The Bogomils, Cambridge 1948, repr. Twickenham 1972
—— 'Papa Nicetas: a Byzantine dualist in the land of the Cathars', Harvard Ukrainian Studies vii (1983), 489–500
O' Callaghan, J. F., A history of medieval Spain, Ithaca–London 1975
Ourliac, P., Les Pays de Garonne vers l'an mil, Toulouse 1993
—— 'Note sur les coutumes successorales de l'Agenais', Annales de la faculté de droit d'Aix lxiii (1950), 253–8
Pacaut, M., Louis VII et les élections épiscopales dans le royaume de France, Paris 1957
Painter, S., 'The lords of Lusignan in the 11th and 12th centuries', Speculum xxxii (1937), 27–47
—— The reign of King John, Baltimore 1949
—— 'The houses of Lusignan and Châtellerault, 1150–1250', Speculum xxx (1955), 374–84
—— 'Castellans of the plain of Poitou in the eleventh and twelfth centuries', Speculum xxxi (1956), 243–57
Papy, L., La Côte atlantique, de Loire à la Gironde, Bordeaux 1941
Parisse, M., 'Qu'est-ce que la France de l'an mil?', in Delort, La France de l'an mil, 29–48
—— and X. Barral I Altet (eds), Le Roi de France et son royaume autour de l'an mil, Paris 1992
Passerat, G., 'Cathares en Bas-Quercy: entre l'église de l'Agenais et celle de l'Albigeois', in Europe et Occitainie: les pays cathares, Carcassonne 1992, 149–65
Paterson, L., The world of the troubadours, Cambridge 1993
Paxton, F. S., 'The Peace of God in modern historiography: perspectives and trends', Historical Reflections/Refléxions historiques xiv (1987), 385–404
—— 'History, historians and the Peace of God', in Head and Landes, Peace of God, 21–40
Pegg, M., The corruption of angels: the Great Inquisition of 1245–1246, Princeton–Oxford 2001
—— 'Historiographical essay: on Cathars, Albigenses, and good men of Languedoc', JMH xxvii (2001), 181–95
Peters, E., Heresy and authority in medieval Europe, Philadelphia 1980
Petit-Dutaillis, Ch., Étude sur la vie et le règne de Louis VIII, Paris 1894
—— Les Communes françaises: caractères et évolution dès origines au XVIIIe siècle, Paris 1947
Plieux, A., 'Récherches sur les origines de la ville de Condom', RA i (1874), 385–95
Poly, J.-P., La Provence et la société féodale (879–1166), Paris 1976
—— and E. Bournazel, La Mutation féodale: Xe–XIIe siècles, Paris 1980

—————— and E. Bournazel, *The feudal transformation, 900–1200*, trans. C. Higgitt, New York–London 1991

Powicke, M., *Stephen Langton*, Oxford 1928

—————— *The thirteenth century, 1216–1307*, 2nd edn, Oxford 1962

Puech, H.-C., *Le Manichéisme: son fondateur – sa doctrine*, Paris 1949

—————— 'Catharism médiéval et Bogomilisme', in *Oriente e occidente nel medio evo*, Rome 1957, 56–84

Remensnyder, A. G., 'Un Problème de cultures ou culture?: la statue-reliquaire et les *joca* de Sainte Foy de Conques dans le *Liber miraculorum* de Bernard d'Angers', *CCM* xxxiii (1990), 351–79

—————— 'Pollution, purity and peace: an aspect of social reform between the late tenth century and 1076', in Head and Landes, *Peace of God*, 280–307

Reynolds, S., *Fiefs and vassals*, Oxford 1994

Rezak, B., 'Women, seals and power in medieval France', in M. Erler and M. Kowaleski (eds), *Women and power in the Middle Ages*, Athens, Georgia–London 1988

Ricaud, A., *Marmande*, 2nd edn, Bordeaux 1975

Richard, A., *Histoire des comtes de Poitou, 779–1204*, Paris 1903

Riché, P., *Les Grandeurs de l'an mille*, Paris 1999

Riley-Smith, J., 'Family traditions and participation in the Second Crusade', in M. Gervers (ed.), *The Second Crusade and the Cistercians*, New York 1992

—————— *The First Crusaders, 1095–1131*, Cambridge 1997

Roquebert, M., *L'Épopée cathare*, Toulouse 1970–89

—————— *Les Cathares de la chute de Montségur aux derniers bûchers, 1244–1329*, Paris 1998

Rosenwein, B., *To be the neighbour of Saint Peter: the social meaning of Cluny's property, 909–1049*, Ithaca–New York 1989

Runciman, S., *The medieval Manichee*, Cambridge 1947

—————— 'The crusade of 1101', *Jahrbuch der Österreichischen Byzantischen Gesellschaft* i (1951), 3–12

—————— *The crusades*, 5th edn, London 1991

Russell, J. B., 'Les Cathares de 1048–54 à Liège', *Bulletin de la Société d'art et d'histoire du diocèse de Liège* xlii (1961), 1–8

—————— 'Interpretations of the origins of medieval heresy', *Medieval Studies* xxv (1963), 26–53

—————— *Dissent and reform in the early Middle Ages*, Berkeley–Los Angeles 1965

Samaran, C., *La Gascogne dans les registres du Trésor des Chartres*, Paris 1966

Samazeuilh, J. F., *Histoire de l'Agenais, du Condomois et du Bazadais*, Auch 1846–7

Šanjek, F., 'Le Rassemblement hérétique de Saint-Félix de Caraman (1167) et les églises cathares au xiie siècle', *Revue d'histoire ecclésiastique* lxvii (1972), 767–99

Sargent, S., 'Religious responses to social violence in eleventh-century Aquitaine', *Historical Reflections/Réflexions historiques* xii (1985), 219–40

Sayers, J. E., *Innocent III: leader of Europe, 1198–1216*, London–New York 1994

Schmittlein, R., *Avec César en Gaul*, Paris 1970

Sénac, R.-A., 'L'Évêché de Gascogne et ses évêques (977–1059)', in *Études sur la Gascogne au moyen âge*, Paris 1981, 131–44

—————— 'Essai de géographie et d'histoire de l'évêché de Gascogne (977–1059)', *BPH* (1983), 11–25

Sharenkoff, V. N., *A study of Manichaeism in Bulgaria with special reference to the Bogomils*, New York 1927

Shaw, I.P., 'The ecclesiastical policy of Henry II on the continent', *Church Quarterly Review* cli (1951), 137–55

Stevenson, J. (ed.), *Creeds, councils and controversies: documents illustrative of the early Church, AD 337–461*, London 1966

Stock, B., *The implications of literacy: written language and models of interpretation in the eleventh and twelfth centuries*, Princeton 1983

Stoyanov, Y., *The hidden tradition in Europe*, London 1994

Studd, R., 'The marriage of Henry of Almain and Constance of Béarn', in S. D. Lloyd and P. R. Cross (eds), *Thirteenth century England*, iii, Woodbridge 1991

Sumption, J., *The Albigensian Crusade*, London 1975

Tabacco, G., *The struggle for power in medieval Italy*, trans. R. B. Jensen, Cambridge 1989

Taviani, H., 'Naissance d'une hérésie en Italie au xie siècle', *Annales: économies, sociétés, civilisations* xxix (1974), 1224–52

—— 'Le Mariage dans l'hérésie de l'an mil', *Annales, économies, sociétés, civilisations* xxxii (1977), 1074–89

Taylor, C., 'Innocent III, King John and the Albigensian Crusade (1209–1216)', in J. C. Moore (ed.), *Pope Innocent III and his world*, Aldershot 1999, 205–27

—— 'The letter of Héribert of Périgord as a source for dualist heresy in the society of early-eleventh-century Aquitaine', *JMH* xxvi (2000), 313–49

—— 'The year 1000 and "those who laboured" ', in M. Frassetto (ed.), *The year 1000: religious and social response to the turning of the first millennium*, New York–Basingstoke 2002, 187–236

Theis, L., *Robert le Pieux, le roi du l'an mil*, Paris 1999

Tholin, G., 'Causeries sur les origines de l'Agenais', *RA* xxii (1895–6), 140–62, 433–50, 516–28

—— 'Notes sur la féodalité en Agenais au milieu du XIIIe siècle', *RA* xxiii (1896), 45–58, 537–46; xxv (1898), 144–56, 171–8, 257–65; xxvi (1899), 62–78

—— 'Documents relatifs à l'Agenais', *AHGi* xxxv (1900), 12–14

Thompson, K., *Power and border lordship in medieval France: the Perche in the eleventh and twelfth centuries, 1000–1226*, Woodbridge 2001

Thompson, S., 'The problem of Cistercian nuns in the twelfth and early thirteenth centuries', in D. Baker (ed.), *Medieval women* (SCH subsidia i, 1978), 227–52

Thomson, J. A. F., *The western Church in the Middle Ages*, London 1998

Thouzellier, C., 'Hérésie et croisade au xiie siècle', *Revue d'histoire ecclésiastique* xlix (1954), 855–72

—— *Un Traité cathare inédit du début du XIIIe siècle*, Louvain 1961

—— *Catharisme et Valdéisme en Languedoc à la fin du xiie et au début de xiiie siècle*, Paris 1966

Tillman, H., *Pope Innocent III*, trans. W. Sax, Amsterdam–New York–Oxford 1980

Töpfer, B., 'The cult of relics and pilgrimage in Burgundy and Aquitaine at the time of the monastic reform', in Head and Landes, *Peace of God*, 41–57

Torchia, N. J., *Creatio ex nihilo and the theology of St Augustine: the anti-Manichean polemic and beyond*, New York 1999

Trabut-Cusac, J. P., *L'Administration anglais en Gascogne sous Henri III et Edouard I, de 1254 à 1307*, Paris–Geneva 1972

Tucoo-Chala, P., *La Vicomté de Béarn et le problème de sa souveraineté dès origines à 1620*, Bordeaux 1961

——— (ed.), *Histoire de Pau*, Toulouse 1989

Turner, R. V., *King John*, London 1994

Van Meter, D. C., 'Eschatological order and the moral arguments for clerical celibacy in Francia around the year 1000', in Frassetto, *Medieval purity*, 149–75

van Mingroot, E., 'Kritisch Onderzoek om trent de datering van de Gesta episcoporum cameracensium', *Revue belge de philologie et d'histoire* liii (1975), 281–332

Venarde, B. L., *Women's monasticism and medieval society: nunneries in France and England, 890–1215*, Ithaca–London 1997

Verbeke, W., D. Verhelst and A. Welkenhuysen (eds), *The use and abuse of eschatalogy in the Middle Ages*, Leuven 1988

Verdon, J., 'Les Moniales dans la France de l'ouest au XIe et XIIe siècles', CCM xix (1976), 247–64

——— 'Recherches sur les monastères féminines dans la France du sud au IXe–XIe siècles', AM lxxxviii (1976), 117–38

——— 'Le Monachisme en Poitou au Xe siècle', *Revue Mabillon* lix (1978), 235–53

Verger, L. and others, *Agen: hier et aujourd'hui*, Agen 1979

Vicaire, M. H., *Histoire de Saint Dominique*, Paris 1957

——— *Saint Dominique et ses frères: évangile ou croisade?*, Paris 1967

——— 'L'Action de Saint Dominique sur la vie régulière des femmes en Languedoc', CF xxiii (1988), 217–40

Wade-Labarge, M., *Gascony, England's first colony, 1204–1453*, London 1980

Wakefield, W., 'Heretics as physicians in the thirteenth century', *Speculum* lvii (1982), 328–31

Warren, W. L., *King John*, 3rd edn, New Haven–London 1997

Werner, E., *Häresie und Gesellschaft im 11. Jahrhundert*, Leipzig 1975

White, S., '*Pactum legem vincit et amor judicium*: the settlement of disputes by compromise', *American Journal of Legal History* xxii (1978), 281–308

——— 'Feuding and peace-making in the Touraine around the year 1100', *Traditio* xlii (1986), 195–265

——— *Custom, kinship and gifts to saints: the laudatio parentum in western France, 1050–1150*, Chapel Hill, NC 1988

——— review of Barthélemy, *Vendôme*, *Speculum* lxxi (1996), 116–20

——— review of *Conventum*, *Speculum* lxxii (1997), 429–31

Widengren, G., *Mani and Manichaeism*, trans. C. Kessler, London 1965

Wolff, P., *Histoire de Toulouse*, Toulouse 1958

——— *Voix et images de Toulouse*, Toulouse 1962

——— 'L'Aquitaine et ses marges', in W. Braunfels (ed.), *Karl der Grosse: Lebenswerk und Nachleben*, i, Düsseldorf 1966, 269–306

——— 'La Noblesse toulousain: essai sur son histoire médiévale', in P. Contamine (ed.), *La Noblesse au moyen âge, xie–xve siècles*, Paris 1976, 154–74

——— *Regards sur le Midi médiéval*, Toulouse 1978

Wolff, R. L., 'How the news was brought from Byzantium to Angoulême; or, the pursuit of a hare in an ox cart', *Byzantine and Modern Greek Studies* iv (1978), 139–89

——— and P. Wolff, *Évêques et comté d'Agen au XIe siècle*, Villeneuve-sur-Lot–Agen 1962

Wood, I., *The Merovingian kingdoms, 450–751*, London–New York 1994

Zerner, M., 'Au Temps de l'appel aux armes contre les hérétiques: du *Contra Henricum* du moine Guillaume aux *Contra hereticos*', in Zerner, *Inventer*, 119–56

────── 'Introduction', to Zerner, *Inventer*, 7–13

────── *Inventer l'hérésie? Discours polémique et pouvoirs avant l'inquisition*, Nice 1998

Zimmerman, M. (ed.), *Les Sociétés méridionales autour de l'an mil*, Paris 1992

Unpublished theses

Dutton, C. M., 'Aspects of the institutional history of the Albigensian Crusade, 1198–1229', PhD diss. London 1993

Ellis, J., 'Gaston de Béarn: a study in Anglo-Gascon relations (1229–1290)', DPhil. diss. Oxford 1952

Frassetto, M., 'The sermons of Adémar of Chabannes and the origins of medieval heresy', PhD diss. Delaware 1993

Martindale, J., 'The origins of the duchy of Aquitaine and the government of the counts of Poitou, 902–1137', DPhil. diss. Oxford 1965

Mullinder, A., 'The crusading expeditions of 1101–2', PhD diss. Swansea 1996

Porter, J. M. B., '*Compelle intrare*: monastic reform movements in twelfth-century northwestern Europe', PhD diss. Nottingham 1997

Solt, C. W., 'The cult of saints and relics in the romanesque art of south-western France and the impact of imported Byzantine relics and reliquaries on early Gothic reliquary sculpture', PhD diss. Catholic University of America 1977

Wands, F. T., 'The romanesque architecture and sculpture of Saint Caprais in Agen', PhD diss. Yale 1982

Index